Netanyahu and Likud's Leaders

This research discusses the second-generation Likud leaders, known as the Princes, who have dominated Israeli politics for most of the last three decades: their relations with their parents and the extent to which they have followed in (or diverged from) their footsteps.

The main theme seeks to explore the unique, perhaps unprecedented, socio-political phenomenon of generational duplication in a western-type democracy. This volume examines the ways and means through which the disciples of Zionist leader Ze'ev Jabotinsky managed not only to maintain lasting control of their mentor's creation – to transform after Israel's establishment from a small opposition party into the country's dominant and ruling party – but also hand down this political pre-eminence to their descendants. Prime Minister Benjamin Netanyahu is the son of Ben-Zion Netanyahu, "foreign minister" of Jabotinsky's movement. President Reuven Rivlin is the son of resistance warrior Rachel Rivlin. MP Benny Begin is the son of Menachem Begin. Former Prime Minister Ehud Olmert, Tzipi Livni and many others were also part of those "Princes".

A breakthrough in the world's inter-generational research, the book is for readers interested in political science, sociology, and the politics of Israel and the Middle East.

Gil Samsonov is a managing partner in one of the top advertising firms in Israel, graduated from Tel-Aviv University, and got a PhD from King's College in London University. Samsonov has led numerus national and local election and general campaigns in Israel, and he is a senior political and marketing commentator in the Israeli television, radio and press.

Israeli History, Politics and Society

Series Editor: Efraim Karsh
King's College London

This series provides a multidisciplinary examination of all aspects of Israeli history, politics and society, and serves as a means of communication between the various communities interested in Israel: academics, policy-makers; practitioners; journalists and the informed public.

The Jewish Origins of Israeli Foreign Policy
A Study in Tradition and Survival
Shmuel Sandler

Israel, the Arabs and Iran
International Relations and Status Quo, 2011–2016
Ehud Eilam

The Arab – Israeli Conflict, 1956–1975
From violent conflict to a peace process
Moshe Gat

Hamas and Ideology
Sheikh Yūsuf al-Qaraḍāwī on the Jews, Zionism and Israel
Shaul Bartal and Nesya Rubinstein-Shemer

The British Army in Palestine and the 1948 War
Containment, Withdrawal and Evacuation
Alon Kadish

The US, Israel and Egypt
Diplomacy in the Shadow of Attrition, 1969–70
Yehuda U. Blanga

Netanyahu and Likud's Leaders
The Israeli Princes
Gil Samsonov

For a full list of titles in the series: www.routledge.com/middleeaststudies/series/ SE0790

Netanyahu and Likud's Leaders
The Israeli Princes

Gil Samsonov

Translated by Kaeren Fish

Routledge
Taylor & Francis Group

LONDON AND NEW YORK

First published in English 2020
by Routledge
2 Park Square, Milton Park, Abingdon, Oxon OX14 4RN

and by Routledge
52 Vanderbilt Avenue, New York, NY 10017

Routledge is an imprint of the Taylor & Francis Group, an informa business

Published in Hebrew by Kinneret Zmora-Bitan 2015.

British Library Cataloguing-in-Publication Data
A catalogue record for this book is available from the British Library

Library of Congress Cataloging-in-Publication Data
Names: Samsonov, Gil, 1957– author. | Fish, Kaeren, translator.
Title: Netanyahu and Likud's leaders : the Israeli princes / Gil Samsonov ;
    translated by Kaeren Fish.
Other titles: Nesikhim
Description: Abingdon, Oxon ; New York, NY : Routledge, 2020. |
    Series: Israeli history, politics and society ; 67 | Includes bibliographical
    references and index.
Identifiers: LCCN 2019051587 (print) | LCCN 2019051588 (ebook) |
    ISBN 9780367133689 (hardback) | ISBN 9780429026119 (ebook) |
    ISBN 9780429643637 (adobe pdf) | ISBN 9780429640469 (epub) |
    ISBN 9780429637292 (mobi)
Subjects: LCSH: Likud (Political party : Israel) | Irgun tseva'i le'umi—History. |
    Loḥame ḥerut Yiśra'el—History. | Politicians—Israel. | Revisionist Zionism. |
    Revisionist Zionism—Israel. | Israel—Politics and government.
Classification: LCC JQ1830.A98 L55813 2020 (print) | LCC JQ1830.A98
    (ebook) | DDC 324.25694/04—dc23
LC record available at https://lccn.loc.gov/2019051587
LC ebook record available at https://lccn.loc.gov/2019051588

ISBN: 978-0-367-13368-9 (hbk)
ISBN: 978-0-429-02611-9 (ebk)

Typeset in Times New Roman
by Apex CoVantage, LLC

Motto

"That which was inscribed in blood and sweat will not be expunged by perfidious pens."

(Uri Zvi Greenberg's words to my grandmother, Malka Samsonov, at Aaronsohn House [the Nili museum] in Zikhron Yaakov)

To my father, Jomik:

The personal example set by you and your generation, and your dedication to the Jewish People and the state, are what inspired us, the second generation. In the spirit of the words of Stern's anthem, we were all "committed for life" to having the history books tell the truth about your generation – the generation of the underground movements – about its bravery and its contribution to Israel's independence. A generation mighty enough to raise a generation of heirs.

Contents

Figures

Acknowledgments

To my darling Tali: You are the most patient, unselfish, encouraging and loving person in the world.

To Jomik, the underground fighter, my father: Only when you read the book will you understand how deeply the personal example set by you and your generation.

I am grateful to my partners at the Glickman-Shamir-Samsanov- Publicis advertising agency – Hanan Glickman, Yigal Shamir, Ronen Goldschmidt, Roi Gefen and Adi Bruner – for the freedom that they gave me to write. Special thanks to the one and only studio manager, Einat Shevo; to my friend and planner, Yoni Flint, who was a great help to me; and to Sara Levy, my Assistant with a capital "A" and my partner in every stage of writing my books.

To Eli Cohen, Yaron Dekel, And Hanan Kristal, the experts that helped tremendously with the fact check. To my dear friend Seth Eisenberg for his friendship and wisdom that guided me along the way

To my supervisor, Professor Efraim Karsh: I have no words to express my tremendous gratitude to you. It was worth going all the way to Kings' College at the University of London for the opportunity to encounter true academic excellence. Thanks to you, we produced ground-breaking research in generation studies.

I owe much to Tel Aviv University and Prof. Yonatan Shapira o.b.m. who led me to achieve an outstanding grade in my M.A. thesis.

Many thanks to the heirs who dedicate their lives to commemoration: to Herzi Makov, Yossi Ahimeir, and Professor Arye Naor, directors of the Begin Heritage Center and the Jabotinsky Institute, who helped me, via Rami Shtivi and Amira Stern, to locate the photographs. I am deeply grateful to the Jabotinsky Institute for the scholarship from the Alex Refaeli Fund that enabled me to pursue my doctorate. By means of this fund, Ester Refaeli and her children – Assi, Lona, and Karni – perpetuate the legacy of Alex Refaeli, one of the Irgun founders.

Many thanks to the photography department of the Government Press Office and its director, Nitzan Hen, for searching through their wonderful collection for me, and to my friend, photographer Malka Shani, for going to great lengths to help me.

I am grateful to the book's editors, Yuval Elazri and Sami Douanis, and to Eran Zmora, Executive Director of Kinneret Zmora-Bitan Dvir publishers and his staff, especially editor-in-chief Shmuel Rosner, who read, liked, believed in and advanced the book with professionalism and efficiency. To English translator Kaeren Fish, who devoted her time and talent wholeheartedly.

Thanks also to Taylor & Francis Group for choosing to publish this book, and to their highly professional and efficient representatives, Titanilla Panczel and Balaji Karuppanan for managing the process all the way to the happy end.

Without all these friends, partners, and family, I could not have realized my thirty-year-old dream of publishing a book that would be the beginning of a life's project. To my dear friend Seth Eisenberg for his friendship and wisdom which guided me along the way.

Introduction

Snapshot 1: Zikhron Yaakov of the 1960s, in all its simple, stirring beauty. A walk along the main road, its appearance mostly unchanged since the early days of the town – the period of the First Aliya.[1] The families of both my father and my mother, Jomik Samsonov and Edna Abramowitz, lived here.

I was ten years old, a student at the Nili school.[2] I enjoyed visiting my grandmother Malka Samsonov, who was director of Aaronsohn House, the Nili museum. I would sit in the guest room of this building in which the Nili underground still lived and breathed, listening to grandmother's stories. From time to time a thin, well-groomed elderly woman would come in. It was Rivka Aaronsohn, who always struck me as being frozen in time, still living through the First World War, with her brothers fighting in the ranks of the British army. In her free time, each of these two old women would tell me about the Nili underground, which had come into existence right here, in this house. They talked about their siblings: the leader, Aharon; the sister, Sara, who lost her life just a few meters from where we were sitting.

Often I would accompany Grandmother Malka on her slow walk back to the old Samsonov family home. Listening to her wander from one subject to the next, passing backwards and forwards through periods of time, I was enthralled, even though many of the stories were familiar to me from the books I read at night. I listened to her praises of Menachem Begin, and her sorrow over Dov, the blond warrior, revered friend of my father, who fell during the War of Independence. I imbibed her rage at those who had handed over their own brethren to the British, and her reverence for the legacy of those executed in the name of the struggle for the Jewish homeland. I memorized what the poet Uri Zvi Greenberg had told her: "That which was inscribed in blood and sweat will not be expunged by perfidious pens."

He referred to the pens of the ruling Mapai party (later to become the Labor party), which had erased the self-sacrifice of the underground movements (other than its own Haganah) from the public record.

Once, as we reached the back of the yard, Grandmother pointed to a corner of the storeroom and said, "Here, underground, there was a 'slick' (weapons cache). Actually, a double slick. Over here," she pointed, "is where your Grandfather Emmanuel hid weapons that belonged to the Haganah, and here," she turned and pointed, "on the left side of the cellar, your father, Jomik, hid weapons for Lehi;[3] he was the local commander." Grandfather knew nothing of his son's activity, Grandmother added, and the look in her eyes told me that she had known exactly where her seventeen-year-old son disappeared to at night. Afterwards the neighbors would discuss the operations that anonymous parties had carried out against marauding Arabs.

On this particular day Grandmother gave me five jars of jam wrapped in paper (covered with biblical verses scrawled in her illegible hand) and asked me – told me, rather – to go and deliver them. The next afternoon I set off by bus for Tel Aviv and the Veterans' Neighborhood in Ramat Gan. Along the way I couldn't resist reading (with great difficulty) her messages of support, and I also discovered the bank notes she had stuck to the bottom of each jar. The notes were neatly folded into small squares and concealed: a discreet form of charity. I did not know most of the people whose homes I travelled to, but some of the names were familiar to me from Grandmother's stories: there was the Irgun commander Yisrael Eldad, whose employment as a Bible teacher had been curtailed by the powers-that-be. There was Uri Zvi Greenberg, the poet and visionary, and his wife, the poetess Aliza Greenberg, also known by her pen-name Ein Tur Malka. Thus I became aware of the persecution and ostracism of the people whom my grandmother held dear.

Snapshot 2: Deputy Minister of Education Aharon Yadlin came to visit my school, Pardes Hana Regional High. It was 1972; I was fifteen, in ninth grade. The students were assembled to listen to the honored guest. Everyone sat in his place, staring dully at the speakers. I sat with them, tense and ready. I harbored a long-standing grievance against the Ministry of Education and its history books, and I waited impatiently for question time.

I was the only student who raised his hand to ask a question. I was invited to speak, and I hurried up to the stage. I didn't want to ask from my seat; I wanted to stand next to the deputy minister so that I could be seen and heard. Instead of asking a question, I started reading out excerpts from the history book that taught the Mapai party's truth – to me, a series of terrible lies: "Fascists in brown uniforms" (Irgun fighters); "the Stern gang" (Lehi underground); "a dangerous terrorist" (its leader, Yair Stern); "separatists" (Jabotinsky and the Revisionists); "the fascist who tried to carry out a putsch with the *Altalena*" (Begin and the Irgun); "endangered the Yishuv (the pre-state Jewish population of the Land of Israel) under Turkish rule" (the Nili underground). . . . The deputy minister of education stood there silently. From up close the Party seemed sympathetic and human. But not enough to ease my burning question: "Does it seem fair to you, Mr. Deputy Minister, that my country forces me to study these insults and lies about my forebears, the early immigrants who built communities in this desolate land; about the brave members of Nili; about the members of the Irgun and Lehi who fought underground and later in the IDF for Israel's independence?!"

The principal indicated that I had said enough. I walked off the stage, the proudest I have ever been of myself. Many years later I discovered that I had not been alone. Hundreds of children of Irgun and Lehi veterans experienced the same frustration and anger over the content of their schoolbooks – their first encounter with the seemingly all-powerful Mapai party.

Snapshot 3: A long drive with my father, Jomik, from Zikhron Yaakov to Jerusalem, where a gathering of Irgun and Lehi veterans was to take place at the Diplomat Hotel. This was already the early 1970s, but the sense of injustice still rankled with the underground fighters, who for years had been depicted as members of fascist gangs.

At the event itself the atmosphere was surprisingly different. Former fighters – men, women, brothers- and sisters-in-arms – were dressed in their finery. Crowds of children played on the small grassy hills in the hotel garden. One big family. A close, proud, connected group. It was only later on that I heard them referred to explicitly as the "fighting family".

At the center of the scene were two youngsters, thin and tall (from my childish perspective), surrounded by dozens of Irgun veterans who were speaking to them, their eyes filled with admiration. I asked my father, "Why do they look to those two with such love and respect? Who are they?" My father answered, "The sons. Benny Begin and Dan Meridor. The successors. The heirs." About a decade later, that formative image became the subject of my research.

Snapshot 4: Tel Aviv University, 1982. Dr. Yossi Beilin was a lecturer in the Department of Political Science, and his course was devoted to the changeover of generations in the Mapai (later Labor) party. He almost enjoyed my antagonistic behavior and political barbs, which made his classes more interesting. Beilin was already the renowned spokesman of Shimon Peres and the Labor party. I was the head of the Likud student cell at the university.

As Beilin spoke about studies conducted around the world focusing on changeovers of generations, the previous snapshots floated through my mind and connected with more updated snapshots of my political life: my first visit to Metzudat Zeev.[4] A meeting with MK Michael Dekel, who, instead of talking to me about politics, as I had expected him to, asked me whether I knew the words of the Beitar anthem. A meeting with the Likud treasurer MK Eitan Livni (father of Tzipi Livni), whom I approached to request a budget for the student cell, and who shared his Irgun memories from Shuni Castle and from Zikhron Yaakov in the days of the underground.

It was only when Beilin started expounding on the theories explaining changeovers of generations that it dawned on me that I knew the sort of generation he was talking about. Not a collection of individuals, but rather an entire generation – the generation of the Revolt – that was in search of its future, its heirs. This generation had no interest in mundane conversations about politics. It was looking for youngsters who were still pained over the *Altalena* affair; it probed to discover whether they belonged to families of Irgun members from Hatikva neighborhood or families of Polish immigrant Jewish prisoners executed by the British. It wanted to ascertain that the youth to whom they entrusted the future remembered the names Meir Feinstein and Moshe Barazani,[5] and were familiar with Jabotinsky's doctrine. It was a generation that was suspicious of anyone entering Herut/Likud headquarters lest he seek power rather than legacy. It was a generation that yearned for heirs who would take the oath of the Revolt and the rectification of history.

At the doors of the permanently broken elevator at Herut/Likud headquarters, that generation came face to face with the generation of heirs. A generation of sons and daughters who came from the Yemenite Kerem HaTeimanim neighborhood, from the Veterans' Neighborhood, and from Moshav Nahalat Jabotinsky. A younger generation that was worthy of trust, that would eventually sit in the Knesset, and later on in the government. A generation that included Roni Milo, Dan Meridor, Benny Begin, Uzi Landau, and Ruby Rivlin, Tzahi Hanegbi, Limor Livnat . . . and later on also Tzipi Livni and Benjamin Netanyahu.

***

The book you are reading, which tells the story of the heirs, was conceived before the concept of "heirs" (in Hebrew, *nesikhim* – literally, princes) became a familiar one in Israeli political discourse. In the early 1980s only two "quasi-heirs" were serving as Members of Knesset (Roni Milo and Ehud Olmert), while the other "children of" were occupied with external battles against Shimon Peres's Labor party and internal struggles against "invaders" who were perceived as seeking to seize the movement from the hands of the veteran underground commanders – our childhood heroes.

My research set me off on a fascinating journey. I embarked on my MA at Tel Aviv University, focusing on the generation of the Revolt. This was no ordinary academic inquiry. Using a research method based on personal experience as an observer-participant, I was able to plumb the depths of the inter-generational relations in the Likud. The movement was open to me, and my colleagues and friends were cooperative. I held about two hundred interviews and personal conversations, mostly with the movement's beloved veterans, most of whom are no longer with us today. I spoke with some of the older veterans, who had been close to Jabotinsky himself; with Irgun and Lehi commanders and fighters; with their children – the heirs, born around the time of Israel's independence; and with their grandchildren, born in the '70s and '80s. I spent hundreds of days and nights with the veterans at stormy – sometimes violent – political conventions; I spent anguished nights with them when they feared that the movement was going to fall into the hands of Sharon and Levy; I was with them when they decided who would represent them in the Knesset in 1984, in 1988, 1992, 1996, and even in 2013. I heard them speak truths that that they would not reveal to strangers. They shared their fears of losing the movement that had become their home, and their concerns that their heirs would not know the Beitar anthem.

It was the heirs whom I wanted to write about.

Who are the heirs?

There are different categories of heirs. Some are considered heirs by all accounts: Begin, Meridor, Livni, and Landau – the sons and daughters of Irgun commanders and of MKs representing the Herut/Likud party. The children of Lehi commanders – Yair Shamir and Tzahi Hanegbi – are also referred to as heirs, as are the children of rank-and-file fighters, like Livnat, Rivlin, and Olmert. Then there are the children of the ideological and political leaders of Jabotinsky's movement, such as Yossi Ahimeir, son of Abba Ahimeir, one of the trio that founded the militant Brit ha-Biryonim (Strongmen's Alliance) faction. The most prominent among this group of heirs is Benjamin Netanyahu, whose father was Jabotinsky's confidant and the head of the movement's political wing.

How, then, do we define an heir?

The heirs are, quite simply, those recognized as such by the veterans; those who, to their view, are loyal to Jabotinsky's teachings and pass the Beitar anthem test. Those whom they supported, wordlessly, at the voting booth. Those who reached the Knesset. Those who were loved, chosen, anointed.

We find inter-generational continuity in many spheres and occupations. We find it among farmers and journalists, and we also find it in politics: in the US, the Bush and Kennedy families, for example, produced generations of leaders. There are families like that in Israel, too: Dayan, Rabin, Burg, Sneh, Baram, Weizman, and more recently also Herzog and Lapid. Both in Israel and around the world, this phenomenon occurs sporadically, among individual families, in different political parties, and at different periods in time. There are individuals who inherit a name and a reputation, sometimes also a fortune. The heirs we discuss here represent a different phenomenon: not a private family affair, and not something that happens once in a decade or two. We are talking about an entire generation of underground fighters that produced an entire next generation of statesmen and lawmakers. A generation followed by another generation. All together, all from the same party, all in the same period.

Most of the parents of the heirs were not well known. Rivlin, Milo, Netanyahu, Livnat, and even Meridor, Olmert, Livni, and Landau were names that at first were not familiar to the public – not like Dayan, Weizman, Herzog, and, later on, Lapid. But in this case there was no need for the family name to ring familiar to the public ear. It was enough that it was familiar to the veterans of the underground. It wasn't fame that mattered. What mattered was loyalty to the ideological path, which was something that only the veterans could assess and affirm. It was they who designated the heirs – in one place, one building, one party, and one era, among one distinct group. They represent an altogether unique phenomenon, and they changed the face of the State of Israel.

My aim in my research was not just to seek out historical facts, but to connect with the perspective, the subjective "truth", that both generations carried with them. The powerful emotions described here hardened the resolve of the veterans to fight for their reputation and to aim for dominion. The bitter resentment of the heirs whose parents had suffered injustice was largely what motivated this younger generation, arousing in them a powerful desire to prevail and to inherit the government, bringing honor to their parents. The mosaic of emotions produced actions, and these actions wrote history, even though the fury towards the previous government had dimmed by the time they reached power. My research tells a story that started a century ago with Ze'ev Jabotinsky and continues over the two generations of his successors. It is a story that was born with the generation of the underground fighters in Poland and in the Land of Israel in the 1920s and '30s, and it continues into the new millennium. It is a story that is critical for an understanding of Israel.

Notes

1 The "First Aliya" refers to the major wave of Zionist immigration following the Russian pogroms of 1881–1882.
2 Named in honor of the first Jewish underground, which operated during the First World War. The Hebrew acronym Nili has its origin in 1 Sam. 15:28–29.
3 Lehi: the group that split from the Irgun Zionist paramilitary organization in 1940 in order to continue fighting the British during World War II. Led by Yair Stern and referred to pejoratively by the British as the "Stern gang". The Irgun, whose full name translates as "National Military Organization in the Land of Israel", and which operated between 1931 and 1948, was itself an offshoot of the older and larger Haganah Jewish paramilitary organization.
4 "Zeev's Fortress", named after Jabotinsky. Herut/Likud headquarters.
5 Underground fighters sentenced to death by the British. At Jerusalem's Central Prison, a few hours before they were to be executed, they embraced and blew up a hand grenade that was lodged between them.

Part I

Pain and pride

This part deals with the birth of the resistance movement Menachem Begin will lead, which featured both in the towns and cities that were burning in Poland and in the Land of Israel (then known as Palestine). During the pogroms, where defenseless Jews were butchered by their Arab neighbors, the Jewish leadership chose to maintain a policy of restraint. Europe was characterized by the frightening and threatening rise of the Nazi Party and the establishment of the Nazi regime.

Ze'ev Jabotinsky rebelled against the Jewish passive leadership in the diaspora and established the first Jewish fighting forces in two thousand years (both in Israel and Russia). He was so charismatic that he swayed a large crowd of youngsters (from Begin's generation, including Begin himself). This generation was the first one to grow on an active, militant, and Zionist education. They rebelled against the Jewish leadership, arrived in Israel, and rebelled against the British mandate which had closed the gates of Israel to the millions of Jews that were being ruthlessly murdered in Europe. Far too many of these hapless Jews facing extinction were among the families of these rebelling youngsters who had now chosen armed combat fighting.

The new State of Israel which was established in 1948 was led by the socialist party, which crushed every opponent and presented these "rebels" as dangerous fascists, threatening the stability of the newborn country. Begin's generation "withdrew", organizing themselves into what will become known as the "fighting family". They worshipped the warriors and leaders, and a deep and lasting mutual respect among the friends was developed. Children were raised according to this doctrine of the "fighting family", and they developed tremendous respect for and pride in their parents, their "uncles", in Jabotinsky and Begin. They stuck closely to their parents' ideology, became active, and basically duplicated Begin's generation (later on, when they take their parents' place in the party, they will be given the title "Princes"). In the elections of 1977 Begin used the help of those "Princes", now young leaders themselves, to operate in the universities and streets and to promote the first political turnover in Israel.

1 Children seared by legacy

They were born in the 1940s and '50s into a world that was trying to recover from immense, cataclysmic, apocalyptic wars, in between a monstrous World War that included the unspeakable Holocaust, and a heroic War of Independence fought by the fledgling State of Israel.

Their battle-scarred parents had served in the paramilitary Jewish Irgun and Lehi underground organizations, fighting against bloodthirsty Arabs and the British administration that sided with them. They had sacrificed the best years of their lives for the sake of establishing a Jewish state in the Land of Israel, only to discover, once the war was over, that their contribution was contemptuously ignored and rejected by political adversaries who were in power. The struggle for their legacy and their good name had only just begun.

These parents, veterans of the underground movements, young in years but old in spirit, were persecuted by the socialist government led by Ben-Gurion's Mapai (later to become Labor) party. The absolute control wielded by Mapai both prior to and after the establishment of the state has no parallel in any western democracy; similar conditions are to be found only in Communist or totalitarian regimes. Mapai power encompassed the national institutions, the economy, the labor market, the army, the media, and the educational, health, and legal systems. In short, it exerted almost absolute control over the lives of Jewish citizens of the country.

The Revisionist parents suffered calumny and denigration, and were excluded not only from the mechanisms of power and influence, but also from the national narrative taught in the schools. With most workplaces under state control, they were turned away from jobs. The press branded them as "gangs", "fascists", "hooligans". The commander and leader of these underground veterans, Menachem Begin, was regarded with contempt and was demonized in the Knesset and in the partisan press.

The parents therefore preferred to live close to each other, in small groups of former fighters, in non-socialist, modest, middle-class urban neighborhoods such as Rehavia in Jerusalem, the Veterans' Neighborhood in Ramat Gan, central Tel Aviv, and the traditional Yemenite neighborhoods (Hatikva, Kerem ha-Teimanim, Mahaneh Yehuda).

With the establishment of the state, the departure of the British, and the attainment of independence, the parents shed their uniforms and turned to the task of raising their families. When their former commanders identified the political arena as the new focus of their efforts and established the Herut movement (later to become Likud), the parents were struggling to keep their heads above water and support their families. While life was hard for everyone in this small, new, embattled country, the former fighters of the underground movements faced significant additional hardships. In addition to the economic challenges of the new state, they had to deal with the callousness and despotism of the establishment towards anyone who was not part of itself. The underground veterans nevertheless remained loyal to the movement and to the memory of the fallen fighters, whose sacrifice had been scorned.

The sons and daughters of these former fighters shared not only the common fate of their parents, but also names: names that eternalized the early Revisionists, the brothers-in-arms who had fallen in battle, and their parents' underground aliases. Their names were codes, signaling commitment to the mission and the obligation of memory. The most common name, Zeev (Zeeva, for girls), commemorates the founder of the Revisionist movement, Ze'ev Jabotinsky. The names Binyamin (Benjamin), Zeev, and Herzl all recall the father of modern Zionism. Yair (Yaira, for girls) was the nom-de-guerre of the legendary commander of Lehi, Avraham Stern. The name Raziel (Raziela) honors the commander of the Irgun, David Raziel, and the names Shlomo and Yosef recall the first Jewish prisoner to be hanged by the British: Shlomo Ben-Yosef.

The children who were given the name Zeev include former minister Benny (Binyamin Zeev) Begin, who is named after both Jabotinsky and Herzl; Ze'ev Jabotinsky, namesake of his famous grandfather and a member of the right-wing faction of the Likud; MK Zeev Boim; Zeeva Ahimeir, the first baby girl in Israel to be named after Jabotinsky; Zeev Perl, former mayor of Safed; Zeev Levanon; and many others. The most prominent bearer of the name is the movement headquarters, known to this day as Metzudat Zeev ("Zeev's Fortress").

The "Yairs" include Yair Stern, former director of Israel Television, who carries the underground name of his father, the Lehi commander executed by the British. "I felt an obligation to carry this name," he once said in an interview. "It's as though I'm carrying the torch." Yair Hamburger is the son of a staunch Revisionist who emigrated from Germany; he owns the Harel insurance company (and has a bust of Jabotinsky on display at the entrance to his office). Yair Shamir, a colonel (res.) in the IAF, son of Lehi commander and Prime Minister Yitzhak Shamir, and a minister in Benjamin Netanyahu's third government, recounts: "Once I was asked why I was named Yair. I explained that 'Yair' is the commitment to the past, and 'Shamir' is commitment to the future."

I bumped into renowned basketball coach Pini Gershon in April 2010, when a mutual friend was in hospital. As we waited together in the corridor, I told him about my research. Without a word, but full of emotion, he took out his identity card and showed me his full name as it appears there: Pinhas Yair Gershon. Then he told me about his home in the Nordia neighborhood of Tel Aviv, about his

Revisionist father, and about his sister, Raziela Gershon, who was named after the Irgun commander David Raziel.

There are many other names that are full of significance in terms of the movement and Israeli history: Herzl Makov, director of the Menachem Begin Heritage Center, is named after the founder of modern Zionism. Sallai Meridor, former chairman of the Jewish Agency and ambassador to Washington, carries the underground name that was used by his mother, Raanana; his elder brother, Dan Meridor, carries the underground name of his father, former MK Eliyahu Meridor, a member of the Irgun high command and a long-serving MK. Yaakov Ahimeir, a well-known television personality, is named after Yaakov Raz, who was killed by Arabs in Jerusalem; his brother, former MK Yossi Ahimeir, was named after Yosef Katznelson. Prime Minister Benjamin Netanyahu's brother, Yoni (Yonatan), killed in the Entebbe Raid in 1976, was named after both his grandfather, Zionist leader Natan Milikowsky, and Colonel John (Jonathan) Peterson, who was commander of the Hebrew Brigades together with Jabotinsky.

Over the years, the underground veterans' children got to know each other. They met on the street, in the Beitar youth movement, at memorial ceremonies. In some cases they attended the same school; sometimes they lived in the same neighborhood; some were quite at home in each other's houses. When the adults met to share their troubles, to discuss politics, or to reminisce, the children would head out to the yard to play, or would sit quietly on the sidelines and listen to the stories.

They would hike together to Shuni Castle[1] or to Acre Prison.[2] David Stern (Yair's brother) and his wife Hinda owned a small truck, and they would pick up their friends Yitzhak and Shulamit Shamir. They would head to Masada or to Avdat, and while the parents spent the journey discussing the Revolt and the contemptuous treatment that the underground veterans received from the state, the children – Avi and Amira Stern and Gilada and Yair Shamir – would play, all the while listening and taking in the vistas of the land their parents had fought for.

Of course, they knew all their parents' old friends, and both the real names and aliases of the "uncles" and "aunts" who comprised the fighting family. At the gatherings that took place year after year, they heard stories about their parents' childhood; about the marches held by the Beitar youth movement in Poland; about the fellow fighters who had fallen in battle or who had been tortured and executed. They heard about Yair Stern, commander of Lehi (known by the British as the "Stern gang"), who was caught in hiding and shot like a common criminal, and about David Raziel, commander-in-chief of the Irgun, who had lost his life fighting the Nazis, in British uniform. They were larger-than-life characters in a story that was still unfolding, day after day.

In their minds the children reenacted the battles and heroic operations that their parents had undertaken. They were proud to be the sons and daughters of a courageous generation of fighters. The rejection by the establishment only amplified their admiration for their parents, which overshadowed the usual adolescent need to rebel.

One of the heroic stories that was engraved in their consciousness, and which reflected the shared destiny of all the members of the fighting family, was that of Meir Feinstein and Moshe Barazani. Feinstein was a nineteen-year-old Irgun fighter; Barazani, aged twenty-one, belonged to Lehi. In 1947 they were both sentenced to death for their involvement in sabotage activities against British targets. They were imprisoned together, and shortly before they were to be hanged, they placed a hand grenade, which had been smuggled into the prison for them, between their chests, embraced each other, and blew themselves up. They became a symbol of the unity and the blood bond not just between the sister-underground movements, but also between Jews of Ashkenazi[3] and Mizrahi[4] backgrounds.

In the years leading up to the establishment of the state, the core of the fighting family comprised no more than six thousand or so members – five thousand affiliated with the Irgun, and one thousand with Lehi. They included native-born "Sabras" along with immigrants from Europe and from the Arab countries. They were youngsters who joined the underground movements and risked their lives in daring guerrilla operations against the British army, smuggling weapons and ammunition, helping illegal immigrants to enter the country, hiding friends wanted by the authorities, and defending Jewish settlements from Arab gangs. This core of fighters grew into a hardened, driven family. Many were sole survivors of families that had been wiped out in the Holocaust. Fighting side by side forged them into an intensely committed group.

In his book,[5] Eitan Livni, the Irgun operations officer, recalls that the oldest of the children were called the "underground babies". Some of them suckled as their mothers concealed ammunition or warned of approaching hostile forces. Some grew up with adopted families, or in safe houses. Many grew up with no childhood memories of their father. Father was the man in the photograph beneath the glass on the table in the sitting room. There were some children who suspected that Father lived in the postbox, since that was where they found the letters he left for them.

Esther Raziel-Naor, one of the "mothers" of the fighting family, sister of Irgun commander David Raziel, and later a Herut MK, recounts:

> When we were arrested, our two young sons, Arye and David, remained with their grandmother. I didn't see them even once during the seven months that I was in prison. I refused to have them brought to me there. I was not prepared to have the memory of barbed wire fences and prisons engraved in their minds. When David saw me for the first time after my release to house arrest, he asked, "Is this the Mommy lady?"[6]

There were also children who were born shortly after their fathers had been executed or had fallen in battle. Yair Stern was six years old when he heard about his father for the first time. He told me:

After my father was killed, my mother couldn't find work. As the wife of a "terrorist", no-one wanted to hire her. [. . .] When the state was born, they took me to a memorial ceremony and they showed me a big stone with the name 'Yair' inscribed on it. They told me, "That's your father." I was surrounded by hundreds of people I had never seen before, and suddenly they were all my "aunts and uncles". They came over to me and caressed me and talked and told stories. To this day they are my family.

Gilada Diamant, daughter of Lehi leader and future Prime Minister Yitzhak Shamir, says of her brother Yair (a future MK):

> When Yair was a year old, our father was exiled by the British. Afterwards our mother was caught, too; she was imprisoned in the Bethlehem jail and she declared a hunger strike. For a whole year Yair had no parents; for three years he had no father. He got to see our father only when he returned, with the establishment of the state. This [absence] left its mark on him. He is very similar to our father. He has great inner resilience; I believe it developed at that time. All in all, [this period] left its mark on the entire family.[7]

Yair Shamir himself says:

> My father was arrested and exiled to Eritrea, and my mother moved from one hole to the next. She couldn't rent a place anywhere because of who she was. She was on the move with a baby. We lived in quite a few laundry rooms in the roofs of buildings in the Ramat Gan area. [. . .] At some stage she was arrested, and I went to a different family that cared for me.[8]

When Israel celebrated its first Independence Day, Shamir had a difficult time because of his father's underground activity: "I was the 'son of the terrorist'," he told journalist Amira Lamm, his anger palpable even sixty-five years later. "There were quite a few run-ins about this. . . . When anyone made a comment, I would react. I wasn't a quiet child. I fought back."

The conflict between the Zionist-Socialist camp (the Mapai/Labor party, which controlled the Jewish Agency from the mid-1930s and, later on, dominated the government) and the Revisionist camp (Jabotinsky's movement, Herut, the ideological right-wing, the eternal opposition) originated in Europe, and then shifted to the Holy Land, where it continued to rage over decades, like the fierce disputes between the Left and Right in Europe. The confrontations between Jabotinsky and the chairman of the Jewish Agency Executive, the moderate political Zionist Chaim Weizmann, were still being perpetuated two decades later by David Ben-Gurion, the all-powerful leader of the Mapai (Po'alei Eretz Yisrael) party (later to become Labor) and first prime minster, and Menachem Begin, Irgun commander and leader of the Herut movement (later to become Likud).

The Revisionists were a stubborn stain on the socialist order, and an ideological, political, and military opposition to Ben-Gurion. During the years of the British Mandate they refused to accept the authority of Ben-Gurion and the leadership of the Haganah – the official military wing of the Yishuv (the collective name for the Jewish community in the Holy Land prior to the establishment of the state) – and were harshly critical of their response to Arab attacks (which the Revisionists viewed as feeble). The underground fighters regarded Ben-Gurion as collaborating with a hostile Mandatory administration which blocked persecuted Jews from seeking refuge in their homeland. The military force that they established in the early 1930s, known as the Irgun (in Hebrew, *Etzel* – an acronym for *Irgun Tzvai Leumi* – National Military Organization) was an underground army that opposed

Figure 1.1 Abba Ahimeir, the spiritual leader of the Revolt generation who was persecuted by the government, with his wife Sonia, and their son Yaacov (right), who later will become a television anchor, and Yossi, who will later become MK of the Likud party.

Figure 1.2 Benny as a child with his father, Head of Opposition Menachem Begin, his mother Aliza, and sisters Chasia and Leah. The father and son will serve fifty years combined in the Israeli Knesset.

the establishment's "restraint" and responded to Arab attacks. (Lehi, pejoratively known in English as the "Stern gang", split from the Irgun in 1940 and continued to fight not only the Arabs but also the British Mandatory forces.)

When the state came into existence, the government was in the hands of left-wing parties whose red flag symbolized, in the eyes of the Revisionists, the world-wide Communist enemy of the Jews; in addition, it now represented a repressive system which had erased and eradicated the contribution of the Irgun and Lehi fighters to the establishment of the state. As the sons and daughters of these fighters grew up, they were confronted with a searing and humiliating reality: their parents – their devoted, admired heroes – had been rejected and forgotten. Teachers did not mention them in the classroom; radio broadcasts disregarded their sacrifice, and they were persecuted by the socialist government because of their

Figure 1.3 Lehi leader Yitzhak Shamir on a stroll with his son Yair Shamir, who followed his father in military leadership roles, Knesset, and in the government.

Figure 1.4 Ze'ev Jabotinsky, the leader and founder, with his son Ari, the first "Prince" and future MK.

Figure 1.5 Tzila and Professor Bentzion Netanyahu, who served as Jabotinsky's secretary, with their children, Israel's hero Yoni (right) and his brother Benjamin.

Figure 1.6 Tzhachi Hanegbi with his mother Geula Cohen, Lehi fighter. Together they served forty-five years in the Israeli Knesset.

Figure 1.7 The legendary underground warriors of the Etzel, Sara and Eitan Livni. The father was MK of the Likud party. Later on Tzipi Livni, their daughter, carried on to become MK, minister, and leader of the centrist party.

Figure 1.8 Me and my parents, Edna and Jomik Samsonov, a founding family of the new Israel. I absorbed my legacy from my grandmother Malka and from my father, a commander in the Lehi underground movement, who fought in the War of Independence.

political affiliation. Their representatives in the early Knessets – a small right-wing island in a left-wing sea – were slandered in the press. At every family meal the children imbibed their parents' bottled-up anger; in every discussion among the extended fighting family the children sensed their parents' profound frustration. They did not forget and were not quick to forgive.

Ostracization consolidates the "fighting family"

Mapai and its powerful leader, Ben-Gurion, built a fortified wall of isolation and hatred around the Revisionist parents, using the tools of government: party newspapers, national radio, and a force comprising tens of thousands of clerks, teachers, and army officers. Even before the state had come into existence, the Revisionists were blamed for the murder of socialist leader Chaim Arlozorov (1933); underground fighters were handed over to the British during the "Hunting Season";[9] they were persecuted following the King David Hotel explosion (1946); they were presented as bloodthirsty killers in the wake of the battle over the Arab village of Deir Yassin (1948); and then they were isolated and blocked from integrating into the mechanisms of government. They suffered economic discrimination over four decades.

The resentment that the parents felt towards the eternal ruling party accumulated over many years. In response to their government-imposed isolation, they closed ranks behind high walls of their own which separated them from the repressive regime. Behind these walls they could share warmth, fraternity, and glory.

The sinking of the Irgun ship *Altalena* off the coast of Tel Aviv was the symbol seared most deeply in their consciousness. The episode took place on June 22, 1948, just a few weeks after the declaration of the state. The ship, carrying illegal immigrants and weapons procured by the Irgun and meant to support the war effort against the Arabs, was shelled opposite the Tel Aviv coastline at Ben-Gurion's orders. The veteran fighters who were on board on that fateful day, and those watching fearfully from the beach, would recount over and over how Begin had adamantly rejected the pleas of his fighters to return fire towards their fellow Jews who were shooting at them. Shortly afterwards, with the Haganah commanders well aware that the Irgun commander was on board, the ship took a direct hit; it caught fire and began to sink. Begin escaped death that day (not for the first time) thanks to Yosef (Yoske) Nahmias, who pushed him off the deck. Sixteen Irgun members and three IDF soldiers were less fortunate. That was the toll in lives on that black day. In the last interview given by Yehiel Kadishai, in 2013, this pleasant and good-natured man, who had been Begin's personal secretary for many years, said that "Ben-Gurion's order was the most appalling act ever committed in our time. It was the result of causeless hatred, hatred directed towards brothers." What he meant was that the Prime Minister had tried to kill the head of the opposition.

The early "heirs" – Ruby Rivlin, Uzi Landau, Ehud Olmert, and others, who had been young children when the state was born, and who went on to become Likud MKs and government ministers – later described the incomprehensible gap between the story of the *Altalena* as they had heard it in their childhood from their "uncles" in the underground, and the official version. What the underground veterans called the "bloody cannon" was referred to by Ben-Gurion as the "holy cannon" at a special meeting of the Provisional State Council,[10] claiming that it was the cannon that had prevented civil war. The deplorable expression "holy cannon" was later removed by Mapai officials from the official protocols, but the painful memory of the event itself remained and was bequeathed to the next generation. Some of the most senior Irgun personnel had been involved in the incident, including some who were parents of next-generation leaders. Those on board included, inter alia, Menachem Begin and Eliyahu Lenkin (commander of the ship and great-uncle of MK Yariv Levin), along with Martin Locker and his brother, both Holocaust survivors (the father and uncle of Major-General (res.) Yohanan Locker and Harel Locker, Prime Minister Netanyahu's bureau chief), and the head of Beitar in Romania, Shabtai Nadiv, whose brother had drowned with the sinking of the *Struma*. Another brother, Zvi Hermon (father of Amos Hermon, one of the heads of the Jewish Agency) was on the beach at Kfar Vitkin, where he had just unloaded some of the weapons from the ship. Six of the participants in the *Altalena* episode on both sides later served as Members of Knesset; three of them became Prime Minister; two served as Chief-of-Staff (David Ben-Gurion, Yigael Yadin, and Yitzhak Rabin, on one side, and Menachem Begin, Eliyahu Lenkin, and Yaakov Meridor on the other).

The parents told their children over and over again about Begin's self-restraint, about the tearful speech that he delivered immediately upon reaching the shore, and about his call that "there shall not be a civil war." Ben-Gurion and his spokesmen on national radio mocked Begin's tears. The Revisionists remembered Ben-Gurion's scorn, which continued to gall them. As though the murderous shells had not been enough, Ben-Gurion added his harsh, unforgivable verdict: "Blessed is the cannon that shelled this ship."

When I was a child, my father told me how he and his friends – Irgun fighters who were serving in the IDF by the time of the *Altalena* episode – were instructed by their commanders to remain at their bases, for fear of the potential rebellion that they might instigate. Moshe Ronen, today a prominent leader of Canadian Jewry, recalls how the events of that day changed the lives of himself and his family. His father and uncle, Mordechai and Shalom Markowitz, were Zionists and members of Beitar in Hungary. Mordechai, the father, was on board the *Altalena*; he saw the blood and he was enraged. He and his friends desperately wanted to return fire. Begin stopped them. The father maintained (although this was not corroborated by other witnesses) that he remembered Begin standing on the ship, waving a pistol in the air and threatening to shoot anyone who returned fire. The brothers fought in the War of Independence but could not forget the horror of seeing Holocaust survivors shot at by fellow Jews. They felt victimized by the regime and feared that they stood no chance in the young state. Like some other former Irgun members, they left the country of their dreams. Half a century later, when the son, Moshe, purchased an apartment in Israel, he announced proudly that he had chosen a building on the Tel Aviv coast, right opposite where the *Altalena* had sunk.

The sense of persecution among the parents' generation was not a baseless delusion born in the minds of conspiracy-seekers. The entire fighting family knew the story of the commander of the *Altalena*, Eliyahu Lenkin. In 1944, at the height of the "Hunting Season", Lenkin had been caught by the Haganah and handed over to the British. He was exiled to Eritrea, but managed to escape and fled to Europe. Here, following herculean efforts, he managed to arrange for the *Altalena* to set sail for Israel, with the immigrants and weapons on board. As the ship reached the coast at Kfar Vitkin he stood proudly on board – until he saw his friends falling around him, culled by IDF fire. Despite this trauma, and despite the fact that in the wake of this episode he was sent to prison for two months, Lenkin acquiesced to Begin's request and enlisted in the IDF. He was rewarded with a humiliating induction: this senior commander was forced to undergo an officers' course in order to earn his rank. Sixty-three years later, MK Yariv Levin, a relative of Lenkin, spearheaded the initiative to haul the remains of the *Altalena* out of the sea to serve as a symbol and a reminder that Jews dare not shoot at fellow Jews.

When the children of the underground fighters went to school and opened the Education Ministry history books for the first time, they discovered, to their astonishment, that their parents' heroism and sacrifice had been erased from Israeli history. Their contribution was scorned, as though they were a wild, extremist, dangerous fringe group. The official textbooks described them as members of violent gangs and bloodthirsty cells. The teachers at schools explained that Irgun and Lehi fighters were not only unconnected to the struggle to achieve independence, but that they had actually hindered it.

Even seemingly simple and self-evident concepts such as "Israel Defense Force" (*Tzva ha-Hagana le-Yisrael*) were fraught with painful connotations. The choice to include the name of the Haganah organization in the official name of Israel's army was interpreted by some as a poke in the eye by Mapai. The fathers would return from their reserve army duty proud of their service, but among themselves they preferred to refer to the "Israeli army", rather than using its official name. In his speeches Begin spoke of "our magnificent army" in order to avoid any mention of the word "Haganah".

The newspapers of the Labor movement and the Histadrut (Israel's Labor-affiliated trade union center), both before and after the establishment of the state, heaped scorn on the Revisionists. The slanted national radio (and later television) presented the graduates of the Beitar movement as members of a radical fascist-nationalist stream. They called them "separatists" and "terrorists", and accused their leaders of harboring an affinity for and empathy with European fascism. Socialist newspapers pointed to a similarity between the brown uniforms that the parents had worn in their youth, in the Beitar movement, and the infamous Nazi brownshirts. There were some who claimed that the Lehi leader Avraham Stern had cooperated with the Nazis (Stern had tried to convey to Nazi Germany a message that killing the Jews was not the only option; they could be sent to the Holy Land). The children heard and read all these accusations and insults, and found it difficult to believe their eyes and ears.

Membership in the fighting family came naturally to the next generation. The children joined in willingly. They had grown up among the "uncles" and "aunts" with the feeling that their parents' stories were their own; that their parents' truth was not the "truth" of the radio, the newspapers, and the official textbooks. Their childhood oscillated between the admiration they felt for their parents' generation, and the humiliation they suffered for their loyalty to them.

When other children went off with their parents to the seaside, they went on hikes that included memorial ceremonies for the Jewish underground prisoners who had been executed by the British. As babies they had imbibed the Beitar anthem with their mothers' milk, and they sang it at the annual memorial for those who had lost their lives on board the *Altalena*:

> "From the pit of decay and dust/With blood and sweat/
> Shall arise a race/proud, generous, and fierce [. . .]
> To die or to conquer the hill/Yodfat, Masada, Beitar."

Outside, they were persecuted, but within their circle they stood by one another. Outside, all they could hear was the distorted and dishonest one-sided party media, while among themselves they spoke their truth. Surrounded by the forces of a hostile establishment, the loyalists converged and told hair-raising stories of courage and valor.

On the outside, it was the "Reds" who were in control – the camp they perceived as supporting the Bolsheviks and the Communists, betraying and informing against Jews, persecuting brothers, and shooting at Holocaust survivors and freedom fighters. Their flag was that of the kingdom of Evil – the Soviet Union – which had armed the Arab forces immediately after the establishment of the state. In their eyes, it was unforgivable to sing the *Internationale* – the workers' anthem sung by Stalin and Khrushchev. It was unconscionable to mark May Day – the workers' holiday instituted by the Marxist Communists.

As the walls of seclusion and isolation grew higher around the fighting family, their ideological zeal grew increasingly intense, including faith in the Greater Land of Israel, stretching from the Mediterranean to Transjordan. Every Irgun veteran's home displayed the organization's symbol: a map of Greater Israel, including both banks of the Jordan, overlaid with the image of an arm holding a rifle, and the inscription below: "*Rak Kakh*" (Only Thus).

Discrimination and disrespect for the dead

Under the regime that they referred to among themselves as the "Labor democtatorship", isolation and persecution were the Revisionists' day-to-day reality. "When we returned home from vacation, we would find signs of fresh paint in all sorts of places where they had hidden listening devices," recounts Aryeh Eldad, the son of Yisrael Eldad, a Lehi leader. Many years later, Brigadier-General Aryeh Eldad, now a retired Brigadier-General and former MK for the right-wing National Union party, discovered that the Shin Bet (General Security Service) had kept his parents' home under observation.

At every encounter among the parents there was some new story of injustice, provocation, or inexplicable hard-heartedness on the part of the "Bolsheviks". The children listened to accounts of blows, curses, and battles lost against tens of thousands of Labor workers, the Histadrut, the Jewish Agency, the kibbutzim, the government, and the army. To them, these bodies were a tightly-knit, vengeful clique that would stop at nothing in its attempts to break its opponents.

Many of the parents were unable to find work, since they did not carry a "red book" – the Histadrut membership card – which was a prerequisite for any job in the public service, in the army, or in schools. Others were dismissed from their jobs once their political affiliation became known. Moshe Arens, who later served as an ambassador, Minister of Defense, and Foreign Minister, was twenty years old when he arrived in Israel in its early years. He was a well-educated young man with valuable engineering experience (thanks to his service in the US army's engineering corps), but his application to work in the military industry was rejected over and over, owing to his having served in the past as head of the Beitar movement in the US. Martin Locker, who arrived at Israel's shores aboard the *Altalena*, was forced to work in Europe since it was all but impossible to find employment in the Jewish homeland without a red book.

Moshe Savorai and his wife Tova had fought in the Lehi ranks and had hidden Stern in their home, where he was killed. Moshe had his teaching license revoked and was unable to find a job. He was forced to work as a driver until he completed his studies and became a lawyer, no longer dependent on the regime to make a living. The case of Yisrael Eldad is more widely known, and even more absurd. This former Lehi leader was stripped of the right to be a teacher in the state whose establishment he had fought for.

A journalist who interviewed Yair Shamir (son of Yitzhak Shamir) described his anger over events that had happened sixty years previously: "He remembers the distress of his parents, who were his heroes. They [his parents] couldn't find work. [. . .] Even when his father opened his own company, he tells me, the company was blacklisted; they got no work." His sister, Gilada Diamant, describes her father's situation in a similar way:

> He couldn't integrate into the Israeli establishment; they wouldn't let him. [. . .] He tried to find work in the public sector, but there was a firm decision not to accept him into any government office. That was Ben-Gurion's policy: Lehi people were to be left outside. [. . .] We felt excluded.

After Yitzhak Shamir's death, Nahum Barnea, writing in *Yediot Aharonot* newspaper, recounted how, in the early '50s:

> Shamir faced a difficult financial situation. In effect, he had no income. He found a notice in a newspaper advertising a course that was about to begin for clerks at the Ministry of the Interior. He passed the entrance tests, participated in the course, and graduated. Just as he was about to be accepted for work, the Minister of the Interior at the time summoned the ministry's director-general. After locking the door of his office he showed him a note, signed by Prime Minister Ben-Gurion: "This terrorist is not to be accepted for work." "What should I do?" asked the minister. "He completed the course; there's no way we can't accept him," answered the director-general. The minister saw things differently, and Shamir was not accepted for work.

Barnea concluded, "The story illustrates the rough-handed, Bolshevik side of the Labor government during the early years of the state." Ultimately, a few years later, Shamir and others were recruited into the Mossad. This was due to the insistence of Mossad head Isser Harel, who appreciated the experience and abilities of the former Lehi leader.

It is difficult to understand the depth of the commitment that developed among the younger generation without an appreciation of the many facets of the grave injustice that surrounded their families' existence. The most upsetting aspect of all, perhaps, was the callous attitude of the state institutions towards the bereaved families of Irgun and Lehi fighters.

The discrimination between Haganah casualties and those affiliated with the Irgun and Lehi, and the efforts exerted by the establishment to erase the latter from the national memory, was especially galling. Ben-Gurion prohibited display of the IDF symbol on their graves, and the media conspicuously ignored the memorial ceremonies held for them. The IDF was ordered not to send soldiers to attend these ceremonies, and while senior state figures (including Presidents and Prime Ministers) frequently participated in events commemorating the fallen fighters of the Haganah, they refused to attend commemorative events for Irgun and Lehi fighters.

According to Dr. Udi Lebel,[11] this policy of estrangement extended to the rights of bereaved families to state compensation and moral support, as well as the listing of the names of the fallen on state monuments and at official memorial events. Irgun and Lehi fighters who had been injured in the War of Independence were even denied the funding provided to other soldiers for surgery and other medical treatment. Lebel explains that the state assistance to these families and soldiers was funded by deductions from the salaries of Begin and the other Herut MKs.

The personal stories that Lebel cites in his book illustrate what many of the children of these families saw, heard, and experienced during those years. The mother of Yehiel Dresner, who was executed by the British in April 1947, was forced to keep the memorial ceremony a secret, "lest the Haganah people inform the British that our family belonged to the Revisionist underground." The mother of Menachem and Shlomo Gelbgisser, both of whom lost their lives in defense of the country, received a letter of condolence over the death of Menachem (who fought in the IDF after the incorporation of the Irgun battalions), but not for the death of Shlomo (who had fallen as an Irgun fighter). Sara Zuckerman, a bereaved mother, discovered that the face of her son, Shmuel, a Lehi fighter, did not appear among the photographs displayed at a monument for fallen soldiers.

Thus, the fighting family was committed, first and foremost, to its internal needs. The veteran fighters helped each other to find work, to fund medical treatments, to raise money for bereaved families, and to pay bills. In the early years, the majority of Israel's citizens were penniless immigrants, and only the Labor leadership had the power to distribute the contributions made by Diaspora Jewry (and, later on, German reparation payments). Most of the public was dependent on the government: not only as recipients of welfare payments or food stamps, but also as teachers, soldiers, clerks, suppliers, and contractors. The underground veteran families were simply kept out of the circle.

Eitan Haber, a long-time commentator from a Revisionist family, told me,[12] "As children, we felt persecuted. Within the movement there was always a sense of family closeness, because of this persecution." He remembers his father devoting much of his time to the rehabilitation of wounded underground fighters, collecting donations for this purpose and to support bereaved families. He recalls accompanying his father to the synagogue located at the Herut headquarters to participate in the Rosh Hashana (Jewish New Year) prayer service together with the veterans. "Begin came to pray; everyone came, the entire Irgun family," he recalled. "All crammed together, in the suits they wore for the occasion, smelling of mothballs."

The parents avoided discussing with the children the pain and affront they endured. Even in their later years, they did not share the humiliations that they had suffered. Nevertheless the children understood and took it all in. And for this reason they did not rebel against their parents as youngsters usually do, but rather rebelled together with their parents against the establishment.

The parents actually tried to dissuade their children from taking an active role in the party, and steered them away from politics. They warned them against exposing themselves as Herut loyalists, with all that this would entail. They hoped that their children would not suffer as they had, that they would not pay the same price. But the teachers at school managed to offend the children, and the history books infuriated them. The ignominy that the parents suffered was a humiliating but formative experience for the younger generation. More than half a century later, almost all of them still speak of it with pain that is evident in trembling voices and tears in the corners of their eyes. As though it all happened just yesterday.

Notes

1 The base for Irgun military operations against the British.
2 The site of one of the best-known Irgun operations. On May 4, 1947, Irgun fighters broke through the walls of Acre Prison and freed twenty-eight incarcerated Irgun and Lehi members.
3 European.
4 Middle Eastern/North African.
5 Eitan Livni, Ha-Ma'amad (Jerusalem: Idanim, 1987).
6 Ester Hagar, "An Evening of Tribute to Women Fighters" (Hebrew), in Be-Eretz Yisrael (Tel Aviv: January–February 1988), 18.
7 Yediot Aharonot, July 13, 2012.
8 Yediot Aharonot, September 13, 2012.
9 The "Saison": a code name for the Haganah campaign to suppress the Irgun and put an end to its activities.
10 Israel's temporary legislature from shortly before independence until the first Knesset elections.
11 Udi Lebel, Ha-Derekh el ha-Panteon: Etzel, Lehi u-Gevulot ha-Zikaron ha-Yisraeli [The Road to the Pantheon: Irgun, Lehi, and the Boundaries of Israeli Memory] (Jerusalem: Carmel, Sapir, Begin Heritage Center, 2007).
12 Interview with the author, July 21, 2007.

2 A generation of heirs

In all the world's political history, there is no instance comparable to that of the sons and daughters of the underground fighters in Israel who, as a group, continued their parents' legacy and, as a group, replaced them as leaders of the movement, the party, and eventually the state.

In no other modern democracy do we find a group of one single generation (in Israel's case, the generation of the underground fighters) retaining its dominant position in a party (whether directly or indirectly) over the course of more than seventy years. And we are not speaking of a generation of royalty that nurtured a crop of heirs. This was a generation that spent decades in the opposition before taking the helm of government, securing its position, and bequeathing power to its sons and daughters. The one-time, unique wonder that the underground fighters in Israel managed to pull off was an act of regime replication via generational reproduction.

There is no shortage of examples of political leadership maintaining power over time by means of loyal successors (in democracies) or biological descendants (in monarchies or tyrannical regimes). Over the course of history there have been many instances in which children of politicians continued their parents' path, sometimes advancing by virtue of their lineage all the way to the top. The Adams, Kennedy, and Bush presidential dynasties in the US come to mind, as do the Chamberlain and Churchill families in Britain. Israeli political history offers its own examples, but they span different parties and the entire seventy-year period: Prime Minister Rabin (his mother, "red" Rosa, was a Mapai activist; his daughter, Dalia, served as an MK after his assassination); Chief-of-Staff and Minister of Defense Moshe Dayan (both his father and his daughter were MKs); President Ezer Weizman (his uncle, Chaim, was Israel's first President); Chairman of the Jewish Agency Yitzhak Herzog (his father was President of Israel); and Chairman of the centrist Yesh Atid party Yair Lapid (his father, Tommy, was also chairman of a centrist party, and a government minister).

However, there is a striking difference between all of these examples and the generation of the Herut heirs. While the earlier-mentioned "sons and daughters of" took office as individuals, in different parties, and in different periods, our case involves an entire group of the same generation who came to power during the same period, and in the same party. Most of the parents were unknown to the general public – they were not Prime Ministers or Presidents (with the exception of Begin and Shamir), and it was not their political nurturing that propelled their children to power. The children themselves rose through the ranks – sometimes even against their parents' wishes – with the support of their "aunts and uncles" in the fighting family.

Of the hundreds of sons and daughters with childhood stories similar to those of Netanyahu, Rivlin, Livni, and Benny Begin, only a few dozen entered the Knesset and became well known. Their later prominence was, for the most part, arbitrary: hundreds of others had also started out as activists in the various regional branches, universities, and campaigns. Hundreds like them had been elected to student unions, city councils, movement bodies, and positions in the Jewish Agency. It was by dint of time and place that these particular figures entered the Knesset and the government, from among a horizontal, widespread wave of contemporaries who shared a similar background and who served alongside them in public positions in the party, municipal leadership, the Jewish Agency, academia, the media, and the army. In light of this, our focus should be on the entire group of peers, rather than particular names. A riddle surrounds the political "genetic code" of the generation as a whole, not just that of specific candidates.

Almost twenty heirs have served in the most senior public positions in Israel over the course of the last four decades: Prime Ministers, chairmen of the Knesset, ministers, deputy ministers, party chairmen, directors of bureaus, and government secretaries. They were all "heirs" (by definition) even if they were sons and daughters of rank-and-file fighters. Only one was real "royalty" – the son of a Prime Minister (Begin); about half were sons and daughters of MKs, ministers, and underground leaders, while the other half were children of fighters and commanders who were unknown to the public, or children of intellectuals and prominent activists. All, however, were children of the fighting family.

In the new millennium, Israel is led by heirs whose parents were senior party members in their time. Benjamin Netanyahu, who is serving his fourth term as Prime Minister, is the son of Professor Bentzion Netanyahu, secretary and confidant of the founder and leader of Revisionist Zionism, Ze'ev Jabotinsky. Reuven Rivlin, Israel's President, is the son of two Herut candidates for the first Knesset: Rachel (Ray) Rivlin, an underground activist, and Middle East scholar Professor Yosef Yoel Rivlin. Former Prime Minister Ehud Olmert is the son of MK Mordechai Olmert, chairman of the party's moshavim; Tzipi Livni, a former minister and head of the Hatnuah movement, is the daughter of the legendary Irgun Operations Officer and Herut MK Eitan Livni.

Seventeen "full" or "partial" heirs have served in the Knesset. At first, the appellation "heirs" was bestowed only on the children of Irgun and Lehi leaders and MKs representing Herut/Likud (Benny Begin, Ehud Olmert, Dan Meridor, Uzi Landau, Tzipi Livni, Yair Shamir, Tzahi Hanegbi). Since then it has come to be used with reference to children of senior and veteran Revisionist leaders (Benjamin Netanyahu, Yossi Ahimeir, Aryeh Eldad), as well as children of fighter families or supporters (President Reuven Rivlin, ministers Yariv Levin, Roni

Milo, Limor Livnat, Zeev Boim). In this book I include in the category of "heirs" anyone whom the party veterans regarded as such. In other words, anyone of the younger generation whom they felt was part of the fighting family and carried with him/her its ideological heritage, pride, and passion. Twelve of the heirs who served in the Knesset were ministers. The last three Knessets have included between eight and eleven heirs – around ten percent of the total of 120 MKs, representing no less than four political parties, ranging from the extreme Right, via the Right and the Center, to Center-Left.

The title "heirs" (in Hebrew, "*nesikhim*" – literally, princes) first cropped up in the public discourse in the 1980s, with the meteoric rise of the sons and daughters of the underground veterans. This was a period of struggle of succession following Begin's retirement from political and public life, and the speedy materialization of the heirs at center stage drew the ire of their opponents – self-styled successors Ariel Sharon and David Levy. Journalist Uri Dan, a confidant of Sharon, explains how the title came to be used.[1] In an article that he wrote in the wake of a visit, together with Sharon, to the Likud headquarters in the mid-1980s, he attached this title as a pejorative description of those known to be the children of underground activists.

> Only gradually did it dawn on me that the anti-Sharon camp surrounding Prime Minister Shamir shared the aspiration of the [younger] group that called itself the "heirs" to skip over the next generation of the party's leadership – Sharon first and foremost among them, as well as David Levy. Dan Meridor, Roni Milo, Ehud Olmert and others flattered Shamir as a way to disparage and besmirch Sharon, believing that this would ultimately advance them to the Prime Minister's seat.

Dan used the term to express the disdain that he and his hero, Sharon, felt towards the members of this group, who were Sharon's adversaries. As he saw it, they were nothing more than "children of" – inexperienced and untried youngsters who had yet to prove themselves.

In 1988, when the "prince of heirs", Benny Begin, was elected to the Knesset, representing Likud, the appellation became widely used. Over the years, growing numbers of progeny of former MKs joined the political field. The initial core of heirs, which included the future Israeli leaders Olmert, Rivlin, Milo, Meridor, Landau and Livnat, broadened to include Netanyahu, Hanegbi, Ahimeir, Boim, Livni, Sallai Meridor, and later also Aryeh Eldad, Ze'ev Jabotinsky (grandson of the party founder), Yariv Levin, and Yair Shamir.

From cell-mates to neighbors

Most of the heirs were born during the course of a single tempestuous decade, around the time of the establishment of the state. The eldest member of the group, Reuven Rivlin, was born in 1939, in Jerusalem. The youngest, Tzipi Livni, was born in 1958 in Tel Aviv. The thousands of sons and daughters born to underground fighters in between those years have left their mark not only on politics, but also in the spheres of public administration, education, the media, and the military.

After 1948, the fighting family was concentrated in three locations: the suburbs of northern Tel Aviv (and the Veterans' Neighborhood in Ramat Gan); the Rehavia neighborhood in Jerusalem, and agricultural communities in the Sharon (central plain) region.

Begin, who maintained (almost) uncontested control of the movement for forty years, made his home in a rented apartment in central Tel Aviv, within easy walking distance of the party headquarters. Here his wife Aliza raised their eldest son, Benny (1943), and their daughters, Hasia and Leah.

Many of the parents chose to live close to Begin, their venerated commander, and thus many of the heirs grew up in the area around the party headquarters: Roni Milo (1949), son of Begin's underground confidant, industrialist Nahum Milkowsky; Tzahi Hanegbi (1957), son of Geula Cohen, a fighter and right-wing journalist (a rarity), renowned as the Lehi broadcaster and later a prominent MK with a firm right-wing stance concerning the Land of Israel; Tzipi Livni (1958), daughter of Irgun fighters and symbols Sara and Eitan Livni; Yair Shamir (1945), son of the Lehi fighter and commander Shulamit and Yitzhak (respectively) Shamir. Journalist Eitan Haber (1940) was also born in the same neighborhood, as was Major-General Yohanan Locker (1958) and his brother, Harel Locker (1965), and many others. Many of the children – and certainly the parents – prayed together in the crowded Herut headquarters synagogue. Eitan Haber and Harel Locker remember their parents praying with their comrades-in-arms and with their neighbor and leader, Begin, on festivals.

Many of the underground veterans chose to make their home in the Veterans' Neighborhood in Ramat Gan, bordering on Tel Aviv (some living right next door to each other). An example is Chaim Landau, head of the Irgun General Staff, a friend and confidant of Begin over half a century, an MK representing Herut for twenty-eight consecutive years, and eventually Minister of Transport in Begin's first government. After his death in 1981, Begin replaced him as a Minister of Transport with another Irgun commander – Chaim Corfu, who appointed as director of his bureau none other than Dr. Uzi Landau, son of the previous minister, Chaim Landau. Uzi Landau's appointment was highly symbolical, but he also came with an impressive professional resumé, holding a doctorate in engineering from the prestigious MIT. Landau Jr. (1943) eventually served as an MK for twenty-seven years, and as a minister for eight. The father and son – strongly similar in their physical appearance, their manner of speech and their uncompromising views – spent fifty-five years in total in the Knesset. Another neighbor was Yaakov Meridor, Deputy Commander of the Irgun and later a minister (his daughter, Rachel Kremerman, was a prominent "heiress"). So were Azriel Livnat, a Lehi fighter, and Shulamit Livnat, the underground songstress, who moved to comfortable Ramat Gan from the "red", hostile city of Haifa (their daughter, Limor [1950] would later serve as a minister); Yisrael Eldad, one of the three leaders of Lehi and of the political faction to the right of Herut (his son, Brigadier-General and

MK Aryeh Eldad, was born in 1950), and Shmuel Tamir, an Irgun commander and later a minister, lived there, too.

The neighborhood was also home to the founders of the right-wing intellectual faction within the party – Abba Ahimeir (father of MK Yossi Ahimeir) and poet Uri Zvi Greenberg. In addition, of course, there were the Revisionists who were supposed to succeed Jabotinsky – until they were pushed aside by the "youngsters" of the Irgun, Lehi, and Herut, led by Begin. When their political path was cut off, they turned towards a different form of public service – the media. Here they achieved prominence in the non-Labor newspapers, *Yediot Aharonot* and *Maariv*. Interestingly, in this realm – as in politics – the next generation continued in their parents' footsteps. Aryeh Disenchik, one of the founders of the Beitar youth movement, and later an aide to Jabotinsky, was a founder and later the editor-in-chief of *Maariv* (succeeded by his son); Dr. Herzl Rosenblum, editor-in-chief of the rival *Yediot Aharonot* between the years 1949–1986, who wrote the paper's typically right-wing, nationalist editorial column for many years, was one of Jabotinsky's earliest followers and among the founders and leaders of the movement (succeeded by his son); Guttman Rabinovich, a Revisionist who was seriously injured as a member of the Beitar Western Wall Platoon, later became the general director of *Maariv* (his son, Professor Itamar Rabinovich, eventually became Israel's ambassador to the US and President of Tel Aviv University). The sons and daughters studied together at the Ohel Shem High School and grew up in an environment which, unlike most other places in Israel, was pluralistic, open, and tolerant. In this neighborhood the underground families enjoyed legitimacy and respect.

Other heirs grew up in the Jerusalem neighborhoods of Rehavia and Katamon. Two of the most prominent among them are Benjamin Netanyahu (1949), son of Professor Bentzion Netanyahu (head of the movement's political wing and Jabotinsky's personal secretary); and Reuven Rivlin (1939), son of Irgun activist Rachel (Ray) Rivlin. Others included Arye Naor (1940), son of Irgun founders Yehuda Naor and MK Esther Raziel-Naor; and brothers Sallai and Dan Meridor (1947), sons of Raanana and Eliyahu Meridor (close friends of Begin; Eliyahu was a senior Herut MK, serving from the party's founding); Ido Nehushtan, son of the well-known Irgun commander Devora Nehushtan and Herut MK Yaakov Nehushtan; and more.

The Revisionist aristocracy in Jerusalem (the children of the Netanyahu, Meridor, Naor, and Rivlin families) studied together at the Hebrew Gymnasium, a prestigious high school in Rehavia that produced many leaders in the military, intelligence, legal, and economic spheres in Israel. The heirs were a fierce and combative Revisionist minority in this school, whose staff and student population identified generally with the values of Labor Zionism. "I was a conversationalist," recounts Reuven Rivlin, "in a friendly, artistic spirit. I was a leader, but far removed from the positions of the teachers and my friends' parents."

Another group of heirs grew up in the movement's moshavim in the Sharon area, especially the tiny Moshav Nahalat Jabotinsky ('Jabotinsky's Estate'). Their environment was different: this was a closed, warm, traditionally religious,

Revisionist community. The parents here had grown up in the Beitar movement, fought in the Irgun, and lived in Shuni Castle, before moving, in 1946, to the small moshav near Binyamina. As Irgun veterans and farmers, the parents belonged to the National Labor Federation (NLF), founded in Jerusalem in 1934 as a Revisionist alternative to the Histadrut and complementing the movement's political arm, the Herut party. During the Revolt, many of the moshav members had been exiled to Africa by the British; all were central activists in the movement. Their children grew up in the Beitar youth movement and later achieved prominence in public life. This small moshav produced no less than seven senior figures in Israel's government and the Jewish Agency, including Prime Minister Ehud Olmert (1945); Minister Boim (1943–2011); head of Beitar and head of the Begin Heritage Center, Herzl Makov; head of Beitar and JNF Chairman Shmuel Gervitz; and Moti Kirmeir, head of the Binyamina municipality.

The childhood stories recounted by the heirs over many hours of interviews with the author and other interviews published in the press display several recurring elements: the searing de-legitimization of and discrimination against their parents; tremendous, profound admiration for the parents' activities; the spirit of activism that animated the younger generation from a young age; the close relations among members of the fighting family; and, in general, the desire on the part of the parents to keep their children out of politics and to allow them as normal an upbringing as possible. However, the children saw past this professed desire. They sensed the true will that emanated powerfully, albeit silently, from the parents: to restore their pride and dignity. To realize the ideology of Jabotinsky, their teacher.

Heirs not to royalty, but to persecution

For the older underground children, born during the Revolt against the British, war was an inseparable part of childhood. In 1943, when Aliza Begin gave birth to her eldest child, Benny, her husband had just been appointed commander of the Irgun. Menachem Begin had only recently arrived in the country. Having left Poland, his birthplace, in the wake of the Nazi invasion, he had been imprisoned in Lithuania as an "agent of British imperialism" and sent to a labor camp in the Soviet Union. Following his release he joined the Anders' (Polish) Army, with whom he was sent, via the Persian Corridor, to the Holy Land. Immediately upon his Irgun appointment, he became a wanted man and was therefore forced to be constantly on the move from one safe house to the next. To avoid any risk to his safety, Irgun member Yisrael "Aviel" Epstein was listed in the hospital records as the baby's father. Epstein, who was Begin's closest friend, became the child's favorite "uncle". In 1946, when Benny was three years old, Epstein was killed in the wake of an Irgun operation against the British embassy in Rome.

For the Begin family, underground life and family life were inextricably intertwined. At first, Begin Sr. decided against living with his wife and son, but owing to their perpetual harassment by British investigators, they ended up joining him and moving with him from place to place. A photograph published in the *Mideast Mail*, which was printed in Cairo at the time, shows the man at the top of the British "wanted" list, standing by his infant son's crib, holding a toy elephant.

Benny grew up with a mother whose name and identity were not fixed (at one time she was supposedly the wife of Rabbi Yisrael Sasover; at another time, the wife of Yisrael Epstein), and a father who, in addition to his name and identity, also periodically changed his outward appearance. He was Benny Halperin, a lawyer; then Rabbi Yisrael Sasover; then Yonah Koenigshoffer. In his autobiography, *The Revolt*, Menachem Begin wrote:

> Benny knew me only by the sound of my voice. [. . .] Every "uncle" that visited our home had a special name by which Benny knew him [. . .] so that the child wouldn't blurt out at kindergarten the well-known names of wanted figures.[2]

Further on, Begin describes the close bond that developed between his young son and Yeruham (better known by his Irgun name, "Eitan") Livni, father of Tzipi Livni. "Eitan would show Benny the funniest tricks. Benny called him 'Uncle Moshe'. [. . .] One day, three-year old Benny asked me, with a knowing smile, 'Dad, where is Uncle Moshe whose name is Yeruham?'"[3]

Shraga Elis, commander of the Irgun's fighting force, built a hideout for Begin in a small cupboard above where his wife and son slept. Years later, he recounted his meeting with Begin's son: "A serious child of about four, his arms folded over his chest. He looked like a little soldier who knew all the house's secrets and who, if arrested, would give away nothing – like any member of the underground."

Dan Meridor, too, was born into the reality of war. His mother, Irgun fighter Raanana ("Hagit") Meridor, recounts that her son was conceived on the night of the bombing of the King David Hotel (July 26, 1946). She is quite certain as to the accuracy of the date: her husband, Eliyahu, was the Irgun commander in Jerusalem, and the next morning he was arrested and deported.

> Dan was born nine months after the bombing, during the curfew that was imposed after the suicide of the two Irgun and Lehi fighters, Feinstein and Barazani, in prison in Jerusalem. In the middle of the curfew I started feeling contractions.[4]

It was a neighboring friend of the family, Professor Yosef Yoel Rivlin, who called the ambulance.

The Meridor household in Rehavia, Jerusalem, just a few meters away from the Prime Minister's Residence, symbolizes the duality that characterized the childhood of many second-generation Revisionists. It was an educated, liberal, open home, both parents being intellectuals (a professor of classical studies and a lawyer and MK). Although the home was firmly planted in the heart of the establishment, the Meridor children could recite Jabotinsky's poems by heart. Visitors to the home included the country's most senior legal minds, along with former underground leaders, some of whom (first and foremost among them, Menachem and Aliza Begin) were close friends of the Meridor parents.

In an newspaper interview,[5] Dan Meridor described his feelings as the child of parents who were well known and respected in Jerusalem, but associated with a de-legitimized movement and leader:

> There was solidarity with the rebels, with the parents. [. . .] I felt that Ben-Gurion had handed over, persecuted, hurt my father's generation. [. . .] I believed that anyone who belonged to the movement was straight and honest, while members of the Labor establishment were evil; that the establishment was corrupt.

Uzi Landau, born (like Benny Begin) in 1943, set eyes on his father, Chaim, for the first time at the age of five. Landau Sr., Irgun chief of operations, was wanted by the British and, like Begin, lived in hiding. "My father didn't live at home," Uzi Landau told me. "We lived with my grandmother, in Haifa. I remember him [appearing] all at once, after 1948."[6]

Landau told me about the sense of mission that had developed within him from an early age:

> My mother tells me that at the age of three, I went to the store on Herzl Street, in the middle of Hadar Carmel in Haifa. I went up to some British soldiers and asked them in Hebrew, "Why don't you let Jews into the country?"

Like other children of underground fighters, Landau, too, read the books by Begin (*The Revolt*) and Yaakov Meridor (about his escapes from British prisons), as well as "a lot of Zionist and Jewish history, Bible, and the party newspaper, *Herut.*" At the age of ten, after moving with his family to the Veterans' Neighborhood in Ramat Gan, he joined Beitar.

Reuven Rivlin, as the eldest of this younger generation, is the only one who has a clear memory of events from the Revolt years. He claims that the childhood event that had the greatest impact on him was the death of Asher Benziman, a young Irgun fighter and a family relative. Benziman, the first Irgun casualty of the Revolt, was killed during an attack on the British Intelligence headquarters in Jerusalem. Eitan Livni and Eliyahu and Raanana Meridor were also involved in the operation. "He and his photograph were in my mind throughout my childhood," Rivlin recalls. "All I wanted was to be like him."[7]

In the long (a few dozen hours in total) and fascinating conversations that I had with him in his capacities as MK, Minister of Communications, and chairman of the Knesset, Rivlin recounted his family's story with emotion and admiration. As the son of an Irgun-fighter mother and a renowned academic father, he was drawn into the movement's activities early on, along with his siblings. At the age of six he joined the Irgun Children, the underground's youth movement. He helped to carry hand grenades while his elder sister, Ettie, was already fighting against the British, alongside her mother.

The most influential figure in Rivlin's childhood was his mother, Rachel (Ray). Born to a family that had been expelled from Hebron in the wake of the murderous Arab riots of 1929, she joined the ranks of the Irgun without her husband's knowledge.

> My father, Professor Yosef Yoel Rivlin, was a renowned Middle East scholar who supported Jabotinsky's movement. He used to sit at home teaching Arabic to the British High Commissioner. In the next room, my mother and sister would be disassembling Sten submachine guns. My father was engrossed in his teaching; he had no idea what was going on, until one day my sister Ettie was arrested by the British, after being informed on by Teddy Kollek (a senior Haganah Intelligence officer, later mayor of Jerusalem). My mother asked my father to intercede with the High Commissioner to have her released. She didn't tell him what the charges were. My father spoke with the Commissioner and managed to obtain the release, but he was surprised to discover the reason for her arrest from his friend and student, who suggested, "You'd better keep an eye on her." When he found out that his family was fighting in the ranks of the Irgun, he signed up, too.

During his childhood, Rivlin ran into many political quarrels with those around him.

> I had arguments about the "Hunting Season" (a code name for the Haganah campaign to suppress the Irgun and put an end to its activities) in the playground in Rehavia. After the *Altalena* affair, when I was already nine, I demanded that Ben-Gurion be put on trial. I wanted to study law just so that I could be the prosecutor for his case in court. The constant posture of "defense through attack" made me more mature than my friends, although physically I looked younger than them. I felt an uncompromising hatred towards Ben-Gurion. I viewed the Labor as an enemy of the Jews. [. . .] In the Rehavia Gymnasium I was the Revisionist spokesman in any argument. And there were many; almost always against teachers who were Labor supporters. I had to continue defending and attacking.

Haggai Segal, a Religious Zionist journalist, recounts[8] how he grew up with his parents' bitterness over the murder of his father's brother, Irgun fighter Yedidya Segal, aged twenty-two. Yedidya was abducted by the Haganah in January 1948, during the "Hunting Season", and tortured to death. The cause of death was obscured, and the Haganah left his corpse in the Arab village of Tira to create the impression that he had been murdered by Arabs. The episode sent shock waves throughout the Yishuv. An Irgun poster blamed the Haganah for Yedidya's death, while the Haganah argued that he had indeed been abducted, but then released, following which he had been captured and murdered by Arabs. As the war of words escalated and appeared to be heading towards violence, the grandmother issued a call to avoid a civil war. Today, Yedidya's name appears on the Ministry of Defense's list of casualties, along with both versions of the circumstances – that of the Haganah and that of the Irgun.

Amos Hermon grew up in the Beitar moshav of Nordiya in the Sharon (central plain) region. His parents met in the Beitar company commanded by his father. His father, along with some of his companions, were exiled for three years to Eritrea, while his mother was imprisoned after she was caught with a baby carriage transporting explosives for the Irgun, to be used to blow up a ship (the couple eventually spent seven years together in prison). In the room that later became baby Amos's, Begin wrote part of his autobiography. He was very close to both Hermon parents and tried to persuade the father to take a place on the Herut list for Knesset. The father preferred to devote himself to managing the moshav. His son continued his parents' tradition by joining Beitar and eventually becoming secretary of the moshav, head of the Beitar leadership, and a member of the Jewish Agency directorate.

Among the childhood stories, those of the "moshavnik" children stand out. Unlike most of the children of Revisionist families, who grew up in a politically mixed environment in towns and cities, the children who grew up on the Herut-Beitar moshavim, such as Nahalat Jabotinsky and Nordiya, grew up in a more insular, more strongly ideological Beitar environment.

The Olmert, Gervitz, Makov, and Boim children grew up in tiny Nahalat Jabotinsky. "All in all, a single road, with twenty-eight families," as Zeev Boim described it to me in 2007.

> We conducted ourselves strictly as a community cooperative. We were cut off from Binyamina. We all studied together at the same local school, but after school we kept to our neighborhood. My younger brother, Lazie, studied in the same class as Ehud Olmert, and I studied with Ehud's elder brother, Yirmi. A sort of blood bond developed among us.

The moshav's single road conveyed a sense of lonely isolation and economic deprivation. The parents' political affiliation with the Revisionist Party – the sworn enemy of the workers' parties – blocked economic resources and doomed them to poverty. However, the frustration of the generation that grew up in Nahalat Jabotinsky was exacerbated by other factors. It was intensified by the enviable situation of the nearby veteran farms and kibbutzim, whose members lived off the largesse of the Labor government. It was deepened by the attitude of Begin, the leader of their own party, who attached little importance to agriculture and did not act to alleviate their problems. The battle for survival, waged simultaneously vis-à-vis the institutions of the Labor regime and those of the Herut movement, left a lasting impression on the moshav's younger generation, including its most prominent representative, Olmert.

A notable element in the childhood stories of the underground veteran children who grew up in the cities is the liberal education they absorbed at home. Many of the parents, who were portrayed in the media as representing the extreme – even fascist – right-wing, chose to raise their children in an open and tolerant environment, in middle-class areas where most of their neighbors worked in the free professions. The parents, who were forced to support themselves outside of the gargantuan government system, practiced law and opened private businesses; many dedicated themselves to educational public service. As noted, many of the parents wanted to leave the war behind them and to allow their children to grow up without feeling the same ostracism and isolation that they suffered.

Limor Livnat, born in 1950 in Haifa to parents from both camps (her father belonged to Lehi, her mother to the Palmach – the elite fighting force of the Haganah), had no childhood contact with the heart of the fighting family in the center of the country. Her father, Azriel, worked in the Haifa municipality and kept a low political profile. Livnat learned of his past as a Beitarist, an underground fighter, and a prisoner from stories she heard outside of the family circle. "My first political memory is only from about the age of eight," she told me.

> My father took me to see the May Day parade. We climbed a hill and he said, "You see? They [pointing] handed me over to the British." It's a memory that remains with me to this day.[9]

Even the families who were more rigid in their Revisionist ideology (for example, Netanyahu, Ahimeir, Begin, and Meridor) raised their children in an open, non-dogmatic milieu. They did not press their children to join the struggle. Often, the opposite was the case: they sought to keep their private family lives separate from the national and political conflict, and to avoid involving their children in tensions that existed outside of the home. "Although my father was always an ideologue, I grew up in a non-doctrinaire household," reports Yossi Ahimeir, son of Abba Ahimeir, who founded the radical ideological group Brit ha-Biryonim (Strongmen's Alliance). Benny Begin recalls, surprisingly enough:

> I don't remember any sense of persecution. Not as a personal experience. There was something else that was more important: attesting to the truth in public, even when you belong to a small and despised minority. In the end, the truth prevails, even if it takes a long time. What amazed us was, where did all this hatred for the Revisionists come from? How could it be possible to hate so much?[10]

Uzi Landau told me that his father expressed reservations about his entry into politics, arguing that "one politician in the family is enough." Dan Meridor, too, told me that "our parents actually didn't push us in the direction of politics." Ido Netanyahu (brother of Prime Minister Benjamin Netanyahu) says, "My father didn't even tell us who to vote for." And so it happened that, in contrast to the fighter parents, who had created and maintained separatist ideological groups in their youth, the younger generation was exposed to the range of views and ideas prevailing among the Israeli public, and most (Begin, Netanyahu, Milo, Hanegbi, Meridor, and Ze'ev Jabotinsky – the grandson) were not members of the Beitar youth movement. Jabotinsky Jr. recalls that his father had not wanted him to join:

"My father didn't want me to be ostracized. [. . .] He sent me to the Scouts (a youth movement more closely affiliated with Labor)."[11] Those who did join Beitar found a weakened, shrunken movement that was financially strapped and in no position to absorb and educate new members. Thus, whereas the parents had received a militant, dogmatic education within the Beitar framework, the children were exposed to the Beitar ideology not as members of the youth movement, but rather from home.

Rivlin reports that although he joined Beitar ("naturally"), he kept his options open and attended Scouts meetings, too.

> At Scouts camps I meet kibbutzniks. There I learned about the Left. If you don't fight for your views and refute the lies, you are liable either to be swept into the other camp, or to give in to despair.

Tzipi Livni, too, combined Beitar activity with involvement in the Scouts in north Tel Aviv.

Tzahi Hanegbi, among the youngest of the heirs, also grew up in Tel Aviv, in the 1960s and '70s, arguing with his teachers and protesting the offensive history books. However, he, too, recalls a regular childhood with his contemporaries: "I grew up in the heart of the elite. [. . .] I didn't feel that I had walls around me."[12]

Notes

1 Uri Dan, Be-Sodo shel Ariel Sharon [Ariel Sharon's Confidant] (Rishon Lezion: Yediot Ahaaronot and Hemed, 2007)
2 Menachem Begin, Ha-Mered [The Revolt] (Tel Aviv: Ahiasaf, 1977), 104.
3 Ibid., 187.
4 Yediot Aharonot, May 8, 1998.
5 Yediot Aharonot, December 28, 2001.
6 Yediot Aharonot, May 8, 1998.
7 Interview with the author, May 23, 2002.
8 Interview with the author, April 18, 2002.
9 Interview with the author, July 5, 2002.
10 Ha-Ir, April 26, 1996.
11 Yediot Aharonot, November 25, 2008.
12 Interview with the author, April 18, 2001.

3   The beginning
Jabotinsky

The underground fighters – the parents' generation – were born in the early twentieth century (1913–1928). They, too, were born into a world caught up in political turmoil, persecution, and war. By the 1930s, with antisemitism intensifying in Poland, they were in their teens and twenties. Many belonged to the Beitar Revisionist youth movement, which grew quickly and reached its peak, in the mid-1930s, with a membership of some seventy thousand youth, about half of them in Poland. Their activities included marching through the streets of Warsaw, wearing the brown Beitar uniform, decorated with the insignia of their different ranks, and proudly bearing the movement's symbol – the menorah. For the first time after two thousand years of exile, Jewish youth were not afraid to display their national identity, despite the growing hatred around them. They adopted the teachings of the movement's leader, Ze'ev Jabotinsky, underwent brief military training, and became an energetic and courageous force inspired by a right-wing, militant Zionist ideology. They wanted to emigrate to the Land of Israel, to fight for Jewish independence in their historical homeland. They were the first generation of Jews who recognized and demanded their own right to independence and self-defense, and they set themselves a clear goal: the establishment of an independent Jewish state in the historical Jewish homeland.

In between the two world wars, Europe was torn between great, absolute ideologies. Adherents of the respective camps recognized no middle path, no shades of grey. The world was divided between black and white, good and evil, right and wrong, Right and Left. Arguments turned very bitter and often descended into violence. Sadly, the hatred that prevailed between the ideological camps seeped into the Jewish communities in Europe, and in the Holy Land, too. The Yishuv witnessed a shift of power from the liberal stream to the workers' parties, which, already by the mid-1930s, were at the center of the coalition that governed the Zionist institutions and controlled their resources, both in the Land of Israel and around the world. This coalition kept the Revisionists – a scorned minority persecuted by the Histadrut and by Ben-Gurion – far from positions of power.

After making their way to the Holy Land from Poland and other European countries, the Beitar graduates joined demonstrations against what they viewed as the conciliatory policy of the Yishuv leadership towards the British administration and the Arabs. They detested the Labor Zionists' socialist symbols, which for them were closely associated with the Communist regime. In the streets they encountered youngsters their own age, who were graduates of the left-wing establishment youth movements. They exchanged slurs – "Fascists!" "Communists!" Such encounters routinely developed into physical skirmishes, especially during May Day parades.

The conflict reached its climax in 1933, when Chaim Arlozorov, one of the leaders of the workers' movement and the Jewish Agency's "foreign minister", as it were, was shot dead while walking with his wife along the Tel Aviv beachfront. Ben-Gurion and the workers' parties attributed the shocking murder to the Revisionists. The logic behind this accusation was that Arlozorov had been in fierce conflict with the Revisionists owing to the negotiations he was conducting at the time with the Nazi leadership, with a view to saving German Jewish property. The workers' media pointed its collective finger at the Brit ha-Biryonim (Strongmen's Alliance) – a small, radical group on the Revisionist right. The group's members vehemently denied their involvement, calling the campaign a baseless blood libel aimed at sullying their public image and weakening their struggle. Two young Revisionists were charged with the murder but were later acquitted, since there was only one witness – the wife of the deceased – who claimed to identify them despite the darkness and the suddenness of the attack. Eight decades after the incident, journalist Dan Margalit revealed that his grandfather, who had been a loyal Laborite, had arrived at the Histadrut headquarters and conveyed to Dov Hoz, one of the Labor leaders, a testimony that contradicted that of Arlozorov's wife. He had heard a reliable report from an Arab from Jaffa, who asserted that it was Arabs who had killed Arlozorov. However, his party chiefs had chosen to ignore this information and to bash the Right.

Arlozorov's murder shook the Yishuv and was the subject of fierce controversy for decades. Calumny was heaped not only on the two men accused of the murder, but also on Abba Ahimeir, on the rest of the group, and on the entire Revisionist movement. For many years, the Labor leadership continued to accuse the movement and Begin, its leader, of killing a fellow Jew. Brit ha-Biryonim fell apart, and the hard-core Revisionists became a reviled, oppressed group. The charge of murder rankled so painfully that fifty years later, newly elected Prime Minister Begin appointed an official committee of inquiry, chaired by Judge David Bechor, to investigate the affair. The commission acquitted the two main suspects of all charges and found that the movement had not been involved in any way. But it was fifty years too late.

Revisionism was born in the very heart of the Russian-Jewish intelligentsia, and Ze'ev Jabotinsky (1880–1940) was its most prominent representative. Jabotinsky was a product of the golden age of Odessa, a bustling and exhilarating cosmopolitan Russian city. His socio-economic worldview was influenced by the optimistic liberalism of the late nineteenth century. Odessa was both physically and culturally far removed from the insular Jewish communities of Poland, and Jabotinsky and his peers received a secular, liberal, assimilationist education. They studied at university, wrote prolifically, published articles and songs and books, toured Europe, and documented what they saw in the newspapers. These trips, departing from comfortable Odessa and bringing them into direct contact with the suffering and distress of the Jews in Europe, changed their lives.

Two central events shaped Jabotinsky's worldview. The first was a wondrous occasion that swept him up in electrified fascination: history's first Zionist Congress, convened in Basel, Switzerland, in 1897. The congress was organized at the initiative and under the direction of Dr. Benjamin Zeev Herzl, whom Jabotinsky and his friends regarded as an outstanding leader and visionary. The second event was traumatic: a wave of pogroms against the Jews of Russia at the beginning of the twentieth century. This savage wage of antisemitism prompted a huge wave of Jewish emigration from Russia, headed mainly for the US. Only a small trickle reached the Land of Israel, representing what came to be known as the Second Aliya.

At the age of twenty-three, Jabotinsky was exposed to the massacre of the Jews of Kishinev, in 1903. This liberal journalist from Odessa arrived in Kishinev (today, the capital of Moldova) and was shaken by the depth and the extent of the cruelty that he documented. Following his visit, he translated into Russian a poem by the Jewish nationalist poet Chaim Nahman Bialik, "In the City of Slaughter" (the English version is entitled, "A Tale of Nemirov"), so that millions of Russian Jews would know what had happened. Indeed, the immortal lines appalled the Russian Jewish communities. The Kishinev pogroms were a turning point for Jabotinsky and his young intellectual friends: they renounced the Diaspora and joined the Zionist movement, as described by Professor Eri Jabotinsky ("son of", a senior Irgun member and eventually an MK) in his book, *Avi* (My Father), *Zeev Jabotinsky*.[1] They turned their backs on assimilation and defied the traditional Jewish leadership. Their first step was to establish a self-defense society for the Jews of Odessa – the first Jewish military organization.

Jabotinsky's charismatic personality attracted a huge following of youth who gathered to hear him speak at gatherings throughout Eastern Europe. In fact, the Revisionist movement grew and developed out of Jabotinsky's multi-faceted personality, his multi-disciplinary activity, and – especially – the tremendous admiration that he inspired. His hundreds of appearances in towns and villages captured tens of thousands of Jewish hearts, and particularly the youth, who were starting to reject exilic conventions and Jewish passivity.

At first, Jabotinsky and his colleagues published their views in the Zionist press, especially the Jewish journal *Rassvet*. In 1923 they bought the journal and turned it into a mouthpiece for new and different Zionist views – a sort of right-wing intellectual opposition. Within a short time they had created an activist camp that was ready to rebel against the prevailing Jewish and Zionist mindset, which they regarded as weak and passive. This led to the birth of the Revisionist Party, in 1925, which became the first (political) arm of Jabotinsky's broader movement.

His followers were at the forefront of the militant wing of Russian Zionists at the Seventh Congress of Russian Zionists, in 1917. Eight years later, Jabotinsky resigned from the World Zionist Organization Executive and established his independent Revisionist Party. The Revisionist movement, as its name indicates, sought a "revision": a new way of looking at reality that would put an end to the conciliatory approach of the Zionist Executive chairman, Chaim Weizmann, towards the British Mandate. It was a courageous act of defiance against the most powerful figure in the Zionist movement.

Jabotinsky was held in esteem by many Jews throughout Europe but endured systematic defamation owing to his criticism of the passivity of the Zionist leadership, which he regarded as criminal negligence in the face of the danger posed by growing antisemitism. Owing to his views he was depicted as an extremist and violent nationalist. In reality, Jabotinsky had another, lesser-known side to him. He was a multi-faceted Renaissance man who appreciated culture and literature, translated poetry, and wrote fiction and commentary on current affairs; he was a secular liberal, a feminist, and a crusader for human rights, whose (non-socialist) social manifesto included five basic necessities that society must provide to those in need: food, housing, clothing, education, and healthcare.

His well-developed doctrine rested on the dual foundations of grandeur and resolve. He was born into grandeur – liberalism, enlightenment, and human rights. The resolve developed as a result of the bloodthirsty reality that his people endured. It was the unrest and upheavals in Europe that brought him to a nationalist, Zionist awareness and absolute dedication to the Jewish People. On his travels as a journalist through the killing fields of the First World War, he reached the conclusion that there could be no reliance on the mercies of other nations, and his was the first voice calling to establish a Jewish army. He believed in and pursued association with a Great Power as a lever to achieving the dream of a Jewish state.

Jabotinsky was a political meteor who rocketed his way into the Zionist Executive, earning great respect for his activities in Europe and in the Land of Israel. In 1915, together with Trumpeldor, he founded the Jewish Legion – an official Jewish military formation that operated within the framework of the British army and helped to expel the Turks from the Land of Israel. Jabotinsky believed at the time that aiding Britain would ultimately pay off and help to achieve Jewish independence. This hope was gradually extinguished as the British abandoned support for the Jews over the course of the years in favor of the more aggressive Arab side.

By virtue of his words and actions, which introduced a new spirit of Jewish nationalism, Jabotinsky quickly became one of the foremost figures of world Zionism. Within just a few years of his arrival in the Holy Land, he achieved prominence in the Yishuv and was regard as a likely successor to Ben-Gurion. In 1920, with the outbreak of the first Arab riots, Jabotinsky and Pinhas Rutenberg organized the youth of Jerusalem, along with ex-Jewish Legion soldiers, into a defense force (later to become the Haganah) to protect the city's Jews. The British occupiers viewed this as a challenge to their authority and arrested Jabotinsky. He was sentenced to fifteen years' imprisonment with hard labor, but this raised a storm of protest throughout the Yishuv and abroad, and so the sentence was reduced: he was expelled from the country, thereby distancing him from the Yishuv and from the political mechanism that had started to develop. As a result, he lost the chance to play a leading role within the Yishuv. One can only imagine what a different course history might have taken had Jabotinsky remained in the country.

Jabotinsky sat on the World Zionist Organization Executive, alongside Chaim Weizmann and Nahum Sokolov, representing the General Zionist camp, and Ben-Gurion, from the socialist camp, but he soon found himself vociferously opposing what he viewed as their restrained and submissive approach. In 1922, in response to a decision by the Zionist Executive to accept the British White Paper which awarded two-thirds of the territory covered by the Mandate to the Arabs (the Kingdom of Jordan), he resigned from the body. In Eastern Europe, which was seething with antisemitism, his messages inspired great hope for change, in contrast to the socialist leadership, which seemed timid and unresponsive. Jabotinsky's vision was especially attractive to the youth, and a military Zionist youth movement was established in the spirit of his ideology. The core members were groups of students – Aharon Tzvi Propes, Aryeh Disenchik, and others – at a gymnasium in Riga, Latvia, who called their new movement Beitar. The name had dual significance: it recalled the ancient city of Beitar, the last stronghold of Bar Kokhba, the Jewish hero who led a revolt against the Romans, and was also an altered acronym for "Brit (Covenant of) Yosef Trumpeldor", recalling the contemporary hero who had fought with Jabotinsky in the Jewish Legion. In 1923, Jabotinsky made an official announcement introducing the Beitar youth movement, eventually to become the Revisionist movement's educational arm. In 1925 he established the Revisionist movement itself. The movement ran in the Zionist Organization elections, and for a short time Jabotinsky rejoined the Zionist Executive but maintained his uncompromising oppositional stance. Ben-Gurion, whose political strength among the Yishuv had grown, identified Jabotinsky as his main personal and ideological competitor. Each saw the other as a sworn enemy, whose path was dangerous and treacherous for the Jewish People.

Jabotinsky and his followers therefore remained active in Europe, while the socialist movement established itself in the Land of Israel over the course of the 1920s and '30s. Physically distant from the centers of power in the Yishuv, Jabotinsky called for the establishment of a Jewish state in the Greater Land of Israel – on both sides of the Jordan River. This demand stood in opposition to the view of the mainstream Zionists, who opposed setting the Jewish state as an explicit and clear goal, lest it anger the British, who might then put a stop to the gradual and quiet process of settlement that was taking place.

Although life for Jews in Eastern Europe was becoming unbearable, all attempts at cooperation among the opposing Zionist camps failed. Following considerable efforts, the two profoundly hostile leaders, Ben-Gurion and Jabotinsky, met at a fateful summit in London with a view to joining forces, against the background of Hitler's rise to power. Surprisingly enough, the leaders reached a promising historical agreement. This agreement was accepted by the opposition – Jabotinsky's movement – but was rejected by Ben-Gurion's camp. The rejection of this compromise, coming on top of the Arlozorov affair and the ideological chasm between the parties, led Jabotinsky to finally pull out of the World Zionist Organization. This was such a dramatic step that it led to a split within his own movement. Most of the core founders of the movement broke with him and formed a new faction, leaving Jabotinsky alone.

This was the first of several rifts that divided the Zionist opposition, which lacked the ability of the dominant parties to distribute favors to their members. The new faction comprised most of the party's executive – in other words, those who had been destined to succeed Jabotinsky and continue his path, first and foremost among them Meir Grossman, Jabotinsky's deputy. Thus, the first generation of Jabotinsky's heirs was lost – a generation of activist, energetic Zionists who were educated, liberal, intellectual, experienced, and worldly. They were not made of the same stuff as Jabotinsky, who foresaw disaster and would not compromise with those whom he regarded as meek, acquiescent, and blind to the annihilation that would come if a Jewish state did not arise. The separatists believed in compromise and advancing their goals from within the Zionist Organization institutions, while Jabotinsky refused to be an irrelevant and powerless minority within a body that lacked the courage to define as its aim the establishment of a Jewish state in the Land of Israel. He thus remained alone and isolated in terms of the Zionist institutions, but enjoyed the support of the Revisionist public and its younger generation – the Beitar movement. In the elections held within the movement, Grossman's faction received twelve thousand votes, while Jabotinsky received the overwhelming support of the party with some ninety-six thousand votes. He had emerged victorious, but the party had been severely weakened, losing most of its leadership along with the precious resources of power: the immigration certificates awarded by the British for allocation at the discretion of the Jewish Agency.

The new faction called itself the Jewish State Party and remained within the Zionist Organization, while in 1935 Jabotinsky established the New Zionist Organization. However, this alternative body was incapable of serving as a counterweight to the established Zionist institutions that were already so well known and enjoyed the support of Jewish communities throughout the world as well as in the Holy Land. The main reason for its lack of traction was that along with its senior leadership, the Revisionist movement had lost its potential partners – the General Zionists and the Religious Zionists. The separatists and potential partners alike chose to cast their lot with the dominant Labor Zionists, and all the power and resources that they commanded, rather than with Jabotinsky, who charted an oppositionist course of blood, sweat, and tears, and remained isolated and slandered as a nay-sayer and divider.

The vast leadership vacuum created by the departure of the party founders was filled by the "Jabotinsky youth", the disciples who had been swept up in the intense following that grew around Jabotinsky a decade earlier, and who had established Beitar and led the youth movement to this point. In the wake of the rift, these figures, now in their late twenties, became the Revisionist movement's new leadership. The youth that the founders had led in the early years of Beitar (Menachem Begin's generation) replaced them at the helm of the youth movement's various branches.

The situation deteriorates – the rise of the generation of Revolt

By the mid-1930s, Beitar was flourishing. It drew in more and more Jewish youngsters, and within three years its membership had quadrupled from 16,500 in 1930 to 65,000 in 1933. At its peak the movement comprised some seventy thousand members in four hundred branches, about half of them in Poland. Beitar drew its inspiration from the Jewish Legion established by Jabotinsky and Trumpeldor within the British army during the First World War. They adopted the same symbol – the menorah (seven-branched candelabrum) – and the movement's brown uniform was a military uniform for all intents and purposes, including ranks and insignia. The Beitar commanders offered Jewish youth something that was new and exciting: military instruction.

Throughout the 1930s, Beitar spread like wildfire over the expanses of riven, hate-filled Europe. Its revolutionary vision attracted children and youth who were drowning in a sea of despair and helplessness in the face of the boundless violence of the Nazis, fascists, and Communists. When the founders of Beitar joined Jabotinsky in the top leadership of the Revisionist movement, their earliest followers replaced them as leaders of the youth movement. For the first time, Beitar was now led by a cadre of "new Jewish youth", who had received an intensive Zionist, activist, revolutionary, and military education. The movement changed its face – not only in the wake of this new leadership, but also in response to the dramatic changes taking place in Europe. From a movement whose focus was education and ideology, it became a movement that was oriented towards military training, immigration, and settlement. And as Beitar, under Begin and his generation, continued to grow, the Revisionist movement – both in the Land of Israel and in Europe – was transformed along with it: from a Russian-based movement it became Polish-based; its adult membership was increasingly outnumbered by youth; and its range of aims coalesced into a single focus: a state, at all costs.

The younger generation had a different perspective from its educators. The youth were in a hurry. The ground in Europe was burning and there was no more time for compromise, for long-term planning. They took to heart Jabotinsky's own warning: "Destroy the diaspora, or it will destroy you." Unlike the leaders of the other Zionist movements, Jabotinsky seemed to enjoy watching his rebellious protégés challenging the older leaders. From this point, the Revisionist movement had two autonomous centers of power: the older political party and the younger, militant Beitar youth movement. The first Beitar youth who moved to the Land of Israel established the movement's second arm – labor and settlement – as part of their vision of settling and cultivating the land.

The 1930s witnessed a murderous struggle in Europe among conflicting ideologies: Left and Right, communism, Socialism, liberalism, and capitalism. This struggle manifested itself in the Yishuv, too, in the conflict between Socialism and Revisionism; between Ben-Gurion's powerful Histadrut, which exercised complete control over the job market, and Jabotinsky's labor and settlement endeavor. The struggle was characterized by a mutual burning hatred, expressed in both verbal and physical violence in the streets. In November 1932, Jabotinsky published an article entitled, "Ja, Brechen!" (Yes, Break It!). In the article, which appeared in the most popular Jewish newspaper in Poland, *Haynt* (Today), Jabotinsky called for breaking the Histadrut monopoly on organized labor – a monopoly which, to his view, was obstructing economic development and strangling the private sector. For many years afterwards, his words were used against him, with the claim that he had called to "break" the workers themselves. Both he and his movement became irreversibly identified in the public mind as enemies of the workers.

This represents the background to the third arm of the Revisionist movement – the National Labor Federation (NLF). This body was established by workers who were disillusioned with the socialist Histadrut and repelled by its communist orientation, along with Beitar immigrants from Poland. The vision of the Labor movement was a situation in which there would be no labor outside the framework of the Histadrut, while the Revisionists viewed organized labor as a form of communism that precluded private initiative and subjugated all workers in the Land of Israel to the absolute control of the Labor movement.

Thus, while Europe suffered the convulsions leading up to the Second World War and the Yishuv endured Arab attacks, the Jewish political movements in the Holy Land were busy fighting each other – as though their common enemies were not threatening to annihilate all the Jews. The Left viewed the Right as fascists; the Right viewed their rivals on the Left as Communists. In the violent clashes that broke out in the streets on May Day, the Beitar immigrants from Poland played a conspicuous role. They viewed this day not as a workers' holiday, but rather as the Communist-Stalinist holiday of the enemies of the Jews. The Polish Beitar figures who stood out in these skirmishes became the movement's leaders for the next fifty years.

The fourth and final arm of Jabotinsky's movement was the Irgun – the movement's military arm in the Land of Israel.

Over the course of his adult life Jabotinsky participated in the establishment and command of four different military organizations. At the same time, he always believed in the superiority of diplomacy and maintained that these organizations had to be subservient to political strategy. He viewed military power as important not as an end in itself, but rather in the service of an idea and a policy.

The first initiative – the first Jewish military organization since the revolt against Rome – focused on self-defense for the Jews of Odessa. Then, during the First World War, Jabotinsky established the Jewish Legion, together with Yosef Trumpeldor. The Legion was important, but its purpose was political: it operated within the framework of the British army, with a view to creating British commitment towards the Jewish People once victory had been achieved and the spoils of war could be divided. Disappointingly, this hope did not materialize.

Next, during the Arab riots of 1920, Jabotinsky organized the Jews in Jerusalem to defend themselves, with the approval of the Yishuv leadership. In effect, this was the origin of the Haganah. (Later on, the Haganah was made subservient to the Histadrut, and the official story came to be that the Haganah had been established by the Laborites.) Jabotinsky's aim was simple: to enlist former Jewish Legion soldiers to protect Jewish lives from the marauding Arabs. No longer would the Jews wait for and depend on British protection; they would now defend themselves. This was a rather revolutionary idea, since most of the Jewish leadership relied on the British and were reluctant to anger them. As noted, Jabotinsky was arrested and imprisoned for this military activity, and it was only public pressure that led to his sentence being commuted, along with the sentences of all those arrested during the riots. However, he was forced to live in exile, and the focus of the Revisionist Party became the salvation of European Jewry from its bitter fate.

After seven years of relative quiet, during which the Yishuv felt that the British were offering protection and a wave of immigration doubled the Jewish population of the country, came the riots of 1929. Sixty-seven Jews were slaughtered and burned, with no intervention by the British police. With this the policy of self-restraint was broken. The Yishuv was deeply shocked by the total of 130 Jews who had been killed in the riots between 1920–1929 (proportionately to the size of the population, this would equal 5,000 people in the State of Israel in 2018, or 200,000 American citizens, relative to the population of the US). The Haganah was accused of inaction and of yielding to the pacifist spirit of the 1920s. Jabotinsky, far away in exile, expressed his support for Haganah commanders who had now had enough of restraint, and sought a Jewish military response. Many Haganah youth demanded action, and when their demand was not met, they took independent action. In 1931 a group separated from the Haganah to establish the Haganah Leumit ("National Haganah", also known as Haganah B) as an alternative. In the next set of riots, in 1936, this group would change its name and its purpose, calling itself Etzel (*Irgun Tzvai Leumi* – National Military Organization, known in English by its abbreviated name – the Irgun). This signalled an important shift from "*haganah*" (defense) to an organization that was openly "*tzvai*" (military).

The Labor party newspapers depicted Jabotinsky as an extremist, but in truth the Revisionist leader set limits on his commanders, insisting that their activities remain within the scope of limited, local self-defense responses. He declared over and over that his aim was not a military underground but rather a unified "Hebrew Brigade" defense force, operating with British approval. However, after failing to receive British support, he sided with the youngsters who demanded a response to Arab violence. His view remained strategic: he feared that Jewish restraint was being interpreted by the Arabs as weakness.

As noted, the Zionist movement split in 1935, and with it the Haganah Leumit. The other parties that made up the Haganah Leumit coalition (the General Zionists and the Mizrahi Religious Zionist party) chose to remain part of the Zionist institutions, with all the resources that they had to offer, rather than heading for the wastelands of the impoverished and beleaguered opposition. Once their demand that the Haganah command be transferred from the Histadrut to the Zionist institutions was accepted, the General Zionists and the Mizrahi party rejoined the Haganah, along with commander Avraham Tehomi and his headquarters, and the population of the moshavot (the farmers of the First Aliya). The Haganah was

Figure 3.1 Abraham (Yair) Stern, later to become leader of the Lehi movement, in a photo
from 1918 with his young brother David, who would become a leader in the
Lehi movement and an MK of the Likud party.

restored to its former status as a large, official, and representative organ of the
Yishuv, while the dissenters who remained part of the Haganah Leumit became
part of Jabotinsky's movement.

The murderous pogroms of 1936–1939, known as the "Arab Revolt", could
legitimately be called a war. Some four hundred Jews were killed. This was a
bloodbath, and a sign of things to come – the great war a decade later.

The years of the Arab Revolt were full of pain and frustration: first, because of
the deadly attacks on many Jewish settlements; secondly, because of British policy,

Figure 3.2 Etzel commander David Raziel (right) riding in Jerusalem. Raziel's sister
Esther Raziel Naor was also a commander in the Etzel and served later as MK.
Her son, Arye Naor, was a secretary in Begin's government.

finding expression in the Peel Commission and the White Paper of 1939, which
placed heavy restrictions on Jewish immigration and forbade the sale of land to
Jews throughout most parts of the country; and lastly, because of the continued
policy of restraint on the part of the Haganah, whose leadership chose immigration and settlement as their first priority, rather than military confrontation.

Even before the Arab Revolt, the Irgun witnessed a changeover of generations
and a change of orientation. As noted, at first the organization was headed by adult
commanders, who respected political authority. Later on, however, there was a

wave of resignations and dismissals of the older commanders, who were accused of yielding to the establishment. The new, "native" commanders were Raziel and Stern. Alongside them were young commanders who had been fighting since a young age. The character of the fighters was different, too: now the organization counted more fighters from the Yemenite neighborhoods and more new Beitar immigrants. The Beitar graduates from Poland began to mold the Irgun into a resolute military organization.

Jabotinsky retained the title of head of the Irgun. He was the responsible, restraining adult, while the commanders were young people who were appalled at the bloodshed in the streets. Their generation had no patience for the moderation of far-away leaders who thought in terms of statesmanship, rather than in terms of the urgency of putting a halt to the butchery. On April 30, 1937, while on a speaking tour in South Africa, Jabotinsky dispatched a telegram that signalled a change in policy: "My order, in current circumstances: if the riots resume, and if they show a tendency to target Jews, too, do not hold back."[2] On November 14, 1937, Raziel led an operation that included attacks in Jerusalem; this marked the end of restraint. The chairman of the Jewish National Council, Yitzhak Ben-Zvi, called it "Black Sunday".

The 1930s were characterized by conflict on the international and local level between the social Left and Right. The end of the decade brought a change in focus and agenda in the defense realm.

Notes

1 Eri Jabotinsky, Avi, Zeev Jabotinsky (Tel Aviv: Steimatzky, 1980).
2 David Niv, Ma'arakhot ha-Etzel [The Irgun Battles] (Tel Aviv: Hadar, 1980), vol. 1, 300.

4 The parents
Generation of the Revolt

Three dramatic events that occurred during the 1930s and '40s changed the agenda of the Revisionist movement.

The first was the outbreak of the Arab Revolt (1936–1939). As described earlier, in view of the Haganah's restraint, the Irgun adopted a policy of military activism. Its change of name, from Haganah Leumit (National Defense) to Irgun Tzvai Leumi (National Military Organization), reflected this shift. In the midst of the Arab Revolt, Britain issued the White Paper of 1939, which placed additional, harsh restrictions on Jewish immigration and settlement – and did nothing to calm the Arab violence. This, for the Irgun commanders, represented further justification for the organization's independent existence.

The second dramatic event was the Second World War, which brought profound upheaval and placed Jewish survival in real and terrible danger, especially in view of the fact that the gates of the Holy Land were now almost locked to Jewish refugees from Europe.

In between, there was a third dramatic event: the sudden death of Ze'ev Jabotinsky, at the age of sixty. This unexpected development dissolved the links that connected the various arms of the movement. In view of everything else that was going on, Jabotinsky's death bestowed independence on the impassioned, activist military youth, rendering all the other, older heirs of Jabotinsky's legacy irrelevant.

This was the stage when Revisionist publicists were replaced by fighters, as the poems and articles penned by Jabotinsky's protégés paled next to the rivers of Jewish blood. The educated founders and ideological leaders of Beitar, who were now in their thirties, appeared old and out of touch in relation to the sixteen-year-olds, who now grasped what seemed to be the only possible solution: the rifle. There was no more time for words, for lessons, for ceremonies. The fighter youth's time had come. It was a new era.

Jabotinsky's final days – victory of the rebels, and their division

The third Beitar conference, in 1938, witnessed an emotional and symbolic confrontation that reflected the inter-generational rift in Jabotinsky's movement: the

Figure 4.1 The spiritual fathers of the Revolt generation: the "Strongmen's Alliance". From left to right: Abba Ahimeir, Uri Zvi Greenberg, and Yehoshua Yeyvin, 1917.

chasm separating the middle generation from the younger one. At this critical moment, just prior to the outbreak of the Second World War, representatives of the two groups found themselves at loggerheads over the movement's path forward. On one side there were the young Beitar members, who had travelled to the conference from around Europe – especially Poland – and from the Land of Israel. On the other side were Jabotinsky's "natural" successors, representing his party and the older Beitar establishment.

During the conference, the young leaders, led by Begin, Raziel, and Stern, sought to change the Beitar oath. To replace the words, "I shall ready my arm for

Figure 4.2 Ze'ev Jabotinsky (right lower corner) among leaders of Beitar in Poland, including Menachem Begin (left lower corner), 1933.

the defense of my people, and I shall raise my arm only in defense", the young Menachem Begin, head of Beitar in Poland, wished to add just two Hebrew words: "I shall ready my arm for the defense of my people and conquest of my home-land". The move to change this formula expressed the growing insistence among the young to conquer the land by force. This distanced them further and further from the older leadership, which still believed in diplomacy and the subservience of military force to political strategy.

Jabotinsky took the side of the older leadership. For the first (and only) time, he faced down his prized protégé, Begin, commenting acerbically on his vehement address: "Your speech, Mr. Begin, was like a squeaking door." He concluded his words by saying, "If you, Mr. Begin, do not believe that the world still has a conscience, you have no choice but to take yourself off to the deep Visela River."

By the end of the conference, however, Jabotinsky had acceded to his young followers, just as a year previously he had yielded to Irgun pressure and had permitted a breaking of the policy of restraint. He changed the Beitar oath, as Begin requested. The conference participants went home with a sense that the future leader, Jabotinsky's heir, had made his appearance.

Jabotinsky's untimely death – from a heart attack, during a speaking tour of the US – came as a shock to his supporters and opponents alike. He had been held in great esteem and was the movement's supreme authority. With his passing, his

followers in Europe were left orphaned, bereft of any part in the Zionist organizations from which they had seceded. In the years following Jabotinsky's death, as
the Second World War grew more intense, everything was caught up in the chaos
of annihilation. A great many activists, including founders of the movement and
leaders of both the older and the "middle" generation, perished along with their
families.

The Holocaust put a halt to the rapid spread of the Revisionist movement in
Europe. In the absence of any overall authority, the movement's center of gravity
shifted to the Holy Land, where the younger generation was waging a determined
struggle against the Arab Revolt and would soon also be fighting against the British, who, at the most critical hour of need, closed the ports to Holocaust refugees.
The militaristic rebel youngsters were the leaders of the remnant of the movement
that had not been exterminated. It was their worldview and their organization that
now became dominant. The Irgun and Lehi were, for all intents and purposes,
the Revisionist movement. The other organizations had lost their members and
had no relevant agenda in this age of bloodshed. From a heterogeneous, multi-
faceted, pluralistic movement with a diverse leadership, Jabotinsky's movement
had become a much narrower and more focused movement, under the leadership
of the young Beitar fighters – the generation of the Revolt.

The Second World War led to a third rift within five years between the (relative) "moderates" and the "militants" within the Revisionist movement, which
was vilified in any case by the Yishuv establishment. The Irgun now split into two
underground movements: Stern and most of the Irgun senior commanders seceded
and formed Lehi (*Lohamei Herut Yisrael* – Fighters for Israel's Freedom), taking
most of the membership (some eight hundred fighters) with them. They supported
a continuation of the struggle against the British, even though Britain was now
fighting against Nazi Germany. Stern had lost faith in the British, viewing the
White Papers as evidence of their hostility towards the Zionist enterprise and their
bias towards the Arabs at the expense of the seemingly weaker Jewish side. Stern
was not convinced that Britain would permit the Jews to establish a state, and he
viewed British opposition to the immigration of Jewish refugees from Europe as a
betrayal. He and his faction decided to fight Britain as though there were no Nazis
and to fight the Nazis as though there were no Britain.

David Raziel, commander of the Irgun, upheld Jabotinsky's call to strengthen
the alliance with Britain in view of the war. He retained his ideological loyalty and
the Irgun name, but only a small number of commanders and about a third of the
fighters remained with him. The generation had had its say: this was a time for the
sword. Jabotinsky died in August 1940, with his underground divided.

Stern and Raziel, the two close friends who had together, brought about the
split from the Haganah in Jerusalem, and had together established the Irgun, now
parted after a decade of fighting together with great courage and powerful fraternity. Hundreds of brothers-in-arms suddenly found themselves in two opposing
camps – fighting against Britain, or supporting Britain.

Within a mere eighteen months, almost all the commanders of both underground
factions had disappeared. Some were killed in action, others were imprisoned,

and some resigned. Raziel was killed on a British intelligence mission to Falluja, Iraq in 1941. His deputy, Yaakov Meridor, fought alongside him in Iraq and then returned to the Land of Israel to lead the Irgun. Just ten months later, in February 1942, the Lehi commander, Stern, was captured in a safe house in south Tel Aviv, and was killed in cold blood by British intelligence officers. *Davar*, the Histadrut newspaper, reported his death: "Avraham Stern, the head of the gang that was recently engaged in acts of robbery and murder [. . .] was killed yesterday in a clash with the police. [. . .] As he tried to flee, the police were forced to shoot him. [. . .] He viewed all means as legitimate, and during the war he even pressed for associating with the countries that are annihilating Jews."[1] Four months later, Stern's only son was born and was given his father's nom-de-guerre: Yair.

The circumstances of the deaths of Raziel and Stern, the leaders of this generation of the underground, epitomized the paradox in which the underground fighters found themselves during the years of the Revolt. One hero was killed wearing a British uniform and fighting the Nazis, while the other was killed by police officers who also wore British uniforms.

The Revolt of the Irgun and Lehi – Begin and Shamir vs. Britain

The leadership vacuum that followed the deaths of the "Sabra" (native-born) leaders, Raziel and Stern, was filled by a core group of Beitar leaders from Poland – the "Jabotinsky youth" who had managed, by the skin of their teeth, to leave Europe as Poland went up in flames. The underground fighters in the Land of Israel, now bereft of their commanders, welcomed the renowned Beitar leaders from Poland with open arms. The most prominent among them was Begin, whose fame had spread far and wide, and who was considered a central ideologue and acknowledged symbol of Beitar. The underground fighters who had grown up with him, and whom he had educated within the movement, were energized and cheered when he finally arrived in the country, following a long and dangerous migration via Russia, Iran, and Iraq.

Although the Polish immigrant commanders had grown up not as underground fighters but rather as members of a youth movement, they adopted a tough and unforgiving position vis-à-vis the Great Power which they regarded as having broken its trust with the Jews. These survivors of the Nazi onslaught were the fiercest and bitterest adversaries that the British faced during the Mandate period. The new underground leaders arrived in the Land of Israel believing that only through force could the Jews survive and the land be redeemed. For them, this was a holy war, honoring that which was most precious to them: the memory of their family members who had perished.

And so it was that despite the rift, and despite the fact that the reason for this rift was the attitude towards Britain, both the two factions found themselves fighting against the British occupiers – each in its own way, using its own methods. Shamir, Eldad, and Natan Yellin-Mor continued Stern's legacy and headed Lehi in its guerrilla warfare against the British even though the British were fighting the Nazis, since they were also preventing Jews from escaping Europe to the Holy Land. Meridor and Begin ended the cooperation that had been maintained with the British army at the beginning of the war and turned against the traitors, to their view, who were preventing Jewish refugees from entering the country. In effect, this was the end of the Jabotinsky era: four years after his death, Begin was leading his fighters in a struggle against Britain, just as Stern had advocated, albeit using different methods, and on a different scale.

The underground fighters were fearless in their revolt. As survivors who had lost all that was dear to them and who now had nothing more to lose, they fought with no constraints. They had a single goal: a Jewish state in the Land of Israel, right away. Not through statesmanship, not by persuading the world powers, not through demonstrations or symbolic acts. There was only one way that they could achieve their goal, and that was through force.

The fire raging around them, both locally and abroad, served to meld them into a single body, a cohesive fighting family (as they would later refer to themselves). They held their marriage ceremonies in secret, gave birth underground, exchanged identities, and evaded pursuers – both Jewish and British. While the underground factions were originally made up mostly of native-born, mainly Sephardi Jews, whose families had lived in the Land of Israel for decades and sometimes even centuries, the ranks came to be filled by Beitar graduates from Poland, who had arrived in the country traumatized by the Holocaust and their personal and communal losses. They were joined by "Sabra" fighters – veteran immigrants from Poland and Yemen, new immigrants from Iraq, Syria, and Lebanon, and immigrant survivors from Germany, Czechoslovakia, Romania, and Lithuania. Thus, the revolt was waged by an underground comprising a hodge-podge of nationalities and ethnic groups. The older neighborhoods of Yemenite immigrants in Tel Aviv, Petach Tikva, and Jerusalem were the locations of most of Begin's hideouts.

The Revolt waged by Lehi, later joined by the Irgun, was a revolt of the few against the many. It was the struggle of a small band against a mighty external Power, as well as a hostile, oppressive Jewish leadership. They fought the British and targeted British personnel, but at the same time were persecuted and hunted themselves by the Yishuv establishment, including its media and security arms, in every city, neighborhood, and organization. They lived with the knowledge that at any moment the person sitting next to them on the bus, or a neighbour in the same building as one of their safe houses, could inform on them. At any moment, someone might recognize their face from the "wanted" posters and hand them over. They lived with a constant awareness that at any hour, on any day, they could be arrested, put on trial, imprisoned, or exiled, like hundreds of their friends, or even hanged on the gallows, like their martyred fellows Shlomo Ben-Yosef, Eliyahu Hakim, Meir Nakar, and Dov Gruner.

It is difficult to describe the emotional intensity of the fighters. The "Poles" carried with them a most profound sense of personal and national bereavement. They arrived bursting with Zionist fervor and hatred for the world that had turned its back on them. They saw their situation as a choice between victory and death, the second option no longer frightening them. They had left behind their murdered families and communities, their treacherous neighbors, and even their former names. They were now new Jews: freedom fighters with nicknames that gave them a new identity. They fought alongside "Sabra" youth who were suffused with the tradition of Sephardi Jewry and of the ancient community of Jerusalem, or with the rootedness of having grown up in the colonies established by the First Aliya. For this latter group, bearing arms was familiar and natural. They had grown up living in their homeland and defending themselves. They had no knowledge of an exilic existence, of apologetics and restraint. They hated the Great Power that had hanged their friend, Shlomo Ben-Yosef. They sang the Irgun anthem (later to become the Lehi anthem), "Nameless Soldiers", composed by the commander and poet Avraham (Yair) Stern, fully identifying with every word:

> Anonymous soldiers are we, without uniform,
> Fear and the shadow of death surround us
> We have signed up for life:
> Only death will discharge us from the ranks.
> Through days red with pogroms and blood,
> Through nights black with despair,
> In cities and towns we raise our flag,
> Declaring defense and conquest.

When these fighters were drafted into the new IDF, despite their vast fighting experience, only a few were designated as junior officers. Many of them had a Beitar background of weapons and uniforms as children; they had smuggled hand-grenades in their youth and had fought against an imperial army at the age of sixteen. They were consummate soldiers and commanders that any army would want to enlist – committed, determined, and ready to fight at any price. But the Labor leadership kept them away from senior army positions. Their colleagues from the Haganah were appointed instead – even though many of them lacked fighting experience. Despite all this, the former underground fighters acquitted themselves with valor in the War of Independence, in besieged Jerusalem, in the battles to liberate the Negev, Ramle, and Jaffa. They suffered casualties in the "Faluja pocket" (today, Kiryat Gat), in Beer Sheba, and in Jerusalem, and dedicated themselves to their role in establishing a Jewish state with defensible borders.

*

Generation research around the world offers no more conspicuous instance of the creation of a "sociological generation". Theoreticians Karl Mannheim, Lewis Feuer, and Jonathan Shapiro define a sociological generation as a specific age-group that experiences traumatic events which cause its members to lose their faith in the leaders of the older generation and to consolidate a new worldview – and, in some cases, also an organizational framework of their own.

The traumas and catastrophes experienced by the Jewish People during the 1930s and '40s – years of persecution, antisemitism, and genocide – left their mark on every sector of the population. However, their impact was perhaps most dramatically apparent among the underground fighters, the Zionists in uniform. They declared their Revolt and were ready to die for their vision of Jewish independence. As a new sociological generation, they felt that the previous generation had failed in ensuring the future of world Jewry, and that all traditional conventions had gone up in the flames of the crematoria in Auschwitz. They had nothing but scorn for the Labor leadership of the Yishuv, which appeared blind to the terrible reality and apathetic towards the horrors taking place in Europe, feeble in combatting Arab aggression, and weak in its response to the shutting of the gates to the Holocaust refugees. They despised the establishment system of the older generation, which seemed self-satisfied, smug, and concerned only with its cronies and its following, not with the Jews who were being exterminated in far-off Europe. They rebelled against all that was adult, old, established, conservative, and restrained. They suffered a loss of confidence to an extent that surpassed that of any sociological generation described by Mannheim or Feuer anywhere in the world. They developed a new, different, mutinous worldview, the likes of which had not been seen in the Zionist movement. It was a vision of boundless insurgency and bloody struggle that would end either in death or in independence. They insulated themselves within their organizations and scorned all other Zionist bodies. Everyone else, in their eyes, belonged to the materialistic, here-and-now, decadent establishment; they were all traitors to the Jewish martyrs.

The experiences of the fighters during the years of the Revolt bound them with cords of pain, bereavement, fury, hatred, and a sense of betrayal. While the theoretical literature describes the bond among the rebellious generation as an organizational connection, there is no comparable instance in which the organization became a family, replacing the family that had been lost. The underground became their world after the world that they had known – their past, their relatives and friends – was gone. They would now not be parted; they were one single extended family that was also a military unit. As in the words of Stern's poem, "Only death will discharge us from the ranks."

Political isolation and convergence of the fighting family

The establishment of the state brought no change in the attitude of the Labor government towards the former underground fighters. The families of Irgun and Lehi fighters who had been killed in battle were not entitled to state compensation, and so their brothers and sisters in arms mobilized to collect funds. They created a civil-political organization, which they called Herut (later to become the Herut political party, which in turn came to be called Gahal and later Likud). The aim was essentially to maintain a common framework for the thousands of fighters whose war effort and contribution were disdained, and who were vilified in the public discourse. This framework offered them support and dignity, and ultimately became the core of a broader framework that emerged during the years immediately after the establishment of the state: the "fighting family". It was this informal social framework, never clearly defined, that bound the parents' generation together.

The "fighting family" would meet regularly, celebrating their children's births, helping each other in finding work, taking care of bereaved parents, widows, and orphans. Herut, although poor and isolated, sought to reflect the values of the Revisionist movement and the principles of Beitar. Begin and the other founders adopted a supreme goal that was not part of the platforms of other parties: the liberation of all parts of the Land of Israel, on both sides of the Jordan. While the ruling Labor coalition could agree to a tiny Jewish state as set forth in the UN Partition Plan (the borders achieved in the wake of the War of Independence were slightly less constricted), the Herut headquarters featured a map of the historical biblical Land of Israel, including Jordan, with a unified Jerusalem at its heart.

Another area in which Herut differed from the other parties related to social, economic, and political justice. Begin and his cohorts viewed the Labor regime as dictatorial, denying basic rights – including work and freedom of opinion – to anyone not associated with the party. In light of this, Herut prioritized human rights issues that today are regarded as self-evident. At a time when the individual and his or her rights were subservient to the state and the (ruling) party, the Herut platform highlighted individual rights that were as yet unfamiliar to the young state: negation of political and economic totalitarianism; negation of discrimination on an ethnic, socio-economic, or party basis; ending public monopolies; promoting private initiatives; and more.

The natural leader of Herut was Begin, the last commander of the Irgun. After the establishment of the state, Begin had signed an agreement to dissolve his army and announced to his fighters, via the underground Irgun ratio channel: "There is no need for a Jewish underground. We will be soldiers and builders in the State of Israel. We will obey its laws, for they are our laws. We shall respect its government, for it is our government." The fighters gritted their teeth and followed his orders.

In anticipation of the first elections, held in 1949, the movement was split once again. Three parties that emerged from Herut ran separately. The first, HaTzohar (acronym for *Brit ha-Tzionim ha-Revisionistim* – Union of Revisionist Zionists) comprised the old guard that had built up the Revisionist party and the National Labor Federation – the "middle generation" which had viewed itself as Jabotinsky's heirs. HaTzohar fared badly in the elections, failing to pass the Knesset's electoral threshold, and was disbanded shortly afterwards. The other two parties represented the generation of the Revolt. Halochamim (the Fighters' List), representing Lehi, received one Knesset seat but did not compete in the 1951 elections. Herut, headed by Begin, represented the Irgun and enjoyed the support of founding members and ideologues such as Abba Ahimeir and Uri Zvi Greenberg. The internal battle over Jabotinsky's legacy had been decided. The factions disappeared, and there remained one single successor party, Herut, with fourteen Knesset seats.

Begin and his companions were deeply disappointed by the lack of public support. The results of these (and future) elections showed that the smear campaign waged by Ben-Gurion and his party mechanism had been effective. The Arlozorov affair, the bombing of the King David Hotel, and the *Altalena* had been

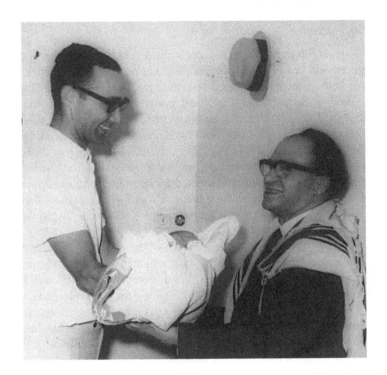

Figure 4.3 Menachem Begin, the godfather of the entire fighting family, with the happy father, Uzi Landau, at his son Giora's circumcision, August 1970.

Figure 4.4 Menachem Begin, known by the parents' generation as "the commander", marrying the Princes, here at the wedding of the "prince" Roni Milo with his wife Elisheva. In 1977, four years after the wedding, the twenty-eight-year-old Milo was elected to the Knesset.

enlisted to paint the underground fighters in the public consciousness not as free-dom fighters who had brought independence, but rather as separatist extremists, while Ben-Gurion and his party took full credit for the establishment of the state.

In the decades of roaming the political wilderness that followed, the fighters maintained their loyalty towards their charismatic and noble leader, while Prime Minister Ben-Gurion derided him from the Knesset podium. He even refused to address Begin by name, instead calling him "the man sitting next to Dr. Bader" (a fellow Herut MK). For the parents' generation, Begin symbolized the Revolt and Israel's liberation, and therefore they voted for him again and again, even when his stubborn stance in the opposition aroused widespread criticism. Any under-mining of his leadership provoked fury among his followers: Begin was them, and they were Begin.

Begin was the "commander", the patriarch of the family, a sacred symbol for the parents and children alike. When a former fighter couple got married, Begin participated in the ceremony. When a child was born, Begin was the *sandak* (god-father). When a boy celebrated his bar-mitzvah, Begin stood alongside him with his parents who had fought under his command. One of the many marriages that Begin attended was that of the future "heir" Roni Milo. Likewise, he was the *sandak* at the circumcision of future heir and government minister Yariv Levin, whose mother's uncle had been the commander of the *Altalena*, and of Giora Landau, grandson of Chaim Landau, and son of the future heir and government minister Uzi Landau.

Even after defeat in one election after the next, the fighting family maintained its fierce loyalty to and defense of Begin. The blind support of his followers, despite the rejection of Begin by the broader Israeli public, is understandable in light of the bond that had developed between the fighters and their commander; in their eyes, he had brought Israeli independence. He was the voice, the symbol. Replacing him was unthinkable.

Note

1 Davar, February 13, 1942.

5   Rebellion against teachers, admiration for parents

Unlike the underground fighters – the parents' generation – who, in their youth, had rebelled against the older generation and its "exilic" worldview, the generation of the heirs did not rebel against their parents' views. On the contrary, the profound identification and solidarity which took root during their childhood grew even stronger as they reached adolescence and served to draw them into the struggle. They somehow skipped the stage where children start to question the supreme authority in their life and begin to develop their own independent view of the world.

Thus, the rebellious parents, who had turned their backs on the docile, compliant stance of their own parents, found the next generation to be staunchly steadfast and faithful. Some of the children volunteered to distribute flyers during elections campaigns. Others accompanied their parents to public demonstrations. There were those who undertook "guerrilla" activities such as taking down the red flags from the roofs of Histadrut branches on May Day. There was no questioning, no doubt, no argument with the parents concerning the justness of the struggle against the regime, or the ways in which it was pursued.

The bond that grew between the former underground fighters and their children is a rare phenomenon in the research of generations. From a young age, thousands of children from different families, in different regions of the country, developed a commitment to their parents' political path and joined their struggle, some of them eventually taking up senior positions in the Herut (later Likud) party and being elected to the Knesset. This testifies to a symbiosis and an intense solidarity between the two generations. The Revolt – the very life-blood of the Revisionists – was always directed outwards, towards an external foe that threatened the camp.

*

Roni Milo, one of the first heirs to make his public debut, recalls accompanying his parents to hear Begin's speeches in Mughrabi Square in Tel Aviv.[1] He testifies that he was "the only openly Herut-supporting student" at his school in Tel Aviv, and he speaks of his bitter arguments with his teachers over the *Altalena* affair and the "Hunting Season". Tzahi Hanegbi remembers fiercely defending Jabotinsky's teachings during his high school years in Tel Aviv. Once he engaged in a public debate with the daughter of Eliyahu Golomb, a founder and senior commander of the Haganah. As he describes it, "She represented the Labor movement, while I was the representative of the 'fascists'."[2]

Thus, the antagonism and rebellion of the fighters' children was directed not towards their parents but rather outwardly, towards the establishment, and specifically its representatives whom they encountered on a daily basis: their teachers. These educators were the official spokesmen of the false history propagated by the Labor movement which excluded the underground fighters from the totality of soldiers and heroes to whom Israel owed its independence. History and civics lessons often became shouting matches between teachers and students whose parents had fought in the underground movements.

Although most of the fighters' children studied at government schools, and although many of them developed close friendships with children from elite Labor families, it was always clear to them which political camp they belonged to: the underground family, the Herut party. As the accusations against the parents grew increasingly strident over the course of the 1950s and '60s (they were branded as despised "separatists" and "hooligans"), so the children's identification with their parents' pain and valor grew stronger. This adults' war became very personal for them, and the enemies were clearly identified: the "red" regime, the educational system, the biased press. In a radio interview in 2007, Tzipi Livni said, "We rebelled – but it was a rebellion against the Labor, against the school. [. . .] We rebelled not *against* our parents, like most other youth, but rather *with* our parents."

There were far fewer political arguments between these children and their classmates and peers – children of families identified with the socialist and Liberal Zionist camps. The Labor's younger generation was full of self-confidence and self-satisfaction, on one hand, but at the same time became increasingly embarrassed by the growing corruption of the parents' parties in government. In the late 1960s and the 1970s, the children of the Labor leaders were a contented generation that showed little interest in the dirty politics that seemed to consist largely of scandals, fights, and divisions. Their apathy allowed the Herut younger generation to conduct itself freely and openly, despite being a minority, without being swallowed up and disappearing.

Tzipi Livni's story typifies the dual background of the heirs' generation. Her home was an ideological underground bastion, located in a bourgeois Tel Aviv suburb which allowed her to integrate with the local youth. Livni was a well-liked student and a talented basketball player; on Saturdays she would go boating on the Yarkon River. In her parallel world, throughout her entire childhood and youth, she accompanied her parents on family legacy hikes and participated in events organized by the fighting family.

Livni was born a decade after the establishment of the state, and grew up in a Liberal-leftist area of Tel Aviv. Her parents were well-known Irgun figures: her mother, Sara (née Rosenberg) came from a religious family in Haifa. In the wake of the execution of Shlomo Ben-Yosef she had joined the Irgun and was given the name "Yael". A courageous fighter, she was caught and imprisoned by the British, and the story of her escape became an underground legend. Her husband, Tzipi's father, was the venerated Irgun operations officer. He was the only member of the movement who was appointed a battalion commander in the IDF during the War of Independence, and following his discharge he was a Herut/Likud MK in three successive Knessets. Born in Belorussia as Yeruham Bezozovich, he eventually changed his name to his underground nom-de-guerre – Eitan Livni.

Livni's parents both participated in the operation known as "Night of the Trains" – a daring sabotage of the British railway in which the underground fighters made off with 35,000 liras (the currency at the time). Three couples formed in the wake of this operation, including Eitan and Sara Livni. Their wedding was held on May 16, 1948 – just two days after the declaration of the state. It was a quick ceremony, with no photographer or guests, since the groom had just one day's leave from the war front. When the Herut party was formed, the Livnis were active members and part of the core of the fighting family. They were close to Begin and were held in esteem by their companions. "We grew up on less 'Red Riding Hood' and more stories about the Irgun," Tzipi Livni said in an interview published in *Maariv*.[3] As she tells it, the Israeli ethos as developed over the state's early decades was

> the story of the establishment organizations – the Haganah and the Palmach. The Irgun and Lehi were regarded as separatists, as bloodthirsty. [. . .] The whole group that my parents belonged to was different. They had different names, they listened to different songs, they had Beitar uniforms (which you didn't see on the streets) and they told stories that no-one ever wrote in the schoolbooks. [. . .] All their operations, everything they did, none of it ever appeared in any book. It wasn't part of what students learned, or what people spoke about on the radio.

The secular-Liberal elite environment of north Tel Aviv did nothing to blur or obscure the family past. The Livni children grew up on their parents' heroic escapades, Beitar songs, the trauma of their mother's imprisonment, and the searing sense of betrayal that accompanied it: one day in October 1946, about six months after Eitan Livni was arrested and sentenced to fifteen years in jail, Sara was sitting on a bus, carrying confidential Irgun documents on her person. All of a sudden, one of the other passengers pointed to her and shouted, "Here's a Beitar member who isn't in prison yet!" An uproar ensued, the police were called, and a body search of Sara exposed the documents. She was arrested and jailed, but shortly afterwards she managed to escape. The story circulated among the underground fighters, but it was given media coverage only after Sara's death in 2007: she had self-injected boiling milk to raise her body temperature, as a result of which she was transferred to a hospital in Haifa. There she jumped out of a window and escaped.

Two years before her death, during an interview that was published in *Maariv*,[4] Sara's eyes glistened as she described how her young daughter "caught the political bug" as a child: "We were constantly talking politics at home [. . .]

I taught them all the Beitar songs and brought them up on the Irgun stories, so that they would be patriotic." As a young girl, Tzipi accompanied her mother to demonstrations.

Sara became a legendary figure not only by virtue of the story of her escape but also because she was the "little Sara" eternalized in the poem "Manning the Barricades" by Irgun fighter Michael (Mike) Eshbal. This became the Irgun anthem; it was sung prior to operations, before the executions of Irgun members, and at fighting family gatherings for decades afterwards. I remember how surprised the guests were to hear the Irgun song at the bar-mitzvah celebration of Tzipi Livni and Naftali Spitzer's son, and to see grandmother Sara, full of pride at her daughter and grandson who were continuing the tradition some fifty years later:

> *Manning the Barricades*
> by M. Ashbel
>
> Today, little Sara,
> We'll meet as I go off to war
> To set up a state
> On both banks of the Jordan.
> Cut off your braid
> And tighten your belt,
> Hug me, take up a Sten
> And come and join the ranks with me!
> Manning the barricades we shall meet, we shall meet!
> Manning the barricades we bring freedom with blood and fire
> Rifle to rifle; barrel saluting
> Bullet after bullet clamoring
> Manning the barricades; manning the barricades we shall meet!
> And if on the gallows
> I give my life for the nation,
> Please do not cry
> For that is my fate
> Wipe away your tears
> Press the Sten to your heart
> Choose yourself another
> Of the men of my squad,
> Manning the barricades

Tzipi's teachers at Dubnov School did not have an easy time. In the late 1960s, during a history lesson that focused on the Haganah, Tzipi voiced her objection, pointing out that two other underground movements had operated in the Land of Israel: the Irgun and Lehi. When the teacher asked how she knew this, she answered proudly, "From home. My parents fought in the Irgun."

In an interview with *Maariv*, Livni recalled other classroom memories:

> The teacher asked us to name ships that brought illegal immigrants. [. . .] The name I gave was "*Altalena*". Afterwards she wrote on the board, "Write about our great leader, Ben-Gurion." So I wrote about the "Hunting Season". [. . .] There was no friction with my classmates. They were fed up with politics, with the Labor corruption. They weren't the least bit interested. [. . .] It was only with the teachers – adults – that there were confrontations. They were hostile towards the underground movements. I was angry. [. . .] Emotionally, I had very hard feelings towards the adult teachers. But not towards my friends.[5]

The establishment's disdain for and ignoring of her parents' efforts made her very angry, but also very proud. "The schoolbooks killed our parents' heroism," Livni stated in the same interview.

> They compared the brown Beitar uniforms to those of the Nazis. [. . .] I went home devastated. My mother told me that the uniforms were brown like the soil of the Land of Israel, and later blue, like the skies of the Land of Israel. Incidents like this left scars.

On May Day each year, when all the other children were enjoying their holiday, Livni used to go to school, in protest. As noted, she belonged to two youth movements – the Scouts and Beitar. Once, as she participated in a Beitar march, wearing a brown uniform, someone walking by on the main road yelled at her, "Fascist!" That moment left a lasting impression.

Her most passionate moments in Beitar were unquestionably the occasions when she went to wage battle against the symbol she hated most of all: the red flag. She told *Yediot Aharonot*[6] newspaper that one May Day she climbed up a tall building in Tel Aviv that was a symbol of the socialist enterprise, and took down the red flag that was flying there in honor of the first of May. Eventually it became an office building, and it was in this building that Tzipi Livni as a government minister chose to have her bureau.

Her older brother, Eli, describes a day when the Livni mother and daughter went to a demonstration against Henry Kissinger, the Jewish US foreign secretary, who after the Yom Kippur War was identified as the figure who had pushed Israel to make concessions. He described how at the demonstration his sister had been beaten by the police.[7] Eli also described how he himself started working at a Histadrut construction company which required all its workers to carry a red Histadrut membership booklet. He risked his job by demonstratively tearing up the membership booklet that they tried to give him.

Commitment to the Irgun legacy simply flowed in the veins of the Livni family. The patriarch of the family, who passed away in December 1991, instructed in his will that the Irgun symbol should be engraved on his headstone, with the map of the Greater Land of Israel and a rifle over it. US Foreign Secretary Condoleezza Rice heard this directly from Foreign Minister Tzipi Livni, a member of Ehud Olmert's government. By means of this story Livni sought to convey the degree to which territorial concessions were difficult for her.[8]

At the same time, the legacy handed down to Livni was not meant to orient her towards politics. On the contrary, like many other former underground fighter families, her parents wanted to keep their children away from involvement in politics and to spare them the frustration that they themselves had suffered. The commitment that the Livni children absorbed in their home involved first and foremost preserving the memory of the Revolt and its heroes, the martyrs. "[We would discuss] neither deal-making nor parties," Livni recalled in an interview she gave a short time after her mother's death. "But values – yes. My mother conveyed that all the time: modesty, integrity, morality, and equality. To be a good person."

The death of her mother, Sara, in October 2007 caused Tzipi to open up: she was interviewed in the media and spoke with uncharacteristic candor about her parents' home. It was very important to her to tell the story of her mother's struggle and her heroism, since activity in the public sphere was a realm that Sara had left to her husband. The personal interviews that Tzipi granted exposed her mother's profound commitment. "It was terribly important for me to tell my mother's story," she told visitors during the traditional seven-day mourning period.

> People always spoke about my father; they didn't know what a "woman of valor" my mother was. It was important to me that people should hear about and remember my mother's heroism, as she deserved. Especially now, with all the talk about women serving as combat soldiers, I think about her and her friends. They were fighters. They did amazing things.

She viewed her father, Eitan Livni, not only as a venerated operations officer but also as a model for emulation. "My father was a personal example to me. Integrity is more important than nationalism. [. . .] His handshake was more reliable than any contract. [. . .] He had respect for people, integrity, honesty, majesty."

It is remarkable that in all their conversations, speeches, and written materials, the heirs never raise a word of criticism about their parents' generation, its views, its positions, or its path. This is an important observation, because it is rare to find assertive and opinionated public figures (and in the case of the heirs, there are certainly some who answer to this description) who have never expressed criticism of the previous generation. Unquestionably, this attests to profound admiration for the parents' heroism, which has not received the public recognition that it deserves. The children of the underground fighters remain full of admiration for the superhuman strength and tenacity of those who fought on behalf of the nation and were persecuted by their brethren, and many of whom were imprisoned, exiled, and even executed.

The level of respect and admiration that the younger generation felt towards the parents bordered on hero-worship. Although the heirs are adults and have their own opinions – in many cases, different from those of their parents and their "aunts and uncles" in the fighting family – they still never speak out publicly against the generation of the Revolt (with the exception of Ehud Olmert, whom I discuss further on). Even those of the heirs who have reached the most senior positions of leadership in Israel do not enjoy the same level of respect and admiration on the part of their own children – but they do not expect it. They understand that the new generation is different, perhaps more "normal" than they themselves were in their youth.

The same respect and loyalty displayed by the heirs from their formative years, via their early forays into politics in university frameworks, to their senior administrative positions, have been maintained even when the heirs have left the Likud for other parties, where they continue to insist that their worldview is inspired by Jabotinsky. They emphasize at every opportunity that they have not turned their back on their upbringing, and that their more moderate or more extreme stance (in relation to the Likud) actually flows from Jabotinsky's teachings, and not from the wellsprings of the progressive Left or the messianic Right. When Meridor, Milo, Livni, and Olmert shifted leftward, they justified their move on the basis of Jabotinsky's principle of "grandeur". When Benny Begin and Uzi Landau took up positions to the right of the Likud, they pointed to Jabotinsky's principle of "resolve". Even when the veterans of Herut/Likud expressed anger towards the "aberrant" heirs who had shifted leftward, there was no counter-attack. The heirs continued to show respect for their parents' generations under all conditions.

President Reuven Rivlin always speaks with childlike admiration of his father: "My father was extraordinary. My father translated the Quran. [. . .] He revived the Hebrew language, while also valuing and appreciating Arabic. . . . A man of the world, but also a man of his place." In June 2007, when Rivlin contended for the appointment as President with Shimon Peres (and lost to him), he refrained from speaking about himself and his own abilities (a rather unusual phenomenon in and of itself), preferring to elaborate, in every interview he gave, on the greatness of his father, Professor Rivlin, who was rejected as a candidate for President in 1952 because he belonged to the "wrong" political camp. He told a *Haaretz* correspondent, "My father deserved to be President. [. . .] He didn't get to be President, and I have always lived in that shadow."[9] Between the lines one senses Rivlin's powerful desire to correct this injustice.

Benny Begin has spoken less about his father, and is zealous in protecting the privacy of his memories as a child growing up in the shadow of a father who was also a national leader. He spoke proudly and publicly of his father only when he cited him as an example of restraint in the face of the betrayal of his fighters during the "Hunting Season", and in his call to avoid a civil war after he and his companions aboard the *Altalena* were fired upon by fellow Jews. Begin Jr. also recalled how, on June 1, 1967, in view of the emergency situation in Israel, his father had overcome his personal reluctance and had joined Israel's first unity government as a minister without portfolio.

After all the de-legitimization and ostracization over the course of twenty years, Begin went to Ben-Gurion – the pariah went to the figure who had blacklisted him – and offered to support his [Ben-Gurion's] candidacy for Prime Minister.[10]

Yair Shamir, son of former Prime Minister Yitzhak Shamir, told an interviewer of his feelings towards his father. Shamir Jr., who at the time of the interview was already CEO of a company and a well-respected businessman, spoke with unusual admiration of the underground movement that his father had led:

> As I see it, Lehi is the symbol of something eternal that existed before I was born and will continue after I am no longer here. [. . .] It's about trailblazing, endless dedication, fortitude, and the ability to sacrifice everything for the sake of your freedom.[11]

Yair Stern Jr., who also participated in this joint interview, spoke about his father, the Lehi commander: "Only once in several generations does someone like that appear. [. . .] I understood that there was no chance that I could come anywhere close to being like him."[12]

The biological and ideological parents were regarded by the younger generation as living legends, as commanders who should be followed unquestioningly. Many members of the younger generation developed close bonds with "aunts and uncles" in the fighting family.

Dan Meridor told how Journalist Hen Kots-Bar described a visit by Menachem Begin to the Suez Canal after Israel's victory in the Six Day War: "As he approached one of the positions, a young tank officer appeared in front of him, pulled himself to attention, saluted, and said: 'It's me, sir. Eliyahu's son. At your command.'"[13] The young officer was Dan Meridor himself, and Begin was a close friend of his father. But Begin was always the "commander", and that was how the fighters and their families addressed him to the end of their days.

The esteem that was felt by the entire younger generation of the fighting family towards their parents found expression in different ways. In a rare interview granted by Professor Raanana Meridor, mother of Dan Meridor, she said: "All his life he [Dan] imitated his father. [. . .] Dan admired his father from the day he was born. [. . .] He continued his father's path."[14]

Yossi Ahimeir, another heir, has dedicated his life to preserving his father's ideological legacy. This son of Abba Ahimeir was a journalist; he was director of Prime Minister Shamir's bureau from 1988–1992, and he also served as an MK. Since 2005 he has focused on his life's project: the Jabotinsky Institute. Together with his brother Yaakov, he converted his parents' apartment into a public archive. To date he has published six volumes of his father's writings. When I asked him why he had abandoned his career in journalism, he answered, "It is a great privilege to be continuing my father's legacy after his death. [. . .] I regard my father with awe, with admiration and appreciation."

The admiration and respect of the younger generation for the parents is eloquently described by the most prominent of the heirs: Benjamin Netanyahu. Over the course of many conversations with him I came to learn how deeply he was influenced by the worldview of his father, Professor Bentzion Netanyahu. He expresses admiration not only for his father's idealism and assertiveness, but also for his political, social, and intellectual mind-set. "At home I absorbed a deep appreciation of Jewish history and our national values," he told me. "Like my father, I am able to ask unusual questions. If you pay attention, you'll understand that they are highly relevant. [. . .] I think that that's a quality I inherited from him." It is surprising to discover the extent to which Netanyahu, who is generally not self-effacing, humbles himself when he talks about his father: "The big ideas started with him. I understood that my father sees things, that he has almost prophetic abilities. [. . .] Because he's an historian, he sees the mosaic of history."[15]

Benjamin Netanyahu was born in 1949 and grew up in Jerusalem as the second of his parents' three sons. His elder brother, Yonatan (Yoni) (1946–1976) was commander of the renowned elite General Staff Reconnaissance Unit. He was killed during Operation Thunderbolt, the hostage rescue mission in Entebbe, Uganda, in which he commanded the rescue force. He was posthumously awarded the Medal of Valor, Israel's highest military award, and the daring operation was renamed in his honor: Operation Yonatan. The family's youngest son, Dr. Ido Netanyahu (1952), like both his brothers, served in the General Staff Reconnaissance Unit, and he is a doctor, a writer, and a playwright. The Netanyahu home was close to the homes of both the Rivlin and the Meridor families, and like their friends, the Netanyahu brothers felt accepted and integrated. Their father, too, was a well-known and respected figure, and their home, too, was open to Jerusalem's high society. When it came to election time, however, Netanyahu recalls:

> I always knew that my parents voted differently from the parents of most of the other children. The other parents generally voted for Labor, but I knew that my parents didn't vote Labor. I was different, but that didn't affect my social life as a child.

In an interview that he granted in April 2009, upon his son's election as Prime Minister for a second term, the elderly Bentzion Netanyahu said:

> The fact that I wasn't made a professor here didn't hurt me at all, since I was appointed to great universities abroad. [. . .] It just pained me that I wasn't able to educate a generation of Jews the way I wanted to. [. . .] But the leftists were afraid that I would harm the image that they wanted to nurture. [. . .] I ask myself, Why have most of my books and studies not been translated into Hebrew?[16]

Professor Netanyahu's astute political insight is a subject that came up often in the conversations I have had with his son over the past thirty years. Benjamin Netanyahu mentions his father frequently, especially in the context of deliberation and making fateful decisions. He always expounds on his father's ability to view the overall historical picture from a distance, and is proud of the fact that it was his father who persuaded Jabotinsky to transfer the center of the movement's activity from Europe to the US.

> In 1939 my father went to Jabotinsky and said, "You're working incorrectly. Your perception of the importance of activity in England is misguided. The Great Power is the US." He convinced him [. . .] and Jabotinsky did indeed travel to there, taking my father from the Holy Land with him.

In one of our conversations Netanyahu told me:

> Only when I grew up did I really understand what my father does, and I learned to appreciate his tremendous, limitless knowledge. [. . .] With the years I discovered that most of the things that my father predicted were right; that his predictions usually materialize. [. . .] It took me a long time to understand that he understands politics much better than I do. He has in-depth knowledge of the politics of the nineteenth century, of the Middle Ages, of the Second Temple Period. When we discuss politics of the past – and we discuss it in great detail – I understand that my father really understands the present. [. . .] He is endowed with a rare ability to foresee the future. In 1938 he wrote about the danger awaiting the Jews of Europe. Who saw it then? Millions of Jews were living there in the shadow of that churning volcano that was Nazism, and they didn't see the danger.[17]

Netanyahu Jr. has never had any doubt that his father was the last disciple of Jabotinsky, who, to his mind, was the greatest Jewish leader. "Jabotinsky understood the essence of a state; a nation. He died trying to bring 'Rome' (i.e., the Great Powers) to our cause, after Rome was always against us."[18]

Netanyahu's profound love for his father – who lost his son and, later in life, his wife – was immensely moving for me, watching from the side, especially during his father's final years. Up until 1988, when I accompanied Netanyahu in his early steps in Israeli politics, he would take every opportunity to visit his parents in Jerusalem, and he would stay for hours at a time. The presence of his mother, Tzila, illuminated the home for him.

During his first term as Prime Minister (1996–1999), and again after his return to political life after a three-year break, Netanyahu would always share his deliberations with his father and seek his counsel. His father served as a sort of personal advisor – a confidant who was not motivated by personal, political, or economic interests; a guide who viewed the national good as a supreme value, even where this involved a risk to one's status and position.

In March 2012, I participated in a meeting with the Prime Minister at his office in Jerusalem. At the end of the meeting, as I was already at the door, I told Netanyahu that I was adapting my doctorate for publication as a book about the Revisionist movement's parents and children. Right away I saw his reaction; he was seized with emotion. Not usually one to show his feelings, Netanyahu told me that his father was approaching his 102nd birthday, but he was already in poor health.

I could hear in his voice his love for his father, his concern for his health, and his battle to come to terms with the fact that they would soon be parted. A few weeks later, Bentzion Netanyahu passed away.

Notes

1 Interview with the author, April 21, 2002.
2 Interview with the author, May 31, 2002.
3 Maariv, October 1997.
4 Maariv, December 16, 2005
5 Maariv, June 18, 2004.
6 Yediot Aharonot, March 1, 2005.
7 Maariv, October 19, 2003; Al Ha-Sharon, May 4, 2007
8 Interview with the author, February 22, 2007.
9 Haaretz, April 6, 2007.
10 Ha-Ir, April 26, 1996.
11 Yediot Ha-Sharon, May 7, 2009.
12 Ibid.
13 Interview with the author, April 10, 2002.
14 Yediot Aharonot, May 8, 1998.
15 Interview with the author, December 2003.
16 Maariv, April 3, 2009.
17 Interview with the author, December 2003.
18 Ibid.

6   In the wilderness of the opposition

After the War of Independence, in 1949, the former underground fighters found themselves facing a new struggle – a war of everyday survival, including finding work, making a living, building a home, and integrating into society. Along with the difficulties that all citizens of the young state had to contend with (a housing shortage, security threats, the strict ration system, and more), the underground veterans also had to deal with discrimination and persecution on the part of the Labor government. Now that it controlled the official state organs and institutions, Labor's power was greater than ever, and it wielded this power unhesitatingly against its political adversaries.

Over the course of three decades, the Herut representatives in the Knesset, led by Begin, waged a war of political survival against all odds. Begin and his companions were defeated time after time by a towering left-wing coalition of workers' parties, along with the Histadrut under its control. They became accustomed to the political wilderness and the opposition benches. Throughout this time Herut was led single-handedly by Begin. On several occasions this led to the loss of natural partners from the non-Labor sector, as well as walkouts by groups within the movement who disagreed with his dogmatic path. The underground veterans, however, representing the core of the movement, continued their stubborn and unwavering support of Begin, even when his rigid policy left them in the opposition, and even when the movement began to age and to lose the intellectual brilliance that had characterized it in Jabotinsky's time.

The veterans, along with their children, aided Begin in every election campaign, even when Herut faced certain defeat. With almost religious devotion the generation of the Revolt maintained its loyalty towards their hero and former commander for thirty-four years, from the first Knesset (1949) until Begin's dramatic departure from the Prime Minister's Office (1983). The veterans' party was defeated in eight consecutive elections – until Begin restored their honor in 1977, the year of the historical "Upheaval".

Like Jabotinsky in the 1920s and '30s, Begin remained loyal to his ideological path despite the heavy price that this entailed – consignment to the slandered, penniless, lonely opposition. Just as Jabotinsky had chosen to follow his principles and part with the World Zionist Organization, even though this meant losing the trappings of power and most of his potential partners, so Begin followed his principles and maintained his struggle in the opposition, refusing to part with the dream of the Greater Land of Israel.

Both Jabotinsky and Begin believed in their path and scorned compromise. They endured defeat and rejection year after year, election after election, and remained mired in the opposition, rather than giving up their faith in the totality of the homeland. They embraced proudly an ideology that knew no concession, spurning groups whose principles were more flexible.

Jabotinsky and Begin had something else in common: the same small, faithful army of Beitar graduates who became Irgun fighters. They had been the "children" and followers of the movement's founder, and they became the soldiers and activists of his successor, their contemporary.

The first Knesset included fourteen MKs representing Herut (contrasting with the sixty-five Knesset members representing the two Labor parties). Eight of them had been senior Irgun commanders, including Begin, his deputy Meridor, Chaim Landau, *Altalena* commander Lenkin, Aryeh Ben-Eliezer (uncle of future MK Gideon Gadot), and Esther Raziel-Naor, sister of David Raziel. Three others represented the Irgun's "foreign office" (Shmuel Merlin, Hillel Kook, and Eri Jabotinsky), and the list was rounded out with three symbolic veterans: the poet Uri Zvi Greenberg, economist Dr. Yohanan Bader, and Avraham Recanati, among the founders of the Revisionist movement.

The loyalty of the underground veterans continued in the parliamentary setting. Begin was loyal to his comrades from the Irgun and from Poland, and they were loyal to him. Many of these commander-MKs almost realized in their political lives the promise of the underground anthem, "Only death will discharge us from the ranks." Five members of the Irgun senior command served in seven or more Knessets: Begin (no less than ten terms), Landau (eight), Yaakov Meridor (seven), Esther Raziel-Naor (seven), and Aryeh Ben-Eliezer (seven). Nine Irgun/Lehi veterans set records for length of service, including Eliezer Shostak (ten terms), Dr. Yohanan Bader (eight), Yitzhak Shamir (six), Moshe Arens (six) and Geula Cohen (five). The fourteen legislators boasted an average of twenty years or more in the Knesset. This phenomenon knows no parallel in any democratic parliament anywhere in the world.

The walls surrounding the fighting family grew higher and thicker during the 1950s and '60s, as a national ethos developed in Israel that was tailor-made to fit the socialist government. The official chronicle of valor trumpeted the contribution of the kibbutz pioneers and the fighters of the Haganah and the Palmach. The Irgun and Lehi fighters continued to be treated as members of insurgent, rabble-rousing gangs that had sabotaged the national interest. Not only did the hurt not heal with time; it grew increasingly acute. Half a century later, journalist Yaakov Ahimeir[1] noted that Israel's public broadcasting service, his place of employment, had never interviewed his father, Abba Ahimeir. He added, sorrowfully, that he himself had been entrusted with editing the official news item concerning Ben-Gurion's resignation speech, which included a reference by the departing Prime Minister to Abba Ahimeir as "a disciple of Hitler and Mussolini".

On the twentieth anniversary of Begin's passing, Yaakov Ahimeir described to *Haaretz* how the Upheaval of Begin's victory in 1977 had been received at his workplace, the public television broadcaster: "It wasn't disgust or disappointment with the election results, but rather real hatred towards the new Prime Minister." In a different interview he reported quite candidly, "I remember that I covered Menachem Begin's funeral, on the Mount of Olives, and then there was a television critic who wrote, in a rather malicious tone, that one could 'hear the sorrow in my voice'."[2]

I can testify to the same feeling myself. On the day of the general elections in 1981, I arrived at the Herut headquarters as a student activist, to monitor the results. I left in the middle of the night, happy with Begin's re-election even though the media had already declared Shimon Peres, the eternal Labor candidate, as the winner. Elimelekh Ram, at the time the political correspondent for Israel's only television channel, was walking alongside me. He did not know me and obviously took me for a random youngster that happened to be walking down King George Street. He was distressed over the results. I shall not repeat here what he said. Suffice it to say that I was amazed that this person who appeared on my TV screen night after night could harbor such a profound abhorrence for Begin and his government. We parted ways, each disappointed for a different reason.

It was perhaps as a result of the intensity of hatred towards the fighting family that this group guarded its cohesiveness so fiercely and kept away anyone who was opposed to the leader's path. Begin preferred to remain in the opposition with a small, disciplined, and harmonious Knesset faction, backed by a devoted and disciplined voter base. The growing frustration with prolonged relegation to the opposition gave rise to pockets of bitterness over the years, but these were handily suppressed by Begin's faithful supporters. He remained the irreplaceable chairman of the party, with the same group that controlled the Herut movement throughout the years of wilderness in the opposition.

Only Begin supporters are elected as leaders

During the 1950s, all the Revisionist groups that had not originally been associated with Begin and the Irgun resigned or ceased activity in the movement. Although most of these groups had shown varying levels of support for the Irgun during the revolt, their leaders gradually disappeared from the Revisionist camp.

The series of internal rebellions and resignations from the movement or from political life can be attributed to various factors: the frustrating isolation in the opposition, the Labor's closure of opportunities in the job market and the military, and later on the internal struggles and attempts to oust the leader who would seemingly never win an election. One way or another, Herut gradually lost all its non-Begin-aligned elements, gradually shedding all the partners and allies that did not speak the language of Beitar and of the Irgun, with the result that it became clear that Herut was run by Begin's loyal core group. Most of this group had been born in Poland, had received a Beitar education, had immigrated in their youth, losing their families in the Holocaust, and had been part of the Irgun revolt.

The first layer to be shed consisted of the old Revisionist establishment, whose party had lost to Herut in the 1949 elections. Most of its members headed in the direction of cultural and journalistic activity, but never parted with Jabotinsky's worldview. Another group of founders, also contemporaries of Jabotinsky, granted their imprimatur to the party by participating in the first elections, and then moved to the "back benches" while still remaining loyal to the Herut ideology.

The next leadership group to leave Herut consisted of the "Bergson group" headed by Eri Jabotinsky, Hillel Kook, and Shmuel Merlin, who were members of the first Knesset. Their group also included Yirma (Yirmiyahu) Helpern, who was among the founders of both the Haganah and the Haganah B, and Dr. Alex Refaeli, editor of the Revisionist newspaper *HaBoker* in Jabotinsky's time, a founder of Beitar in Riga, and one of the first Irgun members in Jerusalem. This was the first group from among the generation of the Revolt to part with the movement, following a direct confrontation concerning its leadership and path. The Bergson group had functioned as the Irgun's "foreign office" in the US, where it ran highly visible and successful campaigns. Even then, the group had run into conflict with the organization that had dispatched it. Begin regarded its members as subservient to and serving the Revolt, while the Bergson group viewed itself as the diplomatic leader of the military revolt. Thus, now that the political/diplomatic era had come about, its members wanted to lead, rather than being subservient to Begin.

The third leadership group to part ways with Herut came from the Labor Federation, which served as the economic, medical, and employment backbone of the underground fighters and of the movement throughout its existence. This group was led by Eliezer Shostak and David Melamdowitz, Polish-born Beitarists whose families had perished in the Holocaust. Following nearly three decades of knotty relations, with repeated separations from and reunions with Herut, they rejoined their Irgun and Lehi brethren in the Likud in the 1970s.

The fourth group to leave from the very midst of the Irgun ranks consisted of the young Israeli-born second-tier commanders of the Revolt (Shmuel Tamir, Amihai Paglin, Eitan Livni), who were not included in the Herut faction in Knesset. They left Herut not for a different party or worldview, but rather as a departure from political life. Thus, the Herut faction gradually aged, since over the course of two decades there was no turnover of leadership. The party leaders were still the same "Poles", just older.

The home-grown Irgun commanders had been disappointed already during the War of Independence, when they were not integrated in the army chain of command. They had fought courageously in battles against both Arab enemies and powerful British installations. And yet, when the newborn state desperately needed experienced and courageous commanders, they were humiliated and placed in low-level positions or even turned away, while Haganah personnel – even junior officers – were awarded senior positions in the new IDF. Their own party offered few meaningful positions, only in the Knesset, and these were filled by Begin's experienced and well-educated companions from Poland: commanders like Meridor and Landau, and Revisionist activists who supported the Irgun, such as Dr. Yohanan Bader.

A fifth group had effectively seceded when Lehi split with the Irgun to fight separately, but this faction had fallen apart after faring badly in the first elections. Its members began to seek other occupations but quickly discovered that they were outcasts, excluded from workplaces and ineligible for any public position. Former underground commanders Shamir and Yellin-Mor established a construction company that never stood any chance of succeeding in the Labor-controlled economy. They were forced to set aside the ideological vision upon which they had been educated, and for which they had fought over twenty-five years, for the sake of feeding their families. Yisrael Eldad was forced to earn a living as a Bible teacher at a school until he was dismissed even from this position upon orders from the "higher-ups", who feared that he might poison the minds of the youth.

Lehi had been established by right-wing Beitarists, but during the revolt some of its members were influenced by liberation movements elsewhere in the world that followed left-wing ideologies. This resulted in phenomena such as the splitting off of the extreme left-wing minority group led by Natan Yellin-Mor, and the shift by Eldad, Shamir, and Geula Cohen to parties ranging from Herut to the extreme Right. Lehi fighters generally voted for Herut, especially after Shamir and Cohen later joined the party's leadership.

"Herut" = Irgun, and the Irgun is loyal to Begin

The splitting of Jabotinsky's movement brought about a situation whereby in the 1950s Herut looked very much like Begin's Irgun. This happened because in the young state virtually all resources and jobs were in the hands of a single party, which controlled the Histadrut, the army, the Mossad, the Shin Bet (General Security Service), the Jewish Agency, the municipalities, the government, and the Knesset, as well as the country's economy and industry – and, to some extent, the other parties that sought its comity. Herut was an outcast, devoid of influence and devoid of income. Israeli citizens were afraid of any contact with the movement, lest they lose their jobs. And as Herut became increasingly isolated, so Begin's centralized leadership grew more firmly entrenched. During the Revolt he had been the supreme commander while his subordinates had been more outwardly dominant and influential. During the decades spent in the opposition, he was a sole leader surrounded by his contemporaries. Anyone who sought a path that was even slightly different either moved away of his own accord, or was removed.

The movement entered the 1960s with little energy or hope. Having been defeated in five consecutive elections, the Herut party remained in the opposition with no more than seventeen mandates. The party coffers were empty, and Begin was depicted as an extreme nationalist who was cut off from reality. While the government was trying to protect the tiny country within the 1949 Armistice borders, Begin, Meridor, and Landau spoke of the Greater Land of Israel, the unification of Jerusalem, and Transjordan. The media portrayed their ideology as dangerous for the fragile state.

The Revisionist movement shrank and grew weaker. From a movement that had boasted several arms and organizations operating in dozens of countries, it became a medium-sized party with a small and destitute youth movement. Its moshavim struggled for their very survival, while neighboring moshavim and kibbutzim made the most of their connections with and representation in the government and the Knesset. While in the past the Revisionist movement had published several newspapers, employing hundreds of writers, there remained only one. Even the party's sole economic pillar – the National Labor Federation – was weak and generally in conflict with Begin.

In the mid-1960s the party's economic situation took a turn for the worse. The party headquarters emptied out and grew dilapidated. While the population of Tel Aviv began to enjoy the fruits of the economic growth driven by German reparation payments, the Herut headquarters was populated by older, serious-looking men wearing old-fashioned suits and hats who still declared the same old slogans. Limor Livnat describes her first, traumatic encounter with the place as a twenty-year old student: "Metzudat Zeev (Herut headquarters) is desiccated. Everyone is old. A group of old men sitting in a smoky room, making decisions."[3]

Just two decades after they themselves had been the "youngsters" who pushed the "old men" out of the Revisionist movement, the generation of the Revolt had aged. Its members were mired in opposition politics and continued to repel any internal opposition to Begin's leadership. Repeated defeat at the ballot box paled into insignificance beside the absolute loyalty to the fighting family in general, and its leader in particular. In the natural course of events a party's leader would be replaced after the first or second failure in national elections; certainly after the fourth or fifth. The Irgun fighters, in contrast, defended Begin with all their being. Rarely was a negative word said about him. A condemnation of Begin – even a hint to his advancing age or his failure to lead the party in the direction of relevance and influence – would cause a ring of former Irgun fighters to all but pounce on the speaker. The slightest criticism was treated as a desecration of a sacred loyalty, as though the speaker identified with the slander of the party's enemies. For the fighting family, Begin and the Irgun had led the Revolt and had emerged victorious, and thus were fully deserving of their full confidence. For them, electoral defeat was not the fault of the leader, the party, or its ideology, but rather solely the result of the brainwashing of the public. The problem lay in the distorted picture of Herut presented by the Labor government. Begin was the beloved patriarch and leader, the true victor, Jabotinsky's successor. He represented the roots, the community, the family that had been annihilated in Poland. His life's story was the very embodiment of the story of the underground fighters themselves.

The 1966 Revolt: Israeli-born commanders vs. the old "loser"

Thus, contrary to what one might expect, five consecutive electoral defeats did not result in the ousting of Begin; seventeen years of isolation and denigration in the opposition did not produce any serious rebellion against the leader who had lost at the ballot box. The fact that no such outcome happened testifies to the degree to which Herut was essentially a movement and a family rather than a party. It was only in 1966, following yet another defeat, for the sixth Knesset, that the younger generation of commanders took the initiative. Even now there was no direct show-down with Begin, but rather some dissent that set itself limited objectives, which then turned into a confrontation and was depicted as a revolt. The dissent arose in the wake of the election results, which were especially painful in light of the fact that this time Herut had run together with the centrist Liberal Party, representing small business owners and private farmers who yearned to free themselves of the socialist control that imposed a centralized, corrupt economy and hijacked the state's resources. The unified party (Gahal, later to become Likud) had held about a quarter of the Knesset seats, and in the 1965 elections was finally poised for significant growth – and yet it retained the same number.

The murmurings became, quite unintentionally, a general revolt at the party conference that was held at Kfar HaMakabiya in June 1966. It all started with the bitterness of the home-grown commanders who had been pushed to the margins by Begin's people, and their displeasure was directed towards Begin's circle. They were immediately joined by most of the student leaders, who were eager to replace Begin's non-fighter, older Polish-born comrades. Everyone admired Begin, but it made no sense to anyone that there was no renewal among the rest of the senior leadership. The dissent deteriorated into a revolt against both Begin and his close circle, which ultimately did not contribute to any improvement in Herut's political situation. What it managed to achieve was the most significant schism in the movement since the split between Jabotinsky and Grossman in 1933.

There are different versions as to what exactly the dissenters were trying to bring about, but what actually happened is clear: there was an inter-generational confrontation between Begin's circle and the popular Sabra Irgun commanders: Shmuel Tamir, deputy commander of the Jerusalem region; Amihai (Gidi) Paglin, operations officer; Mordechai Raanan, commander of the Jerusalem region; and the Polish-born Petahya Shamir, commander of the Tel Aviv region. These men had had enough of the aging Polish leadership which had elbowed them out of what they believed was their rightful place, and viewed Begin's advisors and con-fidants as those responsible for the party's electoral defeat.

Behind the scenes the dissent was supported by three of Begin's discontented contemporaries: the heads of the National Labor Federation and the moshavim, Eliezer Shostak, David Melamdowitz, and Mordechai Olmert.

A new and surprising group comprised another element of the opposition – student leaders from the Hebrew University of Jerusalem, who had been invited to the Herut convention with a view to nurturing a more youthful cadre. It was these student children of Herut members who turned the dissent at the conference into a major conflagration. What sparked the blaze was a speech unprecedented in its ferocity, delivered before the conference participants, including Begin, by a twenty-one-year-old student named Ehud Olmert.

The revolt divided the Jerusalemite students into two camps: a minority that supported Begin, and a majority that revolted. Begin's supporters were the chil-dren of senior Irgun members: Arye Naor, Rachel Kremerman (daughter of

Yaakov Meridor) and, along with them, Reuven Rivlin and Yoram Aridor. Behind the scenes there was also the party chairman's son, Benny Begin.

The rebel student leaders were youngsters whose parents had been part of the various groups that had split from or opposed Begin's core circle – Amiram Buk-shpan, David Kolitz, and Ehud Olmert, who had an old account to settle: his father, MK Mordechai Olmert, held a personal and ideological grievance against Begin, who had removed him from the Knesset after two terms, following Olm-ert's support (as head of the Herut moshavim) for legislation proposed by Laborite agriculturalists.

The leader of the revolt, Shmuel Tamir (born in 1923), was a decade younger than Begin. His family, originally Katznelson, was well known in Jerusalem and throughout the Yishuv. His mother was an MK representing the Liberal Party; one uncle was a senior member of the Labor party; while another, Yosef Katznelson, had been one of the founders and leaders of Revisionism and the Irgun in Israel. Tamir was widely considered to be Begin's future heir. He was young, a former senior Irgun commander, and the scion of Revisionist nobility, as well as a char-ismatic and articulate speaker and a well-known lawyer who fought against and exposed corruption in the Labor administration, in widely publicized trials.

Although his future succession of Begin was almost certain, Tamir was impa-tient. He regarded Begin and his companions as essentially exilic in their think-ing and conduct, and he was unwilling to wait for the leadership to pass into his hands in the natural course of events. He engaged in a decades-long roundabout campaign of love-hate relations, repeatedly breaking with and rejoining the party. He left, established another movement, and then returned, in 1952, in 1957, and in 1964. On the eve of the 1965 elections, with Herut running together with the Liberals and anticipating a political turnaround in light of Ben-Gurion's departure and the splitting of the Labor movement, Tamir was included on the Herut list for Knesset as a star who could be relied upon to attract young voters. The election results were a huge disappointment; it seemed that Herut would never come to power.

A few months later, in June 1966, the party's eighth conference was held, under a cloud of despair and disillusionment. The discontent was directed towards Begin's close circle. Criticizing Begin himself was still taboo; no-one would dare call for the removal of the leader who had lost a sixth consecutive election. Tamir arrived at the conference on a wave of support as the movement's hope for a bet-ter future. This was a classic clash between two completely different generations: young vs. old, Sabra vs. exilic, Israeli vs. Polish. Tamir's speech at the conference brought a new message: "The future belongs to the young." Begin's speech essen-tially said, "Cast me not off in old age."

As mentioned, however, the star of the show was Olmert, whose speech marked the first step on the road to the Prime Minister's Office forty years later. This young student dared to stare directly at Begin and say, "If six times Mr. Begin has not succeeded in leading the movement to victory, he should have reached the obvious conclusion." Unlike other heirs of the fighting family, Olmert had grown up with his father's hostility towards Begin. He had absorbed the criticism expressed by his father and his friends – staunch believers in settlement and labor – for Begin and his group, who placed the vision of the Greater Land of Israel above all else.

The offensive speech of this upstart against the movement's idol produced a commotion at the conference, leading to physical blows. This first direct attack on Begin from within Herut aroused fury among the underground veterans. Even if just an hour or two earlier there had been whisperings that perhaps the "time had come", and maybe Begin could stay on as a sort of president while allowing the younger generation to take the helm, the attack on the leader they revered so highly, this modest man who was a Holocaust survivor and the symbol of their Revolt, catapulted the veterans to the stage. A correspondent for *Maariv* described the turmoil: "A few delegates burst onto the stage. There were shouts of 'Get down, ruffian!'"[4] Arye Naor yelled at Olmert, "Put off your shoes from your feet!"[5] Begin, for his part, applauded the speech and demanded that the young man be permitted to continue. He threatened that if Olmert was not allowed to finish, he himself would leave the hall. The threat had its effect, and Olmert continued his merciless attack:

> The Herut movement needs a different approach. Thus far Mr. Begin has led us into the opposition. One gets the impression that he views the role of the opposition as a holy mission. Tens of thousands of people want a leader who will lead us to power.

Begin responded with an elegant and sharp barb meant for Olmert Sr.: "My dear Ehud, I'm sorry that I've disappointed you since you were two years old." The veteran fighters would not forgive Olmert or forget the episode even forty years later.

The conference took a turn when Begin unexpectedly announced his resignation as chairman of the movement, with immediate effect. His supporters refused to accept this move. "The delegates rose to their feet," reported the *Maariv* correspondent. "There were cries from all sides: 'We won't accept it!' 'We don't agree!'"[6] The chairman of the conference committee refused to accept Begin's resignation, arguing that he was "not a private individual, but rather belongs to the nation and to the movement, and is part of the nation's history."

Ultimately, Begin's camp survived the conference. Their victory was clear after two votes which were supported by a large majority of the opposition. The shift began with anger at Olmert's attack and continued in the wake of the leader's threat to step down – a nightmare scenario that no-one wished to contemplate. Following an emergency mobilization of Irgun veterans with an impassioned, almost imploring call to "keep Begin", his supporters achieved a slim majority. The counting of the votes was accompanied by vociferous claims on Tamir's part as to pressure being exerted and irregularities in the voting mechanism.

Following six months of hostility, Tamir and Olmert and their rebels were expelled from the party, and they went on to establish the Free Center, which comprised three Revisionist groups: the National Labor Federation, the young

Irgun commanders, and the students. In the 1969 elections many expected that the new party's results would outshine the aging Herut. As it turned out, the rebels received only two mandates, while Herut maintained the same level of representation. Once again the group that had split off to the Left suffered defeat, as had the moderates who had split with Jabotinsky in 1935 and the Revisionist parties that competed with Herut in 1949. Four years later the Likud was established, and the members of the Free Center rejoined Herut under Begin's leadership.

The group of Jerusalemite students led by Olmert was the only group of Herut heirs in the history of the movement to rebel as a group against Begin and his generation. Although these youngsters were not children of Irgun commanders, with hindsight they are the exception that proves the rule.

Notes

1 Makor Rishon, May 2002.
2 Globes, September 2014.
3 Interview with the author, July 2002.
4 Maariv, June 1966.
5 Interview with the author, August 20, 2014. The call is an allusion to God's command to Moses, "Put off your shoes from your feet, for the place upon which you stand is holy ground" (Exodus 3:5).
6 Maariv, June 1966.

7 The children are enlisted for life

Most members of the younger generation – the sons and daughters of the underground veterans – enlisted in the IDF. They grew up in patriotic homes and were committed to meaningful service to the state whose independence had been won by their parents' efforts. The broader population of thousands of Jabotinsky youth was active already at school: they were heads of class committees in elementary school, and heads of student councils in high school. Now they carried proudly the tradition that they had received from their parents, which meant first and foremost to act for the nation, the state, and Zionism. Thus, thousands of Jabotinsky's "grandchildren" proudly performed their military service, and many went on to hold positions in the public service.

Israel has been exposed to the dozens of Revisionist sons and daughters who headed for the political arena. Less is known of the hundreds who were central Herut/Likud activists, heads of branches, and mayors. Little attention has been paid to the hundreds of Jabotinsky's "grandchildren" who continued their public service in the areas of education, the military, the media, museums and other legacy institutions, and academia. The familiar political core maintained its connection with and loyalty to the party and its ideology for many years. There was something about the Revisionist homes that led the younger generation to swear allegiance to the state, to the military, to education, and to dedicate its life to the people of Israel. While it may sound mawkish, when one speaks with "Jabotinsky grandchildren" who are involved in business and commerce, one hears their frustration at not being involved in the greater service of the nation, even among those who devote their free time to volunteer activities and initiatives. The fire never goes out.

Enlisting for combat duty

Thousands of "Zeev"s and "Yair"s enlisted in the IDF during the period that saw three wars within six years: the Six Day War (1967), the War of Attrition (1969–1970), and the Yom Kippur War (1973). This short period began with euphoria and ended in despair and grief.

The children whose parents had fought so courageously during the revolt against the British could not imagine evading military service. Along with their

Figure 7.1 The young officer Ruby Rivlin. Like most of the "Princes", he served as a combat officer in the IDF.

peers born in the 1940s, the heirs participated in the heroic battles that changed the face and the borders of the state. Unlike their parents, they integrated smoothly into the IDF and achieved prominence. Dozens of outstanding officers, children of underground veterans, were decorated and went on to build illustrious military careers. Parents who had been de-legitimized and excluded produced no less than four major-generals, along with ten senior officers, decorated officers, and hundreds of combat officers.

The Netanyahu brothers – Yoni, Bibi (Benjamin), and Ido – all served in the General Staff Reconnaissance Unit and led daring operations in the Six Day War

Figure 7.2 Uzi Landau (wearing uniform) with his father Chaim and brother Avner. The
father and son, a genetic and ideological clone, served sixty years (combined)
in the Knesset.

(Yoni), the War of Attrition (Yoni and Bibi together) and Yom Kippur (all three
brothers). Lieutenant-Colonel Yoni Netanyahu, commander of the General Staff
Reconnaissance Unit and of dozens of special operations, decorated with the
Medal of Distinguished Service, was killed in 1976 during the Entebbe Raid. He
had been one of a very small group of outstanding officers who, as lieutenant-
colonels, were already being primed as possible candidates for the position of
chief of general staff in the future.

His brothers, Ido and Benjamin, honored his memory with *The Letters of Jonathan Netanyahu* (published in Hebrew in 1978), a collection of the letters that
Yoni had sent to family and friends. The letters were warmly received by the
Israeli public, and the book became a staple in homes throughout the country. It
became required reading for youth movement members prior to their army enlist-
ment, since it describes in vivid and true colors the path that Yoni followed from
the time of his high school graduation: his military service as a combat soldier
and commander in the Paratrooper Brigade, his training and operations during the
Six Day War, his marriage to Tuti (Tirza) (whom he later divorced), his studies at
Harvard and at the Hebrew University, his return to military service in the General
Staff Reconnaissance Unit, his command during the Yom Kippur War, his life as

commander of the elite unit, and his last letter he wrote to his girlfriend. The universal appeal of the book in Israel lay in the description of Yoni's emotions and the special relationships that this tough commander maintained with his friends, girlfriends, commanders and subordinates, parents, and brothers. Yoni lives on in the collective Israeli memory as a distinguished figure in Jewish history. The book also exposed to the public his family, including his younger brothers, who would come to be known throughout the world.

Reuven Rivlin was honorably discharged from the army with the rank of major after fighting in the Six Day War. Dan Meridor, a captain in the armored corps, was injured in battle on the Golan Heights during the same war. Zeev Boim commanded a tank company, and his neighbor and classmate from Nahalat Jabotinsky, Yirmi Olmert (Ehud's brother), served in the IDF for decades before his honorable discharge with the rank of brigadier-general.

Uzi Landau, son of MK and minister Chaim Landau, joined the Airborne Nahal battalion and was injured by a bullet during a training exercise, which led to a lengthy period of recovery and marred his dream of a military career. Nevertheless, during the Six Day War he participated within the Paratrooper Brigade in the battles to liberate Jerusalem, and during the War of Attrition he was stationed on the heavily bombarded banks of the Suez Canal. He halted his studies at MIT in Boston to fight in the Yom Kippur War and spearheaded the division commanded by General Ariel Sharon. (Benjamin Netanyahu, also in the midst of his studies at the time, also returned to Israel to fight.) Major Uzi Landau continued to perform reserve duty in combat intelligence for decades, even while serving, in his forties, as an MK.

The children of Irgun commanders Shamir and Eldad also built impressive military careers: Yair Shamir served as a pilot, engineer, and senior IAF commander with the rank of colonel. His sister, Gilada Diamant, was a senior Mossad agent, like her father. Future MK Aryeh Eldad, son of the Lehi commander who was dismissed from his humble schoolteacher job, served as a doctor in the army, reaching the rank of brigadier-general as the chief IDF medical officer. Jabotinsky's grandson was an IAF helicopter pilot.

The parents of Major-General Ido Nehushtan, commander of the IAF, were Irgun commanders Yaakov and Devora Nehushtan, among the most prominent underground couples. Ido grew up in a home suffused with stories of bravery. His father, Yaakov, had joined the Irgun immediately upon emigrating from Bulgaria. He fought in Jerusalem, was imprisoned by the British, and was exiled to Eritrea and Kenya. After the establishment of the state he became a lawyer and served as an MK for Likud in the seventh Knesset. Yaakov Nehushtan served the Likud government as a representative in the Israeli embassy in Washington (he was eventually replaced by the son of his neighbors – Benjamin Netanyahu). His mother, Devora, was already a second-generation Revisionist, and she fought in the Irgun alongside two brothers and two sisters. She was injured in the operation to blow up the oil pipeline near Haifa; she participated in the attack on a British army camp in Tel Aviv. She was also part of the operation on the airport in Lod and was arrested upon her return from a sabotage operation on a railway installation in the south of the country. During her trial she delivered a fiery speech in which she declared that she did not recognize the British occupation regime. Sentenced to fifteen years' imprisonment, she shared a cell with Lehi fighter Geula Cohen and was one of the leaders of the women prisoners' revolt, which resulted in their transfer to the prison in Atlit. She escaped two months later, wearing a British policewoman's uniform, and rejoined the revolt. Ido, the son, completed a pilot's course with distinction, served as a combat pilot, participated in many operations deep in enemy territory, commanded flight squadrons, and eventually was appointed commander of the IAF.

Not only the children of the commanders and senior leaders of the movement left their mark on the IDF. The three children of Tzila Amidror, an Irgun fighter and Herut activist, rose through the ranks: Major-General Yaakov Amidror, Binyamin Amidror, and Colonel Ahuva Yanai. Ahuva was the IDF public appeals officer; Yaakov started out in the Paratrooper Brigade during the Six Day War; during the Yom Kippur War he served as a division intelligence officer on the Egyptian front and was appointed head of the Directorate of Military Intelligence Research Department. Later he served as commander of the military academies and then became head of the National Security Council for Netanyahu's second government.

The fifth major-general was Dr. Avichai Mandelblit, who was the chief military advocate general, later cabinet secretary, and is currently Israel's Attorney General. His father, Micky Mandelblit, was an Irgun fighter, a veteran Herut activist, and a colorful and popular Beitar soccer player. His clothing store was located next to the Herut headquarters, which was his second home.

Herzi Makov, from Nahalat Jabotinsky, head of Beitar in Binyamina and head of the student council in high school, went on to serve for seven years in the IAF. Amos Hermon, a former senior figure in the Jewish Agency from the Herut moshav Nordiya, served in an elite Navy unit. Major-General Yohanan Locker, son of Martin Locker, who arrived in Israel aboard the *Altalena*, served in the IDF for thirty-seven years. Inter alia he was the first navigator to command an operational combat squadron of Phantom planes, commander of Hatzerim Air Force Base, head of the IAF Training & Doctrine Division, and military secretary to Prime Minister Netanyahu.

Many children of Irgun and Lehi fighters fought on the frontlines in Israel's wars, and the list of casualties includes a great many fighting family names. David Tamir, son of Shmuel Tamir (the deputy Irgun commander in Jerusalem who revolted and then returned as an MK and government minister) was killed during his IAF service. The Halevy dynasty in Jerusalem started with the grandfather, H.S. Halevy, who was among the founders of the Irgun and its deputy commander in Jerusalem; it continued with his son, Hertzi Halevy, who was killed in the battle for Jerusalem on the last day of the Six Day War. His brother, Momo, a second-generation Herut activist in Jerusalem, named his son, who was born shortly thereafter, in honor of his brother. This Hertzi Halevy II was eventually appointed commander of the General Staff Reconnaissance Unit, commander of the Paratrooper Brigade, head of Military Intelligence, and, in 2018, head of Israel's Southern Command. His brother, Amir, also continued the tradition, serving as head of the Herut student cell at Tel Aviv University, deputy mayor of Tel Aviv, and director general of Israel's Ministry of Tourism. The story of Lieutenant-Colonel Avi Lanir, son of Irgun fighters Yakov and Malka Lenkin, and nephew of the *Altalena* commander Eliyahu Lenkin, is one that continues to stir emotions in Israel to this day: he was the most senior Israeli pilot to fall into captivity, maintaining his silence to the end and refusing to disclose military secrets to his Syrian captors. Lanir was posthumously awarded Israel's Medal of Courage. Journalist Eitan Haber, a fellow heir, wrote of him, "This young man could have become the Chief-of-Staff, or Prime Minister."[1]

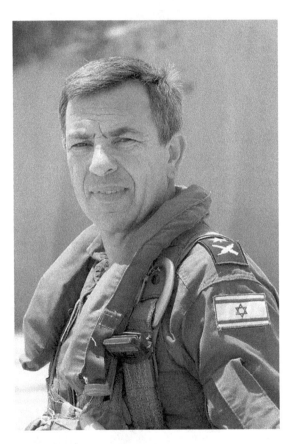

Figure 7.3 Ido Nehoshtan, former IDF Air Force commander. His mother Devora Nehoshtan was a daring commander in the Etzel Organization. His father was an MK of the Likud party.

Figure 7.4 Yaakov Amidror, retired general and former national security advisor, son of Tzila Amidror, Etzel warrior and senior activist in the Herut and Likud parties.

Figure 7.5 PM Benjamin Netanyahu with the "princes" brothers, Harel Locker (on the left), CEO of the PM office, and General Yohanan Locker (in the middle), military secretary of the PM.

Figure 7.6 So similar in appearance and perspective: Yitzhak and Yair Shamir. The son
followed his father's steps, from military service to public service.

Committed to public service and commemoration

If there is one sphere that has always united the younger generation of Revisionists, and continues to unite them to this day, it is their intensive activity to commemorate their parents' generation and the Revolt. Even those who left or are
no longer active in the movement continue to point to Jabotinsky as the source
of their worldview. Begin, the Revolt, Jabotinsky, and the martyrs have been
engraved on the pages of Israel's history thanks to the work of Herut/Likud ministers, MKs, and mayors. The initiative to commemorate Begin brought together
Olmert (who, as mayor of Jerusalem, advanced the establishment of the Begin
Heritage Center) and his adversary, Reuven Rivlin (who had initiated the Begin
Commemoration Law).

The profound commitment to memorializing Jabotinsky and Begin led some
Likudniks in the direction of museums. Yossi Ahimeir, as noted, established the
Beit Abba (Abba's House) museum in his parents' home. He is also the director of
the Jabotinsky Institute. His colleague, director of the institute's archive, is Amira
Stern, whose father, David, fought together with her uncle – Yair Stern of Lehi.
The institute's academic committee is chaired by Professor Arye Naor, whose
uncle, mother, and father were among the founders of the Irgun. Dr. Karni Rubin,
a granddaughter of Ze'ev Jabotinsky, sits on the board, and the institute's bursary

fund is headed by two generations of the family of Dr. Alex Refaeli, who was a member of the Bergson Group.

Herzl Makov established the Menachem Begin Heritage Center facing the walls of the Old City of Jerusalem; the chairman of its executive committee is Amos Hermon, son of Zvi Hermon (one of the founders and leaders of the Beitar moshav Nordiya). One of the executive committee members is Ariella Ravdel, who was the first Herut representative to win an election for chairman of a students' association. The museum's public council includes Ilana Silver, whose father, Shlomo Friedrich, was leader of the Revisionist Movement in France; Naftali Dresner, brother of Yehiel Dresner, who was hanged by the British; and Rachel Kremerman, the first heiress to emerge from the Revisionists' second generation. The head of the organization for the commemoration of the Lehi legacy is Yair Stern Jr., who proudly shares the story of his father and the underground in the Lehi Museum.

It is interesting to see how many sons and daughters of underground fighters have become prominent Israeli journalists, making their mark on Israeli society via the media that dealt so unjustly with their parents, just as their peers chose to make their impact in politics, the military, or the educational system. Most of these media figures are the sons and daughters of Revisionist journalists from the middle generation, between Begin and Jabotinsky. (Some were mentioned previously, in the description of the Veterans' Neighborhood in Ramat Gan.) Some of them have drifted away from the worldview maintained by Jabotinsky's political heirs in the Likud. The list is rather long, and therefore I offer here only some examples.

For many years the respective editors-in-chief of the two largest mass-circulation newspapers in Israel were sons of editors with roots in the Revisionist movement: Moshe Vardi, son of Dr. Rosenblum (*Yediot Aharonot*), and Ido Dissenchik, son of Aryeh Dissenchik (*Maariv*). Israel Rosenblatt, who was for many years a senior editor at *Maariv*, is a descendant of Zvi Rosenblatt, who was one of the Irgun members accused of Arlozorov's murder. Eitan Haber, as noted, is a senior journalist and commentator at *Yediot Aharonot*. Haggai Segal is editor of the right-wing newspaper *Makor Rishon*. (His uncle, Yedidya Segal, was the Irgun officer who was kidnapped and killed by the Haganah, as recounted earlier on.) Haggai's son, Amit Segal, is the political correspondent for Israel's leading television station.

Several of the younger generation of Revisionists have achieved prominence in the Israel Broadcasting Authority, including Yair Stern Jr., Yaakov Ahimeir, and Emmanuel Halperin (the son of Begin's sister) in the sphere of television, while on state radio there is Dan Kanner, son of Rabbi Dr. Yisrael Zvi Kanner, an Irgun officer, and Avshalom Kor, whose father, Shlomo Kor, was one of the veteran leaders of Likud.

The children of other Irgun figures – and especially members of HaTzohar party – have achieved prominence in the academic sphere. Examples include Professor Itamar Rabinovich, who was President of Tel Aviv University; Professor Arye Naor, politics and communications department chair at Hadassah Academic

College; Professor Zeev Tzahor, the first President of Sapir Academic College; Professor Amram Olmert, a renowned expert in agriculture; Professor Moshe Amirav, at the Institute for Urban Studies in Jerusalem; Professor Ilan Avisar, an associate professor in the film and television department at Tel Aviv University; Professor Mordechai Tamarkin, head of the Tami Steinmetz Center for Peace Research at Tel Aviv University, whose father, Eliyahu Tamarkin, was the founder of Ramat Tyomkin, the first Revisionist moshav (today part of Netanya); and Professor Moshe Maoz, an Irgun member in his youth, who was a colonel in the IDF and a lecturer at the Hebrew University of Jerusalem.

Sallai Meridor, Amos Hermon, and others engaged in education through leadership of the Beitar youth movement, proceeding to leadership of the Jewish Agency and of the Jewish National Fund. Roni Milo and Ehud Olmert became mayors of major cities. Three other municipal leaders emerged from the Revisionist moshav Nahat Jabotinsky: Brigadier-General Yirmi Olmert, mayor of Givat Shmuel; Zeev Boim, who was mayor of Kiryat Gat before he was elected to the Knesset; and Moti Kirmeir, mayor of Binyamina. Others who have served in important administrative positions include Professor Itamar Rabinovich and Sallai Meridor (both served as ambassadors to the US); Yardena Meller-Horovitz, secretary-general of the Knesset, whose father, Yossi Meller, participated in the Irgun kidnapping of two British sergeants. Oren Hellman, also with an Irgun background, was director of the Government Press Office and an advisor to Netanyahu. Dani Dayan, Israel's general consul in New York, and his wife, Einat, represent a unification of Revisionist families: Dani is a fourth-generation Revisionist (his great-grandfather was chairman of the movement in Argentina); he himself was among the leaders of the sister Tehiya party and the dominant leader of the Council of Judea and Samaria Communities (Moetzet Yesha). Einat is a third-generation Revisionist who is among the founders and administrative directors of Ariel University in Samaria. Ofir, their daughter, was head of the Beitar youth club in the Karnei Shomron settlement and later was elected President of the SSI (Students Supporting Israel) organization at Columbia University.

An interesting example of the older generation passing the political "bug" on to the next generation is Rahm Emanuel, a second-generation Revisionist whose father moved to the US. Rahm, currently mayor of Chicago and formerly the White House Chief-of-Staff and a member of the US Congress, is the son of Irgun fighter Dr. Benjamin Emanuel. The father changed the family name in honor of his uncle, Emanuel Orbach, who was killed during the 1930s by Arabs in Jerusalem, and he named his son Rahm in memory of a friend who fought in Lehi. Rahm grew up in Chicago, spoke Hebrew at home, and volunteered in the IDF during the period in between his two degrees. He volunteered again for two months during the First Gulf War, when Israel was attacked with Iraqi missiles.

It is difficult to miss the similarity between the life stories of Rahm Emanuel and Benjamin Netanyahu. Both are sons of Revisionist parents who moved to the US during the period of Labor hegemony in Israel. One came back to Israel and eventually became Prime Minister; the other remained in the US and reached the White House as Chief of Staff.

Mobilization on campus, victory, and the pull towards politics

A great wave of youth from underground fighter families entered the universities during the mid-1960s and '70s, highly motivated to bring justice to the cause. Many became political activists on campus, but their intention was not to become politicians; rather, they sought to continue their parents' old struggle.

It was during this time that Herut came to the end of its isolated, independent existence. In a desperate attempt to extricate itself from the opposition benches, it joined the Liberal Center party to form the Gahal/Likud list. During these years the general disgust towards the Labor government grew especially intense, especially among the youth, and as a result the university campuses became centers of much agitation and turbulence. The future heirs, who were accustomed to finding themselves politically isolated (at school, on the street, in the army), were surprised to discover a great many like-minded peers. Those who during their childhood years had not met many other children of Irgun fighters found themselves gravitating naturally to the Herut/Likud student clubs at the universities, where they felt completely at home with each other, recognizing in each other the ideology and influences that had molded them.

They were comfortable in the right-wing student cells that were eager to conquer the Student Union. They were also pleasantly surprised to discover growing numbers of students who were not genetically part of the fighting family but nevertheless loathed the Labor establishment and were intent on wresting the Student Union from its control.

The activity generated over two decades on the campuses – starting at the Hebrew University of Jerusalem, and later also at Tel Aviv University – was powered by the loyalty and determination of the underground children and their supporters. Hundreds of them came together to form a young, vibrant, self-confident, and upbeat group. The children of Irgun fighters from Safed and Jerusalem came to know children of fighters from Nahalat Jabotinsky and from Tel Aviv. All were united by a powerful faith in their cause and animosity towards the establishment that persecuted their parents. Their success in spearheading a political upheaval at the universities strengthened their confidence and pointed the way to a new future for their beloved but aging, marginalized, and down-and-out movement.

Many of the younger generation – including Rivlin, Olmert, Meridor, Milo, Hanegbi, Livni, Levin, Harel Locker, and others – studied law. Perhaps this decision was motivated by an urge to fight against the despotic regime that hounded the underground fighters – including those who had been injured during the Revolt – and the bereaved families. For Rivlin, who had dreamed as a child of prosecuting the culprits of the *Altalena* affair, law studies were an obvious choice. This young Jerusalemite embarked on his studies with an already impressive resumé: upon the establishment of the state, when he was ten years old, he was a full-fledged member of the Bnei ha-Etzel youth movement, and at thirteen he was a prominent Herut activist ("Number-one poster disseminator," Rivlin asserts).[2] At seventeen he managed the operations division of the Herut party for the 1965 elections, and at twenty, during his military service, he was elected to the executive of the movement's soccer team, Beitar Jerusalem. Following his discharge, he enrolled to study law.

It is important to note that the sons and daughters of the underground fighters entered student politics out of pure ideology. At this stage of their lives they had no aspirations to participate in politics on the national level, and they had no political career in mind. The fire that was kindled in them upon entering university was not a calculated move; the revolt that they brought from home still smoldered within. It is possible that the great fire broke out because the children of the underground veterans entered academia right after their military service and were confronted by radical leftist groups. Perhaps it was the result of the encounter with socialist establishment Student Unions, whose attitude towards the children of underground fighters was one of hostility and disdain. Perhaps the flames were fanned by the many scandals and stories of corruption that were exposed during that period. Whatever the reason, what is clear is that the heavy burden borne by the younger generation erupted on the campuses, leading to an influx of youthful energy into the Herut movement.

The Herut younger generation took over Student Unions throughout the country and turned them into political, ideological, aggressive bodies that provided fuel for the rising Likud. The historical victories on the campuses led these youth to the center of the national stage and introduced new names into the public discourse. Finally, the fighting family had leaders who were attractive: young, not aging; energetic, not worn out; winners, not losers; extroverts, not withdrawn; and professional and media-savvy, not old-fashioned and detached.

The new leaders brought about a revolution on a national scale: for the first time since the establishment of the state, the political sphere was challenged by a young generation seeking change. Their student clubs supported the idea of the Greater Land of Israel and opposed the socialist system of discriminating against anyone outside of the Labor camp. They also brought organizational change: while until now Herut had two bases of operations – the party headquarters and the opposition benches in the Knesset – it now had powerful bases on six university campuses, having developed funding resources within the Student Unions that the earlier Herut movement could only dream of.

However, the turnaround at the universities – symbolized most prominently by the victory of the right in the 1969 Student Union elections in Tel Aviv and the 1974 Student Union elections at the Hebrew University – was not a sudden phenomenon. The youngsters accumulated power over the course of a few years, enlisting hundreds of fellow students who were children of former underground fighters, creating a snowball effect. The successes on campuses produced a cadre of young Likud leaders whose confidence grew over the years, along with their appetite for national politics.

The first wave of activist Revisionist "children-of" arrived at the Hebrew University in the early 1960s. The Herut student club at this same university where Raziel and Stern had established the "Jerusalemite Sohba" decades earlier – brought together a group of youngsters in their twenties. The members of this group, including Reuven Rivlin, the future President, Rachel Kremerman (who would later relinquish her Knesset seat), and Yoram Aridor, who later became a government minister, laid the foundations for the next wave of activists, who advanced the conquest of student leadership.

The second wave came in the mid-1960s, including Ehud Olmert; his friend Amiram Bukshpan, who was elected deputy chairman of the Student Union; and David Kolitz, who was elected chairman of the student parliament. This group, which had an immediate impact on campus, also played a prominent role in the 1966 revolt, as described earlier.

A third wave joined the Herut/Likud student society in Jerusalem in 1967, made up of three streams – a harbinger of the alliance that would eventually bring about the Upheaval of 1977: Herut (the right), Liberals (center), and the development towns (new). The core of this wave consisted of children of Irgun commanders, headed by Dan Meridor and David and Arye Naor.

Meridor enlisted the support of his "uncles": the heads of the Herut branch in Jerusalem. Like many other children of underground veterans, he had also distributed Herut posters during election campaigns, and his family lineage caused his father's friends to eye him as a possible candidate for promotion. Following his discharge from the IDF as an officer, and after the death of his father, MK Eliyahu Meridor, Dan was boosted to the narrow executive of the Herut branch in Jerusalem. "They viewed it as continuity," Dan told me three decades later. "A committee of veterans elected me. I didn't ask for it. I was sent."[3]

Their partners in the student society were children of the "nobility" – the Liberal Party – who bestowed legitimacy. Their success in recruiting the Liberals as partners demonstrated to the party veterans that their despair over the failure of the united party list in the 1965 had been premature and misguided. Before their very eyes, the merger of the two parties at the university received broad support.

The third group was a new phenomenon in the young state: student leaders from development towns in the country's geographical and social periphery, to whom the doors of the left-wing student societies were locked. They were the children of Mizrahim: Jewish immigrants from Arab countries who had been settled in towns far removed from the economic and cultural center of the country, and who suffered humiliation and discrimination. These students suddenly discovered a movement that wanted them as partners. In 1969, for the first time, a student of Mizrahi background, twenty-four-year old Moshe Katzav from Kiryat Malakhi, was elected chairman of the Likud-Liberal student society. Soon afterwards he was elected head of the Kiryat Malakhi municipal council, and he later became an MK, a minister, and President, until he resigned under a cloud of scandal (he was eventually sentenced to seven years in prison).

These three groups were motivated by hatred for and anger towards the Labor government. These youth viewed the Labor establishment as a discriminatory, corrupt, and insensitive body. The second-generation Liberals viewed the socialist administration as the enemy of the middle-class, while the students from development towns were driven by a sense of injustice and fury over the administration's assumption of its cultural superiority and the humiliation suffered by their Mizrahi parents. The Herut/Likud student society at the Hebrew University was in fact so dominant that the effects of its activities were felt at the other universities, too. The end of the 1970s saw another wave of student activists, including some who would go on to become central Likud players.

The fourth wave actually brought about the revolution at the Hebrew University in 1974: Ariella Ravdel, a daughter of Lehi veterans and chairwoman of the Right-Likud society at the university, led the society to its first victory in the Student Union elections and became the first Likud chairperson of the Council in Jerusalem. (She was also the first chairwoman of a Student Union anywhere in Israel.)

Ravdel achieved renown as a young leader when, together with her parents and friends, she led demonstrations against US Secretary of State Henry Kissinger, in response to his demands for Israeli territorial concessions. Her mother, Yehudit ("Avigayil") had participated in the underground in an operation against the refineries in Haifa. She was injured in the operation, arrested, and sentenced to life imprisonment (her incarceration ended with the establishment of the state). Her father, Zalman, an Irgun fighter, enlisted in the British army during the Second World War. Following the victory over Germany, he removed his British uniform and proceeded to fight against the British army. He was dispatched to Europe by Lehi. When the British Mandate ended he returned to fight in the War of Independence. After fighting in the Irgun, the British army, Lehi, and the IDF, Ravdel was a Herut activist and a prominent member of the party's Central Committee, where his daughter Ariella eventually joined him.

The position of Chairman of the Student Union was passed from Ariella Ravdel to another Lehi heir: Tzahi Hanegbi. Some of the students who were active during his tenure and afterwards were later active in national politics as MKs and ministers, including Israel Katz, Avigdor Lieberman, and Danny Naveh. At the same time, the Student Union at Ben Gurion University of the Negev was headed by Silvan Shalom, the son of a Beitar veteran. He, too, went on to serve as an MK and government minister for many years.

Getting back to 1969, Tel Aviv University witnessed a revolution that aroused considerable media attention: the first victory for the Herut student society in the Student Union elections. In this secular, liberal, left-wing bastion, this was an outsider victory over a silent, complacent, and apathetic majority. At the center of the clever Herut/Likud campaign was the struggle against Labor corruption. This tactic was of decisive importance in attracting many non-political votes among students and lecturers alike who were fed up with Labor rule. The Tel Aviv society members included future MKs Roni Milo and Limor Livnat, as well as Michael Kleiner, Michael Eitan, and Mikha Reiser. Roni Milo had grown up in a well-to-do Tel Aviv family and was an heir of a different sort. While his father, industrialist Nahum Milikovsky, had not served as a commander in the Irgun, he had supported the Irgun and its fighters during the years of revolt and was regarded as a member of the fighting family to the core. He and his wife, Fruma, also owned the famous Tenuva restaurant. "Irgun veterans would come, and they didn't have to pay," Milo told me.[4] "When Ben-Gurion and his friends came, they paid big-time.

[. . .] The borscht that my father served to Laborites included leftover bones from the plates of the Irgun people." During the years of the Revolt, Milikovsky had offered to smuggle Begin, who was on the run, in the trunk of his American car, which no-one would suspect as being a vehicle in the service of the underground. After the establishment of the state, Milikovsky continued transporting Begin from place to place on a volunteer basis.

In his youth, Roni Milo heard stories of the underground from his uncle, Menachem Melatzky, a prominent Herut activist who had been Irgun commander of the Haifa region and had participated in the Acre Prison break. His stories excited the imagination of young Milo, who absorbed his uncle's ideological intensity and developed an all-consuming ambition to drive Begin's Labor tormentors out of power. At the age of sixteen he submitted his candidacy to lead the student council at his high school, a left-wing bastion – and won. At seventeen he was elected chairman of the national student parliament.

Like Ehud Olmert, Milo also commenced his university studies at a relatively young age. In 1970, at twenty-one, he became chairman of the national Student Union. For the first time in its history, the opposition Herut party took the helm of student politics in Israel. This victory earned Milo extensive media coverage, far exceeding that of his companions Michael Kleiner and Mikha Reiser, who had both served as chairman of the Student Union at Tel Aviv University. Some commentators marked him as one of the most promising young people in politics. When Milo was twenty-three, Begin placed him on the narrow executive of the Herut movement, alongside other members who were twice or three times his age.

Recruiting the "Zeev"s and "Yair"s on campus

The story of how Limor Livnat came to join the Herut student society at Tel Aviv University, eventually becoming deputy chairman of the Student Union, is indicative of the intense enthusiasm of its members. "Right after the army, everything suddenly came to a head," Livnat recalls.

> I went off to demonstrate against the Rogers Plan, which dictated a withdrawal from Judea and Samaria at the orders of the Americans. I wanted to help. They agreed for me to paint posters. [. . .] At the demonstration a tall young man [Michael Kleiner] approached me and recruited me to run for the Student Union elections at Tel Aviv University. The next day I showed up for work at the society, and there I met Mikha [Reiser] and Roni [Milo].[5]

Livnat describes the "underground" recruiting methods of the student activists:

> We went to the Likud headquarters to collect names of veteran Irgun, Lehi and Herut veterans and activists. Then we went to the student registrar at the university and went through the lists by family name. Then we looked for specific names: Yair, Yaira, Zeev, Zeeva, Raziel, Meridor, Eldad, Karni. When we found them, we called them and asked something like, "Why were

you named Zeeva?" [. . .] If they gave a good answer, I would tell them to look out for a woman student wearing a white fur coat [Livnat herself].

The students they recruited in this manner included Chaim Perlok, whose father, Moshe, had been a Beitar leader who appeared with Begin at Beitar branches throughout Poland. That was how he met his future wife Hinda ("Ayala"), who immigrated and fought with the Irgun. (Chaim was a Likud MK in the twelfth Knesset).

Livnat's recruiting efforts accompanied her everywhere: on a bus on the way to university she struck up conversation with a student sitting next to her. Within a few minutes the student – Yossi Kanati – told her that his father had served in the Irgun. Within a few moments he had joined the Herut student cell, and he went on to serve the party for many years.

Almost a decade later I myself was recruited to the Likud student society at Tel Aviv University, in a similar manner. Tzahi Hanegbi, who was chairman of the National Student Union at the time, was looking to replace the body's executive, which was in decline. He consulted with his mother, Geula Cohen, and obtained two names: Ofer Eitani, son of Chaim Eitani, a courageous Irgun fighter and a central activist among the Herut veterans and their "Tagar circle", and me – the grandson of Malka Samsonov and the son of the Lehi commander in Zikhron Yaakov. The warm recommendation of his mother, who had been very close to my grandmother, sufficed for Hanegbi to invite me, over the phone, to join the Student Union executive, despite the fact that I had just arrived at the university following five years of military service and had no experience in student politics. Thus I embarked on twelve years of activity at the university and in the movement.

Later on, as chairman of the Likud Youth, I went to Tel Aviv University to recruit a new leadership for the student society, which had disintegrated. Although this was already the early '90s, I used the same strategy. Even five decades after the Revolt, the best way of finding the proverbial needle in the haystack is to look for the son or daughter of underground veterans. During my search I became aware of a student named Oren Hellman, who had no compunction about voicing views that were quite unusual for the Tel Aviv campus. I scheduled a meeting with him and his friend, David Sharan, at the bastion of the Left – the beautiful coffee shop outside Gillman Building, which houses the Faculty of Humanities.

Hellman spoke up first and told me about his mother's family. The names told me all I needed to know. I decided on the spot that he and Sharan would lead the student society. His mother's cousins were Uri Cohen and Moka Cohen, both renowned members of the "Cohen tribe". Later on, Hellman told me[6] about Yosef Simhon, another of his mother's cousins, whose family had survived the 1929 pogrom against the Jews of Hebron. Simhon had joined Beitar at the age of fourteen and immediately enlisted in the Irgun, where he stood out for his courage in the attacks against the British intelligence in Jaffa, the Qastina airport, and the weapons depot in Sarafand (Tzerifin). He and his comrade-in-arms, Michael (Mike) Eshbal, who composed the Irgun anthem, "Manning the Barricades", were injured and captured by the British. They both refused to defend themselves before the British court, expressing their non-recognition of the British occupation, and both were sentenced to death. Ultimately, they were saved thanks to the kidnapping of two British sergeants by the Irgun, which deterred the British from hanging underground fighters. After the War of Independence, Simhon wanted to join the IDF and serve his country, but was rejected owing to his underground past. Begin placed him on the list of 120 Herut candidates for Knesset, as a gesture of esteem. However, Simhon had trouble finding a job. Ultimately he was killed in a work accident at a drilling facility in the Negev. The rage of his family over the way in which the state had treated a man who had fought on its behalf was bequeathed from generation to generation.

Begin opens the Likud headquarters to student heirs

The student revolution of the late '60s paved the way for the great Upheaval of 1977 and introduced the winning formula. The children of the founders of Herut achieved a first electoral victory for their parents' movement with the new Likud. They brought with them a cadre of winning candidates – leaders of all strata of the population who enjoyed public support and media attention. After years of a dearth of young people in the Herut headquarters, the building began to assume a younger and more energetic atmosphere.

The sudden openness of the generation of the Revolt – a generation characterized by reclusive withdrawal – flowed, to a considerable degree, from the threat embodied by the departure of the young underground commanders and the student leaders following the 1966 revolt. This walkout had effectively cut off the movement's rank-and-file. The leadership was deeply disturbed by the prospect of losing the younger generation altogether.

This fear intensified in view of the support that the seceding youth party, led by Shmuel Tamir, received in the press. The young journalists were fed up with Herut, with its old-fashioned pronouncements and stories of heroism. They were tired of Begin's preaching about the right to the Greater Land of Israel, and the endlessly repeated quotes from Jabotinsky's doctrine. The free press was mesmerised by the young, brilliant, and educated lawyer. Begin was therefore forced to find a youthful alternative, to counter Tamir and Olmert.

Following the 1969 elections, in which the party maintained its power but failed to enlarge it, Begin decided to open up the Likud headquarters to the students. He also accepted back those who had departed, in his characteristic noble and respectful manner, giving no indication of bitterness or anger over the putsch at Kfar HaMakabiya. He replaced his old insularity with a reconciling, unifying approach.

The few youngsters who had remained loyal to Begin during Tamir's revolt received preferential status in the Herut Youth, which from this point onwards became a dominant body within the movement. Its early leaders were Rivlin, Aridor, and Kremerman; they were followed by the age-group represented by Moshe Katzav, the Herut pioneer of the development towns, along with Dan Meridor and Arye Naor. Afterwards the reins passed to the Tel Aviv student leadership: Milo and Livnat, with Kleiner, Reiser, and Michael Eitan.

The heroes of the student revolution received a warm embrace from Begin. For the first time, promising young candidates were not required to "speak Polish" in order to advance in Herut. New faces began to appear at meetings of the Herut Central Committee and in the party's institutions and branches. For the first time, young people could climb the staircases in the Herut headquarters without encountering suspicious expressions on the faces of former underground fighters, who were constantly on the lookout for Labor spies. It was in fact the older activists and MKs who urged the youngsters to enter the party's councils, branches, and institutions, and indeed these political rookies found themselves nominated to these bodies even before they understood exactly what their function was. The older activists did not view the young people as a threat. On the contrary, they had full faith in the children of their former commanders. They had watched the heirs since their childhood; they were proud of the sons of Begin, Meridor, and Raziel. They were also full of admiration for the students who had triumphed in the Student Unions (from Roni Milo and friends to Tzahi Hanegbi). Menachem Begin and his number two, Ezer Weizman, who had served as commander of the

Figure 7.7 Tzahi Hanegbi and his future wife Randy in the struggle against the withdrawal from Sinai following the peace agreement signed by Begin with Egypt (April 1982).

Figure 7.8 "Princesses" Limor Livnat, daughter of a Lehi fighter (sitting), and Rachel
Kremerman, daughter of an Etzel fighter (standing behind her).

IAF and as Deputy Chief-of Staff before joining the Herut, understood the opportunity that the newcomers represented. They identified the tremendous energy and
potential that the student leaders brought to the party. They were also well aware
of the electoral importance and value of the contact that had been forged between
the student leaders and Israel's younger generation. It pointed to the possibility of
attaining the almost impossible dream: defeating Labor in general elections and
bringing about a reversal of the political order.

At the festive reception held for Milo and the heroes of the Student Unions,
Begin granted the young leaders membership in the narrow and exclusive Herut
Central Committee. Begin beamed with satisfaction, believing that the student
victory expressed a more profound mood. He was like a father proud of his
children – Milo, Livnat, Reiser, and Kleiner, all of whom later became MKs.

The older leadership embraced the hundreds of youngsters whom the student leaders brought with them to the desolate Herut headquarters.

Begin did not fear them for a moment. They were thirty or forty years younger than him, and were no threat to him and his Polish friends, who had accumulated considerable parliamentary experience. In addition, it seemed that Herut no longer included subversive elements that could influence the youngsters.

The student victories at the universities breathed new hope into many veteran underground families. In tens of thousands of homes throughout the country, the stories of the young heroes who had brought the color back to Begin's cheeks were devoured with great interest. Begin himself seemed suddenly younger, more vigorous, like someone who had trudged through the desert for many years and finally sensed that he was nearing his destination. Begin was also beginning to enjoy increased legitimacy among diverse sectors of the population, from development towns to the veteran neighborhoods.

I remember myself as a twelve-year-old child in Zikhron Yaakov, cutting out articles from the student newspaper. The headlines announced the Herut victories at the universities. Any victory of "us" over "them" was rare, new, and exciting, and was perceived in my family as a victory of good over evil, of justice over corruption. And I dreamed of the day when I could follow in the footsteps of these children of underground fighters. Similar dreams were floating in the minds of hundreds of other Herut children.

Notes

1 Yediot Aharonot, February 29, 2004.
2 Interview with author, April 18, 2002.
3 Interview with the author, April 10, 2002.
4 Interview with the author, April 21, 2001.
5 Interview with the author, July 5, 2002.
6 Interview with the author, August 12, 2014.

8 Ladies and gentlemen
A first political revolution

During the latter half of the '60s, the Herut movement began to enjoy increasing legitimacy among outside circles and established itself as a major party in Israeli politics. This change came about in the wake of a series of important events, the first of which took place on July 9, 1964.

In a will that he wrote in 1935, more than a decade before the establishment of the state, Jabotinsky stipulated that if he died and was buried abroad, he wanted to be reinterred in the Land of Israel only "at the orders of the Jewish government of the country when it arises." Ben-Gurion, as Prime Minister, refused to issue such an order, and he had his reasons: his heartless decision apparently reflected his understanding of the political effect that such a step would have. Levi Eshkol, Ben-Gurion's successor as Prime Minister, eventually agreed to bring Jabotinsky's bones for burial in Israel, earning the eternal gratitude of the underground veterans.

Jabotinsky was reinterred in Israel twenty-four years after his death, in an impressive demonstration of the fighting family's emergence from its isolation. The event, which Begin entitled "Zeev Jabotinsky Returns to His Homeland", included a funeral procession of hundreds of thousands of Israelis and concluded with a burial ceremony with the President, Zalman Shazar, in attendance. This was in fact the first open mass demonstration of Jabotinsky's supporters in Israel – a very powerful, quasi-mystical event that brought about a change of consciousness both within the movement and on the Israeli street. Jabotinsky's casket was placed in Tel Aviv, and the line of those who waited to pass by it and pay their last respects wound its way through the neighboring streets. Thereafter the casket was brought for burial to Mount Herzl in Jerusalem. While Jabotinsky was buried outside the area reserved for the great leaders of the nation, his grave is located on the path leading towards the grave of Herzl, overlooking the Yad Vashem Museum which commemorates the Holocaust that Jabotinsky warned of, to no avail. The casket was covered with soil from Mount Zion, Mount of Olives, the gravesites of Sara Aharonson and Yosef Trumpeldor, and the gravesites of fallen Irgun fighters.

*

The retirement of Ben-Gurion, Israel's eternal leader, from the Prime Minister's Office (June 1963) contributed most significantly to the strengthening of

Herut. With the departure of his sworn enemy, and the dramatic weakening of the absolute control wielded by the despotic regime, the door was opened for Begin to form new alliances and even to join the coalition. While the alliance with the Liberals did not produce the desired results in the short term, it contributed greatly to the legitimacy of Herut and launched a process of reunification between Herut and groups that had seceded from it, such that within a few short years they were amalgamated into a single party: the Likud. While these mergers did involve some ideological friction, and some Knesset seats had to be awarded to the new partners, there were enormous benefits in terms of image. Begin finally began to be perceived as a worthy leader to serve as Prime Minister.

The national responsibility that Begin demonstrated in June 1967, on the eve of the Six Day War, when he entered a unity government alongside his bitter adversaries, helped to expose the public to his political integrity. His proposal that his historical enemy, Ben-Gurion, lead the government (a proposal that was not accepted by Ben-Gurion's adversaries in his own former party) revealed the fact that Begin was the only figure during the period of moral decay who transcended his personal animosity. And the incredible victory in the Six Day War served to inscribe him in the public consciousness as one of the heads of the unity government that had won the war.

While his main ideal – the territorial integrity of the Land of Israel – had been regarded up to this point as a dream, a fantasy detached from reality, the war brought his vision to realization. Finally, after decades, the far-off dream coincided with the reality. The members of Jabotinsky's movement, under Begin's leadership, who had been viewed and treated over the years as wild-eyed lunatics who dreamed of the Western Wall and the Cave of the Patriarchs in Hebron, suddenly took on the appearance of a centrist stream whose aim had been realized. Suddenly, Begin was a legitimate leader, who spoke regularly with his bitter enemy, Ben-Gurion, and was close to the much-admired military leader, Moshe Dayan. He was at the very heart of the national consensus.

The press, too, started treating Begin differently. These were years in which party newspapers were in decline, and private media began to flourish. Private newspapers such as *Yediot Aharonot* and *Maariv* were major influences on public opinion, which now refused to blindly accept whatever the government and its official organs said. The influence of the prominent Revisionist journalists who had left politics and party newspapers, and were now writing for and editing the leading private newspapers, was now felt. They were not disciples of Begin (some in fact viewed themselves as Jabotinsky's "rightful heirs"), but they held similar views. They, too, were Zionist activists strongly influenced by Jabotinsky's teachings. Their education and heritage found expression in their writing. Thus, after decades in which he was slandered in the party press and on Israel's sole radio station, Begin was finally depicted in the free press as an esteemed and authoritative leader. Previously labelled a fascist, a gang-leader, and a dangerous dictator, he was now granted legitimacy and began attracting supporters from new sectors of the population.

Opening the ranks to the generals, and conquest of the cities

The dissatisfaction that manifested itself among the Herut ranks every few years made it clear to Begin how greatly his party longed for victory. Even if he himself could remain in the opposition for the rest of his life, if necessary, the party hungered for a change. As the movement grew larger and stronger, so its members yearned to attain power and influence. This caused Begin to change direction and to open up the party, building coalitions with disgruntled members who had left as well as with new partners.

In the early '70s, the former Lehi fighters threw in their lot with Herut, the intervening years having blurred the differences between the two underground movements. Yitzhak Shamir, who had left the Mossad, joined already in 1970. He was followed by David Stern, brother of Lehi commander Avraham (Yair) Stern. Other fighters and commanders came aboard, including, in 1972, Lehi radio announcer and journalist Geula Cohen. Next in turn were the younger Irgun commanders, such as Eitan Livni and Moshe Arens, who had previously left the party in order to support their families.

The climax of this reunification process came in 1973 with the formation of the Likud, which included even some activist elements of Labor origin. The appearance of these disciples of Ben-Gurion, some of whom were central figures at the heart of the Labor and military establishment, granted even greater legitimacy to Herut. This in turn led to the return of the various groups that had seceded over the years, including the Free Center with all three age-groups that it encompassed: Eliezer Shostak and National Labor Federation people; Shmuel Tamir and the home-grown Irgun commanders; and the students and youngsters who had followed Ehud Olmert. Begin never forgot their revolt but agreed to integrate them so as to create momentum for the party. At Begin's side throughout this reunification was Major-General Ariel Sharon, who was an important partner in building the Likud.

With new blood flowing in its veins, the Likud won one local election after another in major centers throughout the country. Major-General Shlomo Lahat ("Chich"), who had served in the Haganah, joined the Liberals and was elected mayor of Tel Aviv-Jaffa. His victory earned the Likud a strategic hold in the city, and over the next two decades Lahat served an important role in reflecting the legitimacy of Begin and the Likud, and the perception of the Likud as a centrist party. With other major cities, too, in Likud hands, the party had new bases of power.

The periphery witnessed a similar and no less important revolution among the youth. Here the development towns were won for the Likud by Mizrahi activists whose immigrant parents had been settled in transit camps and then in development towns. The phenomenon began with Moshe Katzav's victory in 1969 in Kiryat Malakhi. The Labor establishment threw its full weight into a struggle to halt Katzav's progress, and succeeded, by means of an aggressive legal battle, in having him removed. The entire party leadership supported the new candidate in a battle that was given extensive media coverage and turned Katzav into a revolutionary icon. In 1974 he managed to build a coalition that brought him back to power at the head of a local council that was now highly symbolic.

Katzav's precedent was repeated by a wave of young Likud representatives of the second generation in the development towns. These were activists in their twenties who had overcome enormous socio-economic hurdles and had enlisted in the IDF, fought in wars, registered for university degrees, and become active in the right-wing student societies. After Katzav came Meir Sheetrit. Born in Morocco, he had immigrated at the age of nine and had grown up in a transit camp in the outlying town of Netivot, until his family moved to the development town of Yavne. Sheetrit began his academic studies at the age of sixteen and finished at twenty. After organizing a protest over the level of education in his town, he enlisted and fought in the Yom Kippur War. Discharged with the rank of major at the age of twenty-five, he took the helm of a group of young people on a quest for change. They joined Herut, which welcomed them with open arms, while Labor had closed its doors to them. In 1974, at the age of just twenty-six, Sheetrit won a widely publicized victory as head of the Yavne local council. Over the next thirteen years he attracted thousands of career soldiers to Yavne and turned it into a forward-looking and successful town. The strategy focusing on career soldiers as the engine of change was adopted elsewhere.

Next in line was David Magen, another immigrant from Morocco who had grown up in a transit camp, enlisted in the IDF, and reached the rank of major. He, too, headed a body of local youngsters which was warmly embraced by Herut. In 1976, at the age of twenty-seven, he was elected mayor of Kiryat Gat, where he served for many years.

Over the course of the 1970s the same scenario repeated itself in most of the development towns throughout the country, and by the 1980s and '90s it was a firmly established pattern. Ten of these mayors went on to serve in the Knesset, six became government ministers, and one became President.

The Likud was now the dominant party in many towns in Israel. While in the past the movement had at its disposal nothing more than a room in the Knesset for faction meetings and a single building in Tel Aviv, it now boasted strongholds and bases in dozens of towns and at universities. The revolution was well underway.

The surprising recruitment of renowned generals Sharon and Weizman

The legitimacy of Herut was also enhanced by the decorated major-generals who joined the movement's ranks. First and foremost among them was Ezer Weizman, esteemed commander of the IAF, who had led the blitz that paralyzed the enemy air forces in the Six Day War. Although Weizman was known for his right-wing views, and although there were rumors of ties between him and the Irgun from pre-state days, his family name placed him squarely at the heart of the establishment, far from the opposition territory that was home to Herut. It is therefore no wonder that the "defection" of this nephew of Israel's first President, Chaim Weizmann, to the Revisionist ranks in 1969 was greeted with astonishment. The tall, articulate, witty, and charismatic Weizman was a certified Israeli hero of "royal" lineage, and he strode into the Likud headquarters like a victor. The same year, Major-General Sharon, the son of a Laborite farming family from the moshav Kfar Malal, also entered into negotiations with a view to joining the party. The Labor government responded to this alarming development by awarding him the appointment of his dreams – Head of the Southern Command – thereby keeping him in the army. Ultimately this served only to delay by four years the effect on the public consciousness when Sharon made his debut in the political arena, with the establishment of the Likud.

While Weizman and Sharon maintained vacillating relations with the Polish Irgun core of Begin's movement, as popular military heroes they filled the "security" spots on the Likud list and granted Begin a level of broad legitimacy that had previously been unthinkable.

Of course, Begin's openness to old and new forces outside of the fighting family involved some degree of risk. Since its establishment the movement had internal strife each decade or so, leading to a split. Jabotinsky and Begin had steered the movement through six such episodes, with help of their loyal supporters, but each crisis had depleted the reservoir of future leaders. After twenty-five years of isolation, introversion, and parting ways with disgruntled groups and individuals, Begin embarked on a process in the opposite direction: openness, forgiveness, and partnership. He understood that in order to seize power he had to win back the rebels and separatists, and to enlist new, fresh membership.

In 1969 the eternal opposition party joined a national unity government for the second time. For the second time in its history, Herut members held ministerial portfolios and controlled budgets and appointments. Begin chose once again to serve as a minister without portfolio so as to avoid being limited to a particular sphere and rather to influence the government's political path. However, the enticing prospect of power brought struggles over the ministerial portfolios that were up for the offing.

During the discussions about the Herut representatives who would be government ministers, Begin loyalists Yaakov Meridor and MK Yosef Kremerman proposed Weizman as a candidate. They saw Weizman as someone with the potential to lead Begin to power and to succeed him. Weizman was not only a hero of the Six Day War, and not only a decorated pilot, but also a home-grown right-wing hawk, who was also young and energetic, extroverted and charismatic – in short, the opposite of Begin in every way. The movement membership adored Begin but dreamed of an heir – and Weizman was the perfect candidate. Begin saw what they saw, but he was not looking for a successor. Moreover, there was no chemistry between the two men; they spoke different languages. No love would be lost between them; at the same time, there could be an ideological, political bond. Everyone hoped that Weizman would have the patience to maintain it.

When it came to voting for the other Herut minister in government (along with Begin), the Herut Central Committee voted for Weizman – even though he was still officially in uniform. How this came about was via a ruse by Meridor and Yosef Kremerman, who set up Kremerman as a candidate, with the understanding of the voters that upon his election he would resign in favor of Weizman. And indeed, the movement voted for Kremerman (Weizman) rather than the more "natural" candidate, Dr. Yohanan Bader – Begin's close friend. Begin remained neutral and, with much pain, allowed the young general to win. Weizman resigned the next day from the IDF and was immediately appointed Minister of Transport and chairman of the Herut executive. The third Herut minister was Chaim Landau.

*

What Herut veterans refer to as "Weizman's revolt" in 1972 actually started two years earlier, with an ideological difference of opinion: following the establishment of the new national unity government, the question arose whether Herut should remain part of a government that wanted to approve an American plan calling for territorial withdrawal (the Rogers Plan). Begin, a proponent of the Greater Land of Israel, insisted on leaving the government. Weizman, the new star of the party, disagreed. It was a reenactment of sorts of the historical confrontation between Jabotinsky (the Revisionist party's spiritual leader) and Chaim Weizmann (Ezer Weizman's uncle).

Conventional wisdom has it that Begin opposed Weizman not only because of the disagreement over the Rogers Plan, but also because Begin sought to distance Weizman from the resources of power and to minimize his influence. Like the former separatist, Tamir, Weizman appeared to be a certain heir to Begin. Like Tamir, he too was native-born and the opposite of the Polish prototype. Both Tamir and Weizman were a decade or so younger than Begin and had more modern charisma. They symbolized hope and renewal, and the movement's younger membership were drawn after them. Both came from well-known, well-respected families; both had been soldiers and commanders in Israel's wars. It was clear to all that both of these young politicians aspired to take Begin's place when the time came and from there to conquer the Prime Minister's Office.

The Weizman crisis was a second test for the generation of heirs, after Tamir's revolt. Weizman counted among his supporters most of the party's young people, including almost all the student leaders, who were captivated by this Sabra who could liberate them from their party's Polish, exilic image. They felt that Weizman represented the new, open, tough Israel, and therefore they supported his call to remain part of the government. With all the respect they felt towards the founding generation and the vision of the Greater Land of Israel, they preferred to tie their fate to Weizman's star rather than going back to the political wilderness. Begin, and his call to leave, were supported by a majority of the Irgun and Lehi veterans, for whom it was a quick and natural choice to side with their leader, their ideology, and the opposition, which had been the default option throughout their lives. But this time, two of Begin's close and loyal followers from the Irgun generation – Meridor and Kremerman – opposed him. Meridor was the Irgun commander who had willingly and deferentially vacated his seat for Begin. He and Kremerman (to whom he was related through their children's marriage) loved Begin and protected him throughout the years. Now, however, they disagreed with his decision. They were successful businessmen, "doers", and they wanted to get things done. They were not looking for government positions, but they did want their party to be part of the government, as a stepping stone to becoming the government. They wanted their major-general as a minister in government so that he could ripen there as an heir to Begin, ready for the moment when Begin would decide to retire.

Weizman's young supporters included the rising Mizrahi social activist, David Levy, who had been nurtured by Begin, as well as student leaders Reiser and Kleiner, who had just recently demonstrated against the Rogers Plan but now supported a personality rather than a political path. They wanted to remain in government with the next leader, rather than leaving, on ideological grounds, with the old one.

The struggle between Weizman and Begin was therefore, once again, a generational one: young vs. old, Sabras vs. Polish immigrants. Once again, the Irgun veterans faced off against the younger generation.

Begin understood that the youngsters were once again being drawn after a new heir, and he launched a personal campaign to recruit supporters among the youth. He sought out prominent individuals who would have the courage to get up on stage and speak out against their friends at the universities. Faced with this moment of truth, he turned to Dan Meridor and Roni Milo, the sons of his trusted Herut veteran followers.

Meridor, then twenty-four, recalls walking in the street when a car stopped beside him. In the car was Begin, with a surprising and unusual request: to take the podium at the Herut Central Committee and call to leave the government. Four years previously, in 1966, Meridor's father, MK Eliyahu Meridor, had passed away. It was clear to the son that his father would want him to continue following Begin through fire and water, and so he could not refuse. And so it was that he stood at the Herut Central Committee podium and delivered a fiery ideological speech against the Rogers Plan and in favor of leaving the government.

Roni Milo, the twenty-two-year-old chairman of the National Student Union, was also enlisted. For the first time in his life, he, too, took the podium at the stormy and tense Central Committee and spoke emphatically in favor of Begin's approach.

The controversy of 1970 was one of principle and ideology. The personal conflict was not manifest. The vote was held, for the first time, at a joint session of the 120 representatives of Herut and 80 representatives of the Liberal Party, since the decision was to be a joint one. At the last minute, an additional four delegates were added, most of them close to Begin. This would clearly be a tight contest. Most of the Liberals wanted to stay, their natural place being in the government. Begin, sensing that he was going to lose the vote, presented an ultimatum, declaring that he would resign from the government if the decision was made to remain part of the coalition. This was his democratic way of forcing democracy in his direction.

Ultimately, Begin won, with a margin of five votes. As in the confrontation with Tamir, the fear of letting "the commander" down served to maintain Begin's control. Five votes stood in the way of a generational change of leadership. Once again, the party found itself in the familiar, bleak opposition. While Begin was completely at home in this territory, Weizman was lost. He was used to commanding air squadrons and military forces; suddenly, he found himself with nothing to do. He had an office and a title within the Herut hierarchy at the old Herut headquarters, but he could not feel comfortable there like the veterans, for whom this was a real home – Begin's home. Weizmann was like a caged lion, waiting for the next round.

It came two years later, at the Herut conference held in December 1972. Chairman of the movement Begin and chairman of the Executive, Weizman found themselves at loggerheads at this party conference, which was always a hub of infighting over power and positions. Once again, the camps were divided generationally, with the Irgun veterans facing off against the younger movers and shakers. However, unlike the previous confrontation, in which the Liberal Party had also been involved, this time it was an internal Herut affair, and the impatient Weizman did not stand a chance.

He made every possible mistake. He said what he felt, offended Begin (thereby unifying the veterans around him), and then, abruptly and with no explanation, submitted his resignation as chairman of the Executive. Ultimately, he did not even put up a fight. His hasty departure left his supporters powerless and abandoned. An entire, mostly youthful, camp that had looked to him as the heir to the throne was dumbfounded by his unexpected and immediate departure. With their idol gone, they quickly sought forgiveness from Begin, who once again became the supreme leader. Weizman set up shop in Tel Aviv: the former Minister of Transport became an importer of Daihatsu vehicles. He was replaced as chairman of the Executive by Yitzhak Shamir, for whom this represented the first step in the direction of the role that had been meant for Weizman: Begin's successor.

Weizman's departure was a great disappointment for many young people who had hoped and believed that a political upheaval in Israel was on the cards. I remember a certain fifteen- or sixteen-year-old boy who was prompted by these events to board a bus from his home in Zikhron Yaakov, seeking a meeting with Weizman. I was that boy. Somehow – even today I cannot explain this – I gathered the courage and entered his office, and for an hour we held an adult conversation about the possibility of him returning. I sat before this tall major-general who was my senior by more than three decades, and told him, with youthful impertinence, that he had acted with undue haste. I told him that there was a younger generation that had pinned its hopes on him to aid Begin in his revolution and take over the government – and then to succeed him. Weizman explained his decision in surprising detail, but I understood even then that problems of "chemistry" and personal relations could lead to serious mistakes even among adults. Weizman's war-wounded son, Shauli, sat quietly at the back of his office. Even then, I had the sense (I understood better later on) that Weizman saw the world differently since his son had suffered his serious injury. Shauli was there with him as a living, painful reminder of the price of war. The hawkish warrior had become a peace-seeking leader. The conflict with Begin was one of principle and ideology, too.

Five years passed, during which Weizman had no part in decision-making with national impact, and then he returned to politics. He rejoined Herut in its new format as the united Likud, spearheaded the election campaign in 1977, and brought Begin his victory.

In any event, the crisis with Weizman caused Begin to understand even more clearly that only a broadening of the ranks, especially to the younger generation, would ensure that he and his companions would remain relevant. This led him to establish the Likud, to include all the separatists and former potential partners who sought to return, including Major-General Sharon. Even more emphasis was placed on Mizrahi youngsters from the development towns, and students, regardless of whether they had revolted along the way or remained loyal to Begin. Begin knew that Weizman's revolt would be the last. It was now a matter of getting into power or out of the way.

Begin obtains Mizrahi support and promotes Mizrahi leadership

The key to understanding what happened later on lies in understanding the profound emotional bond that developed between Begin and the Mizrahim. This bond had its roots in the years of the Revolt, when Begin was on the run from the British police and found refuge with Mizrahi families. Many of the underground's most dedicated fighters grew up in Mizrahi neighborhoods. About half of the Jewish prisoners executed by the British were from families that had emigrated from Lebanon, Persia, Egypt, and Iraq.

It was natural that this sector, which suffered discrimination on the part of the arrogant Labor establishment and was eager for change, would support Begin. However, the fear of political persecution and retribution caused many to hide their political affiliation; it was only during the 1960s that Begin's followers began openly expressing their support. In 1965 elections, the joint list with the Liberals won an average forty percent of the vote in many Mizrahi neighborhoods. Restaurants in the Yemenite Hatikva neighborhood were adorned with photographs of Begin. At the Carmel outdoor market in Tel Aviv, and the Mahaneh Yehuda market in Jerusalem, there was hardly a stall that did not feature pictures of Begin alongside IDF generals. For the Mizrahim, Herut was a home with traditional Jewish values. More importantly, they were among equals there. Thousands of them began attending Begin's rallies.

The departure of Ben-Gurion (widely admired by the older generation) from the Prime Minister's Office contributed further to the rise of Begin's popularity among the Mizrahi public. The quarreling between Ben-Gurion and his party helped to distance the North African immigrants from the Labor party and drew them towards Begin, who now began to seem to them like the national Jewish patriarch.

Mizrahi support for Begin was further boosted by the opening of Herut branches in the development towns over the course of the 1960s. These branches reflected a different sort of dialogue between Ashkenazi veterans and Mizrahi new immigrants: respectful rather than arrogant, with partnership in faith rather than discrimination. The Herut branches were inundated with a stream of activists seeking to change their destiny, ultimately – as explained earlier – producing new leadership for the development towns and later on for the Knesset.

Begin, with his finely honed senses, understood that the Mizrahi activists were the tip of an iceberg that could bring about a national revolution, and so he devoted efforts to nurturing new, authentic leaders such as David Levy. Levy had been born in Rabat, Morocco, in 1937. At the age of twenty he had moved to Israel and was a construction worker in the northern development town of Beit Shean. At twenty-six he became a Labor activist in the Construction Workers' Association but soon felt that he would not be able to advance there. He therefore approached the small Herut office in Beit Shean, where he was warmly received. Within a year he was elected as a member of the local council and as deputy mayor.

Begin and Levy liked each other. Despite the conspicuous differences between them, each complemented the other. Begin loved and nurtured Levy, but Levy was more than just a protégé. He created a wave of support and brought many others with him to the Herut headquarters. He even created a faction within the Histadrut which he despised, and it enjoyed a reasonable level of support. In 1969, at the age of thirty-two, Levy became an MK.

Begin forgave Levy for siding with Weizman in 1972. He saw Levy's huge electoral potential, and continued to advance him – a privilege not shown to most other rebels. Sheetrit, who became mayor of Yavne, received similar treatment. He, too, supported Weizman, and he too was forgiven and welcomed back. The development town mayors were the jewel in the Herut crown. Begin believed that through them he could attract the votes of their parents, who were sworn supporters of Ben-Gurion – and indeed, he succeeded.

Thus, by means of political and social coalitions, as described earlier, Begin's opportunity began to materialize. The accumulated effect of the merger with the Liberal Center and the recruitment of the Mizrahi population, along with the Religious Zionist sector, the Labor separatists, and the younger generation at the universities, paved the way for Begin to realize the dream of the underground veterans: to attain the leadership and influence that they deserved after their Revolt three decades earlier.

History in real time, a changed Israel

On the morning of May 17, 1977, I was on a routine mission at sea. I was a young navy officer, stationed on the bridge of the missile boat INS *Herev*, with a well-trained team that patrolled the open sea along the Lebanese coastline. Owing to a series of enemy sabotage attempts, we had received an order to block the Tyre and Beirut beaches and prevent the emergence of suspicious mother ships, which could release terrorist dinghies opposite Israel's beaches.

The weather was warm and the sea was calm. I enjoyed commanding the bridge in the open air, under the open sky. It was far preferable to being down below, in the operations room, where the officers and NGOs gathered. It was crowded there, and one felt the turbulence more, especially on the way back to shore, when waves from the north-west would continually rock the stern. We were opposite Tyre when we received the OK to return home. We knew then that when we arrived, in the evening, we would have time to the voting booth and fulfill our civic duty in the elections that were taking place that day; it had not been certain until then whether or not we would be able to vote.

In anticipation of our return trip the commander of the missile boat went up to the top bridge, and I went down to the operations room. On this special day, any political comment could spark a political argument. Indeed, there was one older officer who was slandering Begin in the demagogic and arrogant style that typified the Left's attacks on him. While I usually held my silence in the army when it came to politics, this time I told him what I thought. Soon another crew member – a Mizrahi new immigrant – joined the argument, declaring that he was going to vote for Begin. An instantaneous alliance formed between us, and we found ourselves arguing with the older officer. We were both infuriated by his swagger and contemptuousness.

What was interesting was that most of the men around us seemed indifferent to the debate. With the exception of another older officer who supported the Labor provocateur, none of the soldiers in the operations room got involved. My feeling was that some of them – the regular soldiers, most of whom were Mizrahim – agreed with my position but were afraid to express solidarity, while others – the officers – would be voting Labor as always, but they would be doing so out of inertia and habit, with a sense of dissatisfaction and shame.

On that dramatic night, when Israeli civilians had already finished voting, we came into port and ran to vote at the soldiers' booths. While the population waited with bated breath for the results, we cleaned and prepared the boat, and then remained on standby. I did not hear the live broadcast of the election results. All I remember from Begin's modest victory speech were the words he addressed to his wife, Aliza, which I heard over the radio: "You followed me in the desert for forty years, in a land that was not sown" (an allusion to Jeremiah 2:2). To this day I am moved by these words. I thought about my father and his friends in the underground, and about the fact that they were finally receiving recognition and power. I thought about my grandmother, who had been so close to Aliza Begin and to Begin himself, and who had dreamed of this day all her life. They, too, had "followed him in a land that was not sown" for many years, and now, finally, they were restoring honor to Stern, Raziel, the out-of-work Eldad, Groner, and Kashani – the martyrs. Finally, they had all achieved victory.

However, when I went home on furlough a few days later, I did not encounter the all-consuming joy that I had expected. My father's reaction to the victory was rather restrained. The reason for this was the seriousness of the task that now awaited Begin and his camp. What my father felt was not euphoria, but rather responsibility mixed with a sense of gratification that justice had prevailed and the Labor party had finally been defeated.

I was not surprised by the election results. Over the course of my childhood and adolescence I felt the Revisionist camp growing stronger, and watched the tide of young people joining the Herut/Likud ranks. The change was easy to see in Zikhron Yaakov, where Likud had strong support from both Liberal Center old-timers in the town, and Mizrahi immigrants. I watched the revolution as it unfolded in schools and universities throughout the country, and I knew that my generation would bring about a national revolution. For me, it was entirely natural and clear that Begin would be Prime Minister.

The night of May 17, 1977 is remembered in Israeli history as the Night of the Upheaval; the night marking the end of Labor hegemony. For thousands of underground veterans, this represented liberation and the end of three decades of exclusion and survival in the opposition.

The underground veterans – the parents' generation – were already in their fifties and sixties. They were energized and rejuvenated by the election results, and watched through tears as Begin, their hero, delivered his victory speech on the morning of May 18. He restored honor to the veteran fighters, reintroduced the teachings of their leader, Jabotinsky, into the public discourse, and lauded the valor of those who had been executed by the British or had given their lives for the sake of the Jewish state. From the moshavim of Nahalat Jabotinsky and Nordiya, the Yemenite Hatikva neighborhood, the Mahaneh Yehuda market, the Veterans' Neighborhood in Ramat Gan, and the Herut headquarters, the parents breathed a collective sigh of relief and satisfaction.

At the same time, the sons and daughters of the underground veterans were filled with joy at the sight of their parents, now freed of their mark of shame, and their ostracized and denigrated leader whom the nation had now chosen as Prime Minister of Israel. Names that until now had been familiar only among limited circles, in encounters with "uncles and aunts" of the fighting family, began to make their way into the public space: underground founders and commanders Raziel and Stern; poet of the revolt Uri Zvi Greenberg; the first martyr hanged by the British – Shlomo Ben-Yosef.

For a great many Israeli citizens spread over two generations, this felt like a second Independence Day. It signaled victory for the fighters who had risked their lives and had been erased from the history books, and justice for hundreds of casualties whose memory had been besmirched and whose bereaved families had been abandoned.

The nation listened eagerly to Begin's speech in the early morning of May 18. The dilapidated hall at the Likud headquarters was suddenly in festive mode and crammed with journalists and excited activists. Begin's words conveyed most powerfully the magnitude of this historical moment:

> Today marks a turning-point in the history of the Jewish People and the history of the Zionist movement, the likes of which we have not seen for forty-six years – since the seventeenth [Zionist] Congress, in 1931, in which Zeev Jabotinsky proposed as the aim of Zionism the establishment of a Jewish state in our time. Zeev Jabotinsky devoted his entire life to that aim. He did not live to see the establishment of the state, nor the turning point that has come about today. His followers, who, in the name of his teachings and for

the sake of their realization, fought for the nation's liberation, and continued, with patience and with complete faith in democracy, to aspire to bring about change in our state – through the voter's ballot, and only through the voter's ballot – have reached this day. [. . .] Now I wish to thank my friends and companions, the underground fighters of the Irgun and of Lehi, my glorious, heroic brethren. We have walked a very long road, but they never stopped believing that this day, this night, would come. [. . .] If the voter's ballot today elevated the Likud to the first parliamentary party in line to create Israel's new government, then let the world know that Israel is indeed a democratic and free country. Its citizens are not slaves who cower before the Labor regime, but rather [. . .] free citizens who determine their own fate, in accordance with their own perception, decision, and conscience. [. . .] I shall propose that the Likud leadership approach all the Zionist parties loyal to the State of Israel, with an offer to establish a national Likud government. [. . .] I hope that once we obtain the Knesset's confidence for the new government that we present to it, we shall – with the approval of the Knesset – approach President Sadat, President Assad, and King Hussein, offering to engage in negotiations, whether in rotation among our capitals or in a neutral place such as Geneva, with a view to signing a peace agreement between them and the State of Israel."[1]

Begin, isolated in his government, brings veterans and their children into the PMO

Begin had come to power in less-than-optimal physical condition. In the midst of the election campaign he had suffered a heart attack and had been hospitalized. He had almost no involvement in the campaign, which was run by Weizman.

Surprisingly enough, the leader who had been accompanied by his friends since their days in the Irgun appointed a government that included none of his loyal companions. The main reason for this was that some of his veteran confidants had already passed on, while others had left politics and moved on to other pursuits after many years in the movement.

A second reason was that Likud had won a narrow victory, and in order to ensure a stable government Begin had to offer many portfolios to his coalition partners. In addition, Begin's party was itself an amalgamation of different groups, including former rebels and sworn adversaries, all of whom now wanted a place at the table. First and foremost among them were Weizman and Sharon, both of whom had left and then returned. Although the Herut faction within the united Likud had veterans of the underground as its majority, in forming his coalition Begin chose to award portfolios to his partners, rather than fortifying his government with his old friends. There was no offer of a government ministry to his operations officer, MK Livni, nor to MKs who had fought in the Irgun and now served in the Knesset, nor to Lehi leaders David Stern, Geula Cohen, or Yitzhak Shamir. (Begin appointed Shamir as Speaker of the Knesset – a disappointment for Shamir, who aspired higher.)

Begin's first government was essentially comprised of Labor splinters: no less than seven ministers were former Laborites. Some had moved to Likud when it was established, four years earlier; others were coalition partners whom Begin was forced to include. The most surprising appointment was Begin's choice for Foreign Minister: Moshe Dayan. At the expense of an MK from the Likud, Begin appointed this dyed-in-the-wool Laborite and second-generation MK, with a view to calming both the tense public in Israel and the neighboring Arab countries, who assumed that Begin meant war. Begin was now surrounded by five generals – two from his own party, two representing his partners, and Dayan. In addition, his government included representatives of the Liberal Party and the Religious Zionists, who had joined the coalition. None of these belonged to the fighting family.

The Herut veterans had to pay the heavy price for the coalition that formed around the Likud. Their faction ended up with one single representative in government: Begin himself. It was almost a continuation of Ben-Gurion's guiding principle for coalitions since the establishment of the state: "without Herut and without Maki (the Communist party)."

Begin very quickly began to feel isolated within his own government, and sought ways to bring in his old friends. Later on, he replaced "foreign" or "wishy-washy" figures with right-wing veterans. The first to be brought in was Shostak, chairman of the National Labor Federation, who became minister of health. Begin's sense of isolation was such that he put aside their complicated past relations and embraced Shostak as though they were back in the old Beitar days in Poland. About six months after the elections, Begin brought back Chaim Landau, appointing him Minister of Transport. Two years later, when Moshe Dayan left the government in the wake of political difference of opinion with Begin, Shamir replaced him, too. During Begin's second term (starting in 1981), Yaakov Meridor was appointed minister of economics.

The Prime Minister's Office, in contrast to the alienated government, was a miniature Herut, representing two generations of the fighting family. Yehiel Kadishai, Begin's aide and his closest confidant going back to the days of the *Altalena*, became the Chief-of-Staff of the Prime Minister's Office. Matti Shmuelewitz, a Lehi fighter whose courageous exploits were legend, including his escape from a British prison after being sentenced to death, became director general of the PMO. Shmuel Katz, who had been a confidant of Jabotinsky and a member of the Irgun high command, was Begin's advisor for information abroad. Finally, Amihai ("Gidi") Paglin, the former Irgun operations officer, was Begin's advisor on fighting terrorism. Three out of these five appointees had distanced themselves from Begin in the past, but now Begin felt a moral obligation to share the power and responsibility of government with these symbols of the Revolt. He had more confidence in them than in any expert.

Begin went on to appoint Arye Naor and Dan Meridor, the sons of his closest friends, in succession as government secretary, thereby adding personal warmth to the environment in the PMO. Benny Begin functioned as a close and quiet advisor to his father.

Thus surrounded by staff that protected him like a suit of armor, Begin set out to lead the country and spearhead his revolution. His tenure as Prime Minister lasted six years, with dramatic ups and downs. It began with the historical peace agreement with Egypt and a social revolution that included urban renewal for Mizrahi neighborhoods and bringing representatives of the periphery into government. It continued with the liberation of Israel's closed, socialist economy and a shift to a free and competitive economy. It climaxed with the elimination of the nuclear reactor in Iraq, contrary to the advice and expectations of all the experts, and ended with the controversial and bloody Lebanon War.

The heirs develop an appetite – but Begin advances Mizrahim

The proximity to power aroused the political appetite of the heirs, who were taking their first steps in the national arena in the late '70s. They were stuck behind the scenes and wanted a place on stage.

The pure ideology that had motivated them as youth and as students started to become tainted with personal interests. The anger that had caused them to tear down red flags on May Day, and to defend their parents' past at school, was no longer the only force driving them. In the past, they had been drawn into the movement's internal battles, and they had found themselves at the heart of the revolts by Tamir and Weizman, but ultimately the younger generation of the Meridor, Begin, Aridor, Naor, Milo, Kremerman, and Rivlin families had stood by Begin out of personal and family obligation. Now that Begin had come to power, the heirs began to nurture personal ambition and to bare their teeth. The tension grew with the appearance of new heirs who would join the contest in the decades to come.

The early heirs in the 1970s integrated into the movement's various bodies, strengthened their position in its institutions, and tried to advance themselves to realistic spots on the list of Likud candidates for the ninth Knesset (1977) and the tenth (1981). Three of them, as noted, were in the Prime Minister's close environment; two others, Milo and Olmert, managed to "overtake" peers who were closer to Begin and become MKs: Milo, aged twenty-eight, entered the Knesset in 1977; Olmert had been an MK already since 1974, thanks to the coalition agreement that his splinter group had signed in order to join the Likud.

It is interesting to note that during the internal elections for the Likud list for the ninth Knesset (1977) Begin refrained from supporting the three heirs who were candidates (Meridor, Milo, and Naor). Unquestionably, he loved all three, and admired the capabilities they had demonstrated on the campuses and in the media. He was also certainly well aware that his support for any of them would lead to their success in the primaries. Nevertheless, he expressed no public support for any of them. It was enough for him that they surrounded him in the PMO.

Begin likewise offered no help to Dan Meridor, then thirty-two, although he had considerable experience in elections, enjoyed close relations with the party leader and his son, and was well acquainted with the older voters. From a politico-strategic perspective, too, it is most surprising that Begin did not provide Meridor with even the slightest gesture of support. After all, Meridor had been the most loyal of his followers, remaining with Begin even when most of the heirs had thrown in their lot with Weizman in 1970. Similarly, Begin offered no help to Arye Naor, nephew of Irgun commander David Raziel and son of MK Esther Raziel-Naor, nor to Roni Milo, despite the family connection (Milo's brother married Begin's daughter). As it turned out, Milo became an MK even without Begin's help.

Why did Begin not support the heirs as candidates for the Knesset? It seems that despite everything, Begin still viewed them as youngsters – loyal, talented young-sters with their future ahead of them, who could be passed up in the meantime in favor of candidates who had electoral power and could draw in new sectors among the voters. Begin's loyal secretary, Kadishai, stated flatly that, as Begin saw it, the heirs did not hold real electoral attraction. He preferred to offer Knesset seats to his external partners, to bring back the popular generals Sharon and Weiz-man, and to parachute Levy and then Katzav and Sheetrit into the Knesset and the government, believing that these figures spoke for sizeable groups that had forged a covenant of blood with the Likud and that they deserved representation.

Begin preferred to place ahead of the heirs ten figures who represented the Revolt, including commanders of the underground organizations who had become symbols, among them Eitan Livni, Yitzhak Shamir, David Stern, and Geula Cohen.

In making the choice between the younger Naor (son of) and the older Stern (brother of), Begin preferred Stern as a representative of the fighting family. Stern was a Beitarist from Poland, a senior figure in Lehi, chairman of the Building Contractors' Union, and chairman of the Likud branch in Tel Aviv. His record was simply longer and richer than that of the young heirs.

Faced with the choice between the young Meridor (son of) and the older Shamir (commander of), Begin preferred to see a Lehi symbol like Shamir in the Knesset. The early heirs, as Begin saw it, still had time to mature and fulfill their potential. Thus, the appointments of Naor and Meridor as successive speakers of the Knes-set was a symbolic and professional decision, not a political one. Begin did not want "sons-of" on the Likud list. He just wanted the Irgun heirs close by, because they symbolized their parents, and because they were young and energetic, pro-fessional, and exceedingly loyal.

Other youngsters in the movement – the Mizrahi leaders – did receive Begin's support, and he pushed them all the way into the Knesset. The most preferred candidate in this category was David Levy, who became an MK already in 1969. In 1977 he became a minister, and four years later he was appointed Deputy Prime Minister. Moshe Katzav was next in line: as a symbol of the revolution in the development towns, he was warmly welcomed by the Irgun veterans at the Herut headquarters, who were also delighted with his wife, Gila, whose parents (Ben-Tzion and Rachel Pardani) were their old friends. The generation of the Revolt embraced Katzav and catapulted him into the Knesset after the Upheaval. Four years later, he became a deputy minister. Similarly, the Likud candidates who became MKs in 1981 included the young municipal leaders Meir Sheetrit and David Magen.

Roni Milo – the heir who trail-blazed his way into the Knesset

How did Milo succeed where Naor and Meridor could not? From conversations with movement veterans I learned that Meridor and Naor had indeed tried to canvass Herut Central Committee members to vote for them in the primaries, but they had been certain that Begin would get involved in the vote and advance them. Unsurprisingly, the heirs had expected to enjoy the privilege of being their parents' children – and this was their undoing. Milo, on the other hand, was not relying on Begin. With his fine political intuition he understood that Begin would not interfere – or, if he did, it would be on behalf of heirs more prominent than himself – and he focused his efforts on the Central Committee. He put to good use the valuable experience he had gained in managing an election campaign and building a coalition, and as chairman of the Likud Youth he brought masses of supporters with him. His campaign drew in even the older voters, and thus in 1977 he became an MK. Over the next two decades he was re-elected over and over again, each time with the support of his "uncles" in the movement.

Milo had discovered the "genetic code" of the veterans. He was the first to understand the principle of continuity that was so important to them, and was able to substitute genealogy with praxis. In order to understand the significance of this insight, one has to remember what an elevated status Begin enjoyed as Prime Minister. This was no more the "old" and "antiquated" Begin of the opposition years, but rather a leader who had brought about a revolution and who filled public squares with tens of thousands of supporters. Within this reality, anyone perceived as a member of Begin's "family" enjoyed the immediate support not only of the veterans but also of the masses of Begin's supporters.

Milo took care to paint himself in "Beginist" colors. He recounted the story of his father, Nahum Milikovsky, the businessman who had driven Begin from one hideout to the next during the Revolt. Milo's uncle, Menachem Malitzky, provided the genealogical credentials: the underground fighters had stood shoulder to shoulder with him when he led the Acre Prison break. Milo's brother's marriage to Begin's daughter further reinforced the aura that surrounded him. And so it was that even though Begin did nothing to advance Milo's campaign, the veterans and activists viewed him as a youngster whom Begin wanted in the Knesset.

Over and above all this, Milo came across as a champion of the Right, who spoke out vehemently against the "left-wing mafia". He accused the Peace Now movement of accepting funding from the CIA, and his popularity only increased when the movement reacted angrily with a personal attack on him. He adhered carefully to the political path set down by Begin and later maintained by Shamir, espousing a hardline ideology that won him the endorsement of the "uncles and aunts". One incident illustrating his tactic of "overtaking from the right" took place before my own eyes, when I was still a young student leader. It happened at a Likud Youth gathering in early 1982, which focused on the peace accords that Begin had signed with Egypt, and the imminent withdrawal from the Sinai. Tensions at the convention ran high: would the youth rebel against the party leader?

Would Milo, the youngest MK, announce his opposition to the historical move? Milo delivered a dramatic, radical right-wing speech. It contained not a word in favor of the chances of peace. The young audience, which was mainly opposed to the agreement, applauded enthusiastically, anticipating the obvious conclusion: the young heir's brave opposition to the old leader's concessions. When the end of the speech came, it contained warm words of support for Begin as a great leader.

The heirs overtake from the right

On their way to the Knesset and the government, during the 1970s and '80s the heirs presented themselves as hardline right-wing spokesmen whose positions were completely synchronized with those of their parents. Both generations spoke the same language, including specific expressions (the "iron wall" strategy) and quotes from speeches by Begin and, especially, Jabotinsky. The hardline image was welcomed by the veterans, whose hearts were with these young leaders, while the exigencies of government required the senior party leadership to adopt a more measured style and stance.

Most of the young student leaders at the universities belonged to the activist branch of Herut and the Likud. Throughout the years of the opposition and Begin's government, they consistently stood to the right of the party, to the joy and satisfaction of the proud "aunts and uncles". They fanned the Revisionist coals and remained faithful to Jabotinsky's teachings to a greater extent than the MKs of the Likud, who were bound to parliamentary codes of expression. The more steadfast the younger leaders were, the greater the support they received from the Herut veterans. The more they fought against the Left, the more viciously they were attacked by left-wing opinion leaders in the media, earning them even greater esteem in the eyes of the underground veterans.

On many occasions the heirs were accused of extremism. While their parents had sufficed with expressing support for the vision of the Greater Land of Israel, the younger generation played an active role in promoting the settlement enterprise. While the parents had expressed themselves against their Labor adversaries with grandeur and resolve that would have made Jabotinsky proud, the style adopted by the youngsters was more reminiscent of the intense and ferocious Brit ha-Biryonim (Strongmen's Alliance), the heroes of their youth. The veterans were filled with pride over the militant campaigns waged by their younger generation, the students, and the Likud Youth. For them, this was sweet revenge on their foes – the "socialists", "communists", "informers".

In 1970, the youngsters – like Begin himself – had spoken out against the Rogers Plan (the American framework for Israeli withdrawal from Judea and Samaria) knowing that their opposition would lead to their party leaving the national unity government. The demonstrations against the plan were attended by thousands of children of underground fighters, including the already well-known politician Ehud Olmert, and the young and unknown student Limor Livnat. Dan Meridor headed the Likud Youth who were opposed to the plan and – as described earlier – even delivered his first speech before the Herut Central Committee, excoriating the submission to the US and calling for Herut to leave the government.

In a conversation I had with Meridor decades later, he recalled:

> That was when the settlement in Judea and Samaria began. I went to the Park Hotel in Hebron to support settlement. [. . .] They established the Gilo Field School; we went and helped with guard-duty. [. . .] When they began building Maaleh Adumim, we went to guard over there.[2]

Meridor was not alone. A *Haaretz* supplement from January 2, 2015 records that Arye Naor was also associated with the Gush Emunim settlement movement. He invited the head of the Religious Zionist settlement movement to participate in the circumcision ceremony of his son Michael, along with Begin, who participated in the ceremony of the other twin, Naftali. Most of their Revisionist friends expressed their support for the settlements. While most continued living inside the Green Line, many put their words into action and helped to establish communities close to and even over the Green Line.

Meridor's two siblings, Sallai and Avital, who were both Beitar youth leaders in Jerusalem, helped to set up the Kfar Adumim settlement (along with Herzl Makov and Aryeh Eldad), where they live to this day. Batsheva Hahermoni, daughter of deputy minister Michael Dekel, helped to found Beit Aryeh. Uri Cohen, son of the Irgun commander for Jerusalem, moved to Maaleh Adumim. His cousin, Moshe Meron, moved with his wife Yael to Ma'aleh Mikhmas. The communities of Kokhav Yair and Tzur Yigal, situated on the Green Line, were planned at Herut headquarters by MK Michael Eitan along with central activists from Shamir's camp.

There were even some youngsters who expressed open criticism of the Likud establishment headed by Begin. They claimed that having finally reached power, the party was now making overly generous concessions to the geopolitical reality. The most vocal of the hardline right-wing heirs was Olmert, a young MK representing the splinter Free Center faction that later joined the Likud. According to *Maariv*, the young Olmert "admired the settlers, their enthusiasm, and their determination. He would spend weekends with them in new communities such as Ofra and Elon Moreh."[3] During the Weizman crisis, Olmert had quarreled with the leader of his faction, Tamir, who had accused him of extremism after Olmert appeared in Kiryat Arba at an event where participants swore allegiance to the ancient city of Hebron. During his first term as Prime Minister, Begin was surprised to discover that he had an opposition to the right. After being accused throughout the years of extremism and unwillingness to compromise, Begin now had to explain his pragmatic policy to the young MK who was accusing him of being too moderate. Olmert also opposed the peace initiative with Egypt (1978–1979) and voted against the Camp David Accords, arguing that the Jewish residents in Sinai should not be uprooted. Along with Olmert the activist group that opposed Begin included MK Geula Cohen; her student son, Tzahi Hanegbi; Dr. Shmuel Katz of the Irgun high command (and advisor to the Prime Minister); and Dr. Yisrael Eldad (who was always to the right of Herut). This group broke away in October 1979 to form the new Tehiya party.

Limor Livnat, too, was vociferous in her opposition to the territorial concessions set forth in the peace agreement with Egypt. In 1982, she left the political
arena for two years in protest over Begin's policy.

Tzahi Hanegbi burst onto the public stage when he was elected chairman of
the Student Union in Jerusalem, in 1979. In his capacity as head of the right-
wing student cell, he waged fierce battles against the Communist-Arab student coalition, Hadash, which sided with the Palestinians against the IDF. A year
later, Hanegbi became chairman of the National Student Union, and he served
in this position during one of the stormiest periods in the history of Israeli academia. The press accused him of violence when, in one of the political confrontations on the Jerusalem campus, two members of his society (both future
government ministers) – deputy chairman Israel Katz and new immigrant Avigdor Lieberman – used an iron chain in their fight against Arab anti-Israel students who supported the PLO.

After his term as Student Union chairman, Hanegbi left for a trip to the US, like
thousands of other Israeli youth who set aside time to travel after the army or after
completing a university degree. He was disconnected from the goings-on in Israel
and was thus flabbergasted to hear, by chance, that Prime Minister Begin, leader
of the Herut movement, had reached a peace agreement with Egypt that entailed
a withdrawal from the entire Sinai Peninsula, including the Jewish communities
that had been built there. Hanegbi was certain that such a concession would lead
to an uprising in Israel, and he felt that he had to return. All that he had absorbed
throughout his childhood was suddenly threatened in the face of this betrayal.

Hanegbi threw himself into the struggle against the evacuation of the communities in the Sinai, together with his mother, MK Geula Cohen, who had already left
the Likud in the wake of the peace agreement in 1979 and was among the founders
and leaders of the new Tehiya party. In April 1982, Hanegbi went to Yamit, a town
in the Sinai slated for evacuation, together with 150 students from the Hebrew
University. He and his group (including his girlfriend, Randy, a recent immigrant
from Miami, who later became his wife) barricaded themselves at the top of the
IDF memorial monument in the town. For twenty-three days and nights the students faced off against IDF soldiers. They blocked access roads to the site, surrounded the monument with barbed wire, stocked up on food and gas masks, and
flew a giant blue-and-white flag from the top of the monument. It was a display
of desperation on the part of these ideological young people who were watching
communities being destroyed around them and residents evacuated – in many
instances by force. Only after protracted negotiations, with the fear of bloodshed
in the background, did Hanegbi and the students part with the monument.

Netanyahu: from the ancestors' legacy to the world struggle
against terror

Throughout this time, Netanyahu was following a completely different path. Nevertheless, like his forebears, he was turning the world upside down in an effort to
advance an unconventional activist idea.

Netanyahu and Uzi Landau both studied at MIT. While their peers in Israel were active in Herut and fighting against the Labor party, Netanyahu and Landau were fighting an information war for Israel against pro-Palestinian forces. In the mid-1970s, Netanyahu was the spirit behind the Israeli student cell in Boston. "I could see that he would become an important political figure," Landau would tell me afterwards.[4] "I was happy to connect him with the Likud later on." In the meantime, Netanyahu's distance from the corridors of the Likud headquarters and the Knesset caused a delay of about a decade in his integration into the movement's institutions. Upon completing his studies, Netanyahu turned his focus to the business world, but the tragedy that befell his family, with the death of his elder brother, Yoni, changed the course of his life.

Yoni's death brought out his brother Benjamin's potential, along with the wealth of the legacy inculcated in him by his parents: the pioneering Zionism of the First Aliya, as embodied in his mother, Tzila, and the Revisionist Zionist tradition of more than a century, rooted in Odessa (home to Jabotinsky) and in Lithuania and Poland (home to Netanyahu's grandfather, Natan Milikowsky) which he learned from his father.

While the parents of most of the heirs had been young, brave, action-oriented underground commanders, Netanyahu's father was an historian who researched the deeper processes at work in Jewish history, and for whom day-to-day life was of lesser urgency. The other heirs grew up in the practical, earthly homes of MKs, settlement leaders, and regular business owners trying their best to make a living, Netanyahu grew up in the intellectual atmosphere that surrounded his father and with the legacy of his grandfather, Natan Milikowsky, who had stood at the sides of the giants of Zionism (Herzl, Jabotinsky, Weizmann) at the Sixth Zionist Congress in Basel, in 1903. (More than a century later, as Prime Minister and at the height of the tense election campaign in January 2013, Netanyahu was proud to show me a photograph of Milikowsky at the Congress with the Zionist leaders.)

At the age of twenty-nine, Netanyahu decided to devote his life to an original idea that had begun to sprout in his mind as a youth in his parents' home and developed further when he experienced the war on terror as a soldier and a commander in the IDF. It was the heroic death of his brother in the war on terror that unlocked the torrent that has gushed forth ever since, for four decades. He swore himself to a task seemingly better suited to the leaders of world powers: to persuade the world that terrorism in its familiar sporadic and localized form could develop into a far more dangerous mode of world terror. He anticipated the reality that came about only many years later: the crystallization and solidification of Islamic terror, with the support of terror states such as Iran, Afghanistan, Syria, and Lebanon. While up until that time the world had treated terror as a localized phenomenon, Netanyahu argued that terrorism was backed by patron states that nurtured it, and that therefore it would grow. He insisted that in order to prevent the spread of terrorism, it was necessary to dry up its sources: the Communist Soviet Union, North Korea, Cuba, and – later on – Iran.

This as-yet unknown Israeli youngster proceeded to initiate an international conference against terror. It was held in 1979 in Jerusalem, and was attended by first-rate Israeli and international experts (including US Senator Henry Jackson). In addition, there were a great many senior journalists, who told the world of the danger that Netanyahu was predicting. And thus Netanyahu succeeded in introducing his vision into the headlines of the major world media (inter alia, the *New York Times*, *Washington Post*, *Wall Street Journal*, *Los Angeles Times*, the British *Chronicle*, and the French *Le Monde*).

And the conference was not all. In order to advance the audacious objective he had set for himself – to persuade the world – he established the Jonathan Institute, which studied and published books on terror. The institute, which was the basis for all Netanyahu's activity, was named for his beloved brother, who had lost his life in the war on terror. The books that Netanyahu edited and wrote, in Hebrew and English – *International Terrorism: Challenge and Response* (1979); *Terrorism: How the West Can Win* (1987); and *A Place Among the Nations: Israel and the World* (1992) – carried his voice to the furthest reaches of the globe, to congressmen, and to the US President, Ronald Reagan.

As his father had mobilized masses in the US to support the establishment of the Jewish state, so his son managed to bring his message to the attention of the world's superpower. He managed to convey the understanding that what the world perceived as home-grown terror that was not dangerous to the West was actually Islamic state terrorism, which would inundate the West. He propagated this idea long before the major terror attacks in New York and in the capitals of Europe. In his books, he was ahead of his time in predicting that militant terrorists operating in secret in the West could smuggle atom bombs into democratic countries. Years later, the US watched in horror as terrorists who lived in the US brought down the Twin Towers in the heart of New York.

One of the important supporters of Netanyahu's efforts was his father's good friend, Professor Moshe Arens. Before 1948, when Bentzion Netanyahu served as executive director of the Revisionist organization in America, Arens had been the head of Beitar in the US. Now Arens was Israel's ambassador to the US, and in 1982 he invited the younger Netanyahu to serve as a political attaché to the Israeli embassy in Washington. Netanyahu accepted the offer, and quickly made a name for himself in the Congress and in the US press, where he continued his fight for Israel and against the great threat of world terror. In 1984, while in the US, he organized a second conference on world terror, which brought his message to millions of people worldwide.

Arens was so impressed by Netanyahu's abilities that he worked to have him appointed as Israel's ambassador to the UN. And indeed, the appointment came, in 1984, just two years after Netanyahu had embarked on his political career. This time the appointment came with the backing of Foreign Minister Shamir and the approval of the Labor Prime Minister at the time, Shimon Peres. Peres – a friend of the Netanyahu family whom he had met after Yoni's death, in his capacity as Defense Minister and one of the planners of the operation – was already cognizant of the open ties between Netanyahu and the Likud, but could not withhold the appointment from the brother of the commander who had fallen in battle on his watch. Netanyahu was appointed and became the most conspicuous ambassador

Figure 8.1 PM Begin with David Levi, whom he nurtured to leadership by appointing him a minister and deputy leader. Levi would in the future fight with Shamir and Netanyahu on succeeding Begin.

Figure 8.2 Jerusalem "Princes" Dan Meridor (right) and Reuven Rivlin in the 1980s. Both were Etzel sons, active from childhood and as students. They served as MK and ministers for many years. Rivlin would also become the tenth President of Israel.

Figure 8.3 The Lehi "family" (from right to left): Limor Livnat, the former Lehi commander; PM Yitzhak Shamir; Limor Livnat's dad Azriel Livnat, a Lehi fighter; and her mother Shulamit, the "underground organization's singer".

Figure 8.4 Benny Begin assists his "prince" friend Dan Meridor in the 1992 primaries, after his father retires. The father and son served in the Knesset from 1949–2019 (combined).

at the world body. His struggle to open the UN archive of Nazi criminals received worldwide coverage, and he succeeded in his well-publicized battle to turn Austrian President Kurt Waldheim into a persona non grata around the world after his Nazi past was exposed.

While his peers were engaged in trench warfare in the branches of Herut and the Likud in Tiberias and Beer Sheba, Netanyahu was becoming an international figure. While the young Milo, Olmert, Meridor, and Landau were serving as MKs, Netanyahu was an ambassador who had all of Israel standing proudly behind him, viewing him as a leader of international stature.

Notes

1 Haaretz, May 19, 1977.
2 Interview by author. April 10, 2002.
3 Haaretz, March 2006.
4 Interview with the author, May 23, 2002.

Part II

The Diadochi Wars

With the retirement of the admired leader Menachem Begin, the Likud movement (the name of a number of parties that had been unified and led by Menachem Begin in 1973), entered into a decade of successive battles. Two wings threatened the successor Itzhak Shamir, who was supported by the party elders (of Begin's generation). Shamir was one of the leaders of the Lehi resistance movement, a movement which was even more right-winged than the Etzel. He was a tough and stiff-necked leader but never as charismatic as Begin. This is why he was on the edge of impeachment during the ten years that he was in power. Those who stood by him were the "Princes". Prime Minister Shamir and the party's elders needed the young generation and elevated them to the Knesset, the Israeli congress, and even key positions as ministers. In this way they became young, familiar leaders who began their political career in the 1980s, when they were in their early thirties. Now these Princes (Ehud Olmert, Reuven Rivlin, Roni Milo, Dan Meridor, Uzi Landau, and Benny Begin) followed their parents' footsteps, and at the same time leaned further to the right-wing.

Part II

The Diadochi Wars

9   The end of the Begin era

On Sunday, August 28, 1983, Begin surprised his government by announcing his intention to resign. He waited until September to submit his formal resignation, allowing time for his replacement to stabilize the coalition under his new leadership. Begin's weakness at this point was such that he did not even tender his resignation letter in person, but rather conveyed it to the President via government secretary Dan Meridor. Thereafter Begin confined himself to his apartment. Until the day he died, nine years later, he did not address the nation again. The events surrounding his resignation are best summed up by his own comment, "I cannot go on."

Up until this point, the Revisionist movement had been led by only two men over the course of sixty years (compared with five Labor leaders): Jabotinsky and Begin. Begin had been part of the party's top leadership for five decades and had overseen its various incarnations (Irgun, Herut, Gahal, Likud). For forty years Begin had been a legendary, almost mystical figure within the movement. He was the symbol and source of pride of the underground veterans, and was widely admired among Mizrahi activists in the periphery. As Prime Minister, he was a very dominant figure in national life. He was the first Israeli leader to sign a peace agreement with an Arab country; he ordered the bombing of the Osirak nuclear reactor in Iraq; and he spearheaded the neighborhood renewal revolution, introducing Mizrahi leadership into positions of power. In 1983 he was a last relic of the generation of giants who had brought the state into existence.

Up until 1983, Begin was the Likud, and the Likud was Begin. His resignation therefore heralded a real crisis, especially in view of the fact that the historical events leading up to his resignation had been so painful and traumatic. The crisis was exacerbated by the fact that following his departure, Begin chose to turn his back on the world and to seclude himself at home. It was a complete, absolute, defiant break that pained his followers.

Yehiel Kadishai told me[1] (and he repeated this in an interview he gave shortly before his death)[2] that Begin's decline was sparked by the death of his beloved wife, Aliza, about a year before he resigned. Aliza had been at his side in Poland, throughout the Revolt against the British, and during the unending years in the opposition. She was his loyal and self-effacing friend and companion. Without her, he felt alone; he was bereft of the support he had relied on for sixty years against all adversaries.

Many others have insisted that the explanation lies with Begin's acute distress over the war that Sharon brought upon him. Three senior heirs – Begin's son, Benny, and government secretaries Arye Naor and Dan Meridor – were outspoken critics of Sharon during the war. Three decades have done nothing to dampen Naor's heartache. In an interview with *Yediot Aharonot*,[3] this respected and level-headed professor did not mince his words:

> Begin's decline began with the Lebanon War, as a result of Sharon's actions. [. . .] Looking back, it is clear to me that Begin saw that he was mired in a swamp, having lost all control and looking like a liar who violated his promises to the President of the United States. He mourned the deaths of the soldiers, and held only himself to blame, since it was he who had appointed Sharon as Minister of Defense, contrary to everyone's advice.

Everyone agrees, however, that in addition to all his troubles, what finally broke him were the Peace Now demonstrations outside his home, day and night, featuring a body count of military casualties in Lebanon, blaming him for needlessly shedding Jewish blood. It was a tactic that American demonstrators had used against President Johnson during the Vietnam War.

One way or another, Begin's dramatic resignation in 1983 launched the Likud into a decade of inter-generational battles of inheritance. Only the emptiness left by a leader of such dominance, after such a protracted period, could engender such a savage, all-out struggle, which continued over ten stormy, violent years.

Veterans and youngsters in a war of inheritance against the middle generation

In Begin's absence, the Likud split into different factions and coalitions. Just as the Revisionist movement had split into two underground movements and its two separate constituent generations, so the movement and the party were now on the verge of dissolution. An enormous chasm opened up between the "newcomers" and the veterans and their children. However, the difference was that in the Jabotinsky era the movement had been stuck in the opposition, with no resources in the offing and thus no fight over budgets and positions. Now, having come to power, the party controlled government ministries, bureaucratic hierarchies, budgets, and dozens of municipalities. The conflict now involved not only ideology, but also real assets and interests.

The 1980s witnessed unprecedented infighting. Up until this time, political battles had been waged in closed rooms or at insiders' conferences. Now the battles were fought in the open, in tempestuous sessions of thousands of Likud committee members, in the media, and in hundreds of Likud branches throughout the country. The fighting lacked the veneer of decorum and restraint that had previously characterized political discord. The Likud was now the ruling party, a party of the masses, and this was already the media age. For a decade, Israeli television and newspapers dripped with political blood.

The Likud separated into three distinct generational groups: the veterans, headed by Shamir, Begin's "next in line" successor; the new middle generation, headed by Levy and Sharon, both of whom were competing for the crown; and the younger generation, centering around the early heirs, who remained loyal to the veterans throughout this period.

The veterans were the Irgun commanders and underground fighters of Begin's generation. Just as during the Revolt every commander who was killed or exiled had been replaced by one of his contemporaries, so in the Herut party every veteran who passed away or retired from the Knesset was replaced by a younger veteran of the fighting family. Thus, while the names changed from time to time, the essence and spirit of the party remained fixed. To an external observer, the Herut MKs and leadership of 1949 were identical to that of 1984: they comprised uniformly hardline, uncompromising, ideological underground veterans, faithful to the Irgun legacy and to Jabotinsky's teachings, toughened by Mapai/Labor persecution, and suspicious of any newcomer who was not part of the fighting family.

During the years in government, the MKs who had joined the Likud from the Liberal Party – Sharon, Levy, and Modai – gradually consolidated their position. Viewing themselves as Begin's rightful successors, they became bitter adversaries of the veterans, who objected to their appropriation of power in the party.

The consolidation of the middle generation was augmented by a new element that had become manifest in the Likud. Whereas the wearying years in the opposition had eliminated all but the hardiest idealists, the shift from this austere constriction to the largesse of government gave birth to the phenomenon of political power-brokers.

With the rise to power there had been a change in the internal party election system. Previously, a narrow appointments committee, operating under the auspices of the head of the party, had determined who would serve as MKs. Now the voting involved the party's Central Committee, numbering around a thousand members (later on the number grew to three thousand). This amplified the influence of the power-brokers who functioned as "vote contractors". They supported the middle-generation contenders, who controlled the government ministries' budgets and political appointments. In the wake of the democratization and politicization of the internal elections, the party was swamped by a flood of new members who had no knowledge of or identification with the party's history, and who bolstered the power of Levy and Sharon at Likud headquarters. To the bewilderment of the veterans, who recalled a similar phenomenon from the dark and corrupt days of Mapai rule, the mechanisms of government were now manned with hundreds of political appointments. The movement seemed to be losing its grip on its pure vision and legacy, whose sole and supreme interest was the good of the nation and the state. It seemed that for the self-appointed successors, personal interests were a higher priority than those of the country. Suddenly, wheeler-dealers with no ideological commitment, who could just as easily belong to a different party, were taking over Likud branches. In the eyes of the veterans these were corrupt and dangerous infiltrators who needed to be fought and repelled. This was a war of survival for the movement that Jabotinsky and Begin had nurtured, and for its vision.

In addition to the veterans and the middle generation, there were the thousands of youngsters, including a core of hundreds of children of underground veterans, who had completed their army service as officers and had gone on to become Student Union heads and activists in the movement. They were a capable group, and their "aunts and uncles" in the fighting family were proud of them, but they still held only marginal positions in the internal arena. Even the appellation "heirs" had not yet been used in relation to them.

Looking back on the process of the growth and integration of the heirs in the party, one discovers an interesting phenomenon. Over the course of around forty years, the veterans and the younger generation engaged in a gradual role-reversal: the children started off as foot-soldiers but over the years turned into leaders. The parents were the leaders, but with time they gradually retreated, willingly, allowing the youngsters to take the helm. The close cooperation between the two generations in view of a common enemy – the middle, "outsider" generation – remained firm over time.

As children, the youngsters had imbibed the soul of the Revisionist struggle at home and had willingly embarked on the quest to restore their parents' glory and respect. From the very outset, their political journey had the almost universal support of the "aunts and uncles" – the underground veterans. As mentioned, the biological parents generally did not encourage their children to enter politics; it was usually only after the retirement or even the passing of the parent that the other veterans would prod the youngsters to replace him or her. Without the support and the urging of the "aunts and uncles", who included heads of Likud branches and other central activists, it is doubtful that the younger generation would have got as far as it did in the political realm.

There is no way of knowing who Begin's chosen successor would have been, but we may glean some idea of his preferences from his behavior in his later years. He kept out of the first battle of inheritance, in 1983, between David Levy and Yitzhak Shamir, standing firm against the heavy pressure of the veterans to openly support Shamir so that the movement would continue to be led by an underground veteran. But his non-intervention may be viewed as a calculated, quiet statement: it was obvious and natural that a graduate of Beitar in Poland would support a candidate with the same background; that a disciple of Jabotinsky would support a fellow disciple of Jabotinsky; that one underground commander would support another; that someone who had suffered persecution would support a fellow victim.

At the same time, Begin refrained from declaring his support for his beloved protégé, Levy, although Levy was absolutely convinced that Begin was unreservedly behind him. Notably, Levy's candidacy speech included a declaration long remembered for its pomposity, passion, and faith, assuring Begin, "You have a successor!"

Like other leaders, Begin neither wanted nor groomed a successor. Had he been forced to choose a replacement, it is reasonable to assume that he would have wanted a fellow Irgun veteran. But faced with the two candidates – neither of whom Begin would have picked as his first choice – it is possible that he would have preferred the young Levy. We recall that following the Upheaval of 1977, Begin had appointed Shamir, leader of the Irgun's sister-underground, Lehi, to the somewhat ceremonial position of Speaker of the Knesset, rather as a minister. Only when Dayan resigned as foreign minister did Begin appoint Shamir to this ministerial office. Levy, on the other hand, had been granted the title of Deputy Prime Minister. (Both appointments were made only after heavy pressure).

Either way, what we can be sure of is that Menachem Begin never imagined the flood of ego and passion that would be unleashed upon his departure from the party that he had founded and led.

A stirring among the Mizrahim and their new influence on politics

What would have happened in the Likud if Begin had remained Prime Minister? I believe that he would have continued the process that he embarked on: cultivating a Mizrahi generation as the continuation of the generation of the Revolt. Begin regarded the mayors of the development towns – second-generation North African/Middle Eastern inhabitants of the transit camps – as the natural continuation of his movement. This Ashkenazi Polish leader felt a profound connection with the Mizrahim. He never forgot their courageous exploits in the Irgun. In his heart he carried the memory of the Jewish prisoners who had been hanged by the British, half of whom were Mizrahim. Begin promoted Mizrahi fighters to senior command positions; had the Revolt continued, the home-grown Sabras and the Mizrahim would have become the commanders of the Irgun. Begin felt that the self-satisfied Ashkenazi tribe gave its allegiance to the Mapai establishment, while the underground and the Revisionist movement enjoyed the love and admiration of the Yemenite immigrants and, later on, the immigrants from North Africa. He always remembered where he had hidden as a fugitive and who had risked their lives for the persecuted leader of the underground. During his years leading the opposition he saw how the Ashkenazi tribe – in very general terms, Tel Aviv society – grew ever more distant from Herut, while the "others" – the Mizrahim and the Religious Zionists – flocked to the movement. I remember as a child attending Begin's election rallies (this was before the Facebook era); they were usually held in the poorer Mizrahi neighborhoods and development towns.

A special connection developed between these contrasting sides – Begin, the older, "exilic" Jew with his Polish accent and his "old-fashioned" European manners, and the younger, brash, Middle Eastern native youngsters. It was this unlikely connection that led to the political Upheaval. It led Begin to groom the Mizrahim for leadership, and it led thousands of Herut members from the periphery to feel that the movement was "theirs", and hence to demand representation and influence. Not as a gesture or a favor, but by right.

The 1981 elections proved to Begin and to everyone that Israel had changed, and this had an impact on the Likud and on Israeli politics. The elections showed that Israel was no longer a society in which a dominant Ashkenazi tribe that controlled the two largest parties ruled over "others". Two other major tribes – the Mizrahim of the periphery, and the Religious Zionists – had displayed independence and broken through to center stage.

In the 1981 elections a surprising tension developed between Labor, which portrayed itself as Ashkenazi and secular (and which was perceived by those outside of it as arrogant, disdainful, and closed to new voices and groups), and the new Likud that had opened up and was flooded with Mizrahim and religious voters (as well as the early Russian immigrants). Just prior to the elections, a well-known television personality, Dudu Topaz, proved the claims of discrimination and arrogance when, on stage, he called the Likud voters "ruffians". He also claimed that they did not serve in the IDF – a claim that infuriated hundreds of thousands of Israelis. Begin used this statement to propel the discriminated masses to the voting booths, bringing a surprising victory.

In this highly charged election, Begin, now Prime Minister, returned to the open plazas where he had built up his support in earlier years. The thousands of participants at his rallies proved to him that the Mizrahim and traditionally religious Jews represented the sector that connected most naturally to a nationalist worldview and faith in the Land of Israel. It was they who connected to the pain and the legacy upon which the Revisionist movement had been founded. They were his hope for continuing the Likud and upholding the banner of a just society opposed to the Socialism, which in Begin's eyes, had turned into a monstrous employer that served the oppressive elite. Levy, Katzav, Sheetrit, Magen, and their friends represented Begin's vision for the future; they were the Likud for the new age.

All of this was a prelude to the ethnic tension that later infiltrated from the general elections into the Likud itself. Here, the masses of new members demanded representation in the leadership of the movement that they had helped bring to power. However, within the movement there waited two generations of successors who were happy to welcome these new members as partners but were not willing to have David Levy as their leader.

Notes

1 Interview with the author, March 5, 2007.
2 Yediot Aharonot, May 24, 2013.
3 Yediot Aharonot, January 8, 2013.

10　Round one

Levy vs. Shamir

The climax of the first battle of inheritance came on Thursday, September 1, 1983, in the Ohel Shem hall in Tel Aviv. The small, dilapidated venue was packed with hundreds of Herut Central Committee members who had assembled to make a fateful choice: the election of the new chairman of the movement, the Prime Minister, who would replace Begin.

The battle of inheritance between the representative of the veterans (Yitzhak Shamir) and the representative of the middle generation (David Levy) marked the youngsters' first foray into the jostling and elbowing among the more seasoned members. Unlike Begin, who had avoided placing sons and daughters of veteran fighters in the Knesset or the government, Shamir developed a real dependence on the youngsters who served as MKs during his tenure. They gained experience and expertise and gradually climbed their way up the hierarchy, becoming advisors and aides to Shamir's most senior staff. Shamir, who lacked Begin's brilliance and charisma, was the one who propelled the wave of heirs to the forefront of the movement and of the state, elevating them from the Prime Minister's Office (which he inherited from Begin) to the Knesset and the government. "Children of" – Milo, Olmert, Meridor, Ahimeir, and Hanegbi, along with Mizrahim including Katzav and Sheetrit, owed their breakthrough in national politics to Shamir.

Shamir's battle for political survival was in fact a war of survival of his generation. Shamir was the guardian of the Polish Beitar core, a camp now besieged by "new invaders" and "returning seceders". He was backed by two groups: the underground veterans, who were in their sixties and seventies, and the Herut youngsters, in their thirties and forties, including a core of well-known heirs.

Begin's departure left such a gaping hole that two generations were needed to fill it. A general overview of a decade of infighting shows clearly how the veterans advanced the young heirs in the party's institutions and relied on them as a critical auxiliary force in fending off enemies of the fighting family.

Two candidates presented themselves in the hall. Behind them were two distinct and homogeneous camps. One camp supported the serious-faced Foreign Minister, Yitzhak Shamir – the highly experienced, security-oriented candidate. The other camp supported Deputy Prime Minister David Levy – a new and different star, who was borne on the waves of his supporters' admiration.

This was the first open confrontation in a series of protracted and egotistic battles in the Likud: they were clashes between figures of the present (Levy, Sharon) and figures of the past (Shamir, Arens), between electoral power and the power of legacy. Both camps were well aware that Levy was the only leader in Likud who enjoyed broad popularity among "the people" – the people who had brought Begin to power. And thus, although the Herut Central Committee was the veterans' "home base", the Levy camp appeared confident of victory, while the veterans' camp looked tired and defeated. "They're going to win," I overheard one of the movement's veterans mutter to his grey-haired companion, who replied with pathos, "They're going to take the movement from us. . . . This is the last time we'll be singing Beitar songs here." The Irgun veterans comforted themselves by singing underground songs as they waited.

These sixty- and seventy-year-old veteran fighters – mostly Ashkenazi, some Yemenite – proceeded like a disciplined, quiet, determined army whose mission was to protect Shamir and the Jabotinsky hegemony. They operated with a sense of historical mission. They saw no alternative to Shamir, the representative of their own generation. The other candidate was too young, lacking in political and security experience, and devoid of Revisionist ideological roots. In addition, he was suspected of opportunism, in view of the fact that at the start of his political career he had tried his luck in the Labor party and later on had supported Weizman's revolt against Begin. How could Jabotinsky's legacy be entrusted to someone who did not know the Irgun anthem, they wondered. How could the fate of the state lie with a candidate who had no military experience, whose resume was one of political wheeling and dealing, and who imitated Begin's rhetoric at rallies?

Levy's camp was made up mostly of relatively new activists in the Likud. These were representatives from the periphery who had helped to bring about the Upheaval and now demanded their rightful place. They believed that they were the real Likud, not the "old people" whom Begin had appointed to the Knesset and who represented no more than a few thousand underground veterans. Front and center in the Levy camp was a group of chairmen of Likud branches who had become mayors of development towns.

In the eyes of Levy's supporters, Shamir was an old, grey, exilic, establishment politician, made in the mold of the hated Labor leaders. In the 1960s, while Begin had fired up the masses in town squares, Shamir had been out of the country, serving in the Mossad. He had entered the Knesset only in 1973, after Levy was already there. With all due respect to Shamir and his Lehi activity in the past, Levy's supporters could not understand how he dared presume to steal the inheritance from their candidate. What they saw before them was not Shamir, humble hero of the underground, who had carried out dozens of courageous operations and had eliminated some of Israel's biggest enemies. In their eyes Shamir and his camp were simply old men, lacking in verve and charisma, and pale copies of Begin at best.

Levy had accumulated considerable influence in the Likud. He had consolidated his power in the branches scattered around the country, especially in the periphery and among blocs of younger voters, and had become one of the symbols of the Upheaval in 1977. He approached the showdown with Shamir with an aggressive and organized campaign that was the first of its type in the movement. Levy felt that he was the most suitable candidate to succeed Begin. In fact, he behaved and expressed himself as though Begin had actually named him for the position. He was convinced that his title of Deputy Prime Minister signalled that he was the next in line. He did not see it as a symbolic role, as did Shamir, the veterans, and the media. He was well aware of the level of popularity and love he enjoyed among the public, and was connected to what he called the "true Likud". He and his camp viewed Shamir as "the Likud of the past", a Polish remnant of a distant history who could not break out of the boundaries of the underground, to reach out to the wider population. To Levy's supporters, it was not the fighting family – a few thousand households – that had defeated the leftist Ashkenazi elite and brought about the Upheaval in 1977 and a second victory in 1981, but rather Levy and his generation, including hundreds of thousands of his activists in the faraway towns.

The way the two candidates entered the hall spoke volumes. Shamir, short of stature and sixty-eight years old, entered quietly, almost incognito, as though he was still in hiding from the British or agents of the Haganah. He appeared bewildered by the crowd that gathered around him and by the masses of photographers, and made a show of firmly rejecting the praises heaped on him by his admirers, waving his hand dismissively in his typical style and rebuking them gently: "Leave me alone. Go and persuade the voters." Only after much cajoling on the part of MK Roni Milo did he agree for two younger party members to escort him.

Forty-six-year-old David Levy's entrance was quite different. He was surrounded by a large and boisterous group who clapped, whistled, and exhibited great self-confidence. Levy was younger, taller, and more exuberant than Shamir; moreover, he had a photogenic coiffure. He loved the camera, smiled in every direction, and embraced his supporters. On that evening, too, he behaved as though he was Begin's certain successor.

Levy approached the elections from a well-organized political position. He controlled the movement's Operations Department, its branches, and its financial allocations. As Minister of Housing and Construction, he was the first to introduce political appointments and to award jobs to party hacks – a phenomenon that until now had characterized the Labor Party. His rise from grass-roots beginnings, via the Likud's worker committees in the National Labor Federation, had spurred a wave of branch activists throughout the country towards the movement's institutions. They believed in Levy, they viewed his election as the rectification of an historical wrong, and they believed that his appointment as Prime Minister would signal the end of discrimination against Mizrahim.

The first war of inheritance not only led to cooperation between the veterans and the youngsters, but also united the various forces in the veteran camp. Former Lehi members found themselves once again fighting alongside veterans of the Irgun, the aim this time being to preserve the Revisionist hegemony.

Although the struggle had an ethnic aspect to it, the division was more along generational lines. This was a struggle between the generation of new power-brokers and the two generations of the underground, which included no small number of Mizrahim. While the earliest group of fighters had comprised mainly Polish immigrants, most of these veterans had already retired or passed away, and the frontlines of the battle were now manned by underground veterans who were for the most part native-born Israelis whose parents had immigrated from Yemen, Lebanon, and Egypt, and old-time Sephardim whose families had settled many generations earlier in Jerusalem, Safed, and Tiberias.

The veterans' camp was led by brothers Eli and Yosef Sheetrit, who headed the Tagar Circle (to be discussed later). Eli and Yosef were two out of five brothers who had fought in the Irgun. Yosef had met his wife in the Irgun, too. Their family had immigrated from Algeria nine generations previously. Along with them in Shamir's team was Yosef (Yoske) Nahmias, who had thrown Begin off the *Altalena* as it was being shelled, thereby saving his life. Another key player was Nahmias's friend Chaim Eitani, father of my colleague in the Likud student cell at Tel Aviv University, Ofer Eitani. Chaim had immigrated from Afghanistan via a long journey with his parents and four older siblings that lasted an entire year (1932). Upon reaching the Promised Land, his grandfather refused to carry a "red card" and consequently found no work. When he finally found a job as a laborer in an orchard, he was severely beaten by Histadrut thugs. The memory of the blows remained with him for many years. The grandfather was proud of his two sons who had enlisted and fought in the Irgun ranks. One was imprisoned by the British in Latrun for three years; the other, Chaim, continued his activities and was a respected Irgun fighter.

Two generations of the Ratzon family, hailing from the Yemenite neighborhood in Petah Tikva, likewise stood firmly behind Shamir. The dominant player at this point was the son, Michael Ratzon, chairman of Herut Youth, a lieutenant-colonel in the IDF, and a member of Shamir's narrow circle. His father, Avraham, who remained loyal to the fighting family well into old age, had hidden Irgun ammunition in the taboun oven at his home (so that if the British arrived, they could light the taboun and blow up the cache). His uncle, Yosef, had been a Lehi fighter; another uncle, Chaim, had been in the Irgun and remained a member of the Herut Central Committee throughout his life.

The youngsters were the veterans' hidden weapon. Behind Shamir and his grey-haired companions stood a hungry, aggressive, determined camp: the students of 1969, who were transformed almost overnight into soldiers in this campaign. The Shamir-Arens camp was headed by Roni Milo and the early heirs serving as MKs. Back in the 1970s, Milo, responsible to the Youth Department on the twelfth floor of the Herut headquarters, had tied his star to his eleventh-floor neighbour, Shamir, head of the Operations Department. Milo had dared to bet on this older, quiet, modest newcomer to the building who had completed his stint with the Mossad, and had started to plan with Shamir for the day when Begin would move aside. Now, at the age of thirty-four, Milo was ready to lead the Shamir camp together with his veteran colleagues.

Two prominent heirs who immediately joined Shamir's inner circle were Meridor and Olmert. Government secretary Dan Meridor, who had been a confidant of

Begin, was to be Shamir's closest advisor throughout his tenure. MK Olmert, now aged thirty-eight, finally had his opportunity to rejoin the core of the movement, now that Begin had left the scene. While the savage speech he had delivered at Kfar HaMakabiya seventeen years previously still rankled with the veterans, the real and immediate danger presented by Levy was sufficient reason to forgive him.

Surprisingly, two of the early Mizrahi mayors – Deputy Minister of Housing Moshe Katzav and MK Meir Sheetrit – also sided with Shamir, albeit surreptitiously, lest they be branded as traitors to the Mizrahi cause. They simply felt different from Levy: he was a blue-collar, uneducated workers' leader, while they had served in the IDF, had received university degrees, and had run municipalities. They felt no special affinity for him, while Shamir had cultivated them from the outset, along with their fellow heirs.

The young leadership that had established the victorious Tel Aviv student cell a decade earlier was thus split into two rival camps. The confidence that they had gained in the wake of their sensational victory on campus had aroused their political appetite. Chairman of the student cell, Michael Kleiner, had even once scribbled the placement of his friends in the future government. He, of course, was to be Prime Minister; Livnat was to be awarded the Education Ministry, and Milo was to be Foreign Minister. In the meantime, their paths had separated, and when it came to the Shamir-Levy clash they took different sides.

Milo had no intention of being part of a Kleiner-led government. He aimed higher – and indeed was the first of the Tel Aviv students to become an MK, to the chagrin of his peers. Now he was head of Shamir's campaign staff, and at his side in the Ohel Shem hall sat his fellow student cell member Michael Eitan, and his friends – the Likud Youth and underground children Michael Ratzon, Limor Livnat, and Ariella Ravdel, the latter two choosing to support their fathers' former commander in the Lehi rather than their young friends in the Levy camp.

The Levy camp was led by the new and energetic MKs Reiser and Kleiner. They were joined by the young, aggressive activist David Appel, who effectively controlled Levy's Ministry of Housing and had seized control of the Tel Aviv Herut branch, elbowing out the veterans along the way. Although he was the son of a well-known underground veteran, Avraham (Avrum) Appel (to be discussed at greater length later), he was the engine of the well-oiled and belligerent machine that was aimed against the veterans and the heirs, who became his enemies.

The crowding in the old hall became more acute as the voting began. Some 850 Herut Central Committee members were squeezed inside, and it was clear to all that the vote would be very close. Begin was a presence in the air. Everyone prayed for a miracle – that a single word from him, in favor of one or the other candidate, would decide the issue. Shamir enjoyed the benefit of the doubt, since the prospect of his election was viewed as the natural continuation of Begin's leadership, but Levy's people did not give up. A rumor passed through the hall suggesting that Begin had expressed support for his beloved Mizrahi candidate, but it remained a rumor and no more.

At midnight the results emerged: sixty percent for Shamir, forty percent for Levy. The veterans and the heirs breathed a sigh of relief but at the same time understood how vulnerable their position in the Likud had become. To both generations it was clear that the egotistical display they had witnessed at Ohel Shem was just a sign of things to come. Levy's people were deeply frustrated: their Begin had been warm, loving, religiously traditional, persecuted, and pained – like themselves. Suddenly he had been replaced by this old man who was uncharismatic, tough, calculating, and distant. The Levy camp felt that the vote reflected the demographics of the past, not of the present. Once again, they had come out on the losing side.

Looking back, it was this decisive battle that redefined the party's character and its balance of forces: it marked the shift from a single leader to opposing groups; from one heterogeneous party into three warring camps (with Sharon's camp at this stage still waiting in the wings).

The first war of inheritance was also a baptism of fire for the younger generation, which included the early heirs. The dependence of the veterans on these youngsters had now become manifest, and it became increasingly marked in the contests to come. Shamir and his right-hand-man Arens came to understand that the youngsters brought with them considerable experience in managing election campaigns, as well as excellent representation in the media. Unlike the veterans, the youngsters were happy to be photographed. They exuded success and branded the Likud as a young and attractive party. They were able to steer their journalist friends in the direction of support for Shamir and had no difficulty in presenting their narrative: a squeaky-clean, principled, and ideological camp of older underground veterans and educated youngsters, against an aggressive and corrupt camp of wheeler-dealers looking for favors and jobs. Milo, Olmert, and Meridor were concocting "spin" long before the term became widely used.

11 Round two

Sharon takes the veterans by surprise

Only a year had passed since the contest between Shamir and Levy, and the 1984 general elections were approaching. While it was generally assumed that Shamir would be the Likud candidate with no new internal elections, Ariel Sharon surprised everyone by announcing his candidacy. From his point of view the aim here was not to win but rather simply to reassert his presence following his failure in the first Lebanon War, his removal from the position of Minister of Defense, and his relegation to oblivion.

Sharon was weak politically; he had been all but banished and his legitimacy was low. A minister without portfolio who spent much of his time at his ranch, he had not dared to present himself as a candidate to inherit Begin in 1983. He carried with him the stain of having misled Begin during the Lebanon War. This accusation emanated from the heirs who were close to Begin: Dan Meridor and Arye Naor. Sharon, the respected army general, had become a persona non grata in the press. He was perceived as having deceived Begin and dragged him – and, indeed, the entire country – into a war that cost hundreds of lives.

Sharon viewed himself as the candidate best suited to lead the Likud, better even than Begin himself. He had little respect for Shamir and Arens, who appeared to him weak and exilic, and lacking in battle experience. Levy, to his view, was an inexperienced political hack. As he saw it, not one of his adversaries had his military experience with the victories he had accumulated, nor his real connection with the land, with agriculture and settlement, with the army, and with the people.

Sharon and the veterans – from great admiration to fathomless suspicion

Sharon's relations with the Likud and with the Herut veterans were tricky from the outset, and had many ups and downs. Since his first flirt with the Likud a decade and a half previously, the veterans had shifted from admiration for Sharon, the charismatic general who had brought military victories, to suspicion towards Sharon the politician.

Sharon's personal and family history was completely different from that of both the veterans and the youngsters in the Likud. He was born in 1928 on a Labor-affiliated agricultural moshav. In his youth, in the War of Independence, he had distinguished himself as a commander in the ranks of the Haganah, rather than the Irgun or Lehi. He enlisted in the IDF carrying his Labor membership card, which smoothed the path for those wishing to advance in the army (a fact which the veterans never forgot).

Over the course of a glorious twenty-five-year career Sharon climbed the hierarchy of military command, until his discharge with the rank of major-general. He was founder and commander of the elite Commando Unit 101, which changed the face of the IDF, and became legendary as a brave and implacable – but also willful – commander. His commanders, and even Ben-Gurion himself, accused him of manipulating, misleading, and lying to them. He was among the Israeli generals who brought the great historical victory of the Six Day War (1967) and who were legends in their time (along with Chief-of-Staff Rabin and IAF commander Weizman). In the wake of his decisions and actions in the bleak Yom Kippur War (1973), Sharon was regarded as having almost single-handedly saved Israel from annihilation. He broke army rules, violated orders, and advanced with astounding courage from the Sinai desert, which was under attack, into Egypt, crossing the Suez Canal at a terrible cost in blood but reaching the outskirts of Cairo. The Egyptians, who had been close to victory, were forced to request a ceasefire. From that point onwards, Sharon's soldiers followed him blindly. All of Israel saluted the general who had saved the country.

Admittedly, Sharon was detested by his fellow generals, owing to his excessive independence and ignoring orders. But on the street he was a legend. Tens of thousands of soldiers worshipped him; every child in Israel recognized his photograph from the Sinai in 1973 of him with his head wrapped in a white bandage.

Begin and his circle had set their sights on Sharon and courted him intensively in the late '60s. They believed that the securing of two popular generals, Weizman and Sharon, would represent a significant achievement for the newly-consolidated Likud, in terms of both image and electoral power. However, unlike Weizman, who proceeded to leave the IDF and join the Likud, Sharon decided at the last moment not to leave the army. Begin was rather disillusioned upon discovering that the cunning general had exploited the negotiations for the purpose of obtaining an appointment to the position of Head of the Southern Command.

Four years later Sharon left the IDF and joined the Likud. He was a senior partner in establishing the party in 1973 and even served as an MK (representing the Gahal faction), but after just one year in the Knesset he decided to leave, to the Likud's astonishment and disappointment. They were especially upset when it turned out that he had once again crossed the party lines – with great fanfare, accepting an appointment as advisor on security affairs to the Labor Prime Minister, Rabin. This move was viewed as weakening the Likud and strengthening the Labor Party. Begin and his friends had been let down once again by the deceptive general.

Sharon deceived Begin and the Likud all over again in the period leading up to the 1977 elections. Sharon's right-wing opinions were well-known and sat well with the Likud's political platform, but even when there appeared to be some chance of reaching power for the first time, Sharon made no effort to help Begin.

On the contrary, he surprised him by forming the Shlomtzion party, with the assumption that Rabin was going to win and then he himself – Sharon – could join the government as a minister. Sharon's bet – which included failed contacts with prominent leftists concerning their inclusion on his Knesset list – failed miserably. Shlomtzion received only two mandates, and Sharon managed to squeeze into Begin's government, accepting the relatively minor portfolio of Minister of Agriculture.

Sharon and the heirs – from great admiration to fierce hostility

How, then, did Sharon manage to reinstate himself within the top echelon of the party, which had been so severely disappointed and humiliated by him? To understand this we must bear in mind the profound admiration that Begin and the Herut veterans had felt towards Sharon in the '60s and '70s. He was a highly decorated commander of unparalleled intrepidity in whom thousands of soldiers placed their complete trust. Of course, there was also the electoral consideration: while the Labor Party boasted a seemingly endless list of chiefs-of-staff and generals that it had produced, the Likud offered only "Ezer" (Weizman) and "Arik" (Sharon), the latter now enjoying the broad love and support that until now had been reserved for Begin.

And there was another reason: from the moment Sharon entered politics, he projected a very right-wing image. His tactic was simple and straightforward: to brand himself as even more loyal to the right-wing cause than was the right-wing itself. As Minister of Agriculture Sharon built up an enormous settlement enterprise, supporting government-approved communities and illegal outposts alike, and becoming the father of the settlement movement and the darling of the religious settlers. When later on his drawing of the country into the Lebanon War prompted a harsh leftist campaign against him, including billboards reading "Sharon is a murderer", this merely bolstered his support among the rightist camp, and especially the Irgun veterans, who remembered all too well the experience of left-wing persecution.

The Herut Youth admired Sharon as a general and as a leader in his early days. Some had even served under him in the Yom Kippur War and had witnessed his fearlessness at first-hand. His activity on behalf of the settlements won the hearts of young activists such as Olmert, Landau, Hanegbi, and Livnat, who regarded him as a true partner. When Sharon was appointed Minister of Defense in Begin's government, most of the youngsters gave him their full support. But then came the war, and the IDF was soon mired in the mess of Lebanon. At this point the attitude towards Sharon on the part of two senior heirs – Dan Meridor and Benny Begin – underwent a change. They came to suspect that Sharon had dragged Israel into an ill-advised war by deceiving Begin, who had consequently resigned. The conclusions of the official commission of inquiry, known as the Kahan Committee, confirmed their suspicions. This bone of contention defined the relations between the two men and Sharon for the years to come.

The elections of 1984 – Sharon surprises the veterans

Sharon therefore decided to run for Likud chairman in the party primaries of 1984, as a way of easing himself back into the center of the political arena. Despite his all but non-existent chances, he chose to submit his candidacy in order to show the party members that he was not "finished", as was commonly believed. His core of supporters was small, but he hoped to appeal to Levy's camp, too, which was stacked against Shamir.

In this internal contest Sharon found himself up against a united front of veterans, headed by his replacement as Defense Minister, Moshe Arens, along with the rising stars, MKs Milo and Olmert, and government secretary Dan Meridor and his close friend Benny Begin.

The heirs were assigned to cutting down Sharon in the media. They had close connections with prominent journalists, and the latter helped to present Sharon as a power-hungry hooligan who would do anything to strengthen his position. The liberal-leftist press, which painted Sharon – the settler-general – in demonic colors, was quick to buy the warnings of the young MKs and their claims as to Sharon's extremist right-wing views.

As noted, it was against the backdrop of this clash that the collective term "heirs" became widely used, following its acerbic reinterpretation by Uri Dan, a journalist close to Sharon, in his book *Ariel Sharon: An Intimate Portrait*. He devoted several pages, full of antipathy, to the heirs, going so far as to accuse Benny Begin and Dan Meridor of a blood libel against Sharon during the Lebanon War:

> His adversaries in the Likud began poisoning [the public sphere] against him via the media, and tried to re-circulate the lie that "Sharon misled Begin". [. . .] They were united in their burning aversion to (not to say hatred of) Sharon. [. . .] The struggle against Sharon at the Herut Central Committee in 1984 was spearheaded covertly by Dan Meridor and overtly by Benny Begin.[1]

Sharon had a hard time recruiting high-profile supporters. His adversaries, Shamir and Arens, held the highest and most influential positions in Israel: Prime Minister and Minister of Defense. Even David Levy was reluctant to help him for fear of another competitor for the top spot. And so Sharon decided to run an "underdog" campaign. He appealed to the compassion of the Central Committee members via pleas from his supporters, whose message was, "Just don't humiliate Sharon; don't throw him to the dogs. It's obvious that Shamir will win, so vote for Sharon just so he can maintain his dignity." And indeed, many members of this traditionally underdog party acceded to this request and voted for Sharon. The results were astounding: Sharon received no less than forty-two percent of the vote, while Shamir, the sitting Prime Minister, won a narrow majority of fifty-six percent.

The veterans and the youngsters were flabbergasted. From their point of view, this was a monumental failure. Sharon had proved to all that despite his role in the war, he still occupied a warm place in the heart of Likud activists. His heroism in Israel's wars was still a factor for many of them.

The challenging of Shamir by Sharon and Levy indicated that Herut/Likud was divided into two camps, distinguished from one another in terms of age, background, values, aims, and leadership. There was the camp comprising the veterans and their younger generation, comprising just over half of the Central Committee, and there were the challengers – the party hacks and the Mizrahi youngsters from the periphery, who had advanced within the party and government mechanisms and now comprised close to half of its membership.

A draw, and national unity

Despite a series of colossal crises (Begin's departure, Likud infighting, entanglement in Lebanon, soaring inflation, and the great stock exchange crisis), Shamir managed to prevent a Likud collapse in the elections held in July 1984. Although Labor received forty-four mandates and the Likud only forty-one, the outcome in terms of the major blocs was a draw: sixty to sixty. This led to the establishment of a national unity government. The agreement between the two major parties stated that for the first two years Labor leader Peres would (finally) be Prime Minister, while the chairman of the Likud, Shamir, would be the Acting Prime Minister and Foreign Minister. For the two following years, these roles would be switched. Yitzhak Modai was appointed Minister of Finance, and the defense portfolio was entrusted to Rabin, who actually enjoyed closer relations with Shamir than he did with his fellow Laborite, Peres.

The new government faced complex tasks, including extricating Israel from Lebanon and conquering the runaway inflation, all against the background of the bitter animosity between the parties and among themselves. And in fact, it succeeded. Shamir maintained his status in the Likud even while serving for two years as Foreign Minister, by appointing his adversaries – Levy and Sharon – to central portfolios in the unity government. Levy became Deputy Prime Minister and Minister of Housing and Construction, while Sharon was Minister of Industry and Commerce. However, these men aspired much higher – they desired to lead the Likud, coveting the seat of the leader whom they never accepted, from the start of his tenure to its end.

The ferment in the party continued unrelentingly. In 1986, following two years of organizing and gearing up, the two sides confronted each other once again in an especially violent battle at the Exhibition Grounds in Tel Aviv. This Central Committee convention had reached the moment of truth: would the veterans finally be driven out, or would they prevail over the "invaders"?

Note

1 Uri Dan, *Ariel Sharon: An Intimate Portrait* (London, Hampshire: Palgrave Macmillan, 2006), 189–191.

12 Mobilizing the veterans and heirs for the battle of inheritance

The two wars of inheritance made it evident to Shamir and the Herut veterans that a significant camp, comprising just about half of the party's membership, was fundamentally questioning their leadership. Sharon and Levy challenged Shamir over and over again, and after repeated defeats decided to join ranks. These two men were determined to remove Shamir and his camp. Their opposition was reinforced by hundreds of workers, thanks to the political appointments that they made – Levy in the Ministry of Housing and Construction, and Sharon in the Ministry of Commerce and Industry, which he headed after the 1984 general elections, having received a boost after submitting his candidacy as head of the party.

The danger of the party falling into foreign hands was now very real for the veterans. They felt that their movement, which had served for four decades as a home for the fighting family, and which had finally risen to power and had restored their dignity, was now being appropriated by the newcomers. They were horrified by the ascent of activists devoid of any background, who had never read a word of Jabotinsky's writings and had no experience of the "Hunting Season" and Labor persecution.

Around the Sabbath dinner tables of the fighting family there were emotional discussions about the movement's fearful deterioration in the wake of the flood of political appointments. The veterans could not understand how, having reached the point where they were finally supposed to be able to rest and enjoy the fruits of their labor, they were now in danger of being thrown out of their political home. It was true that the Prime Minister, as well as other ministers and MKs, were warmly received when they paid visits to the veterans' organizations, but they were well aware that if they rested for even a second on their laurels, they would soon discover that the Likud was no longer theirs. The threat to the Beitar hegemony, which had made its appearance already on the eve of Shamir's run in 1983, led to an emergency mobilization of veterans, including even those who had left the party following Begin's concessions to Egypt in the Camp David Accords.

Arens, Shamir's closest partner, was appointed Minister of Defense (replacing Sharon) after a brief but successful term as Israel's ambassador to Washington. He expressed unwavering support for Shamir and helped him to spearhead a campaign recruiting and mobilizing veteran and younger members of the movement.

From this point he was Shamir's loyal ally, waging a determined struggle against Sharon and Levy throughout the nine dramatic years of Shamir's leadership.

The recruitment began with the Likud list for the eleventh Knesset (1984), in which veterans who concluded their political career were once again replaced with other veterans. Thus, even thirty-six years after the Revolt, a third of the Likud faction in Knesset (eight MKs) were underground veterans.

Shamir advances the heirs

The main recruitment efforts were directed towards the large, young, and energetic reservoir that was the Herut's younger generation. From the time he took office, Shamir took care to bring youngsters – and especially fighting family heirs, including Olmert, Milo, Landau, Meridor, Ahimeir, and Hanegbi – into the Prime Minister's Office (PMO) and into the government and the Knesset.

Unlike Begin, Shamir was very eager to have the heirs in the Knesset. He believed in their power, their abilities, and their professionalism, and in contrast to his charismatic and eloquent predecessor, he needed them for dealing with the media. For a battle-scarred and shrewd old-timer like himself, loyalty was a supreme value. The heirs who demonstrated their loyalty were promoted very quickly, to the consternation of Sharon and Levy.

Shamir began with the inner circle – his bureau. Dan Meridor remained the government secretary. He was joined by journalist (and son-of) Yossi Ahimeir, who served as Shamir's advisor, spokesman, and, later on, bureau chief. This was a professional appointment but also a symbolic one: Yossi Ahimeir was the son of Abba Ahimeir, who had been the spiritual father of the Irgun. Shamir also brought back Tzahi Hanegbi, son of his old Lehi comrade Geula Cohen, from the Tehiya party, appointing him in 1986 to the position of bureau chief. Hanegbi and his mother had been a belligerent right-wing opposition to Begin in light of his agreement to withdraw from the Sinai settlements, but in Shamir's eyes this was a fact in their favor. Shamir also brought on board two members of the Beitar moshav Nahalat Jabotinsky – Zeev Mahnai, as an advisor, and Herzl Makov, as an aide.

Moshe Arens turned his own bureau into a fighting family club of sorts, with five children of underground veterans as advisors: Avi Steinmetz, son of an Irgun fighter from Nahariya; Sallai Meridor; Moka Cohen (advisor for settlement affairs); Brigadier-General Yirmi Olmert (military advisor to the Minister of Defense), and me. (I remained his advisor throughout the 1980s.)

Later on, Netanyahu would adopt a similar policy. Over the course of twenty-five years of activity he has recruited no less than nine members of the fighting family's younger generation onto his staff. I was his advisor throughout six internal and general election campaigns; Major-General Yohanan Locker was his military secretary, while his brother Harel Locker served as director general of the PMO. Major-General Yaakov Amidror, son of Irgun fighter and Herut candidate for the Knesset Tzila Amidror, was appointed head of the National Security Council; and the oldest appointment was Netanyahu's cousin and friend, David Shimron, whose mother was an Irgun member and whose uncle fought with Lehi.

All in all, the bureaus of the four Likud heads – Begin, Shamir, Arens, and Netanyahu – recruited a total of twenty-one second-generation members of the fighting family.

Shamir also worked to place heirs in his outer circle: the government and the Knesset. In the 1984 elections he promoted Milo to his deputy in the Foreign Ministry; he and the veterans elected Uzi Landau and Gidon Gadot (another heir) for the Knesset; and they kept Aridor. Olmert, the heir who had been expelled by Begin, became one of Shamir's closest confidants. All in all, the fighting family was well represented in the Knesset: there were five youngsters along with eight veterans, comprising about half of the Herut faction. Three of the young MK heirs were already leaders in the Shamir-Arens camp, and four others were manning Shamir's bureau.

Shamir and Arens also promoted siblings of these first heirs to senior positions outside of the Knesset: the brothers of Meridor and of Olmert were appointed senior advisors to Shamir and Arens. This aroused displeasure in the movement. There was a sense that these appointments represented nepotism at the expense of other activists who were devoted and no less deserving.

The recruiters

The task of recruiting the youngsters was undertaken by dozens of veterans. We shall dwell here on just two symbolic representatives, two men who devoted their later years to the task of replicating their generation: Eli Sheetrit and Avraham Appel. The former was the life and spirit of the Tagar Circle – an organization of Herut veterans that worked to preserve the Irgun legacy and was effectively a mechanism for advancing the heirs; the latter was an old-time party activist who had become legendary for his absolute loyalty to Begin. Following Begin's departure, Appel devoted himself to cultivating the next generation.

Eli Sheetrit, born in 1925, established the Tagar Circle as an association of Irgun veterans. He himself was one of five brothers who had fought in the Irgun. His brother Yosef was a deputy company commander who participated in the attack on the British Intelligence headquarters and in the Acre Prison break. During the War of Independence he participated in the conquest of Jaffa and sustained a severe injury, from which he miraculously recovered. During the war he married his girlfriend, who served with him in the Irgun; the organization's clandestine radio station operated from her parents' house.

Sheetrit enlisted in the Irgun at the age of sixteen and took part in many operations, including the sabotage of the crude oil pipeline near Haifa, for which he was imprisoned for three years in Latrun. Following his release, he fought in the War of Independence as a platoon commander and was seriously injured. He lay recovering in hospital for an entire year. After his recovery, he opened a business supplying spare parts for vehicles in Tel Aviv. He and his brothers were loyal to Begin throughout, protecting him and defending him against anyone who dared to say a bad word about the man who, to their view, had brought independence to the Jewish People.

During the turbulent 1980s Sheetrit's shop became a war room dedicated to saving the movement by advancing the youngsters who would preserve Jabotinsky's teachings about the integrity of the homeland. It was from this small shop that sons and daughters of Irgun veterans emerged and went on to become MKs and ministers, and even a Prime Minister: Netanyahu.

Sheetrit, the Mizrahi Sabra, advanced not only Netanyahu, Landau, Rivlin, and Livni, but also those he referred to as "Mizrahi heirs": development town mayors Moshe Katzav and Meir Sheetrit. He cultivated the younger generation up until 1993, from which point he devoted himself exclusively to the heir whom he himself and the other veterans regarded as possessing the greatest potential: Netanyahu.

The veterans' main annual event was hosted by the Tagar Circle every year just before Rosh Hashana (the Jewish New Year). It was generally attended by over a thousand veteran fighters (the majority of them couples who had fought together), dressed in their finest. The VIP table on the stage was reserved for Tagar Circle honorees, MKs, ministers, and Prime Ministers representing two generations of the movement. From the mid-1980s until 2012, Netanyahu attended this event no less than twenty times.

The other kingmaker who serves as a faithful representative of hundreds like him was Avraham Appel, a mythological activist with Beitar roots who served for many years as chairman of the Central Tel Aviv branch of Herut. Appel was a Holocaust survivor who admired Begin and devoted his life to supporting him during the decades he spent in the opposition. Begin was the godfather of Appel's elder son, Dudi, who eventually took a different path and became the enemy of the veterans and heirs.

After Begin's resignation, Appel became a veritable one-man war machine dedicated to promoting the younger generation. Over the course of three decades, up until the day he died, he fought against what he referred to in a discussion we had as the "seizure of the Likud by external, corrupt, interested forces".[1] He was the only activist who, way back in the early 1980s, dared to say openly what many of the veterans were feeling:

> Labor dropouts are trying to take over the movement by buying power with money, and buying people with government ministry budgets. [. . .] If we don't put a stop to this hostile takeover, the movement will cease to exist; no-one will remember who Jabotinsky was, who Begin was, who Barazani and Feinstein were.

Avraham Appel remained faithful to the legacy of his generation to his dying day. Over the course of thirty years he accompanied the heirs through thousands of meetings and hundreds of Central Committee conventions, waging a personal campaign on their behalf, with boundless faith in the idea of inheritance of the party. He passed the crown from Begin to Shamir and would not rest until he had placed it on the head of the heir, Netanyahu. He viewed Netanyahu as a direct continuation of Ze'ev Jabotinsky, the leader who had inspired the education he himself had received during his childhood. He accompanied, cultivated, and advanced Netanyahu literally until the end of his life.

It was Appel who, as early as 1985, thought up the idea of a conference of all the heirs so that they would advance and take the reins of the movement after the

Shamir-Arens era. He insisted that only the ideological aristocracy of Jabotinsky's movement should attend.

The first and last heirs' conference

On July 18, 1985, the first conference of its kind was held at the Diplomat Hotel in Jerusalem. This was a joint initiative of Avraham Appel and the young brothers Amiram and Eldad Bukshpan. Appel sought an opportunity to recruit more of the fighting family youngsters to the cause, while the Bukshpan brothers envisaged a non-political event aimed at preserving Jabotinsky's legacy. The heir and journalist Eitan Haber, who was already a confidant of the Labor rival Rabin, had made the organizers swear that the event would not be of a political nature. However, he knew that the initiative came as a response to David Levy's growing popularity and support, and that Appel's goal was to recruit more heirs to the political war.

Some seventy-seven youngsters joined the initiative, effecting a unification of the ranks of "Jabotinsky's grandchildren", bringing together the younger generation of all the various Revisionist groups (with the exception of the rebels).

The participants in the first conference of heirs made up an impressive list of office-bearers with a promising future: inter alia they included Israel's ambassador to the UN, Benjamin Netanyahu; the new MK Uzi Landau; Reuven Rivlin, a lawyer and chairman of Beitar Jerusalem; Zeev Boim, who had successfully campaigned and been elected mayor of Kiryat Gat; Brigadier-General Yirmi Olmert, advisor to the Minister of Defense; Professor Arye Naor, cabinet secretary; Yossi Ahimeir, advisor to the Prime Minister, and his brother, Yaakov, a top figure in Israel's Channel 1 TV; Yair Stern Jr.; and other senior personnel in radio, television, academia and politics.

The invitation to the conference was worded in the stately, unifying tone that the Bukshpan brothers hoped to lend to the event. It was adorned with a photograph of Jabotinsky (rather than Begin), and the invitees were defined as "the children of the early members of Jabotinsky's movement" (rather than as "children of Irgun/Lehi members").

> Our parents were among the first followers of Zeev Jabotinsky, and they carried the torch of his teachings and his path in the national movement. Conscious that the memory of their activity and efforts has yet to be awarded due recognition, and aware that their legacy lives on with us, we have decided to establish the "Younger Generation" organization to unite all the descendants of the early members of Jabotinsky's movement.

As appropriate to the occasion, the conference opened with the Beitar anthem, followed by Amiram Bukshpan's opening address:

> We went through crises as children and youth; we were excluded and ostracized, but we proudly bore the yoke. [. . .] We all have a sense that the story of what our parents did – their bravery, their faith, their persistence – has

not been given expression. And we have a task – first and foremost towards our children: "And you shall tell it to your children . . .".[2] We have differing views, but we carry with us the memory of our parents' [generation].

The conference was a success. Despite the old conflicts, more than half the participants joined the activities of the Shamir-Arens veteran camp. The conference was Netanyahu's first political occasion, and his presence reflected his intentions. He came from the USA to participate in the event and delivered a tough policy speech, to the visible chagrin of those who viewed it as a political statement, violating the agreement concerning the character of the conference. But Appel himself was actually quite pleased.

It was here, at this event, that Eitan Haber coined the term "heirs": "When I entered the hall, late," he told me, "I saw the attendees, and I said: 'Aha, all the heirs are here'."[3]

Notes

1 Interview with the author, October 10, 1987.
2 A reference to the biblical command that parents recount the story of the Exodus from Egypt to their children (Ex. 13:8).
3 Interview with the author, February 21, 2007.

13 Round three

Blowup at the party conference

The Herut conference held at the Tel Aviv Exhibition Grounds in March 1986 was the stormiest, most violent, and most important in the history of Herut and the Likud.

After the wars of inheritance between Shamir and Levy (1983) and between Shamir and Sharon (1984), and just six months before Shamir was due to move into the Prime Minister's Office (within the framework of the unity government rotation agreement), an all-out war erupted between two formidable forces. On one side were thousands of veterans and their younger generation; on the other were thousands of activists representing the Herut branches, along with the political appointments made by the Levy and Sharon camps, the latter now united in their frustration and anger over the appropriation of their "natural inheritance" by Shamir and the "old men". This was a large-scale, all-encompassing war whose outcome also determined the results of the smaller wars of inheritance.

This was the first conference held after the Begin era. In accordance with the party's constitution, the event was attended by about two thousand branch representatives, who had been chosen in prior elections held at branches throughout the country. The two thousand conference members were supposed to choose from among themselves the thousand or so Central Committee members (the party's "parliament" and the body authorized to select MKs). The conference was also supposed to elect the chairman of the movement, the president of the conference, the chairman of the Central Committee, and the chairman of the secretariat (the party's "government").

Battles raged over party procedures and roles. While the previous battles had concerned the party leadership and were conducted within the relatively smaller and more familiar body (the Central Committee), this all-out war (at least in its early stages) involved thousands of party members, including new members who had no connection with or loyalty to the Revisionist legacy. The preliminary elections that were held in the hundreds of branches launched the war a few months in advance of the conference. At each branch there was competition over control of the branch and the identity of its representatives at the conference: would they be veterans who had maintained the branch for four decades, or new, hungry forces seeking the trappings of power?

The 1986 conference was also a formative event in the life story of the heirs. For the first time it was they who led the veterans' camp, owing to Shamir's confidence in them and their experience in election campaigns. The heirs adopted an approach that was original, sophisticated, and aggressive on the legal, organizational, and media levels. Their surprising tactics attested to political experience and cunning, and made the veterans exceedingly proud. Unquestionably, without them Shamir and Arens would have stood no chance at all against the unleashed fury of their many adversaries.

Preliminary elections – a clear advantage to Levy

As noted, the conflict started at the stage of the preliminary elections at the branches. The charismatic Levy fired up the masses, aided by the well-oiled mechanism of the Operations Department of the party and his government ministry. With the motivation aroused by Levy's rousing appearances, his camp managed to recruit thousands of activists, who gained control of most of the branches.

Sharon made a comeback after his "exile". In the wake of his unexpected achievement in the contest against Shamir, he was given a suitably attractive portfolio: the Ministry of Commerce and Industry, with its hefty budget, which Sharon held for six years (1984–1990). During this time he built up and expanded his base of supporters, well aware that the road to the top began at the level of the branches.

Levy and Sharon geared up for the conference as though they expected a fight to the death. They even joined forces, following their two previous failures, in a manner recalling "the collaboration between gunslingers in a Hollywood Western", as political commentator Nahum Barnea wrote at the time in the now-defunct *Koteret Rashit* weekly news magazine. "First they get together to eliminate the other characters in the plot, and then turn on each other for the decisive duel."

Levy and Sharon viewed the conference as an historical opportunity to put an end to the veteran-youngster hegemony, to uproot Shamir's support base, and to take control of all the party institutions. They took care to coordinate their moves throughout the primaries at the branches and during the conference. Despite the tense relations between the personnel of the respective camps, their common denominator prevailed over all differences between them.

Jerusalem branch – the surprising victory of the veterans-youngsters camp

The preliminary elections held in anticipation of the 1986 conference witnessed inter-generational conflicts in branches all over the country. On one side were the Sharon and Levy camps, with the movers and shakers who operated on their behalf, while the other side featured a core of veterans, bolstered by hundreds of white-haired comrades who set aside all their other occupations in order to save their movement. Alongside them were cells of second-generation activists, aided by newly recruited "sons and daughters of", who likewise feared for the fate of the party.

The largest branch in the country – Jerusalem – was considered Levy's "bunker". The veterans were set to lose their hold in the capital altogether. MK Yehoshua Matza, from Levy's camp, was the uncontested king of the branch. He presided over a veritable army of hundreds of minions of Levy and Sharon who received wages, budgets, offices, cars, and phones. The economic backing for all this came from the Ministry of Housing, the Jerusalem municipality, and the Likud Operations Department. This giant branch, with its two hundred representatives at the conference, guaranteed a victory for the Levy-Sharon camp.

The Levy camp, which controlled the Jerusalem branch, retained a symbolic representation of veterans (largely thanks to the fact that Matza, the branch chairman, had joined Lehi as a boy and felt a moral obligation towards his "older siblings" from the underground movements). The remaining veterans in this branch were isolated, devoid of resources, and elderly. They were headed by Meir Heller, the eternal branch secretary, who never budged from his tiny office despite the flurry of the young party hacks representing Levy's camp. Heller sat in his office – thin, quiet, alone – appearing harmless enough. He sat night and day poring over lists of names of underground fighters and their families who had passed through the Jerusalem branch over the course of fifty years. To the masses of activists he looked like a living monument to a bygone generation. They had no inkling of the depth and strength of willpower of the veteran underground fighters.

Quietly but determinedly, the Irgun and Lehi former fighters consolidated themselves. A review of the veterans' list takes us back to fifty years earlier, with the founding of the Menora soccer team (later to be called Beitar Jerusalem). On the field the soccer players got on with their game, while on the sidelines they trained with their Irgun weapons. In the 1930s the team included Chaim Corfu, Gershon Abramowitz, Dov Milman, and Asher Benziman ("Avshalom", who became the first Irgun casualty of the Revolt). The team was dismantled by the British and its members were imprisoned and expelled to Eritrea. There, in exile, the fighters founded the Beitar Eritrea group. It was in Eritrea that Gershon Abramowitz received notice of the death of his brother, Aharon, an Irgun fighter, in the King David Hotel. He later named his son after his brother (and Aharon Jr. went on to become director general of the Ministry of Justice).

Fifty years after playing soccer and fighting together in the underground, these Beitar and Irgun veterans mobilized for a political campaign. They had the organizational and political backing of their Irgun veteran friend, Chaim Corfu, who was now Minister of Transport.

The veterans enjoyed a high level of support from the youngsters. The younger group was headed by Reuven Rivlin, who was head of the Beitar Jerusalem soccer team and widely popular among Jerusalemites. Within a few weeks Rivlin had managed to bring on board his good friends and fellow members of the fighting family's second generation. One of them was Yaffa Nakar, whose uncle, Meir Nakar, had been the last Jewish prisoner hanged by the British, on the eve of the UN vote on the Partition Plan (despite his having served for four years in the

British army during the Second World War). Another was the legendary Beitar Jerusalem star, Danny Neuman, whose parents had fought in the Irgun. All in all, they were a fresh, clean, idealistic, and goal-driven group, committed to ridding the Jerusalem branch of aggressive power-brokers.

At the last moment, Tzahi Hanegbi, who was serving at the time as an aide to Foreign Minister Shamir, surprised everyone by establishing a third, even younger, group within the Jerusalem branch. Within a short time he had mobilized his friends from his university student cell days – the same idealistic youngsters who had barricaded themselves atop the monument in Yamit – who now joined the veteran/youngster camp in the elections, against the Levy camp.

The results of the elections in Jerusalem sent shockwaves through the city and the party alike. Against all odds, the naïve but hardworking volunteers on behalf of the veterans and youngsters had defeated the strongest power-broker machine in the country. This successful contest elevated two new heirs to the Knesset and later to the government: Reuven Rivlin and Tzahi Hanegbi.

All of a sudden, the nationwide struggle looked less hopeless.

The youngsters protect Shamir against a hostile majority

From the outset, both camps at the conference were highly agitated. A thick cloud of animosity and suspicion pervaded the hall. Scuffles broke out at the entrance, with insults, accusations, and aggressive elbowing. Hundreds of new members affiliated with the Levy-Sharon opposition arrived, full of real hatred for the "old men" who needed to "go home". These new arrivals had no idea that the people standing next to them were underground heroes; fighters who had lost their brethren and comrades in the quest to establish a state. They looked like ordinary old-timers who had lost their youthful zest and whose time had come to move aside and let others take up the reins.

They were mistaken about these "old men", who had been fighting military and political battles for forty years. They had defended Begin for decades from waves of rebellion. These old men had arrived first at the conference, hours before the opening, laying claim to the front seats in the hall. They were ready to fight, even physically.

Hours before the conference began, the battles were in full swing, as though the participants were not members of the very same movement, but were rather two enemy camps. There were fights over the seats closest to the stage – the seats considered to have special influence on the mood of the conference. Veterans in their seventies scuffled with younger, stronger activists who tried to force them out of their places and push them to the back of the hall. Bentzion Yehudai, Chaim Tasa, and Chaim Gelzer fought for their seats the way they had fought the Haganah soldiers almost half a century earlier.

During the conference the Shamir-Arens-youngsters camp held consultations in a room at the back of the main hall. At the center of these huddled discussions were the young MKs Milo, Olmert, Meridor, and Landau. Surrounding them were Tzahi Hanegbi, Yossi Ahimeir, Reuven Rivlin, and another thirty or so members of the fighting family's second generation, me included. The outer circle was made up mainly of white-haired veterans. Once, they had been the soldiers on the battlefield – in the hall, with their families. To this day I remember how one of the veterans called to his son, "Zeev, come here," and ten or more "Zeev"s turned their heads. It was a camp of Zeevs and Yairs.

Katzav is chosen as chairman of the presidency – the youngsters' first maneuver

The veterans and youngsters were terrified that their last battle was approaching. The conventional wisdom held that the Shamir-Arens camp would be defeated by the Levy-Sharon offensive, which jointly enjoyed a majority of about fifty-five percent.

The navigation of the conference was critical, and so the youngsters implemented their first maneuver. In order to break the majority of the opposing camp, they selected as their candidate for this role an unfamiliar face – Moshe Katzav. Katzav, the development town trailblazer, was already a minister with his own support base, but he also appealed to the youngsters from the periphery who had come with the intention of supporting Sharon and Levy. The result was a narrow but critical majority of fifty-two percent for the veterans-youngsters-Katzav camp. Now Katzav – and, by extension, the Shamir-Arens camp – was at the helm of this riotous conference.

The real blowup between the two camps came on the second day. It erupted over an unimportant function that most of the conference participants had never heard of and knew nothing about: chairman of the mandates committee. In the past, this committee had made adjustments to the results of the preliminary elections in the branches, adding an additional ten percent made up of important members who had lost the contests or had not stood as candidates.

Sharon (in coordination with Levy) announced his candidacy for this symbolic function, and it was immediately clear that he would choose the ten percent from the opposition, thereby seizing control of the Central Committee, which was already split fifty-five percent in favor of Levy-Sharon and forty-five percent for Shamir. Levy and Sharon anticipated dividing the spoils and creating a clear majority at the conference, as a step towards the certain overthrow of the veteran hegemony.

Sharon's brilliant tactic took the Shamir-Arens camp by surprise. The youngsters were well aware that no-one among them had the stature needed to stand up to Sharon. In the back room we scrambled for a candidate who could draw votes from the other camp and thereby build a majority – as Katzav had done the previous day. Shamir and Arens stood down, since it was clear that no-one from the hostile camp would vote for either of them. The young MKs were likewise out of the question as candidates, since they stood no chance at beating Sharon. They simply did not have the same popularity among the public. Gloom settled the heirs and their supporters, gathered in the back room.

Benny Begin is summoned to compete against Sharon

The surprise card that was drawn at the last minute was a familiar and beloved Herut heir: Benny Begin. Unlike the other early heirs, Begin was (by choice) not an MK. He preferred to remain behind the scenes, helping his father – and now also his friends. The love for this modest heir transcended groups and factions. In this crisis, he became the doomsday weapon in the hands of the Shamir-Arens camp.

The desperate initiative of the youngsters – placing Begin Jr. at the forefront of the political stage – emerged out of the realization that only a name with mythical power like "Begin" could match Sharon and prevent the loss of control in the party. The difficulty lay in persuading Begin, who, until this point, had avoided any political contest, and in fact was not even present at the conference. His good friends, Dan Meridor and Rachel Kremerman, took on the task, knowing that there was no alternative. They believed that Begin's genuine concern that the party might fall into Sharon's hands would convince him to join the fight. The underground veterans joined the solicitation, which took place in the hours following Sharon's announcement. They wheedled Begin and begged him not to abandon his father's party. Benny Begin refused at first, citing his abhorrence of politics. Then he stopped and deliberated, turning the question over and over in his mind and weighing up the consequences. Ultimately, he agreed. His friends guessed that he had acquiesced to the request not out of concern that the legacy of Jabotinsky and of his father would be lost, but rather out of bitterness towards Sharon, who, four years previously, had led his father into a war that would haunt and torment him in his old age.

The rumor ("Begin is back!") spread like wildfire and immediately lifted the spirits of most of the conference participants, and especially the veteran-youngster camp. The mere thought that the name "Begin" would be part of the proceedings again was enough. Begin Jr. symbolized the ideological power of the Likud throughout all strata of the movement.

When it came time for the two contestants to address the conference, the air was electric. Silence fell over the hall and the three distinct groups comprising the audience. Close to the stage sat hundreds of veterans aged sixty-plus; at the back, their children, in their thirties and forties, stood tensely or rushed to and fro, with about a thousand opposition activists in their forties and fifties sitting or standing in the middle. The young, slender Begin and the older, hefty Sharon thrilled and electrified them all.

When Begin spoke, there was a powerful sense of excitement among the audience, as though they were experiencing something of the live spirit of their old leader now secluded in his home. After three years of waiting for "Begin's return", here he was, in the form of his son, with the same voice and the same familiar way of articulating his words.

Benny Begin chose to confront Sharon head-on. For the past four years the media had relayed anonymous accusations against Sharon; now this supreme heir finally removed the kid gloves and thrashed Sharon in classic and cynical Begin style. His speech warmed the hearts of the veteran and younger supporters, but failed to win over Levy's camp. They, too, had felt a ripple of emotion at Begin's return, but they wanted him to rejoin the movement out of love, in a positive spirit. They had expected him to embrace Sharon, to unify the ranks, not to arrive and immediately take sides, proceeding to batter a long-time Likudnik like Sharon.

Sharon, for his part, delivered one of his greatest speeches. He touched the hearts of hundreds of members, presenting himself as the underdog, as a commander who had gone to war in Lebanon in the name of the party and the state, and had ultimately been abandoned by those who sent him. In his speech he managed to turn the vote for the role of chairman of the mandates committee into a vote on his return to the top tier of the party. A vote against him was now perceived as an act of removing Sharon from the senior leadership of the Likud.

At two in the morning the votes were finally all counted. Sharon had won a handy victory, with 1,082 votes, in comparison with Begin's 850.

It was clear to the veterans that their worst fear had been realized: they had lost control. Their anguished faces, against the roars of "Arik, king of Israel!" gave eloquent expression to their mood.

Their sole consolation was that they had brought about the return of the ultimate heir, Benny Begin.

Gaston Malka breaks up the conference, saving Shamir and the heirs

Next came the voting for the chairman of the permanent committee – yet another low-profile role which had served in the past for mediation and to choose one thousand representative Central Committee members from among the two thousand conference participants.

This time the vote became a battle over whose candidate would be elected and thereby control the Central Committee that chose the party's MKs. The opposition fielded Levy. The veterans' camp had intended for Arens to compete against him. In light of Sharon's victory over Benny Begin, it was now clear that this scenario was doomed.

Instead of moving directly to the vote, the Sharon-Levy activists became involved in an unrelated row which led a forty-four-year-old, mustached activist named Gaston Malka to charge onto the stage; he assaulted Milo, shouting challenges and throwing tables and chairs as he stormed in the direction of the Herut chairman, Prime Minister Shamir. Shamir's exclamation still rings in the ears of those who witnessed this chaos: "This movement is committing suicide!"

Gaston Malka broke up the Herut conference of 1986, saving the veterans' camp from an ignominious defeat. His aggression significantly harmed the opposition camp, and his name became synonymous with political hooliganism. Of course, the youngsters made the most of this incident, and in their appearances in the media they described their adversaries as using thugs to shut down the conference. In fact, they owed Malka nothing but thanks for saving Shamir. The images broadcast on television showed the hefty, sweating Malka breaking chairs, storming onto the stage, and assaulting the veteran leader. His opponents were respected, older figures including Shamir and Arens, along with popular younger faces such as Sheetrit, Katzav, Milo, and Olmert. The public had little trouble judging the situation. The chairman of the conference presidency, Katzav, took the obvious step of announcing the conference adjourned.

With no more voting, Shamir remained chairman of the movement, and Katzav remained chairman of the presidency. Sharon's hasty and inexplicable resignation from the position of chairman of the mandates committee left the Levy-Sharon camp with no significant role in the conference and the party.

The Shamir-Arens camp remained in control of both the adjourned conference and the movement. The Levy-Sharon opposition, with its majority at the conference, ended up missing what had been a certain opportunity to take over. Not only did these two men leave the Exhibition Grounds with no official position and no authority, but their defeat was marred with the ugly stain of violent and inappropriate behavior.

Splitting of the opposition and victory to the veterans/youngsters

A whole year passed until, in March 1987, a second session was held as a continuation of the Herut convention. By now Shamir was already Prime Minister, under the terms of the rotation agreement, and as such his standing in the party was stronger. It was clear to Levy and Sharon that neither of them now stood any chance of replacing him as chairman of the movement. At the same time, the veterans and the heirs knew that it would be difficult to continue leading the party without allies. The situation demanded another maneuver: a splitting of the Levy-Sharon camp by means of an alliance with one or the other leader.

Dan Meridor and Benny Begin did everything in their power to gain Levy as their ally, hating the prospect of joining forces with Sharon. But Levy doubled down on his insistence that he was the sole legitimate heir, and that Shamir was occupying his seat. There was therefore no choice but to turn to Sharon, who was disappointed with the results of his alliance with Levy and jumped at the chance to gain a foothold in the leadership of the movement.

The results of the voting this time showed a decisive, two-thirds victory for the Shamir-Sharon-youngsters camp. Shamir remained chairman of Herut, Levy scraped enough votes to earn the empty title of acting chairman, and Sharon was voted by a wide margin as chairman of the Central Committee – a position with no real power, but an insurance policy of sorts concerning his status. Arens likewise received a wide majority of the votes for chairman of the Likud secretariat, a position which effectively manages the life of the movement. This affable professor, having learned the lessons of the past, immediately set about clearing the Levy activists out of Herut headquarters and especially the Operations Department, which controlled the party branches throughout the country.

At the Herut conference of 1986–1987 the offensive against the veterans ground to a halt. While the veterans' starting position had seemed hopeless, they emerged from the conference with two Beitar graduates at the movement's helm, for the first time since Begin's departure. This was also the point where the young stars of the movement – the second-generation representatives of the fighting family and the transit camp immigrants – showed their mettle and bolstered their own standing among the leadership of the veterans' faction and the party as a whole.

This was the last major recruitment conference attended by many of the veterans. The younger members of the Lehi and Irgun veteran group, born in the 1920s, who had spent their adult years in their various occupations, had now reached retirement age and stepped up, ready to spend the last decades of their lives providing rock-solid support to their heirs in the party.

14 The heirs are propelled into the government

In the six years following Begin's resignation (1984–1990), Israel entered its first period of political equilibrium between Left and Right. Neither side was able to prevail over the other, and the Likud and Labor were forced to share power. Shamir and Peres took turns holding the title of Prime Minister, with Rabin as their agreed Minister of Defense, and with Arens and Modai also holding senior portfolios. This functional unity did not conceal the differences of opinion, but it did facilitate solutions to major economic and defense crises: the unity government implemented an economic program that stabilized the skyrocketing inflation and the gargantuan stock exchange crisis; it brought an end to the Lebanon War and dealt with the first Palestinian Intifada.

The years of the unity government were a period of relative "peace" with Labor but ongoing struggle within the Likud headquarters, at every level: there was hostility among the administrative departments occupying the various floors of the building, among branches (until Arens took over), among the different generations, and among the leaders. These were years of complete chaos, of burning hatred and hostility.

Shamir and the veterans, now aged seventy-plus, depended increasingly on the second generation of the fighting family and of the transit camps. As the internal struggles continued, Shamir's reliance on his younger subordinates grew. Ultimately it was now they who took charge of maintaining his control of the party. Alongside the heirs there were also the "new" veterans, in their sixties and seventies, who reappeared for the first time since the Revolt against the British. They were just as fierce and determined as they had been then, and now, with all their life experience and their working years behind them, they were able and willing to devote themselves to the movement, its ideals, and its younger generation. This most unusual white-haired corps conducted itself with the energy and dedication of soldiers in their twenties. Their aim now was to ensure that the present and future heirs would reach the pinnacle of the movement and the reins of government.

New stars of the 1988 internal elections – Netanyahu and Begin

The internal elections for the Herut list for the twelfth Knesset (1988) produced a most surprising outcome: the winners of the first round were not the familiar top-brass (Arens, Sharon, Levy) but rather two new contenders, who received unprecedented support: Benjamin Netanyahu and Benny Begin.

At this time the Herut internal elections consisted of two stages. In the first stage (known as the "panel"), the Central Committee members chose the candidates for the Knesset, without arranging them in order of preference. It was usually the most popular names who featured in this round – those who were not controversial and aroused no opposition – rather than those identified with specific groups or camps. The second stage (the rounds of "sevens") was held a week later, and it was then that the candidates selected by the panel were arranged in lists. Against the backdrop of warring camps and internal struggles, this system worked very well for the more "connected" candidates with "backing", who were able to improve their placing on the list by striking deals. It was a complicated system, later to be rejected, owing to events that we shall describe later. The important point is that in 1988 (and even more so in the internal elections of 1992), the second round showed itself to be a defective election system that invited scheming and intrigue.

The surprising surge of support for the newcomers in the first round of voting brought with it a new sense of hope. The generally unsupportive press presented the election of these two heirs as big news. Their names and their faces were all over the newspapers, the television, and the radio. The seventy-three-year-old Shamir, who had endured criticism from within the party as an obsolete and inactive leader, was buoyed by their victory, which bolstered his standing vis-à-vis Levy and Sharon from within, and Peres and the Labor from without.

Netanyahu's victory in the 1988 primaries was without precedent not only in the history of Likud/Herut, but indeed in the history of Israel. At the age of thirty-nine, having just completed a stellar four-year term as Israel's ambassador to the UN, he ran an effective and innovative American-style campaign that swept up the Central Committee members and awarded him the first place in the panel. The media carried the news with huge headlines that conveyed a combination of surprise and admiration. All the news broadcasts reported on this most promising youngster in Israeli politics.

Netanyahu captured the heart and support of the Central Committee by virtue of his charisma, his fresh and new presence, and the techniques he learned from the American elections. He raised donations which allowed him to run a campaign far more sophisticated than the standard in Israel. In front of cameras and microphones he enjoyed a significant advantage over his competitors. Everything about his campaign was calculated, planned, and organized. He was accompanied by a full-time spokesman, and he conducted surveys to assess his situation within the Central Committee and on the street – both privileges which until this time had been reserved for heads of parties and Prime Ministers. Unlike many other Israeli politicians, who would improvise their messages at the podium, he planned every speech thoroughly. He prepared for every meeting with every branch head as though it were an encounter with a head of state: he obtained detailed information about the individual, studied it well, and lavished attention during the meeting, asking about the activist's interests, his family, and so on. He promised that branch head's support would make him a partner in Netanyahu's success (an American-style promise that was in many cases understood literally, engendering high hopes and causing Netanyahu endless problems later on).

While his competitors were forced to hold their meetings in the rather Spartan branch offices, Netanyahu's donation-funded budget allowed him better conditions in a Tel Aviv hotel. His meetings were expertly managed by a team of professional aides including Yaakov Ekst (whose wife was the daughter of an Irgun veteran), Zeev Levanon (son of an Irgun veteran), and Avigdor Lieberman (a quiet new immigrant studying at Hebrew University).

Netanyahu introduced the strategy of penetrating branches in a way that bypassed all the local tensions and hostilities. While the other candidates would visit the warring branches, Netanyahu held regional gatherings in neutral venues, inviting all the members of the rival groups and thereby casting himself as a host who unified all the Likud factions around him.

Netanyahu received enormous support from the veterans, with whom he had maintained contact throughout his diplomatic service. Every time he visited Israel he would participate in a Friday meeting of the Tagar Circle veterans. His speeches stirred their emotions. He did not speak in the "Israeli right-wing" style of the other youngsters, nor in the style of Begin and Shamir. Netanyahu spoke like Jabotinsky, and the veterans identified deeply with his political worldview, which drew from the wellsprings of Revisionism. The son of Jabotinsky's secretary offered a coherent and articulate translation of the Revisionist vision into the language of the new era.

Although he was not the son of an Irgun commander, and although his father had belonged to the old political wing and did not share the experiences of the fighting family, the veterans accepted Netanyahu as a natural heir, and the Tagar Circle embraced him warmly as the choicest of the heirs. The patronage of Moshe Arens, who had "discovered" Netanyahu and advanced him through the diplomatic corps, signaled to the veterans that this was the up-and-coming leader: not only Shamir's future successor, but a pureblood Beitarist and follower of Jabotinsky.

The Tagar Circle was an important force behind Netanyahu. Its members would accompany him to the various veterans' events, escorting him from table to table and introducing him personally to each underground veteran, who would then become a loyal ally. While Eli Sheetrit led the veterans' camp in the struggle to maintain the Shamir-Arens leadership, cultivating the younger generation along the way, for Avraham Appel it was the youngsters themselves – and especially Netanyahu – who were his life's project. For more than twenty years Appel devoted all his energies to this cause, and eventually had the satisfaction of twice seeing Netanyahu elected as Prime Minister. When Appel died in 2010, Netanyahu delivered a moving address at his funeral, speaking of him as a mentor and guide.

On the surface, Netanyahu's victory seemed like an effortless and almost instantaneous achievement. In truth, however, he had had planned it over a long period. Every important Likud activist who visited New York during Netanyahu's term at the UN heard from his friends that a meeting could be arranged for him with "Israel's prominent ambassador to the UN". The activists were excited to be photographed in the ambassador's office, to bask in the presence of someone whom the world media presented as a political meteor, and to listen to the theories of this world expert on terror. Only after his dazzling victory in the internal elections did it emerge, in discussions among the young activists, that each of them who visited Netanyahu's office in Manhattan had not been the only one; the ambassador had acquiesced to the requests of quite a number of sons and daughters of the fighting family who visited New York. They were all mesmerized by this figure who stood before them and spoke about values and ideology rather than deals and interests.

I was there, too, in 1987. As an advisor in the Prime Minister's Office, I met Netanyahu for the first time in New York. I shared with him a political deliberation which was occupying me, and his answer demonstrated his unique approach. Getting up from his seat, he pointed to the map of Israel that was hanging behind him. "We have only one country," he said. "You have to think about what is best for the country." In an instant, he elevated my thinking to the level of the national good. That was not the way his opponents spoke. His manner of persuasion was unique and most impressive.

Netanyahu's new style of campaign raised eyebrows, and issues great and small gave rise to all sorts of comments. For instance, Netanyahu drove around the country with an election team of aides and spokesmen. Another subject of conversation was the collection of ironed blue shirts that he kept ready in his car at all times, so as to ensure that he conveyed a crisp and businesslike impression at every meeting and in every television appearance that might take place during the day. He looked fresh and tidy, morning, noon, and night, a striking contrast to the rumpled image that most Israelis associated with politicians. In the eyes of his opponents and their journalist friends, the ironed shirt was a symbol of "American shallowness".

Nevertheless, Netanyahu's put-together campaign, and especially his huge victory in the primaries, gave rise to competition among the other heirs. This was an altogether natural development, but until Netanyahu's dazzling success, the question of who would advance faster had remained covert. Now, the early heirs – Milo, Olmert, and Meridor – were unhappy. They had been activists in the party, in Israel, and in the Knesset for twenty years or more and were not pleased to have someone "from the outside" overtake their progress. And so Shamir and Arens began to receive suggestions that Netanyahu be advanced in a different sphere; perhaps in the Jewish Agency, which was well suited to a man of the wide world. (A few years later, Netanyahu got his turn to advance two of these rivals to a different sphere – the municipal realm.) In contrast, the newer faces in the Knesset who had not yet achieved senior political status (Hanegbi and Livnat) were drawn to the new star. They saw in him the party's future, and their own.

The second surprise in the first stage of the 1988 primaries was Benny Begin's election to second place on the panel. The process of drawing Begin Jr. into political life – which had started two years previously, when he had competed against Sharon at the Likud conference fiasco – was now complete. Dr. Benny Begin, a geologist by training, left behind his beloved research and dived into politics, seeking to influence the movement and the country.

His modest campaign was completely different from that of Netanyahu. Begin roamed the country with Ruti, his assistant, secretary, and chief-of-staff. He took buses to faraway branches, entered them quietly, wearing his ordinary sandals, and talked about his beliefs and views. Unlike Netanyahu, he had no need to exert himself to receive support. The Central Committee members knew him well. His family name was a code that unlocked hearts. It was for this reason that his candidacy for Knesset, during his father's final years, was so meaningful to everyone in the Likud, especially the veterans. They cried real tears as they heard the familiar voice, with the same diction; the same cynical barbs aimed at the leftists who were ever ready to make concessions. Likewise, he had no need to work hard in order to receive public exposure and spread his name, as his competitors did. The national stature of the son of the beloved past leader gave him instant access to any media at any time.

The second stage of 1988 – and the fourth round in the battle of inheritance

The second stage of the Likud internal elections was held on July 6, 1988, a week after the panel. The Sharon and Levy camps were disappointed with the results of the first round: their candidates had been placed fifth and sixth, respectively.

Levy was furious. In the first round he had been pushed out of the top positions by Arens and the youngsters. When he saw the results of the panel, he stormed out of the voting area, calling out his unforgettable challenge, "See you in the rounds!" He joined up (once again) with Sharon in a secret deal that would allow them (with their combined fifty-six percent of the vote) to arrange the list to their liking.

On the morning of the second stage of voting, Shamir, Arens, and their young colleagues were astounded to discover the deal that now threatened their seats in the Knesset, since at this stage the voting was for individual names, not blocs. All the candidates were now dispersed throughout the crowd, carrying on their personal campaigns, and more than half the attendees were approaching the booths with their choices already marked on the voting slips. Hundreds of public servants from the government ministries under the control of Sharon and Levy carried out what looked like a military operation in comparison with the dozens of other individual competing candidates. This was a sure recipe for a Sharon-Levy victory. A political Pearl Harbor seemed to be looming.

When Arens, chairman of the Likud secretariat, learned of the deal between Levy and Sharon, he took charge and spearheaded a rescue operation. Minutes before the voting began, together with Shamir he drew up a list of the seven most preferred candidates. At the very last minute, hastily procured megaphones blared a call to their supporters to halt their voting and to come and get voting slips. This was a complete break with the rules of the game: Sharon and Levy had come to their agreement in secret, but this was an open announcement that as of now the voting was organized in blocs. This was an unprecedented directive to promote a fixed list, with no room for personal discretion. Perhaps the voters would object to the move. However, it was clear that allowing the voting to continue without organized lists would destroy any chances for the Shamir-Arens camp candidates, since a bad outcome in the first round of sevens would create a domino effect that would affect the rounds that followed.

To everyone's amazement, hundreds of veterans came to the six-sided tent and, with their quiet and accustomed discipline, took their slips. There was no need for lengthy explanations. They understood everything. Every word carried a world of meaning for them: "Levy", "Sharon", "deal", "take control", "list". They voted the same way that they had mobilized during the Revolt. They came back to take voting slips for the second round, with no questions asked. And for the third.

Thanks to the advance planning of the Levy-Sharon camp, the first round of sevens did bring them a partial achievement. Levy was awarded first place uncontested, with the prior agreement of Arens, who relinquished the right to compete in order to lower the level of tension and avoid infuriating Levy on the eve of the general elections for the Knesset. Sharon was placed second, and David Magen (from Sharon's camp) was sixth – a total of three out of the first seven places. As for the Shamir-Arens camp, Arens was in third place, along with three candidates who enjoyed support that crossed factional boundaries: Moshe Katzav (fourth place), Benjamin Netanyahu (fifth place), and Benny Begin (seventh).

The fact that Levy and Sharon headed the Knesset list raised hopes among their camp but also led to a certain passivity. The ensuing rounds of voting indicated that their initial exhilaration had been premature. From the opposite perspective, the results of the first round of sevens aroused great anxiety among the veteran/youngster camp, and this once again galvanized the fighting family into action. All eight hundred supporters of the Shamir-Arens camp presented themselves for the second round of sevens, all holding exactly the same list, and they all voted precisely as indicated. The result was a resounding victory, in the wake of which the candidates of the Levy-Sharon camp began to betray one another. The deal fell apart, and by the third and fourth round the Shamir-Arens camp was firmly in the lead.

A second major initiative to take control of the movement had been averted, largely thanks to the iron discipline of the underground veterans. Levy and Sharon were placed high on the list, but most of their candidates were rejected. Their camps accused each other of back-stabbing. While Levy managed to get eight of his candidates included on the list – representing a third of the faction – Sharon was left with almost no MKs; they were either voted out or, in desperation, joined the dominant camp.

Once again the Shamir-Arens-Katzav-youngsters had escaped an existential threat, by a hair's breadth. Eight hundred disciplined voters beat the more than one thousand supporters of the opposing camps. Once again, the few had prevailed over the many.

The biggest winner of the primaries of 1988 was the group of youngsters. These elections represented a generational revolution, with no less than sixteen youngsters – two-thirds of the Herut faction – placed on the Likud list. Ten of these were heirs: the five already serving as MKs (Milo, Olmert, Meridor, Landau, and Gadot) were now joined by Netanyahu, Benny Begin, Rivlin, Hanegbi, and – towards the end of the Knesset term- Livnat. The youngsters, together with the senior veterans (Shamir, Arens, Corfu, and Shilansky) now represented an absolute majority of the faction. The twelfth Knesset featured fourteen members of the fighting family, spread over two generations.

Despite the relief that came with their victory, the veterans/youngsters camp was well aware that it had defeated the majority of the movement by the skin of its teeth. This led the heirs to implement a fifth maneuver in their attempt to maintain hegemony, this time in the auspicious guise of an historical merger: unification of the Central Committees of Herut and the Liberal Party to form a single joint Central Committee that would make decisions and choose the party's MKs and ministers.

Within the framework of this initiative, in August 1988, three months before the general elections, the eight hundred or so members of the Shamir-Arens camp in the Likud were joined by another approximately one thousand members of the Liberal faction. Now, with eighteen hundred Central Committee members, the veterans and youngsters were able to form a majority of about sixty percent and to undo the Levy-Sharon coalition. Shamir, Arens, and the youngsters were convinced that the city-dwelling, moderate Liberals would join them, rather than the more extremist-right-wing/periphery opposition. They were confident that Liberal ministers Modai, Nissim, and Pat would naturally join them. But this turned out to be wishful thinking.

1988: the heirs join the government

It was largely thanks to the young and impressive list of new political stars that the Likud won the general elections for the twelfth Knesset (1988). As usual in Israel, it was a close victory – forty mandates to the Likud and thirty-nine to Labor – but the equilibrium between the two blocks was broken, with the Right and the ultra-Orthodox together holding sixty-five mandates. Nevertheless, Shamir chose to put together another unity government. Faced with the prospect of dependence on others, whether external (the ultra-Orthodox and the parties to the right of Likud) or internal (Sharon and Levy, who expected senior positions in his government), he preferred national unity and an alliance with his Minister of Defense, Rabin. Their shared understandings were intended to block the political threats from the direction of Peres, on one side, and Levy and Sharon, on the other.

Immediately following the election victory, the chairman of the Likud secretariat, Arens, convened the (now united) Likud Central Committee at the Tel Aviv basketball stadium so Shamir could announce the list of Likud ministers in his government. The choice of venue reflected past experience: it would be easier to maintain order in a closed, walled-in structure in which the seats were bolted to the floor. As expected, tensions ran high. Levy and Sharon feared that their standing would take a blow owing to the rivalry with Shamir and demanded that the selection of ministers be left in the hands of the Central Committee – or at least that the Central Committee be authorized to approve Shamir's list. Shamir refused, insisting that he, and he alone, would determine the list.

When the list was presented, thousands of Central Committee members were dumbstruck. After the predictable names – Moshe Arens, Ariel Sharon, and David Levy of Herut; Yitzhak Modai, Moshe Nissim, and Gideon Pat of the Liberals – there followed five consecutive newcomers. Shamir pulled off a generational revolution that astounded the party and the country. Three heirs were designated as ministers: Meridor, Milo, and Olmert. Netanyahu was to be a deputy minister. The youthful revolution was rounded off by Katzav and David Magen, the latter now taking his final step away from the Sharon camp to join his young colleagues in the central camp.

The astonishment only grew when the allocation of portfolios was announced: Shamir ousted the middle generation from the top government positions and restricted the power of the senior ministers from the three preceding governments. Levy remained stuck with the title of Deputy Prime Minister and remained in the Ministry of Housing and Construction (for a total of eleven consecutive years). Sharon, too, remained where he was, in the Ministry of Commerce and Industry. He was not reinstated in the Ministry of Defense, from which he had been removed and to which he aspired to return. The Liberal representatives, Nissim and Modai, each of whom had served as Minister of Finance, were now appointed to lesser positions.

Moshe Arens was given the most senior Likud position – Foreign Minister – thus effectively being declared Shamir's future successor. Meridor was promoted to the important office of Minister of Justice. Milo and Olmert received their first government portfolios, and Netanyahu was made Deputy Foreign Minister. For Speaker of the Knesset, Shamir chose the Beitarist Holocaust survivor and Irgun veteran Dov Shilansky. All in all, the fighting family, over two generations, now had seven representatives in senior governmental posts.

In the wake of the 1988 elections and the government that was formed, the intergenerational alliance between the veterans and the youngsters was reinforced by a third dependable arm in the form of the development town mayors. This was the sixth maneuver by the youngsters, and it served to shift these periphery leaders from the Levy-Sharon camp to the Shamir-Arens camp, thereby changing the balance of power in the Central Committee. Thus, the popular and powerful MK David Magen, who had become disillusioned with the Sharon camp, was invited to join the government. Similarly, Arens appointed MK Ovadia Eli, mayor of Afula and Levy's most prominent ally in the north of the country, as Deputy Minister of Defense. MK and mayor of the northern town of Migdal Ha-Emek, Shaul Amur, who still fumed over the betrayal of the Sharon camp in the rounds of sevens, also moved over to the Shamir-Arens camp. They were joined by two more disappointed figures from Sharon's camp: Israel Katz and MK Gideon Gadot. Thus, Shamir's camp now boasted fourteen young, prominent MKs and ministers who were well connected among Likud activists, in the large cities, and in the development towns. The base that Shamir and Arens could rely on consisted not only of the old faithful from the underground days but also a gallery of promising, impressive young stars.

However, the rumblings of those whose progress had been thwarted was growing louder. The leapfrogging of the youngsters enraged the middle generation of Levy, Sharon, and now also Modai. Their response was not long in coming.

15 The fourth world war
Constraints

Sharon and Levy, who viewed themselves as better suited than the youngsters to lead the Likud, were frustrated and angry over the results of their struggles throughout the 1980s. Although they enjoyed a larger base of support among the party's Central Committee than Shamir, Arens, and the veterans did, their status around the cabinet table was dwarfed. They watched helplessly as Arens, who became Foreign Minister in 1988, was built up as Shamir's future successor, with all the younger MKs behind him.

Their frustration grew with the promotion of the heirs to center stage. Levy and Sharon watched on television as Milo, Meridor, Olmert, and Netanyahu were interviewed as loyal representatives of the Prime Minister and displayed their proficiency and involvement in state affairs conducted behind closed doors. In the meantime, Sharon and Levy were stranded in their offices, while Liberal Party MKs Modai and Nissim had been left out of the government. Unsurprisingly, they joined forces against the party leadership.

The Levy-Sharon-Modai alliance chose as their strategy an ideological attack from the right, in view of the fact that over the course of fifty years of Jabotinsky-Begin leadership, all ideological initiatives launched from the left or center had failed. The three men saw their chance when Prime Minister Shamir was forced to compromise and show flexibility towards his Labor partners and the Bush administration. US Foreign Secretary James Baker approached Israel as a protectorate of the US that could be coerced into negotiating with the PLO, which was still designated as a terror organization. He insisted that Israel give up what he viewed as its unrealistic vision of the Greater Land of Israel. After Shamir's return from a meeting with the heads of the US administration in Washington, in mid-1989, the government approved what became known as the "Shamir-Rabin plan", centering around reinforcement of the peace treaty with Egypt and the launching of a political initiative for an agreement with the Arab states.

The internal opposition sensed the opportunity to launch an assault on Shamir and the heirs. Although the Shamir-Rabin plan did not include any actual concessions, and although Shamir had managed to come to an understanding with the hostile US administration without committing to any withdrawal, the aim of the Levy-Sharon-Modai alliance was to attack Shamir from the right, as a point of departure for a political attack on the Likud Central Committee.

The rebels demanded that various constraints be put in place for the Shamir-Rabin plan at the Central Committee elections. In this way, they hoped to cause Labor to pull out of the national unity government, thereby freeing up the ministries of Defense and Finance.

It was at this point that Sharon's seemingly symbolic role as chairman of the Likud Central Committee came into play. Sharon, wily as ever, used his authority as chairman to convene the Central Committee, in July 1989, and to pass a resolution concerning the constraints. To avoid a confrontation, Shamir accepted the constraints, but from the perspective of the public he appeared to be submitting to the triumvirate which was conducting itself as a government within the government and dictating the national agenda.[1]

Shamir looked feeble next to the charismatic Sharon, who berated him for his "weakness" towards Baker and his concessions to the PLO, even though in reality Shamir was more firm and stubborn in his right-wing views than was Sharon. Shamir's close circle urged him to fire Sharon so as to distance him and isolate him, thereby breaking up the threesome and demonstrating to the impatient American administration Israel's commitment to political moderation. But Shamir feared that dismissing Sharon would lead to a chain reaction on the part of Levy and Modai, and the government would fall apart. He chose to hold back and continue enduring the poisonous attacks denouncing his spineless policy and personality.

Battle of the microphones

The next major confrontation between the two camps erupted on February 12, 1990, at the Likud Central Committee convention at the Tel Aviv Exhibition Grounds. The convention, which later came to be known as the "night of the microphones", was focused once again on the Shamir-Rabin political initiative. Each of the sides was as determined as ever to prevail. Leading up to the convention, Arens and the heirs made it clear that this time there would be no capitulation; they would take the fight all the way to the end.

The convention opened with an announcement by Sharon that took everyone by surprise: "I hereby submit my resignation. I have decided to resign from the government."[2] He went on to deliver a speech that castigated Shamir:

> Mr. Prime Minister, under your government Palestinian terror is raging. [. . .] The policy of your government has left Jewish lives to their fate. [. . .] Your political plan puts Israel on the road to a Palestinian state.

What the convention participants (and television cameras) went on to witness was one of the most absurd scenes in the history of Israeli politics. Shamir, who lacked both Sharon's sense of drama and Begin's charismatic rhetoric, requested a vote of confidence on the part of the Central Committee: "The public needs to know who represents the Likud: Myself, or my detractors. [. . .] Do they accept my proposal, the chairman's proposal?"

And Shamir raised his hand, indicating his vote in favor of the plan.

This spontaneous vote did not surprise Sharon or his aide, Uri Shani. They were both ready to take control and manage the convention. Shani took out a pair of pliers that he had brought along in his pocket, and disconnected Shamir's microphone, allowing Sharon to announce a vote of his own on the constraints. Both leaders stood on the stage, facing the crowd and seeking its support. Prime Minister Shamir was saying something and waving his arms angrily, but no-one could hear a word; it was like watching a pantomime. Sharon, the burly sixty-two-year-old general, could be heard loud and clear shouting into his microphone. The Central Committee members raised their hands hesitantly, trying to vote, but unsure of whom or what they were voting for. It was the sort of humiliating spectacle that Levy and Sharon set up every so often for the seventy-five-year-old, diminutive, quiet, modest, and uncharismatic Shamir, who kept finding himself in scenes that were quite foreign to his personality.

The Israeli public at large was shocked by this new nadir in Likud conduct. It was clear that the scenario that Olmert and the other heirs had set up for Shamir was altogether unsuited to the Likud chairman; he was not the type to engage in an almost-physical confrontation with the giant general who had an amplification system and ushers on his side. It seemed like a dead end, a battle in which both sides were losing.

However, when the dust settled, it turned out that once again the Shamir-Arens camp had emerged in the stronger position. In the absence of any clear vote, Shamir continued with his negotiations and his plan, while Sharon, who had submitted his resignation, was now out of the government and could no longer direct his wheeler-dealers in the Ministry of Commerce and Industry. The schemers were portrayed in a negative light in the media, which supported the more moderate political view (that of Shamir-Arens), which was more in line with the media bias. The heirs were quick to point out to the public the danger that Sharon and his extremist views posed to the country. All of a sudden, Shamir and Arens were emerging in the press as prudent, centrist leaders. Their rivals were depicted as violent, antidemocratic elements who lacked the most minimal standards of respect. The image of Sharon perspiring and shouting on stage made a lasting impression on the public consciousness, preventing any chance of his election as leader of the Likud for years to come. Following the "night of the microphones" his status went into a decade of decline.

But in Israel, unlike other countries, leaders do not retire. The weakened, defeated Sharon, who had to all appearances come to the end of his political career, waited quietly and bided his time. He knew, as always, that his opportunity would come.

The "dirty trick" breaks apart national unity

Luckily for Sharon, Levy, and Modai, Shamir had an enemy greater than them: Shimon Peres. The political episode that has become known as the "dirty trick" was an attempt on the part of Peres, acting Prime Minister under Shamir, to oust his partner in the unity government and establish a narrow government based on a coalition between the Left and the ultra-Orthodox, dedicated to making peace with the Arabs.

Peres was frustrated by the fact that owing to a tiny margin in the 1988 elections, he had to accept Shamir as Prime Minister. It irked him especially that harmonious relations prevailed between Shamir and Peres's rival in the Labor party, Minister of Defense Yitzhak Rabin. Immediately following the election defeat, Peres embarked on building an alliance with the ultra-Orthodox, who were upset that Shamir had chosen to establish a national unity government with Labor, rather than sufficing with a narrow right-wing government, in which the ultra-Orthodox parties would have wielded considerable power.

At the same time, US Foreign Secretary James Baker was trying, in coordination with Peres, to advance the Baker peace initiative. Shamir opposed the initiative, viewing it as overly accommodating from the Israeli perspective and biased in favor of the Palestinians. Peres deliberately demanded a vote on the plan, knowing Shamir's position, with the intention of bringing down the government in which he himself sat. By the date of the fateful vote he had already come to an agreement with the ultra-Orthodox parties that they would vote with him and would join the government that he would form. Indeed, his plan worked; in March 1990, the Shamir government fell in a no-confidence vote.

On April 15, 1991, Peres was ready to present his new government in the Knesset when, at the very last minute, two MKs from the ultra-Orthodox Agudath Israel party deserted and Peres was publicly humiliated, finding himself unable to obtain the confidence of the Knesset. The "dirty trick" has gone down in Israel's political history as an undemocratic initiative.

Following this episode, which rocked the country, Shamir was awarded the right to form the next government, and in June his cabinet received a vote of confidence from the Knesset. Unlike the two previous governments that he had headed, which had both been unity governments in partnership with Labor, this was now a Likud government. With the departure of the Labor ministers, the Likud ministers advanced their positions. Even the middle generation representatives were promoted, since Shamir now needed every vote in his narrow coalition. Nevertheless, relations remained full of suspicion and resentment. In the hope of obtaining some peace and quiet, after seven years of upheaval, Shamir gave Levy the position he longed for: Foreign Minister. Modai, whom Shamir had pushed aside in the past, exploited the tight majority to demand the Finance portfolio. Sharon returned to the government and demanded the Ministry of Defense, seeking to clear himself of the stain of the Lebanon War, but had to suffice with a broadened Housing and Construction ministry. The Shamir-Arens camp was also in a stronger position: Arens was promoted to Minister of Defense, to Sharon's chagrin, and the heirs were placed in high-profile ministries: Milo became Minister of Internal Security, Olmert was appointed Minister of Health, Meridor remained in the Ministry of Justice, and Netanyahu continued as Deputy Foreign Minister.

After seven years of cooperation, Sharon and Levy were disappointed with each other. Their alliance had failed over and over again, and their public image had taken a beating, each being perceived as power-hungry and focused on narrow interests. They had few loyalists left, and the relations between them were marred by anger, envy, and mutual lack of appreciation. The schism soon turned into a bitter conflict.

The "night of the microphones" was the last joint initiative between Levy and Sharon. From this point onwards each acted alone. The underground veterans/ youngsters camp no longer faced an imposing, unified opposition but rather two separate and weakened factions.

Notes

1 Maariv, October 2, 1989.
2 Maariv, February 13, 1990.

16 From factional wars to
loss of power

The Likud entered the 1990s in the best situation it had ever experienced. After thirteen years in power it appeared unbeatable. Despite all the fierce internal battles, it was a living, breathing, vibrant, and powerful party. For the first time, the Likud was alone in power, without cobbled-together partners and without the burden of unity with Labor. For the first time, the party leaders occupied all the senior positions in the government and the Knesset: Prime Minister, Minister of Defense, Foreign Minister, Finance Minister, Speaker of the Knesset. In addition, this core was backed up by a sizeable group of youngsters with good potential.

The Likud's eternal rival, the Labor party, led by Peres, was once again in the opposition. Peres's "dirty trick" had caused Rabin to lose the defense portfolio, and the already hostile relations between the two men deteriorated further. The Labor party entered the 1990s bruised, weak, and divided. Moreover, the Labor and its left-wing allies had lost their status as leaders of the peace process, now that Shamir and the Likud had acquiesced to the American initiative to convene an international peace conference. The purpose of the conference, which opened in October 1991, in Madrid, was to promote peace talks among Israel, the Palestinians, and the Arab states. During the conference, polls in Israel predicted forty-six mandates for Likud in the coming elections. Political commentators assumed that a Likud victory was a foregone conclusion.

The Madrid conference ultimately produced one single winner: Deputy Foreign Minister Benjamin Netanyahu. Neither Prime Minster Shamir, nor his Foreign Minister, nor any of the Arab leaders, gained any meaningful benefit, but Netanyahu managed to shine. Shamir had not made him a government minister, preferring three other heirs who had rated lower than him in the primaries. Nevertheless, two events propelled Netanyahu to national prominence. The first was the Gulf War, in early 1991. The Deputy Foreign Minister appeared on television screens throughout the world, representing Israel in a manner that aroused pride among the Israeli public. Many still hold in their memories an image of Netanyahu, in a CNN interview, wearing a gas mask and personifying the restraint of his small, beleaguered country in the face of Iraqi aggression. The other event, coming a few months later, was the Madrid Peace Conference. Netanyahu's performance there sealed his image as a major-league political figure, as Netanyahu became the first Israeli leader to appear before dozens of Arab journalists.

The feeling among the Likud was that the general elections were a mere formality. The party fielded several promising candidates as future Prime Ministers, including the development town stars Katzav and Sheetrit, and the heirs – Netanyahu, Begin Jr., Milo, Olmert, and Meridor. The polls continued to show encouraging results up to just a few months before the 1992 elections, predicting a landslide victory for the seventy-seven-year-old Shamir. But in Israel, elections are unpredictable. There are always surprises.

Madrid Conference – Levy is left out

Over the course of the year leading up to the elections, Sharon once again tried to outdo Shamir and Arens (graduates of Beitar, the Irgun, and Lehi) in proving his right-wing credentials. He attacked the two leaders for their weak and yielding posture vis-à-vis the European peace initiatives in which they were involved. He also deliberately contrived a crisis between Shamir and the American administration by generating an enormous wave of construction in the Jewish settlements in Judea and Samaria, under the Prime Minister's nose, in his capacity as Minister of Housing and Construction. This defiant move led to one of the bitterest confrontations between Israel and the US, with the threat that Israel's loan guarantees would be withheld. In view of the fact that the funds in question were earmarked for the absorption of hundreds of thousands of Russian immigrants, this threat represented a real and immediate risk to national economic survival.

Sharon released a string of provocative declarations that infuriated US Foreign Secretary Baker. He announced that three billion shekels would be allocated to the construction of thirteen thousand housing units in the settlements. His aide boasted that each time Baker visited the country, a new settlement was established. Sharon continued to attack Shamir for failing to stand up to international pressure. He criticized the decision to engage in a peace process while the Intifada continued to rage, and he berated the restraint shown by Shamir and his government during the First Gulf War. The US administration had such an aversion to Sharon that during his visit to the US in May 1991, Baker deviated from diplomatic protocol and challenged him – a visiting minister representing a foreign government. He accused him of building in the settlements with a view to sabotaging the peace process, and he threatened economic sanctions.

Sharon vocally opposed the Madrid Conference and demanded that the Prime Minister resign. In response, the heirs demanded that Sharon himself resign. Shamir, as usual, held his peace, preferring not to rock his narrow government as the tempest raged.

Then came a new crisis: Foreign Minister Levy was incensed at Shamir's decision to attend the Madrid Conference in person, even though it was meant to be held at the level of Foreign Ministers. He boycotted the event and was replaced by Netanyahu, who received worldwide attention. Now the humiliated Levy was also resentful towards his subordinate.

On the international level, the Madrid Conference produced no diplomatic breakthrough. Its only significant outcome was Israel's quasi-formal recognition of the PLO, insofar as the delegation that was officially defined as "Jordanian-Palestinian" included PLO representatives. On the local level, in contrast, the Madrid Conference prompted a political earthquake. The only ones who treated the Madrid discussions – and their continuation in Washington – seriously were the right-wing parties. The unrest in Shamir's narrow coalition reached its peak on January 16, 1992, with the walkout of two coalition partner parties, leading to the downfall of the government and the announcement of new elections to be held in June 1992. This signalled a new phenomenon of right-wing MKs bringing down Likud governments.

Rounds of sevens 1992 – Netanyahu weaves a Sharon-Shamir deal

The confrontation that split the Likud took place in January-February of 1992, in the internal elections leading up to the general elections for the thirteenth Knesset.

The first stage saw only a minor blowup: instead of focusing on the contest against Labor, the Likud was forced to spend weeks going through the motions of a predictable vote for the head of the party, and indeed Shamir won with forty-six percent of the vote, while Levy received thirty-one percent and Sharon twenty-two. Once again, the results showed that half of the party was opposed to its chairman.

The Shamir-Arens camp would again have to forge an alliance with one of its two rivals in order to draw up a list for the Knesset. Sharon, in his weakened political state, jumped at the opportunity to join up with the dominant camp. His combined cunning and weakness dictated that he relinquish any and all demands, just to be part of the top leadership. He was willing to ally himself with Arens – Shamir's intended successor, and holder of the defense portfolio that Sharon craved – a mere two years after having accused him of shirking military service. Arens opened the door to Sharon because the mutual resentment between himself and Levy was a chasm that could not be bridged. Within days, the Arens-Sharon axis was consolidated. Behind the scenes, this new united front had been facilitated by Netanyahu.

The results of the first stage of voting (the "panel"), on January 27, 1992, once again showed a convincing victory for the new Arens-Sharon alliance: Shamir, Katzav, Netanyahu, Begin Jr., Arens, and Sharon occupied the first six places, while Levy was pushed down to eighteenth place. This, for him, was an intolerable humiliation.

***

Levy arrived at the second round of the primaries (the "rounds of sevens"), in early February 1992, full of confidence that his camp could now upend the balance of power. Instead, his status was dealt yet another blow by the new, powerful front that was united against him.

These internal elections marked the appearance of a new axis: Arens-Netanyahu-Sharon. After a decade during which Shamir had run his camp with the help of Meridor-Milo-Olmert, the new axis seemed poised to lead the Likud in the era after Shamir. The Arens-Sharon deal had changed the balance of power at the party's top levels: David Levy had lost his "permanent" place on the list (number two), and was now in fourth place (after Shamir, Arens, and Sharon). The new axis also affected the composition of the list: Katzav, Netanyahu, Begin, and Milo occupied places five to eight, respectively. Six of the first eight places on the list belonged to the Shamir-Arens camp. Fix of the six were second-generation members of the fighting family. For the first time, the heirs were awarded an equal standing (politically and in terms of public image) to the top-tier leadership of the party. Levy's power within the Likud's faction in the Knesset went down to between two and four MKs. As throughout the preceding decade, Levy was hurt to the very depths of his being by the movement that failed to appreciate his contribution.

Unlike Levy, Sharon was a seasoned tactician who was able to recognize his own weakness and to use it to his advantage. After a decade of struggles that had got him nowhere, he recognized the ineffectiveness of his aggressive approach and switched it for a strategy of political flexibility. Sharon was realistic enough to understand that he could not defeat the alliance of Mizrahi youngsters and increasingly popular heirs, and so he chose to join them in order to preserve his standing. By this stage he even gave up cultivating a camp and advancing MKs of his "own", preferring to help the heirs who were closer to him (such as Landau, Livnat, and Hanegbi). This amity reached its climax when he walked arm in arm with his bitter adversary from the Lebanon War era, Dan Meridor, who was having trouble getting re-elected after his liberal term in the Justice Ministry – a situation which lasted for several years.

In the wake of the internal elections of 1992, the Likud list for Knesset was made up of four veterans (Shamir, Arens, Shilansky, and Matza) and nine heirs (Netanyahu, Begin Jr., Olmert, Milo, Landau, Meridor, Hanegbi, Livnat, and Ahimeir, who joined later on) – all in all, thirteen MKs spanning two generations, including five who were children of past MKs representing Herut.

Levy's "monkey speech" – nosedive in the periphery

Levy reacted to his resounding defeat in the elections by levelling a shocking accusation at his party. He delivered an unforgettable address, remembered to this day as the "monkey speech", in which he accused Shamir, Arens and the heirs of racism, no less, of discriminating against his camp on an ethnic basis: "Some Likudniks spoke about me as though I were a monkey that just came down from the trees. [. . .] They attacked me, claiming that I am pompous, a demagogue, that I don't care about the real problems".[1] His close circle explained his act of political suicide onstage as an expression of his frustration but also pointed to an alleged scornful reference to him by party veteran Avraham Appel, who was close to Arens, as the final straw.

Levy immediately announced his intention to resign from the government, retracting only after Shamir promised to give him the most senior position that

Likud had to offer in the next government. But his speech had already had its disastrous impact on the sector most loyal to the Likud – the Mizrahi population of the periphery. Only in the 1992 elections did the Likud come to understand how deeply Levy was adored by the Mizrahim, and the extent to which his sensitivity towards discrimination had seeped into the Likud centers where his influence held sway. It happened when Rabin, the Labor candidate for Prime Minister, succeeded for the first time in penetrating the Likud branches in the development towns. Shamir was driven away from these Likud strongholds by Labor activists – this time, with no resistance on the part of Likud supporters.

Levy's speech was a devastating knockout blow after a decade of political infighting: it effectively ended his own political career while tearing a deep rift within the party; it caused the Likud to lose the government, after fifteen years in power; it damaged the historical fraternal bond between Begin and the Mizrahi sector; and it paved the way for the Shas ethnic-religious movement's inroads into the periphery. (Levy could have led an ethnic Mizrahi protest movement himself, but throughout his career he had avoided running alone.)

Following this episode Levy had trouble remaining part of the party leadership. He would return twice more to the government (under Netanyahu in 1996 and under Barak and the Labor in 1999) by virtue of a reserved seat. After that he ran for Knesset as part of the Likud, but was placed low on the list. His consolation came later on, when his own two children became MKs, at which point his resistance to heirs disappeared.

"You're corrupt; we've had enough!" – the Likud defeats itself in the 1992 elections

In the months leading up to the elections a great wave of protest built up among many Israelis who were fed up with the prevailing political norms. Huge demonstrations were held under the slogan, "You're corrupt; we've had enough", demanding immediate changes to the system of governance, which was responsible for a long list of failures, including coalition extortion, corruption, and unbefitting political conduct, from the "dirty trick", via the "night of the microphones" and Levy's "monkey speech", which had brought about a schism with the Mizrahi sector, and culminating in a most severe report by the State Comptroller, accusing Sharon of squandering billions.

The only one who profited from all this uproar was the Labor leader, Rabin. He benefitted from every aspect of the situation: the split in the Likud, the badmouthing of the Likud by Levy, the State Comptroller's report, the demonstrations in the streets, the American sanctions applied by Foreign Secretary Baker, and the public rage towards terror attacks. Rabin himself was perceived as a contrast to this general fiasco: a leader who was upright, centrist, patriotic, and security-oriented.

On June 23, 1992, the Likud was voted out of government. For the first time since the Upheaval of 1977, the Labor party was back at the wheel, alone this time, after earning forty-four seats in Knesset (Likud received thirty-two).

The fall of the Likud played itself out like a bloody Greek tragedy in which each main character kills off another, until, by the end of the final scene, they all lie lifeless on the stage. Shamir and Arens had managed to strike at Levy in the Central Committee, which ended up causing Likud's defeat; Shamir had belittled Sharon, who ended up causing both Shamir and Arens to leave politics. All of them, ultimately, caused the downfall of the Likud, putting an end to the potential for continuous dominance for the long term.

The defeat in the 1992 elections brought about dramatic change within the party. The leadership had taken a beating: the founders' generation had reached the end of its historic journey, the middle generation was burnt out and weakened, and the heirs' generation was entering a challenging period.

Forty-three years of leadership by the party's founders, Begin and Shamir, had come to an end. As the election results were broadcast, on the night of the elections, Shamir announced his resignation as chairman of the Likud. He later resigned from the Knesset as well.

The middle generation seemed to have suffered a knockout. Modai moved to a different party, which soon disappeared; Nissim and Pat, from the Liberal Party, concluded their Knesset careers. Levy, now out of the party leadership, hung on to his Knesset seat for another fifteen years; Sharon kept a low profile, refraining from running for party chairman for the next decade, and avoiding any provocations, as befitting the suspected cause of the Likud's downfall. In other words, all five senior figures who, to all appearances, had been potential candidates for Prime Minister, either resigned or had become irrelevant.

The younger generation was left to fend for itself. The big question was whether the heirs would now have the fortitude to step into their parents' shoes, or whether Rabin's rise to power would signal their disappearance. Within a very short time it became clear that the heirs were full of motivation, energy, and faith in themselves. And they were happy to discover that despite the resignations of Shamir and Arens, the army of veterans gave not a moment's thought to the idea of giving up. They were already prepared and ready to lend the heirs their support.

Note

1   Yediot Aharonot, July 30, 2000.

Part III

From princes to kings

When the Likud party lost the elections in 1992, the long-time leader Itzhak Shamir resigned and the battle between the old and younger generation began. This automatically triggered "fighting" among the different factions within the party of the younger generation.

Benjamin Netanyahu, the rising star, after completing a very successful few years as the ambassador to the UN, surprisingly got the support from the party elders at Benny Begin's expense – Benny Begin, the son of the legendary leader Menachem Begin. Netanyahu won the leadership of the party (and would lead the party for most of the period from 1993 to 2018).

In 1996, when Netanyahu was elected Prime Minister at the expense of the respected socialist Shimon Peres, the Israeli public was completely taken by surprise, in light of left-wing leader Yitzhak Rabin's assassination just a year earlier. With the new situation as the ruling party, the struggle among the "Princes", that generation of the party elders' children, began. For the first time they were divided by the overwhelming dilemmas which they faced in the security, economy, and justice of Israel.

The division and these inner battles led to the fall of the first "Prince's government", in which six of these Princes served as ministers, and the Princes were now scattered among three different parties in the 1999 elections.

17 The battle over Shamir's inheritance

An historical turning point had arrived in the history of the Likud – and especially in the saga of the underground veterans: for the first time since the party's founding, its chairman was not one of them. However, a generation of heirs had grown up within the party, and they were well equipped to take over. The question now was what would become of this divided and defeated party: would the middle-generation leaders, Levy and Sharon, manage to regain their previous status, now that many within the party regarded them as aggressive politicians who had led to the trouncing in the elections? Or would the youngsters, the bearers of the Revisionist legacy, succeed in maintaining the fighting family hegemony?

The two generations of Revisionists faced a party that was battered and in shock. Thousands of activists and Central Committee members who had grown accustomed to power and control had all at once lost their footing. The power-brokers who had been proud to show off the MKs, ministers, and other dignitaries who showed up at every one of their family celebrations were unable to contain their dismay. The Levy and Sharon loyalists, who had railed against Shamir and the veterans, were appalled at the results of the infighting. Likud old-timers had seen the crash coming; they had warned of it, and now they were silent and sad. The elderly underground veterans went home with a sense of catastrophe, as though the legacy of Jabotinsky and Begin had come to an end. The party headquarters went into a new decline as the prospect of sitting in the opposition set in.

It was at this moment that Arens should seemingly have stepped up and taken control. He was the candidate supported by most of the veteran/youngster camp as well as most of the general public.

Arens, aged sixty-seven, a professor and an aeronautical engineer, was a dignified and upright public servant who had served as an MK (for twenty years), a successful ambassador to the US, and a well-respected Foreign Minister and Minister of Defense. He was capable of taking the lead; the veterans were solidly behind him, and he was the accepted, unquestioned candidate in the eyes of most of the young MKs and ministers, including all of the heirs. MKs such as David Magen and Ovadia Eli were very close to him. Even candidates who had indicated that they might run for party chairman in the future, such as Begin Jr., Netanyahu, and Katzav, were likely to support him. Netanyahu told Arens that he would be willing to serve as chairman of his election campaign. In view of such widespread support, neither Levy nor Sharon stood a chance. The two self-appointed successors had finally witnessed Shamir's departure, only to be accused of bringing down the Likud. They were now isolated politically, with their public image tarnished.

But Arens was a Knesset oddball: he was a non-political politician, a non-combative ideologue, a leader devoid of the obsession for power, a quiet and introverted man for whom principles always came before personal interests. Throughout his years in politics, he had not pushed himself to the forefront so much as he had been pushed by his peers. Arens surprised everyone by announcing that he was leaving not only the contest for chairmanship of the party, but also the Knesset and political life. He offered no explanations, no complaints, no accusations; he simply made his announcement and then disappeared, within days, from the political horizon. People surmised that he was sick of the internal struggling; that after a decade of chaos, mud-slinging, and violence he had had enough. He had entered politics not out of hunger for power but out of ideology. This became apparent when, despite his abrupt departure from the political stage, he continued his ideological involvement in the country's affairs for another twenty-six years. He continued to write, lecture, and exert his influence in the public sphere until his death in early 2019.

Begin Jr. and Netanyahu surge forward

New energy began to circulate in the party from an unexpected source: the unassuming MK Benny Begin. After just four years in the Knesset, this young MK announced right away, with no strategic calculation, that he intended to run for party chairman. Some party members assumed that he had been goaded on by the early heirs – Meridor, Olmert, and Milo – who viewed him as an effective obstacle to the rise of another, rather ambitious heir: Netanyahu.

And indeed, Begin Jr.'s move towards center-stage triggered Netanyahu's candidacy. Netanyahu had planned to run for Likud chairman only after Arens, his political patron and mentor, had finished his term. Now, he was forced to bring the plan forward, in order not to lag behind Begin.

Those who had wondered whether the heirs possessed the requisite leadership received a positive answer, in two parts. It was these two newer MKs who surged forward. Those who had served in the Knesset for longer did not dare: they did not feel ready or were not confident that they enjoyed enough support on the national level.

Five candidates prepared for the battle of succession. Along with the eternal David Levy there were four popular youngsters: the two heirs and two second-generation Mizrahi ministers. All in all, Benny Begin (MK), Netanyahu (Deputy Foreign Minister), Moshe Katzav (number one in the primaries), and Meir Sheetrit (former MK and Treasurer of the Jewish Agency) comprised a respectable, young, and diverse cadre of leaders.

For the first time, two heirs were competing for the top spot. The fifty-year-old Begin Jr. was familiar to all. He enjoyed special prestige not only by virtue of his dignified personality but also, of course, thanks to his father's mythological aura which still spoke to the hearts of the nation.

Begin Jr. ran an election campaign that reflected his personality and spirit: it involved no resources, no entourage, no demonstrations of power with roaring crowds. He made few appearances in the media, and therefore his message was not widely disseminated. Those who listened carefully heard how he distinguished himself with articulate precision from the other aspiring heir, Netanyahu. Begin's conduct embodied the old Likud: the humble, popular, ideological, Israeli movement. Netanyahu, to his view, symbolized the new Likud: media-oriented, gimmicky, shallow, wealthy, and "American".

Netanyahu, aged forty-nine, was also something of an outsider among the heirs. He had not developed politically alongside the others and had not climbed his way up the party hierarchy. Rather, he had acquired his experience in the diplomatic sphere, far from the goings-on in Israel. He had been involved in Israeli politics for a mere four years and had jumped straight to the top, over the heads of the early heirs. His modern, sleek, audacious campaign presented a leading candidate who made no reference to his competitors – especially not to Begin.

The ideological difference between the two was almost imperceptible. Only those who listened very carefully identified the different justifications provided for similar positions: Netanyahu offered political and security concerns, reflecting a Jabotinsky-inspired worldview that had also absorbed some of the influence of the conservatism of Thatcher and Reagan. Benny Begin, like his father, argued for the historical Jewish right to the Land of Israel.

The battle to succeed Shamir, in March 1993, split the heirs into two camps. Begin could count on the early heirs: Meridor expressed open support for his old friend, while Milo and Olmert supported him passively, realizing that Netanyahu was going to win anyway. Netanyahu's jump ahead had united them: all three felt that the "visitor" from America had come and grabbed the prize.

Netanyahu had the support of the newer MKs – Landau, Hanegbi, Livnat, and Ahimeir – who were all involved and active in his campaign. Hanegbi had been the first to hitch his star to Netanyahu, way back in 1987 when Netanyahu had been Israel's ambassador to the UN and had only just begun to think about running for Knesset, while Hanegbi was already an MK. Now, Hanegbi was the head of Netanyahu's campaign.

Reuven Rivlin was the only heir who had maintained his support for Levy since the primaries in 1992. Rivlin felt that he had been pushed out of the Shamir-Arens camp by Olmert, his Jerusalemite rival. At the time Levy had welcomed him, supported him, and promoted him to lead his faction after Reiser's death. Had Rivlin known then that Begin and Netanyahu – two heirs whose families he knew and respected – would be competing for the chairmanship of the party, he would probably have supported one of them, most likely Begin, his personal friend who shared his worldview. But for now he was committed to Levy.

The veterans were torn between Begin and Netanyahu. Both were well versed in and committed to the Revisionist path (Begin – in its original form, as he had learned it; Netanyahu – with some upgrades), and both were worthy successors.

The obvious choice of the veterans would seem to have been Begin. After all, he was an heir in the fullest and most literal sense of the word. To appreciate their love and admiration for Begin Jr., we have to go back to the gathering of the underground veterans that I attended with my father in the early 1970s. I was curious to see who was standing at the center of the crowd of dozens of veterans and discovered two young men: Benny Begin and Dan Meridor. Already then I could see how the veterans gazed at the heirs. Benny Begin spoke the same language that they did – "Beginese" – and they all but melted in a cloud of nostalgic pleasure and pride just hearing his voice. Through him, the veterans would be able to fulfil their dream: to duplicate Begin Sr., as it were, and coronate their old-new leader in place of Shamir.

Most of the veterans had known Netanyahu for only six or seven years. Unlike Benny Begin and his friends, Netanyahu had not attended veterans' gatherings during the fifties, sixties, and seventies. He had not distributed voting slips as a child, like Rivlin and Meridor, nor argued with his teachers at school, like Milo and Olmert, nor had he fought for the Student Union, like Livnat and Hanegbi. He had not spent most of the 1980s waging simultaneous battles against violent adversaries from within and a powerful enemy from without – as had Milo, Meridor, Olmert, Boim, Landau, and Rivlin. He had been living far away, in a reality that seemed to the others altogether bright and pleasant.

Nevertheless, the family lineage of Netanyahu, as the son of Jabotinsky's personal secretary and as the bereaved brother of an Israeli hero, earned him the veterans' goodwill. Moreover, they were enchanted by the new spirit that he brought with him to the movement, and they were proud of him and his appearances in the media. The same year that the Americans fell under the spell of forty-six-year old Bill Clinton and elected him as their President, the underground veterans were captivated by Netanyahu, whose charisma was taking Israel by storm.

This decision by the veterans was influenced by the over-arching objective which had already become something of an *idée fixe*: preventing David Levy from taking control of the movement. The veterans perceived Levy as the main threat to their hegemony. From their point of view, the choice could not be between two heirs; it had to be between their heir and Levy, and in this contest Netanyahu enjoyed two clear advantages over Begin.

The first was Levy's poisonous attacks on Netanyahu and Netanyahu alone. These attacks annoyed the veteran, and as they deliberated which of the two heirs to support, every speech in which Levy criticized Netanyahu inclined them further in his favor. The second advantage was that the veterans understood that with Netanyahu, they stood a better chance at beating Levy. Every vote that went to Benny Begin would come at the expense of Netanyahu's chances and might lead to a second round of voting. And in a second round, who could guarantee that the candidates who lost would not give their support to Levy, allowing him to take control of the movement? Who could be sure that if Levy beat Netanyahu, he would not set about (once again) ridding the party headquarters of veterans?

And so halting the "invaders" took precedence over the natural, "genealogical" choice. Replicating the fighting family hegemony was more important than nostalgia and emotion. Once again, the veterans placed continuity as their first priority, over and above ideology.

And so it was that while the veterans retained their love, respect, and admiration for Benny Begin, their vote went to Netanyahu.

***

When the internal elections came around, Netanyahu was ready for the fight – psychologically, financially, and organizationally. The rest of the Likud top-brass, which had become accustomed to and complacent in the cabinet, watched in open-mouthed wonder.

Netanyahu launched his election campaign in November 1992, with a dramatic and revolutionary move. He managed to lead the party to replace the old election system with primaries, thereby shifting the power to choose the Likud chairman and MKs from the Central Committee to the tens of thousands of party members. Instead of the Knesset list being drawn up within a closed framework that invited shady deal-making, it would be opened to the masses.

In a courageous move, Netanyahu stood before the Central Committee members and asked them to give up the essence of their power: the choice of the party's leader and MKs. He won the vote against his opponents, headed by Central Committee Chairman Sharon. It was a surprising victory, and it heralded Netanyahu's rising power.

When Netanyahu approached the podium to present his position, Sharon appeared tired, irritated, and detached from the proceedings. The familiar chant, "Arik, king of Israel" was drowned out by a growing drumbeat call: "Bi-bi! Bi-bi!" It pained Sharon to see his long-time supporters singing songs of praise to the younger leader. He felt the full weight of his political decline and his failure to shake off the label of having "brought down the Likud". He tried to propose putting off the decision about primaries until 1996, citing budgetary problems. Faced with a Central Committee longing for a new leader, he offered an old-fashioned bureaucratic solution: nominating an organizational secretary-general to rehabilitate the party. He then proceeded to offer himself as a candidate for the position. But the Central Committee was familiar with Sharon's maneuvering and was deaf to his efforts to extricate himself from his dismal situation. They were eager for the Likud, for the first time in its history, to hold primaries.

In the Central Committee vote on the question of primaries, Sharon won just seventeen percent of the vote, while eighty percent voted in favour of Netanyahu's proposal. It turned out that the shock of defeat in the general elections and the loss of power was sufficient to persuade the Central Committee members to give up their power in a body that had become synonymous with vested interests and aggression.

Primaries 1993 – Netanyahu's rousing campaign

Israel had never seen an "American" election campaign like the one Netanyahu embarked on for the Likud chairmanship. Hundreds of blue stalls popped up in city centers, all bearing a picture of the candidate along with the slogan, "Netanyahu – go for winning leadership". Hundreds of volunteers manned the stalls, and dozens of coordinators circulated among them, arriving at the campaign center every evening with hundreds of newly filled Likud membership forms.

David Levy put up a surprisingly good fight, signing up dozens of new members who expressed their admiration for him along with frustration over the perceived discrimination against him as the representative of the Mizrahi neighborhoods and the periphery. The high-profile battle was waged in the media, too, with Levy attacking Netanyahu and trying unsuccessfully to draw him into a confrontation. It all came to a head on the day Netanyahu received a blackmail telephone call. The anonymous caller threatened to publicize a "steamy video" showing Netanyahu's involvement in an extra-marital affair. Netanyahu responded by calling a press conference, acknowledging the affair, and pointing an accusing finger at the "bunch of criminals" surrounding Levy. The episode cemented the elections as a contest between just two candidates – a contest brimming with accusations and slander that left both sides with scars that would not heal. Twenty-five years later, Levy's daughter, MK Orly Levy, told an interviewer of the trauma she carries with her from the accusations against her father. She never forgave Netanyahu, and neither did her father. In fact, Netanyahu and Levy's relations deteriorated even further, since Levy refused to accept Netanyahu's leadership, while Netanyahu, a devotee of the American system, believed in the "winner takes all" principle. He had learned from Shamir's period in office not to try to placate the losers in the race with positions that would only whet their appetite for more.

Netanyahu's campaign roused the entire country and contributed significantly to the unprecedented achievement in the Likud census leading up to the primaries: the party boasted 216,000 members. Netanyahu was responsible for some seventy thousand new members, who were his sworn followers in the years to come. Most of his supporters in the party branches were junior or new activists. Every branch was suddenly being inundated with hundreds or even thousands of new members, who campaigned to have themselves elected as branch heads or leaders of major factions in the branches, and as representatives of their cities at the Likud conference. This popular trend changed the face of the Likud and awarded Netanyahu the type of standing that until then had been enjoyed only by Shamir, Sharon, and Levy. The entire enormous operation was overseen by the unknown Avigdor Lieberman, who quickly became the Likud strongman and the all-powerful general director of the Likud headquarters.

Levy, Begin, and Katzav never stood a chance. Netanyahu conquered the Likud in a blitz whose impact lasted for decades. From this point onwards there was a Netanyahu camp – new, loyal, ready, and committed to Netanyahu over and above the Likud.

Victory of the veterans' successor – Netanyahu the heir

The first primaries ever held in the Likud ended with Netanyahu ensconced as the new party chairman, following an illustrious line of legendary leaders including Jabotinsky, the founder of Revisionism, and the Irgun and Lehi leaders Begin and Shamir.

His landslide victory with fifty-two percent of the vote (Levy received twenty-six percent, Begin Jr. received fifteen, and Katzav received seven) reflected the support of some eighty thousand party members. No candidate for any party in Israel had ever received a similar number of votes. Many were enthusiastic young people who saw in Netanyahu the hope of more a professional and photogenic style of politics, far removed from the typical image of the '80s.

The excitement over Netanyahu's success drew attention away from the significant achievements of the other candidates, reflecting their stature among the public. Levy received about forty thousand votes – a number that would have assured him victory in any other party at any time in Israel's history. Even Begin, who ran a drab, low-key campaign, received the support of some twenty-five thousand voters.

Netanyahu's staff wasted no time. Within hours they had taken over the twelfth floor of the party headquarters. Netanyahu did what his predecessors had not dared to do: he set up his office in Begin's old room. He exercised his full authority over the movement, and his right-hand man, Lieberman, took care to ensure that his adversaries had no foothold at headquarters. In this respect, it seemed, Netanyahu had learned and implemented the lessons Shamir had endured.

A few weeks after his victory, on May 17, 1993 (the anniversary of the 1977 Upheaval) Netanyahu convened the new Likud Central Committee at the large Yad Eliyahu stadium, the site of high-profile basketball games and performances. With the help of Lieberman and Hanegbi he persuaded the Central Committee to award unprecedented powers to the party chairman – in other words, himself, and Levy boycotted the gathering in protest. Sharon, too, attacked the move, but with more caution. The message Netanyahu had gleaned from observing the efforts by Levy and Sharon to undermine Shamir's leadership was not to yield, not to appease, and not to placate, since rivals who want the number one seat cannot be placated. He therefore attacked Levy and Sharon in return, accusing them of bringing down the Likud by turning it into a "jungle".

Netanyahu's victory marked the completion of the generational revolution not only in the party leadership but in the national leadership, too. After the generation of the commanders in the War of Independence (Dayan, Rabin) had come to replace the founding generation of the Labor party, a similar process took place within the Likud. The difference was that the generation that replaced the founders of the Likud (Herut) had been born around the time of the establishment of the state and were much younger than their parallel Labor successors.

The generation of the Revolt had successfully replicated itself, in keeping with the model described by generational scholars such as Karl Mannheim, Lewis Feuer, and Gaetano Mosca. Their research indicates that the fundamental motivation of any ruling group is to continue its rule, either in person or through the agency of its successors.[1] And indeed, the Likud veterans celebrated Netanyahu's victory with a month of conventions and gatherings. For them, his victory was the victory of their generation. They had succeeded in warding off the invaders seeking to conquer their fortress. They had placed a purebred and promising heir at the head of their party: a "grandson" of Jabotinsky who was proud of his roots, who did not accede to the dictates of the Left and the elite, and who was not cowed by opponents from within the party.

Note

1 Mannheim, Karl, *The sociology of knowledge* (London: Routledge & Kegan Paul, 1952).

18 Together confronting the Oslo dream of peace

Opposition to the Oslo Accords was the only issue that succeeded in uniting the feuding camps within the Likud. For the first time since Begin's departure, three generations within the Likud stood side by side, united in their struggle.

The framework agreement that Prime Minister Rabin signed with PLO leader Yasser Arafat, on September 13, 1993, shook the Right – not only because of the extensive and painful concessions involving parts of the historical Land of Israel, but also owing to the very fact that secret negotiations had been held with an enemy such as Arafat, leader of a terror organization whose hands were stained with the blood of many innocent victims.

In fact, it was this arch-foe who led to the first and last joining of hands of three generations: Shamir and Arens, who came back to have their say; their bitter middle-generation rivals, Sharon and Levy; and all the heirs: Netanyahu, Olmert, Rivlin, Begin, Landau, Livnat, Hanegbi, and Ahimeir, as well as Meridor and even Livni, who was just starting out in politics.

The Likud leaders recalled the fierce resistance of Jabotinsky and Begin towards the restrained and compliant posture of the Labor Party under Ben-Gurion towards the British. They discovered within themselves the same Revisionist DNA of grim struggle in the opposition, which they carried into the streets in seething demonstrations and speeches denouncing the Left's capitulation. The veteran fighters and their heir, Netanyahu, compared Rabin's concessions to the most catastrophic surrender in modern history: Chamberlain's surrender in the Munich Agreement of 1938.

The generational change of leadership was put to the test at a critical moment, and the new guard turned out to be firm and strong. The heirs opposed the Oslo Accords from day one and issued sharply worded warnings that the move would lead to a terror state in the heart of the country. Some of them spoke out at demonstrations (Netanyahu, Hanegbi, Livnat, Landau); others sufficed with public statements, whether emphatic and forceful (Begin and Olmert), or more muted (Meridor).

Milo – the first to come out of the leftist closet

In the meantime, the two earliest heirs, Milo and Olmert, realizing that the party chairmanship would be closed to competition for the foreseeable future, each decided to run for mayor in one of Israel's two largest cities – Tel Aviv and Jerusalem, respectively. Netanyahu was only too happy to usher them out in whichever direction they wished to go, relieving him of their oppressive presence. He had no doubt that the moment he stumbled, these "brothers" would be the first to bring down the "newcomer" who had overtaken them.

Olmert and Milo ran against candidates who started out with a significant advantage over them in the polls. It took courage for Olmert to compete with the mythological Teddy Kollek of the Labor Party in Jerusalem and for Milo to run against the army general and war hero Avigdor Kahalani, also representing Labor, in Tel Aviv. Both Likud heirs won thanks to brilliant campaigns reflecting their considerable electoral experience. Once installed in the mayors' offices, with the attendant extensive municipal bureaucratic apparatus, huge budgets, and extensive media exposure, they bided their time until they could jump back into national politics and run for chairman of the Likud and Prime Minister.

The atmosphere and character of each city gradually came to influence its mayoral candidate. Olmert, who had started out as a right-wing hawk but with time and experience had become more establishment-oriented and moderate, was drawn back to his early tendencies, reflecting the Jerusalem public, which was largely comprised of religious, ultra-Orthodox, and right-wing sectors. Milo, who had also been identified with the more hardline figures in the Likud, adapted quickly to the secular, liberal, left-inclining energy of Tel Aviv.

The short distance (a few hundred meters) separating the Likud headquarters from the Tel Aviv municipality was enough to draw Milo away from his roots and to appeal (as expected of a mayoral candidate) to his target audience of voters as a leader in favor of territorial compromise, who opposed the settlements and wanted peace, even at the expense of extensive withdrawals.

Milo therefore realigned himself with the Left (at first, in coordination with Netanyahu, who understood the tactical need for an apolitical, liberal city council list). He launched his election campaign with declarations of his willingness to support territorial concessions, all of a sudden revealing that in 1992 he had proposed to Shamir a unilateral withdrawal from Gaza. He also adopted a combative stance vis-à-vis the ultra-Orthodox religious establishment.

The Likud veterans were convinced that all of this was nothing more than a tactic to win the city. They were certain that this son of Nahum Milikowsky, who had fought side by side with them for twenty-four years, would circle back. They watched in amazement as Milo, in his new position as mayor of Tel Aviv, displayed support for the Oslo Accords, flaunted his meetings with the arch-enemy Arafat and with Faisal al-Husseini, and even went so far as to sign a "twin cities" pact with Gaza – all this as terror attacks were perpetrated in his city.

Still, the veterans believed that this was just another tactical move concocted in Milo's creative and brilliant head in order to connect with his electorate. Only when Milo began criticizing Netanyahu, to the glee of the media, did they understand that this son was lost to them. Still, they never imagined that Milo's move signalled a broader shift that would occur among other heirs in the years to come, with the dream of the Greater Land of Israel coming to be replaced by the dream of peace.

Against the world – Netanyahu's struggle against the Oslo Accords

Netanyahu adopted a position of organized and fierce opposition to the agreement with the PLO, which, along with territorial concession, had included arming a Palestinian police force. Over the course of the struggle he joined up with the religious Right, running a giant campaign in the streets and in the media. Then came the explosions on buses and in restaurants in Israel's cities, proving his argument and shattering the illusion of peace. Netanyahu appeared at the mass demonstrations, whose most memorable slogans included "Don't give them guns".

The Likud leadership was united in its opposition to Oslo, although the approaches differed. Sharon was the most extreme and outspoken critic. He assailed his former friend Prime Minister Rabin, and Peres too. As Begin and Olmert, who were among the fiercest critics of the agreement in the media, would not participate in the Right's demonstrations. Meridor, too, was against the agreement, but adopted a far less strident tone, and he, too, kept far from the demonstrations. Most of the other heirs were with Netanyahu and the masses.

On April 6, 1994, eight Israelis were murdered in a suicide attack in the northern town of Afula. A week later, another suicide attack claimed another five Israeli lives in Hadera. While the IDF was pulling out of Jericho and Gaza, as required under the terms of the Oslo Accords, suicide terrorists were being dispatched to Jewish population centers in Israel. On January 22, 1995, twenty-one soldiers and a civilian were killed in the first double-suicide attack of its kind at the Beit Lid junction in central Israel. The country was in turmoil, shaken and incredulous at the duplicity of Arafat, who had reciprocated Israel's concessions with murder. Having shaken hands with Israel's leaders and gaining international praise and acclaim, he had no compunction about sending murderous terrorists to butcher innocent civilians. Spontaneous demonstrations big and small sprang up all over the country. Every Friday, demonstrators stood at junctions handing out stickers denouncing Rabin and Peres ("Prosecute the Oslo criminals!")

Netanyahu was criticized by the Left and the press for "exploiting the blood of the victims for political purposes". The Labor leaders who were responsible for the greatest lapse in the state's history, and the press that enthusiastically and unquestioningly supported their initiative, never acknowledged their miscalculation, nor did they apologize. On the contrary, they aimed their poisonous arrows at those who had warned of the danger of the agreement with a mass murderer. But the Israeli public was largely oblivious to the political argument; it was in profound shock over the collapse of the dream of peace a moment after the signing of the framework peace agreement by the trustworthy, patriotic Prime Minister and general, Rabin. The public began distancing itself from the agreement, support for Rabin fell, and polls from early 1994 showed Netanyahu to be in the lead.

The outcry reached a climax at a raucous demonstration held at Zion Square in Jerusalem on October 5, 1995, following a debate in the Knesset over Oslo II (the Interim Agreement on the West Bank and the Gaza Strip, also known as the Taba Agreement), which was meant to continue the original process, despite the terror attacks. Over the vehement opposition of the Right and broad swathes of the public, the agreement was approved in the Knesset with a slim majority of two votes. Two new MKs had been induced to desert the Right and join Rabin's coalition, in return for appointments as minister of National infrastructures, Energy and Water resources, and deputy minister of Construction. This move enraged the Right, whose stolen votes had facilitated this fateful and controversial agreement. To this day in Israel, the two MKs are regarded as mercenaries and deserters. (One of them was arrested in 2018 and sentenced to a jail term on charges of spying for Iran.)

There were a few lone voices in the Likud – the early heirs, Meridor, Olmert, and Begin – who, while completely opposed to the "peace process", were uncomfortable with the nature of the demonstrations and with the idea of cooperating with the radical Right. Hence, they stayed away from the giant demonstration at Zion Square.

Various speakers, including Ariel Sharon, delivered fiery, impassioned speeches accusing the country's leadership of betraying the people, and blaming them for the bloodshed that had resulted from the agreement. Netanyahu himself denounced the agreement but was one of the only speakers who did not launch a personal attack on his political rivals.

The speakers, who all stood on the balcony of the building overlooking Zion Square, were too far away to hear the shouts of the demonstrators and to see the signs some of them were holding. However, the journalists covering the event from among the crowd saw, heard, and broadcast the incitement: "Rabin is a murderer!" "Rabin is a traitor!" "With blood and fire we'll get Rabin out!"[1] When the demonstration ended, a few hundred participants marched to the Knesset, where they tried to break into the plaza, on the way smashing the cars of government ministers and members of the coalition.

The crew of Israel's state television station was among the crowd and caught an image that would shock the country and leave its impact for years to come: a demonstrator was holding a poster that showed a picture of Rabin wearing a Nazi SS uniform. For millions of Israelis sitting at home in front of their television screens, the implication was that this image characterized the demonstration – in other words, that the same poster was carried by a large number of demonstrators and reflected the mood at the event. The next day, media commentators claimed that Netanyahu was behind the poster. It took some time before the truth came out, too late: the sign had been produced using a desk-top printer. It was the size of a regular page, and none of the speakers standing on the balcony could possibly have seen it. Later, the Shamgar Commission, which was set up to investigate Rabin's assassination, determined that the poster had been the work of a Shin Bet operative named Avishai Raviv, who had infiltrated the Right in order to expose dangerous extremists. This agent had coordinated his provocation (not for the first time) with the television crew. Correspondent Eitan Oren and his team had waited for Raviv and his companions to arrive, so they could give coverage to this extremist poster and thereby cause a public outcry against the "extremist Right".

But by the time this all became known, the damage was done. The pundits' erroneous estimation as to Netanyahu's involvement had made its way into virtually every household in Israel, and the demonstration at Zion Square had become a symbol of incitement. Netanyahu was publicly branded as a dangerous fanatic. The focus shifted from the government's failure and the collapse of personal and national security to accusing Netanyahu of incitement. Later on, in an address to the Knesset, Netanyahu said:

> I issued an initial denouncement immediately upon hearing of this calumny during the demonstration itself. [. . .] It was a handful of thugs; I believe I know which outlawed movement they belong to. Of course, you can't smear an entire public on account of a band of delinquents.

Rabin's assassination – Netanyahu is anathematized

November 4, 1995 marked the blackest incident in the history of Israeli politics: the assassination of Prime Minister Rabin. This was a politically motivated murder of a sitting Prime Minister by a right-wing extremist; the murder of a democratically elected leader; a murder prompted by extreme and violent opposition to a leader's decisions.

Much has been said and written about Rabin's shocking assassination. It was a terrible moment in the life of the country and its people. A subject that has received less attention is the subsequent persecution of the right-wing camp, which, from that dreadful night, was held collectively responsible for the murder. Anyone who was associated with the Right, who wore a skullcap, or who lived in a settlement felt persecuted in the public sphere, marked as an accomplice to the crime. Those who, prior to the assassination, had voiced opposition to the Oslo Accords suddenly found themselves facing accusations by friends and slander by colleagues. Some were summoned for police questioning. The leaders of the Likud, and especially Netanyahu, were viewed as vicariously liable for Rabin's murder.

All at once, the heirs felt their world turning upside down. They found themselves slandered in the press and blamed for witnessing the violence around them at the demonstrations and remaining silent. For the party veterans, the sense of persecution brought back painful memories from an event forty-six years previously: the accusation by the Labor leaders of the murder of Chaim Arlozorov in 1935. The accusations against Netanyahu also brought back memories of the way Begin was accused of violent fascism following the demonstration that he led against the German Reparations Agreement in 1952. The heirs now experienced first-hand what their parents had described to them from the "Hunting Season" during the 1940s. Everything seemed to be sliding back to the dark days when their parents had been accused of a massacre at the Arab village of Deir Yassin and of attempting a coup with the *Altalena*. The next generation was now the target of similar vilification.

The persecution of the Right in the wake of Rabin's assassination gave some of the second-generation Revisionists the final push they needed to enter politics.

Tzipi Livni, a successful Tel Aviv lawyer and the daughter of Irgun veteran parents, embarked on her political career in 1995. She regarded the Oslo Accords as an historical mistake.

After Rabin's assassination, Livni felt that she and her friends on the Right were being incriminated; that a despicable and deranged murder was being pinned on a legitimate and democratic movement.

Less than a decade later, as a member of the centrist faction of the Likud and already on the way to leaving the movement, Livni appeared at a memorial ceremony for Rabin and courageously told the audience, numbering in the hundreds of thousands, of her oppressive feelings during the mourning period following his death. She recalled how an entire public had been denied the right to mourn and how this public had been made to feel responsible for an act which they rejected outright.

Netanyahu, for his part, was trapped. He was denounced in opinion pieces the likes of which had not been seen in Israel for fifty years. The picture of Rabin wearing the SS uniform was shown in conjunction with his name again and again, the implication being that he had been responsible for it. Television and radio broadcasts were devoted twenty-four hours a day to incitement against the Right, the Likud, and – most importantly – the political target: Netanyahu. Again and again Netanyahu was shown at a demonstration that had been held at Raanana junction, with a coffin behind him. The television presenters did not bother to mention that the inscription on the coffin read, "Rabin is killing Zionism"; the symbolic funeral held at the demonstration was meant to depict the death of Zionism and not of Rabin. But in the repressive atmosphere that prevailed in November-December 1995, no media correspondent felt the need to address such trifling details. Any word that Netanyahu uttered was seized by the press as an excuse to depict him as anti-democratic, a fascist, and a murderer of peace. However, since throughout his career (in contrast to other leaders of the Left and the Right) Netanyahu had made a point of avoiding direct personal attacks, no evidence could be produced supporting the claim that his "incitement" had led to the assassination. Many of his supporters felt that what the media was presenting was carefully edited fragments of footage with partial images, including the photomontage of Rabin in Nazi uniform and the symbolic coffin whose significance had been twisted and misrepresented. Nevertheless, Netanyahu's supporters and other opponents of Oslo held their tongues. It was shameful and frightening to dare whisper a word against this witch-hunt. Everyone was afraid, me included: as Chairman of the Likud Youth, Likud spokesman, a leader of demonstrations over three election campaigns, as well as Netanyahu's advisor, with frequent appearances on television, I was afraid to speak out, to be seen, to express my protest. I was afraid that my advertising agency would lose its clientele; that someone would yell "Murderer!" as I sat in a coffee shop or walked in the street. It was best to keep silent during those terrible days of pain and anger for the bereaved persecutors, and pain, injustice, and fear for the bereaved persecuted.

In the months leading up to the 1996 elections, the polls predicted a trouncing for the Likud. To be more precise, they predicted the most devastating defeat in decades. More than half of the respondents expressed support for Peres. Only about a fifth were behind Netanyahu – a gap of about thirty percent between the candidates. The public mood seemed to have reverted back to the days of persecution of the underground movements and Ben-Gurion's shunning of Begin.

With a view to isolating Netanyahu, who represented the "main culprit" and the real threat to Labor rule, the media took a more forgiving and benign approach to the other Likud leaders. Meridor, Begin, and Olmert were cleared of blame for the assassination by virtue of their absence from the infamous demonstration. Even Sharon, who had delivered the most personal and poisonous attacks on Rabin, was politically rehabilitated and was received at the Rabin home while the family sat "shiva" (the traditional seven-day mourning period). Netanyahu was left alone at the pinnacle of the pyramid of guilt. He was not invited to memorial ceremonies and was the target of vicious denunciation, even at official memorial events. Malchei Yisrael Square in Tel Aviv (renamed Rabin Square) was filled with tens of thousands of youth who held nightly vigils, weeping and singing mournful songs. It appeared that this entire generation, which came to be called the "candlelight kids", would never forgive or forget. The old days of isolation and lack of legitimacy in the opposition seemed to have returned. News broadcasts announced arrests of an unending stream of right-wing activists as suspects in the planning of Rabin's murder (which turned out to be the work of a sole assassin and his brother). The hundreds of thousands of protesters who had participated in demonstrations against Oslo felt that they were all on trial. The "Hunting Season" was on again.

For Netanyahu, this was an exceptionally difficult period. He believed with all his heart that he had not engaged in incitement and had been fair towards Rabin, out of the genuine respect that he had felt towards him as Chief-of-Staff during Netanyahu's period of army service. Nevertheless, he found himself facing a barrage of public abuse. For many it was a foregone conclusion that Netanyahu stood no chance in the elections, that his career was over, that he would remain a persona non grata, like his political forebears.

Only those who (like me) spent those dark days at his side in Begin's old office on the twelfth floor of the Likud headquarters – the headquarters that had endured so many defeats and failures, so many years of rejection and disparagement – can testify to the degree of Netanyahu's confidence in his innocence and determination to fight, despite standing almost completely alone against the onslaught of words and images. There was almost no-one who wanted any contact with him. The telephone sat idle, the office was empty, the silence was deafening. Outside, he knew he would encounter a throng of accusing journalists and a cloud of public opprobrium. He had no choice but to remain sequestered in his office: sitting, getting up, reading, listening, pacing to and fro, having his meals delivered to him, like a prisoner.

Netanyahu had no illusions as to his situation. He did not try to persuade himself that this wave would soon pass. He felt the political guillotine close to his neck and was well aware of what the polls were predicting. He also knew that it would not take long for his rivals within the party to take advantage of his weakness and try to elbow him out in favor of a candidate who would be better received among the public. Indeed, within a few weeks after Rabin's murder there were Likud voices calling for his replacement. This was very worrying; Netanyahu was not at all certain that he could withstand a putsch from within the party.

He suspected that the sources whispering in the ears of hostile political commentators were the early heirs. It seemed that they sought to exploit his vulnerability in order to repair the "historical mistake" of his election as party chairman instead of one of them. And so he devoted his time to persuading party members that he was the right candidate and that under his leadership Likud would arise again. The mission seemed impossible: those who were scheming against Netanyahu were ably assisted by a group of senior journalists whose connections with the early heirs had grown strong over many years of cooperation and friendship. As in the days of the popular, moderate leaders, Shmuel Tamir and Ezer Weizman, against Begin the "extremist", these opinion-leaders were eager to "convert" the Likud and replace its right-wing leader with a more moderate figure. A small group of heirs – Hanegbi, Landau, and Ahimeir – stood openly and courageously at Netanyahu's side, braving the hurricane.

A breath away from losing it all

It was a well-known businesswoman (and Likud activist) by the name of Galia Albin who kindled the fire that Netanyahu knew was coming. In December 1995, Albin announced a campaign in support of Dan Meridor as party chairman. The media jumped at the chance to back a different candidate against Netanyahu. All of Netanyahu's opponents among the middle generation and among the youngsters rubbed their hands in glee, waiting for the media to do their work for them. They expected that at some stage Netanyahu would have to do the obvious: take a step back and vacate his position. Within the party, pressure was growing to replace him with someone who had not been involved in any way with the demonstrations preceding Rabin's murder (such as Meridor); otherwise the Likud faced the possibility of utter annihilation.

But Netanyahu had no intention whatsoever of surrendering. From Likud headquarters he waged a battle for his name and his status as though his life depended on it. He knew only too well how fragile the situation was and how easily Albin's initiative could gain momentum and draw in thousands of activists. Despite his reservations, he tried to court another influential heir whose image in the public and in the media was squeaky clean: Benny Begin. Netanyahu offered him to serve as the head of his election campaign, hoping that this would help to dissolve the initiatives to replace him. But Begin refused. He understood that Netanyahu's aim was political in nature and was intended solely to shore up his deteriorating position. Moreover, Begin faced an ideological obstacle: he knew that Netanyahu would recognize the Oslo Accords, as an act of contractual continuity. He was not willing to head the election campaign of a candidate who would honor and continue Oslo. Presumably, Meridor, Milo, and Olmert also discouraged him from any move that would help their rival.

As always, it was the veterans who threw their chosen heir a lifeline. It was they who identified most profoundly with Netanyahu, having been persecuted, slandered, and isolated themselves in the past. They, too, had known the bitter taste of libels concocted by the Left. Their natural instinct was not dependent on some or other poll. Their immediate urge was to embrace a member of the fighting family who was being falsely and unfairly attacked and accused. The Irgun veterans all fell in line at Netanyahu's side, without the slightest hesitation. Avraham Appel and Eli Sheetrit literally moved into the Likud headquarters. They lavished love and support, never leaving his office and tending to his every need.

Sharon was one of three key figures who helped Netanyahu to extricate himself from his situation. As in other crisis situations, Sharon's resourcefulness dictated a strategy altogether different from what might have been expected. Perceiving a real and immediate threat to his political future if Netanyahu were to be replaced by Meridor – Sharon's enemy since the Lebanon War – he took the side of his young rival in order to ward off the putsch.

The second figure who saved Netanyahu was Meridor himself, who, owing to media pressure, was forced to take a clear stand either in favor of the head of his party or against him, as a candidate to replace him. The tension was immense. Netanyahu's staff was deeply concerned that Meridor's statement would create an unstoppable wave within the movement, especially in view of the media coverage that would accompany his run for the chairmanship. Following a nerve-wracking wait, Meridor announced his opposition to Albin's initiative and his support for Netanyahu.

With this, the idea of replacing Netanyahu soon died out. The failure of this initial and unorganized initiative had a neutralizing effect on the putsch. And thus, a few months before the elections, all the senior Likud MKs were united around their candidate for Prime Minister – whether out of genuine support or based on political interests.

The third and most surprising contributor to Netanyahu's recovery was Shimon Peres, who had been appointed Prime Minister following Rabin's assassination. Peres firmly rejected the pleas of his associates to exploit his advantage in the polls and the public hostility towards the Likud and to call an immediate election. Instead, Peres waited and put off the election until six months after the assassination. He wanted to win in his own right, not because of Rabin. He believed with full faith that his advantage was firm and decisive, that the Likud and Netanyahu were finished. He believed the polls, which predicted a victory with a very wide margin, and was confident that an electoral abyss separated Netanyahu from the Prime Minister's seat. (It is my personal belief that once Peres was finally in the Prime Minister's seat, he was not in a hurry to hold elections.)

During the six months until the elections, the Palestinians continued to carry out terror attacks that tore at the nation's heart. In fact, as the elections approached, they seemed to increase. On February 25, a suicide bomber boarded a number eighteen bus in the middle of Jerusalem and blew up twenty-six people. Jewish blood was flowing freely in the capital. A few hours later, while the country was still trying to cope with this horror, another civilian was murdered in the south of the country. A week later, Jerusalemites made a valiant attempt to celebrate the Purim holiday in traditional style, with children in fancy-dress and adults carrying baskets of foodstuffs to neighbors. To Arafat's terrorists this only made the target more attractive, and another suicide bomber blew up another number eighteen bus, this time killing twenty Israelis. Pools of blood stained children's costumes. Scraps of little girls' dresses lay mingled with scorched human limbs.

Israel was convulsed with grief. But before Israelis could digest the news, and while still watching the footage and photos of the many funerals, they were dealt yet another blow. In the heart of secular, fun-loving Tel Aviv, where Purim celebrations had been in full swing, a suicide bomber blew himself up at a road crossing next to the popular Dizengoff Center shopping mall, leaving thirteen dead. The Zionist ideal had called for Jews to return to their homeland in order to prevent the cold-blooded murder of Jewish children. The sight of bloodied, injured, and dead children and youth in the streets was more than the country could bear.

Israelis were seized by a kind of hysteria. The longed-for peace had turned into a nightmare. The public was desperate for quiet after the peace agreement that the reliable, experienced Rabin had approved. Mothers were afraid to let their children out of the house. Fathers thought twice before walking about with their families. Drivers tried to keep far away from buses on the road, fearing explosions. Anyone who entered a coffee shop or restaurant could be a potential suicide bomber. Any suspicious passer-by was a reason to panic. Many Israelis asked themselves what possible strategy could be adopted to deal with terrorists who were willing to kill themselves in the name of blind, bottomless hatred.

Blood politics

On the afternoon of March 4, 1996, I was on my way to the King David Hotel in Jerusalem for a consultation meeting with Netanyahu. I was his election campaign advisor at the time – a position that entailed a degree of risk in relation to my other clients and a fair measure of personal unpleasantness in my social relationships. The social pressure that I was subject to was unbearable. Every word I said and every photograph that showed me anywhere near Netanyahu aroused criticism among my closest friends – not to mention the reactions of others. On that afternoon, however, what concerned me was not what other people thought of me, but rather a news item that I had heard on my way to Jerusalem. The newsreader reported the terror attack on busy Dizengoff Street in Tel Aviv, near Dizengoff Center. The thought of the timing of the attack (the Purim holiday) and the victims (children who were out celebrating) was heartbreaking. I was also anxious as to the welfare of my wife, Tali, and our young sons, Uri and Matan. I called Tali on the clumsy cellphone that was the height of technological progress at the time, but the entire mobile communications system had crashed. As soon as I entered the hotel lobby I tried calling from a public phone, once again – with no success.

Overwhelmed with this national pain and personal panic, I went up to Netanyahu's room, where I found someone else sitting with him: an older, quiet American man. I did not know him, and no introductions were made. He was wearing white socks, with no shoes. The man looked like a friendly Jewish tourist who had suddenly found himself in the midst of chaos in Israel. Netanyahu was speaking to him in English. I paid little attention; I was still shocked by the news of the attack and concerned about my family, and so the stockinged guest did not interest me. It was only a few days later that I asked about the man, and was told that he was Arthur Finkelstein – the renowned consultant who brought American-style brief, repetitive election broadcasts to Israel. This development would have dramatic impact on Netanyahu's election messaging later on.

During my meeting, I witnessed an astounding telephone conversation. Ariel Sharon called, asking to speak with the party chairman. Netanyahu tensed and gestured to me to remain silent. I understood that this was to be a critical exchange. Of course, I only heard half of it – the lesser half, at that, since Sharon did most of the talking. As the conversation progressed, a look of amazement spread over Netanyahu's face. From his reactions I gleaned that Sharon was trying to put together a deal with Peres – while the terror attack victims were still bleeding – to postpone the elections and create an emergency government, in which none other than Sharon himself would serve as Minister of Internal Security. He explained to Netanyahu how serious the situation was, and how it demanded a pooling of forces and a halt to the divisive election campaign. He proposed leaving the elections aside until things were quieter; meantime, he could enter the government and focus on security for the people.

Netanyahu did not need much time to weigh things up. He understood immediately that Sharon was planning a deal that would ensure Peres the premiership despite the fact that terror attacks had shattered the hopes of Oslo and the gap in the polls was closing. He understood that as Minister of Internal Security, Sharon would have a path from the political outback to center stage, where he could overshadow Netanyahu. After a few months, he would no doubt present his demand that primaries be held for Likud chairman. The party members would have to choose between the Minister of Internal Security who had brought the country together, and Netanyahu, whose public image had been gravely undermined. Netanyahu concluded the conversation by promising Sharon an answer. He consulted with us and called back an hour later conveying a polite refusal. The initiative fell away and was almost forgotten. Neither side had any interest in exposing it.

Netanyahu enlists reinforcements – and comes back from the brink

With the intensification of the bloodbath, Netanyahu changed his election strategy. Although his opposition to Oslo had turned out to be correct, and although he had issued withering criticism of the "peace government", he avoided visiting the sites where terror attacks had taken place, did not encourage demonstrations, and did not attack the government. He knew that any word of criticism on his part would be interpreted as "exploiting blood".

In view of the national shock and trauma, Netanyahu decided to adhere to a statesmanlike position. He appeared on television but took care to convey a message of encouragement and fortitude, and to offer hope for a safer future. He called press conferences but used them to call for national unity and cooperation against Israel's enemies. He appeared day after day in the world media but expressed only the Israeli consensus against terror. The public noted and appreciated the messages of solidarity issuing from the head of the opposition. This was a confidence-building measure on the part of a responsible politician who was not seeking to rock the boat during a storm. Netanyahu soon regained his image as a legitimate leader – at least in the eyes of half of the nation.

The 1996 elections were to be the first in Israel where the Prime Minister was elected by direct ballot (along with a separate ballot for a Knesset party list). To the entire country it was clear that despite the slight improvement in his situation, Netanyahu was heading for a colossal loss against Peres. This was evident to all with the exception of one person: Benjamin Netanyahu. Not only did he believe that he could put up a good fight; he fought for every percentage point on the way to a seemingly impossible aim: to climb somewhere close to parity against Peres, who was clearly going to be the next Prime Minster, voted in by a very wide margin.

Netanyahu sought to run as the representative of the entire Right. In other words, he pressed the message that members of each right-wing or religious party could vote for that party's Knesset list while at the same time voting for Netanyahu as Prime Minister. To this end he had to persuade the other right-wing candidates for Prime Minister – former Chief-of-Staff Refael (Raful) Eitan, head of the Tzomet right-wing party, and David Levy, who had left the Likud and started his own party, Gesher – against submitting their candidacy and thereby taking precious votes.

The threat posed by Eitan was not so much quantitative (the potential number of votes) as qualitative (critical votes). Netanyahu managed to talk him out of running and rewarded him most generously, relative to his electoral power: he gave him second place on the Likud list and six places reserved for his faction among the first forty places. The Likud thereby lost some Knesset seats, but its leader gained some critical percentage points in the contest against Peres.

David Levy was, of course, a harder nut to crack. Levy had recently left the movement that had been his political home for thirty years. As he saw it, the Likud had betrayed him by rejecting him as party chairman in favor of his sworn enemy – and all this after Levy had delivered the country's periphery, and thereby the reins of government, to Begin and Shamir. When Levy left, Netanyahu was happy to be rid of this stubborn adversary. But about a year later, with the new system of voting and the general elections drawing near, Netanyahu had to get Levy to withdraw his candidacy so that his voter base of a few tens of thousands of votes (polls predicted around three Knesset seats for Gesher) could support Netanyahu's bid. The savior who entered the picture at this stage was none other than Sharon who, as usual at critical junctures, jumped in, achieved the desired results, and demanded his price. He managed to convince Levy, promising in return seven reserved places for Levy's faction among the first forty Likud places, with second place on the list for Levy himself. Netanyahu managed to get Refael

Eitan to move down to third place. Netanyahu paid an exorbitant, unimagina-ble price that cost the Likud list dearly. But he was not interested in the number of Likud MKs. His priority was every possible percentage point in the race to become Prime Minister.

Netanyahu was now well on the road to return from the political oblivion to which many had been ready to relegate him. On March 12, he held a gigantic show of right-wing unity in Jerusalem. He stood on stage, flanked on one side by Refael Eitan and on the other by his mythological rival, David Levy, along with Sharon, the matchmaker, all raising their arms together in a show of fraternity and unity of purpose.

The Likud primaries, held two weeks later, further strengthened Netanyahu. The event passed in an atmosphere of unusual peace and quiet, and produced a young and impressive list that included twelve heirs. Five were MKs who were also children of MKs.

The veterans were satisfied, having elected the heirs Netanyahu, Begin, Meri-dor, Hanegbi, Livnat, Landau, and the newcomers – Zeev Boim, Livni, Dr. Yossi Olmert, Yossi Ahimeir, Yardena Meller (who currently serves as Secretary of the Knesset), and Rachel Kremerman. It was the veterans, in fact, who paid the price of the agreement to reserve seats for Levy and Eitan: since they had been placed lower on the list, they did not become MKs. Thus, they lost their opportunity to introduce the last new wave of fighting family members onto the list.

The united Right was filled with a new energy. Netanyahu had managed to bring on board two unexpected reinforcements in the security realm. One was Gideon Ezra, who was not a familiar name, but he held an impressive title: dep-uty head of the Shin Bet. The other was Yitzhak (Itzik) Mordechai, who had at one time or another headed all three IDF Regional Commands and was also Mizrahi. The gap between Netanyahu and Peres in the polls now stood at only five percent.

During the primaries, Netanyahu did everything he could to advance Morde-chai, convinced that placing him at the top of the Likud list would create a positive momentum of renewal. And indeed, Mordechai reached first place, the newspa-per headlines announced the victory, and Netanyahu immediately appointed him chairman of the Likud election campaign. This signaled that he was Netanyahu's candidate for Minister of Internal Security, in response to the country's urgent need for an experienced, impressive, tough figure to take on this responsibility. This move had the effect of narrowing the gap in the polls to three percent as Elec-tion Day drew near.

The voters' revenge

Of the entire Likud top-brass and election team, only Netanyahu himself believed and projected confidence in his return to the political playing field as a candidate on an equal footing with Peres. Every morning he visited the campaign office to participate in the daily meeting with senior advertising and media consultants, me included. Netanyahu was proactive, offering ideas and advancing initiatives, but in truth even his team of consultants was skeptical as to the dramatic revolution that he envisaged. Almost everyone that he spoke with listened patiently but then, after he left the office, gestured with their hands or muttered, "The man is delusional. He doesn't understand that he's finished."

The polls that were published immediately before the elections showed a close race, with Peres enjoying an advantage. Israel was strongly under the influence of the message that been repeated by the media for half a year, insisting that Netanyahu's political career was over and that Peres was unquestionably going to be the next Prime Minister.

Only those of us in Netanyahu's closest circle, including Arthur Finkelstein, discerned the sea-change that was occurring far from the media focus. After Rabin's assassination, hundreds of thousands of Israelis preferred not to express their views, or to supply the "correct" answers to pollsters' questions. While on the surface it seemed that the entire country rejected Netanyahu and the Likud, many people were simply reluctant to identify openly with the Right, fearing the accusatory finger that would be pointed at them. An enormous, silent coalition was developing among all those who did not belong to the "white tribe": Religious Zionists, settlers, ultra-Orthodox circles, Mizrahim from the periphery, Ethiopians, Yemenites, Russians, and right-wing secular Israelis. Netanyahu's steady ascent in the polls helped to reinforce the right-wing ranks and encouraged more and more people to make their voices heard.

At some point the change was felt among the Likud leadership. All the heirs stood firmly behind Netanyahu. Meridor, Livnat, and Olmert headed his election campaign and cooperated with Netanyahu and his staff in preparing election broadcasts. Every evening, the heirs gathered in momentary harmony – as in the old days of Begin and Shamir – and deliberated strategies and slogans, evaluated the rival camp's broadcasts, and suggested counter-messages, which went on air the very next day.

Together, they implemented the innovative strategy that Finkelstein had brought with him: brief broadcasts, repeating the same messages over and over. One iconic clip showed a glass breaking against the background of video footage showing Peres walking arm in arm with Arafat. The narrator warned, "Peres will divide Jerusalem!"

This sort of negative messaging balanced the positive slogans, such as, "Netanyahu – making a secure peace." The idea was to take back the term "peace", which had been appropriated by the Left, and reinstate it as the dream of all of Israel, along with the fundamental aspiration towards "security". We created an election slogan that promised both worlds: both peace and security.

In contrast to the casual campaign produced by Peres's team, Netanyahu's sharp and distinct message addressed the diverse population groups that were his potential voters. The Labor campaign relied on the media and its positive polls. Netanyahu's team operated from an underdog position and quickly attracted sectors that identified with this image.

The Labor strategy was based on the old perception that sectorial groups vote for their respective parties. They remained focused on the traditional voter base that they could rely on, failing to grasp that this time, groups such as Religious Zionists, immigrants, ultra-Orthodox, and Arabs could swing the election.

Avigdor Lieberman, the campaign manager, operated independently out of the Likud headquarters. Without attracting any media attention, he and Netanyahu built a politico-organizational strategy that addressed a very wide range of underdog groups – all those who were not part of the mainstream hatred of the Likud. Most prominent among these groups were the immigrants from the former Soviet Union (FSU). Lieberman had been born in Moldova and was fully aware of the scope of Russian electoral power in Israel, long before it was apparent to anyone else. He knew that the 1992 upheaval was attributable to the Russian immigrants. No-one but our team saw that future revolutions in Israel would likewise depend on the votes of the million or so immigrants from the FSU.

A second group was the religious sector: Religious Zionists, the ultra-Orthodox, and – especially – the Chabad movement. In the last days of the campaign, for the first and seemingly last time in history, Chabad got involved in the Israeli elections. Thousands of Chabad activists descended on junctions throughout the country, bursting with energy and armed with huge signs and stickers bearing the slogan, "Netanyahu is good for the Jews". The media, along with Peres's campaign team, scorned this initiative, but it served the purpose of mobilizing the religious public, which suddenly began to volunteer, offering physical assistance, transportation, and more, and which ended up voting like a huge army full of religious fervor. No-one had anticipated this.

Even Milo, who had gone his own way, was enlisted at the last moment. The Tel Aviv mayor, regarded as the most dovish of the heirs, was persuaded by his old Likud friends and the veterans to lend a hand. He acquiesced, appearing on the final elections broadcast on television and endorsing Netanyahu. This was especially effective, since Milo, a liberal centrist, appealed to the undecided voters, convincing them of Netanyahu's genuine intentions to bring about a secure peace.

The Netanyahu miracle

The final blow to Peres's campaign came with the televised debate between the two candidates on the eve of the elections. Peres arrived, relaxed and unprepared for the encounter with a rival who, in the eyes of his circle, was "not in the same league". Both his speech and his body language revealed his disdain. Netanyahu, on the other hand, had prepared himself carefully and thoroughly. He was articulate and radiated a young, fresh alternative to "same old" Peres.

The press was also caught unawares. Most journalists and commentators had ignored or overlooked the fact that all the polls were now pointing to a very narrow advantage to the Labor candidate. The reason for this oversight was quite simply that these correspondents did not encounter Netanyahu's voters, since not many of them were to be found among upper-middle class circles in the Tel Aviv area.

Even on election day itself, May 29, 1996, the polls were misleading. The preliminary results publicized on television awarded a victory to Peres. The smug commentators in the studios ignored the fact that Peres's advantage stood at a mere two percent. And so it was that Israelis went to sleep at midnight believing that Peres was their Prime Minister, and woke up the next morning to a completely different reality. It turned out that many of the respondents in the preliminary surveys had been afraid to state openly that they supported Netanyahu, but at the ballot box they were free to express their preference.

On May 30, 1996 the seemingly impossible became reality: Netanyahu had defeated Peres with a one percent margin (50.5 percent versus 49.5 percent), performing the greatest revolution in the history of Israeli politics: he had closed a starting gap of thirty percent and had come back from the political brink to win the election. The son of Professor Bentzion Netanyahu was Prime Minister of Israel. This second-generation heir had replicated the victory of his parents' and grandparents' generations. That which the previous generations had achieved in the 1977 Upheaval, following fifty years spent in the underground and the political opposition, the younger Netanyahu had achieved after a mere eight years in politics, at the age of forty-seven.

Note

1 Haaretz, October 6, 1995.

19 At the high point, cracks appear

The veterans were euphoric. After two years of a relapse into persecution, they were deeply gratified to see their prized heir rise to power. Finally, as grandparents in their seventies and eighties, they watched as their prodigy swore allegiance to the state as the youngest Prime Minister in Israel's history. At his side stood another seven MK heirs who would serve as ministers, along with another two who were the mayors of Israel's two largest cities. This crowning achievement was rounded out by dozens more sons and daughters of underground veterans who would serve in senior governmental positions, including Tzipi Livni, whom the Prime Minister had appointed Executive Director of the Government Companies Authority.

Every one of the veterans was filled with pride that the familiar, beloved names had made their way into the government and even the premiership. Their dream had come true: the old core of underground fighters had managed to replicate itself. Geula Cohen, the mother who had always been on her guard to protect the Land of Israel, could celebrate with her son, Tzahi Hanegbi; Azriel Livnat, a Lehi fighter who had been persecuted in the underground, now watched as his daughter emerged victorious from the election; the veterans who had broken into Acre Prison, and those expelled to Eritrea, rejoiced as they had not rejoiced since the establishment of the state and the Upheaval of 1977. Chaim Eitani, the brave underground fighter, "father of the heirs" Eli Sheetrit and his brother Yosef, all witnessed their protégés in their moment of stunning victory; Yoske Nahmias embraced the group that had included his comrades for half a century; Hedva Spiegel and Haya Shamir, who had been part of thousands of meetings, conventions, elections, and struggles, watched the television screens in the Likud headquarters at three in the morning, overwhelmed at the sight of the youngsters whom they had hosted in their homes, nurtured, and supported with their votes, and who were the new leaders of the State of Israel.

The elderly veterans were confident that their young dream team would hold onto the reins of power for many years and follow their right-wing, Revisionist path of protecting the Land of Israel and uprooting Socialism.

The elite's revenge

The joy over Netanyahu's victory among the veterans and the Right contrasted sharply with the stony non-acceptance of the election results among the dominant mainstream. While the victory was celebrated in Russian, Moroccan, Yiddish, and Amharic in the development towns, the immigrant neighborhoods, and among religious circles, the mainstream Israeli narrative was one of shock and outrage. In north Tel Aviv, in the kibbutzim, at the universities, and especially in the press, there was righteous indignation: "Have you killed and also taken possession?!"[1] The Israeli elite was dumbfounded. A sense of betrayal and loss of confidence in democracy seized the "white tribe", led by the media, academia, the cultural elite, the business community, and the members of Rabin's family. In their eyes, the country had been snatched from them.

Netanyahu was not aware of the extent to which he lacked legitimacy in the eyes of the Israeli elite. He failed to grasp that the vast majority of opinion-leaders in Israel – government clerks, army generals, the heads of the Shin Bet and the Mossad, the diplomatic corps, television commentators, writers, actors – did not recognize him as their leader. They had all hoped for his downfall and had collaborated against him. And he, new to the job and lacking experience, inadvertently gave them reasons to trip him up.

It was clear to me at the time that Netanyahu stood no chance. I saw then that the only strategy that would allow him to function within the hostile environment would have been to extend a respectful invitation to Peres, who had lost the election; to roll out the red carpet for him and to offer him any government ministry that he chose, in order to connect himself – the unwanted leader – with the elite. But Netanyahu was in a different place. He had won, and he believed that according to the rules of democracy it was the winner, not the loser, who should run the country. This was a mistake. He was denied even a minimal period of grace in which to find his feet. At every turn, with every misstep, he received a barrage of criticism. He was constantly under attack, from those whom he offended through his lack of experience, from those who denied the legitimacy of his leadership of the party and the country, and from the vast camp of those who had nurtured great hopes for the peace process and viewed Netanyahu as having taken an axe to Oslo, to peace, to a happy future.

The ties start fraying

Starting at the high point of the 1996 victory, the heirs' generation began to fray and drift apart. Paradoxically it was when they reached the very top that the personal and ideological fissure that had developed among them began to appear. Of course, the process took many years; it had started already in the 1980s, if not before. Nevertheless, it was the establishment of the first government of heirs that exposed the contours of the process, like a mighty wind exposing the foundations of a house in ruins. Disagreements that had until then been expressed only behind closed doors, in meetings at Likud headquarters or huddled deliberations at coffee shops, moved to the forefront in face of the challenging reality of ruling the country.

What were the sources of the impending split? What caused this distinct and seemingly homogeneous generational group, whose members had imbibed the same values and believed in the same path, to lose its cohesiveness and fall apart?

One factor would seem to be a pervasive sense that the supreme mission of commemorating and honoring the generation of the Revolt had been completed. The supreme mission that had unified the veterans and the younger generation of the Likud, the fuel powering decades of activity, had been the repair of an historical injustice. Their sacred duty had been the rewriting of the distorted history books. Both generations sought to restore to the underground fighters the respect that was due to them for their contribution to the country's independence. This was the true and lofty legacy that had united all members of the fighting family, young and old alike.

In his will, Begin had asked to be buried on the Mount of Olives, alongside the Jewish prisoners who had been executed by the British, rather than in the special section of the Mount Herzl cemetery reserved for the nation's leaders. For Begin, the memory of the heroes of the Revolt was a supreme value. Indeed, immediately upon taking office he had worked tirelessly to correct the historical injustice and to realign the official attitude of the state towards the underground movements and their fighters. He led a revolution in the public consciousness: the murder of Arlozorov ceased to be spoken of as a "Revisionist murder" and was viewed instead as an episode that had sparked persecution of the Revisionist movement; the "holy cannon" that had sunk the *Altalena* became a symbol of Labor's treachery; and the "Hunting Season" was a pejorative name for a dark period of persecution of Jews by other Jews. All the Jewish prisoners executed by the British, who had been "beyond the pale" thirty or forty years previously, were reinstated by Begin and Shamir: streets were named after them, while new towns were named after Jabotinsky, Raziel, and Stern.

Following Begin's resignation in 1983, the torch of commemoration was carried mainly by the heirs. Shamir, his successor Netanyahu, and President Rivlin, along with the other heirs, continued attending state memorial ceremonies, inaugurating memorial sites, and mentioning the Irgun fighters' legacy in media appearances. They laid wreaths on the graves of Jabotinsky as well as those who died aboard the *Altalena* and in the British prisons, and delivered speeches that recalled their leaders and their parents' heroes.

All the heirs continued to point to Begin and Jabotinsky as sources of inspiration, as leaders worthy of emulation, and as fathers of the nation. The mayors of Tel Aviv and Jerusalem, Milo and Olmert respectively, took care to ensure that their cities featured memorial museums, sites, and events.

Tzipi Livni described in a radio interview the joyous day when the Irgun anthem was played for the first time on state radio.

> One day, in 1996, I got a phone call – I think the caller was the son of one of the Irgun fighters – and he told me, his voice choked with tears, "Your mother's song is playing on the radio." [. . .] It was a kind of relief. [. . .] It was only in 1996 that they received recognition.

With Netanyahu installed as Prime Minister, it now seemed that this sacred mission had been completed. The very fact that the heirs now sat in the government meant that their legacy had prevailed over that of Ben-Gurion and his followers. Studies found that Begin had been the most widely respected and most deeply loved Prime Minister in Israel's history. The fiery drive to preserve memory and redress injustice thus cooled, and the heirs left behind their old feelings of discrimination and isolation. They continued quoting and memorializing their leaders, but they were no longer united in a critical, supreme, unattainable quest. It became a privilege rather than an obligation. Thus, the strongest bond that had held the heirs together began to fall away.

From the fighting family to an open, even leftist environment

While the veterans had lived in a relatively close-knit nationalist, activist environment, their children had grown up in homes that were nationalist but open. The generation of the Revolt was introverted, keeping to itself within its own organizations well into old age. This engendered a very intense togetherness and a rare depth of friendship. The younger generation, in contrast, while being educated with the same values and heritage, did not grow up within closed organizations such as Beitar and the Irgun.

The heirs grew up with a dual identity: on one hand, they were the products of fiercely Revisionist homes that hated Labor; on the other hand, they lived in middle-class, secular neighborhoods alongside neighbors who, like their parents, engaged in the free professions.

The parents earned respect and appreciation by virtue of their professional status and activities. Their children absorbed this and were well assimilated in the "regular" world; they studied and played with children from liberal and socialist families. They and their friends were cut off from politics, which was the province of "grownups".

The underground veterans conveyed the legacy of the Revolt to their children but at the same time desperately wanted them to have a normal childhood. They did not want them to be marked and tainted, as they had been. They wanted their children to succeed and advance in the army, in the public service, in education, without being imprisoned behind new walls. And indeed, as we have seen, most of the children did not join the Beitar youth movement; many even belonged to the Scouts. A militant Beitar training was not part of their world.

During their formative years most of the youth were exposed to different political ideas and figures. The open environment in which they grew up left its impression, which began to manifest itself decades later when these heirs joined the government. During their early years they had fought for their ideas and positions, which were not the norm in their socio-economic environment. As the years passed and they grew further from the nuclear family and the fighting family, and spent more of their time in an environment that was hostile to their views, cracks began to appear. They lacked the sort of collective experience that their parents had. They were left fighting for their truth alone, and it became increasingly difficult – especially as they were judged by the media, which attached "good" and "bad" labels differently from the way in which they had been educated.

The common life story of the heirs, as described here, sheds light on the process: they all emerged from a distinct, right-wing reference group to life in a leftist environment that was altogether different. As the years passed, so the heirs felt less of the direct influence of their parents (many of whom were already elderly or deceased) and were forced to cope with a very powerful pull in the other direction. As they became more firmly rooted in their new environment, they were less firmly held in place by the ring that had surrounded them in their childhood: the nationalist environment of the fighting family.

Loss of parents and leaders – the unifying authority

Many of the heirs entered the Knesset and the government after their parents had retired from politics or passed away. After Shamir and Arens left the scene, the heirs were completely independent, with no higher authority imposing party discipline. The heirs were no longer tied to a single ideological path. The vacuum created in the wake of the departure of the veteran leadership marked the loss of ideological, political, and ethical authority and the loosening of yet another cord that had bound the heirs together.

Starting in 1992, with the departure of Shamir and Arens, a fissure appeared that deepened with time. With no "responsible adult" in charge, the heirs fell into a series of struggles that were often characterized by jumps from one camp to another, and a widening gap that revealed powerful personal rivalries.

The practical expressions of this process were manifest for all to see. Milo, who had been Shamir's most loyal supporter, abandoned his allegiance immediately upon Shamir's resignation. Meridor, who had followed Begin unquestioningly and had remained loyal to and supportive of Shamir, had begun to entertain the idea of political compromise already towards the end of the veterans' era but expressed himself only in closed forums. Now he adopted a significantly more moderate stance and gave broader expression to his views, to the point where it became clear that they deviated from the party line. Olmert, who had been a central player in the Shamir-Arens camp, moved from a hardline right-wing position as mayor of Jerusalem, at the beginning of Netanyahu's term in office, to initiatives that included leaving the Likud and joining a different party. Tzahi Hanegbi, another of Shamir's devotees, continued with Netanyahu until he lost the party chairmanship, at which point Hanegbi started to grow closer to Sharon. The further unravelling of the heirs' unity proceeded with political developments, as we shall see.

"Mixed marriages" – Left and Right

Another dramatic difference between the younger generation and the veterans, which also contributed to the ideological rift that developed, relates to the fact that most of the wives of the early heirs had not grown up as part of the fighting family.

The veterans had married during the war, taking as their partners for life the women who fought alongside them in the Irgun and Lehi and who shared their worldview and values (Tzippora and Yaakov Meridor; Raanana and Eliyahu Meridor; Aliza and Menachem Begin; Shulamit and Yitzhak Shamir; Sara and Eitan Livni; and so on). Their children, in contrast, married partners who were part of their social (rather than ideological) milieu. Thousands of younger Revisionists set up households in which two different worldviews came into play. The early heirs married women with roots in the Labor movement. The political influence of the wives grew stronger over the years, molding not only their children but also their husbands. Yitzhak Shamir, for whom ideological loyalty was a supreme value, once commented on the wives of the heirs to his bureau chief, Herzl Makov: "They don't enjoy sitting at events with our people; they prefer to sit with the snobs."

Perhaps the most prominent example of this phenomenon is Aliza Olmert. Ehud Olmert, who grew up in the heart of Revisionist Israel, met Aliza during his studies at the Hebrew University. Aliza (nee Richter) had grown up on Kibbutz Nir David and was a graduate of the socialist youth movement Hashomer HaTza'ir. In a newspaper interview she described the distinctly left-wing education that she had received at home and on the kibbutz – "I don't remember conversations from my childhood about the holiness of Jerusalem, or longing for the Temple Mount or the West Bank" – and proudly expressed views that positioned her squarely on the Left. During the interview she also revealed the difficulty she had accepting her husband's views, especially while he was mayor of Jerusalem: "I couldn't take that rhetoric, talking about Jerusalem as the united and eternal, holy and historical capital."[2]

The wives of the three earliest heirs – Dr. Liora Meridor, Dr. Elisheva Milo, and Ruti Begin – likewise came from centrist or Labor backgrounds.

The wives of Uzi Landau (Naomi) and Reuven Rivlin (Nechama) were from Labor-affiliated moshavim. Like many of his peers, Rivlin met his future wife at university. He was studying towards a graduate degree in law; she was studying biology. He was known as a Beitarist through and through; her moshav belonged to the rival movement. They met at a party held on the festival of Channukah, in 1965, at the Betzalel Academy of Art. Fifty years later, Rivlin recounted:

> I fell in love with Nechama at first sight. [. . .] It took her a little longer to fall in love with me. She was no pushover, and the fact that I was a Revisionist didn't help matters. She came from a prominent left-wing family, and it was hard for her to tell her mother that she was bringing home a Revisionist. When I ran for the Likud list, she voted Likud, but asked that I keep it a secret.[3]

Few of the wives came from backgrounds similar to that of the heirs. An exception was Sara Netanyahu (1958), daughter of Shmuel and Hava Ben-Artzi. Sara grew up in a traditional nationalist Zionist home that was steeped in study of the Bible. Her father was a renowned Bible teacher and poet; her brothers were Bible Quiz stars (as was her son, Avner, later on). Shmuel Ben-Artzi was identified with the Irgun and was buried in the Irgun section of the Mount Herzl cemetery in Jerusalem. Limor Livnat married Elihai Hoenig, who also came from an Irgun family. Randy Hanegbi was a young Zionist from Florida who immigrated to Israel. Along with Tzahi, her husband-to-be, she became a prominent activist in the student cell in Jerusalem, and they were both part of the group that barricaded itself atop the memorial in Yamit in protest against the Sinai withdrawal.

Integration into the elite and the media

In 1996, almost twenty years after the Upheaval, the heirs faced no archetypal enemy like Ben-Gurion. They experienced the power and challenges of leadership, not the trials and tribulations of the opposition, which would have forced them to close ranks. They were now part of the country's elite and maintained contacts with bureaucrats, army officers, journalists, and businesspeople.

The second generation of the fighting family was firmly and integrally part of the country's leadership. Unlike their parents, for whom the opposition was their natural home, the youngsters were well integrated in the army, the universities, academia, the media, politics, the Jewish Agency, and the government. They were exposed to outside influences, and these, along with the status and privileges that their positions offered them, intensified the competition between them and began to drive them apart.

Ironically, then, it was Begin's Upheaval that created the conditions in which divergent personal ambitions could come to fruition. The parents' generation had paved the way for their children to reach the Israeli elite, but with Begin's election, the bond that had held the fighting family together – the internal unity arising from a sense of persecution – was broken. The assimilation into the elite led to a rethinking and revisiting of the ideology that had been imbibed unquestioningly at home, and the consolidation of a new worldview.

The reality of running the country brought the heirs into close contact with the "other side": a camp that had once appeared demonic from afar but now turned out to be human. The main point of contact was the media, which had not been won over in democratic elections. The media comprised commentators, correspondents, newsreaders, and others, many of whom had been born into Labor families, had belonged to leftist youth movements, were supporters of sports teams affiliated with the Left, and hated Begin and the Likud. Most of the media milieu that held the fate of politicians in its hands was leftist in its worldview, opposed Likud positions, and cultivated those heirs whose stance softened with time. Thus, the media became an important reference group for the heirs and was an active factor in moderating the views of some of them.

At the start of their political careers, the heirs were sharply criticized for their right-wing positions. Nevertheless, the media liked these new stars – the sons and daughters who had followed their parents' footsteps – and the story of the generational revolution in the Likud. Meridor, Begin, Olmert, Netanyahu, Hanegbi, Livnat, Livni, and others were impressive and articulate, and were therefore given extensive coverage, even when they voiced firmly right-wing messages that did not sit well with the views generally endorsed by the press. As they grew older and ventured into deeper political waters, the influence of their parents diminished and that of the press increased.

As time went on, the media chose to cultivate the more moderate heirs, who were more closely aligned with a leftist, secular worldview. One of the first to receive positive coverage was Dan Meridor, whose support and exposure in the media rose in inverse proportion to his stature in the Likud (conversely, his troubles in the Likud may in fact have been related on some level to the effusive media embrace). The heirs associated with the Tagar Circle (Hanegbi, Livnat, Rivlin, Ahimeir, and Landau) received far more critical treatment.

In the 1980s the press was strongly supportive of Meridor, Milo, and Olmert, the threesome that surrounded Prime Minister Shamir in fighting off the aggressive and more extremist Sharon. The three heirs were influential in the Israeli Broadcasting Authority, on the radio, and on television, and they connected with the media milieu on the personal and social levels, too. The connections that were formed during those years between the three heirs and leading media figures included eating out together and family introductions, and engendered long-term friendships.

The fate of the heirs lay in the hands of two rival ideological groups: the veterans, on the right, and the journalists, on the left. Some of the heirs chose to attach themselves to the media, thereby distancing themselves from the older generation; others continued to view the media as a non-objective player which simply had to be tolerated. For some time Milo managed to have the best of both worlds: on one hand, he was a loyal disciple of the veterans who fought against Peres, the darling of the press; who established a right-wing weekly magazine (*Hashavua*); and who struggled against the Israeli Broadcast Agency, which was a public body but antagonistic towards the Likud governments. On the other hand, he was constantly featured on television, and the media influence softened him to the point where he eventually decided to relinquish the support of the veterans and to cross the party lines.

Olmert maintained a love-hate relationship with the press. At the start of his political career, and again during his term as mayor of Jerusalem, he was portrayed as blunt and extreme, but at the same time he built up friendships with his critics: influential journalists with leftist-centrist views, such as Dan Margalit, Tommy Lapid, Amnon Dankner, and Yitzhak Livni. With the years their influence on him grew, and Olmert came to feel increasingly at home in the media environment and less connected to the closed group that was his father's generation. In addition, he held senior parliamentary positions already at an early age, and as such he may have felt that discrimination against Herut belonged to the past and that there was no longer any reason to fight Socialism with such vigor, since it had long since declined.

Limor Livnat, too, arrived on the political scene filled with antagonism towards the oppressive Labor establishment. She railed against Labor in the media but nevertheless received broad coverage. When she joined the government as Minister of Communications (1996–1999), she was suddenly in constant contact with journalists, and the situation changed. Livnat commanded widespread respect among journalists and feminist and liberal groups. Having once been described as "Geula Cohen's twin", she was now praised for her professional and liberal functioning as Minister of Communications. The daughter of the shunned Lehi fighter found her place at the heart of the elite.

Ideology meets the reality of government

So long as the veterans and the younger generation were in the opposition, it was relatively easy to maintain rigid ideological unity. Everyone toed the party line, and any gap between the older generation and the younger one was to be found in the tone of speech, not the ideological content.

With the debut of the heirs onto the political stage, they were increasingly exposed to the tension between their vision and reality. Firstly, they witnessed as participant-spectators Begin's lack of success in implementing his ideology as Prime Minister. They watched as their great leader grappled with the reality of government differently from what he had preached for decades. Inter alia, they watched as he signed an agreement that included awarding Palestinian autonomy in Judea and Samaria, and an evacuation of the Jewish settlements in the Sinai Peninsula. Secondly, from the start of their political journey many of the heirs felt that their movement's vision – the vision of the Greater Land of Israel – was not a realistic one, and from the outset they bypassed this issue and focused on decrying the corruption of the Labor administration. They attacked the lack of patriotism of the Left without mentioning the Greater Land of Israel, as though the existence of the political Left (rather than their own political vision) was what defined them as the political Right. In the information campaigns that the early heirs, Milo, Olmert, and Meridor (as well as Livnat and Netanyahu later on) managed on behalf of Begin and Shamir, the issue of security was at the forefront, rather than ideology. They promoted the Likud not by emphasizing the historical and religious connection of the Jewish People with Judea and Samaria (a task which they happily left to Mafdal, the Religious Zionist party) but rather by warning that territorial concessions would lead to existential danger. Begin and Shamir were not happy about the campaigns that omitted what was for them the main and most important message that sanctified the land itself. Shamir chose to ignore the ideological evasion by the heirs, in order to retain power. He chose to live with suppression of the original ideological message, knowing that the message that was being conveyed would allow him to maintain the political status quo and the de facto integrity of the land.

Dan Meridor points to the encounter between the vision and reality as a defining moment. "So long as we were in the opposition, the movement was always right," he told me in one of our discussions.[4] Meridor drew legitimacy for his position from Begin Sr., who, even from his seat in the opposition, had not pushed for a conquest of Jerusalem, and as Prime Minister had not pushed for annexation of Judea and Samaria. Begin, as Meridor noted, did the opposite: he chose compromise in view of reality. For the sake of a real peace he approved the greatest territorial concession ever made in Israel and even uprooted settlements.

Meridor's first term as Minister of Justice was the most liberal and non-political period the ministry has ever known. The Revisionist heir connected to two sources: the reference group of his fellow senior legal experts, and Jabotinsky's teachings concerning liberalism and human rights. "In the Herut movement," Meridor explains, "there was something else that was as important as the Land of Israel, and that was the connection to Jabotinsky: justice and equality. [. . .] The individual over the state. The state for the sake of the individual. Man is the pinnacle of creation."

He was a liberal minister who acted decisively against political appointments and against violations of the law even where security-related considerations were involved. He even clashed with Rabin, the Laborite Minister of Defense, who had advocated "breaking arms and legs" during the Intifada as well as demolition of homes of Palestinian rioters. Meridor gave his backing to liberal legal circles (and enjoyed their support in return), earning harsh criticism from Likud activists. In the 1992 elections he almost missed being included in the Likud list for Knesset.

Journalist Eitan Haber, an heir who crossed party lines, summed it up simply in a single sentence: "It turns out that within the office, inside its walls, the facts fly in the face of Prime Ministers' visions and ideologies."[5] A few years later, he wrote about his former colleagues – and, by the same token, about himself and his roots – in his column in *Yediot Aharonot*:

> Roni Milo, Tzipi Livni, Tzahi Hanegbi, Dan Meridor and, to some extent, Benny Begin, all got stuck. After long years in the wilderness of the opposition, they came to power, and suddenly the words [that they had repeated] didn't match up with the tune [of the world]. They discovered that Jimmy Carter, Bill Clinton, Vladimir Putin and Nicolas Sarkozy had never heard of Jabotinsky and his teachings, and weren't familiar with the song about "Both banks of the Jordan".[6]

The silent, imperceptible drift to the Left

A subtle softening of the worldview of some of the early heirs had commenced already in the 1980s, but it progressed in each of them at a different pace and with differing intensity. For many years this adjustment remained hidden from Shamir and Arens as well as the vigilant veterans, but in off-the-record conversations the early heirs were often heard expressing political views that were more conciliatory than those they expressed in the media. The three early heirs saw that the complex reality could not be resolved merely by quoting from Jabotinsky. They understood that which their parents refused to see: that a full realization of the vision of the Greater Land of Israel would involve ruling over millions of Palestinians and sacrificing a different, greater value: the existence of a Jewish democratic state.

Meridor's understanding of the limitations of power began to take shape after the first Lebanon War. During the war, he had been at the Prime Minister's side, along with Benny Begin. Both observed how Begin was manipulated by an aggressive Minister of Defence (Sharon) and an aggressive Chief-of-Staff (Raful). They saw at close hand the terrible price of war, the schism that it created among the nation, and, of course, the devastating effect on Begin's psychological wellbeing. Even as the war raged, the two heirs functioned as a moderating force in Begin's government but expressed themselves only in the privacy of his office.

That which Meridor and Begin had done quietly and in private other heirs permitted themselves to do openly. The departing cabinet secretary, Arye Naor, attacked Sharon publicly during the war, and later criticized the Shamir government's political stance, going so far as to support Peres openly in the 1984 elections. Dr. Yossi Olmert (Ehud's brother), a scholar of the Middle East at Tel Aviv University, spoke out from every possible platform against Sharon.

By the time the Lebanon War was over, most of the early heirs had a clear idea of the limitations of military might. Four of the five early heirs started drifting towards more moderate positions that placed less faith in physical power and gave more emphasis to the importance of a diplomatic solution. Milo himself told me that the Lebanon War changed his worldview and caused him to adopt a more conciliatory position.[7] In public he continued attacking the Left for its lack of patriotism, and he came across as supporting the war, but he claims that he pressured Begin to get out of Lebanon and was already then, in private, a moderating influence.

A government of heirs – a government of adversaries

On June 18, 1996, Netanyahu's first government was sworn in. Early on in the process of making the government appointments it was clear how much suspicion separated Netanyahu from the early heirs, his rival-colleagues.

Netanyahu was determined to implement the lessons of Shamir's tenure, which had been plagued by struggles between the ministers and the Prime Minister who had appointed them. He therefore chose to stave off and block those who had rebelled against Shamir (Sharon and Levy) as well as those who, he suspected, would never come to terms with the fact that Netanyahu had overtaken them and would use their positions to bring him down (the early heirs).

He went about this in different ways. Firstly, he promoted the younger heirs who showed greater loyalty to him to ministerial positions: Tzahi Hanegbi received the Health Ministry; Limor Livnat became Minister of Communications. Secondly, he announced at the very outset that he intended to award three senior portfolios to external professional figures (who presented no threat to him), as is customary in the US. The Defence Ministry was entrusted to the rising (and at this stage, well-disciplined) star, Itzik Mordechai, who was also chairman of the election campaign staff. The Finance Ministry was reserved for economist Yaakov Frankel, Governor of the Bank of Israel, who appeared on no Knesset list and represented no party. The Justice Ministry was placed in the hands of Yaakov Neeman, who was likewise politically unaffiliated. The two latter appointments testified to Netanyahu's lack of trust in the senior Likud leadership, as well as his lack of experience. He either failed to understand or refused to accept the political norm in Israel, whereby the Prime Minister has to appease coalition partners by "honoring" them with ministerial portfolios.

On the day the government was formed, Netanyahu gave most of his intended ministers a talking-to for which none of them ever forgave him. They waited at the doorway to the Prime Minister's Office, each waiting in tense anticipation of the meeting with him. Each in turn was treated to a speech about his/her office, which fell far below his/her ever-high expectations.

The early heirs were targeted by Netanyahu immediately. At nine in the morning, Benny Begin was first to be summoned to the PMO. Netanyahu told him that he intended to give him the Science portfolio – a low-level ministry in relation to Begin's public status. Begin quickly concluded the meeting. On his way out, he said that he would agree to serve in the government only if Meridor was a member, too. This declaration came in the wake of rumors that had reached him, to the effect that Netanyahu was intending to leave Meridor out.

Sharon, Netanyahu's rival and also his savior in the attempted pre-election putsch, received similar treatment. He was the second to be summoned to Netanyahu's office, and received an offer to return to the same ministry he had left just four years previously: the Ministry of Housing and Construction. Netanyahu's logic held that Sharon would be a troublemaker in any event, but he would cause less damage from within the government than if he were outside.

From Sharon's point of view, this was a humiliating offer. Just as Sharon had aided Shamir's election campaigns in the old days, despite the rivalry, with the expectation of receiving appropriate compensation, so he had mobilized the ultra-Orthodox to vote for Netanyahu as Prime Minister, and he had gained their support for the coalition. Sharon expected the position he desired above all others: Minister of Defense. Now he watched as this most senior ministry was handed to a new player –Yitzhak Mordechai – who was now taking on the role of the "security expert" and threatening Sharon's very political existence. Sharon rejected the offer, declaring that he would be part of the government only as either Defense Minister or Finance Minister. Netanyahu refused, and the negotiations fell apart. Sharon left, offended and disbelieving.

Here David Levy – Sharon's old partner and rival in previous battles – entered the picture. In an instant, Levy, who headed a Knesset faction of five MKs, turned everything upside down: he presented the Prime Minister with an ultimatum, declaring that he would not enter the coalition without Sharon. Netanyahu was forced to capitulate at the last minute and to appease Sharon with a portfolio that was a hodge-podge of leftovers from other ministries and bore the name "Ministry of Infrastructure". Ultimately, this became one of the strongest and most influential ministries in Israel.

Next in line was Meridor. Having held the Justice portfolio and in view of the high esteem in which he was held by the public, Meridor was disappointed and insulted by the possibilities offered to him: the Ministry of Communications, Ministry of Health, or Ministry of Tourism. It was clear to Netanyahu that Meridor would refuse these offers, whose real purpose was to push him out of the government. Meridor exited Netanyahu's office furious and incredulous. He and Begin sat together in his office in the Knesset. Begin repeated his ultimatum: he would not serve in the government without Meridor. He did not shout or threaten; there was no need to. For Netanyahu, Begin was a sort of ideological stamp; the one and only figure in the Likud – and on the political Right – that Netanyahu viewed as a moral, ideological, traditional authority. Netanyahu discerned that Begin was the most authentic representative of the nationalist-traditionalist public, and therefore he wanted him in the government at any cost. He acquiesced to Begin's demand and appointed Meridor as Minister of Finance – the post that he had originally reserved for the Governor of the Bank of Israel. The manner and circumstances of the appointment dealt a mortal blow to the level of cooperation and trust defining the working relationship between the Minister of Finance and the Prime Minister. Meridor knew how much Netanyahu had not wanted him to be part of the government, while Netanyahu was forced to work with a Minister of Finance who had been forced on him and whom he did not trust.

Thus, Netanyahu started his first term in office with a government made up of angry, vengeful ministers. The leaders of the two generational camps that had struggled against each other just a decade earlier now found themselves on the same side and on the margins of the Likud government. The heirs in government (Begin and Meridor) and in the major cities (Milo and Olmert) as well as the leaders of the middle generation (Sharon and Levy) were all, with greater or lesser justification, resentful towards the Prime Minister who had leapfrogged over them, bypassed them, and humiliated them.

From his very first day in office, Netanyahu was wary of the early heirs. He was convinced that they did not recognize his leadership and were working constantly to bring about his replacement. He had no doubt that the two mayors, Olmert and Milo, would at some stage seek to move on from their temporary station and would return to the national arena. He heard some activists who claimed that the two mayors were fortifying themselves in their cities and preparing a putsch – Milo from the left, Olmert from the right. If they were to switch cities, Netanyahu supposed, each would continue attacking him, just from the opposite direction.

The main suspect, he concluded, must be Meridor. This Minister of Finance who had been forced upon him was the darling of the media and the legal system; moreover, as far as director-general of the PMO, Avigdor Lieberman, was concerned, he had attempted a putsch already in the past, after Rabin's assassination. All the extensive negative press about Netanyahu at this time was attributed by Netanyahu's staff to Meridor – and if not to him personally, then to his colleagues, Milo and Olmert, who were chummy with the press.

Unquestionably, the youngest Prime Minister in Israel's history was forced, immediately upon taking office, to deal with thorny coalition challenges of the sort that even the most experienced leader would have had trouble sorting out. Netanyahu lacked experience in the minefield of Israeli politics and was not equipped for coalition-building. Unlike the early heirs, he had not previously been an advisor to the Prime Minister, nor had he run a government ministry. He also lacked a team of loyal professional staff, experienced in government service, who had accompanied him for decades. Even the strongman at his side, Lieberman, had gained his administrative experience at Likud headquarters, not in government. Netanyahu's political experience in Israel added up to a total of eight years, most of which had been spent progressing steadily from one success to the next. Admittedly, he had been a sensational diplomat and an outstanding Deputy Foreign Minister, but all his talent and experience had been limited to the international arena and election campaigns, not the local swamp of coalition politics, where even leaders with considerably more experience had faltered and failed. He had risen to the office of Prime Minister still wet behind the ears and also wafting in the euphoria of his string of victories. I believe that today even Netanyahu himself would agree with this assessment.

His impossible challenge was only exacerbated by the fact that he was up against dozens of enemies who circled him, just waiting for their chance to attack. Outside, the cultural, academic, military, and media elite treated him as having "snatched power" from Peres – the sole legitimate candidate to lead the country, as far as they were concerned. In conversations behind closed doors there were those who expressed (and continue to express) bitterness over the fact that as they saw it, Netanyahu had "both murdered and inherited" – a false and shocking accusation against a man chosen by millions of Israelis in a democratic election. Any misstep by Netanyahu was publicized in blaring headlines; any problem in the country was inflated to catastrophic proportions. The headlines, the articles, and the interviews all painted a black picture of the country under Netanyahu's leadership.

Recognition of the Oslo Accords – the first ideological argument among the heirs

The first government of the heirs was the youngest government in Israel's history, and thus also the least experienced. Netanyahu, full of euphoria and confidence, made many mistakes as he learned the ropes. His cabinet was right-wing in its views and homogeneous in its composition, with no centrist or left-wing counterbalance. The Right-plus-religious coalition held a solid majority that should have assured it a full term in office. However, it had to deal with a complex political and security reality: on one hand, Palestinian terror attacks were occurring on a regular basis; on the other hand, there was pressure to move forward on the diplomatic front, on the part of senior members of Clinton's administration, which had overseen the signing of the Oslo Accords and was not ready to acknowledge the failure of the peace process. In Israel, the Prime Minister was squeezed between the media-legal-business elite, which demanded progress on implementation of the Oslo Accords, and his colleagues in the Likud who wanted the government to turn its back on the agreement that had been stained with Jewish blood the moment after it was signed. Netanyahu was allowed no period of grace in which to seek a way out of this zero-sum situation.

The Oslo Accords were the first real test of the heirs in government. As noted, many of them no longer had their parents as an ideological influence in their lives, and the Revisionist bonds that they had shared in their youth were beginning to weaken. This point marked the beginning of the split and schism between the heirs who now chose the path of political compromise, in view of the reality of the Oslo Accords, and those who reinforced their rigid right-wing stance, in view of the disillusionment that Oslo had brought. Milo was the first sign of the approaching storm.

From its first day to its last, over the course of three turbulent years, Netanyahu's government was formally committed to the agreements that the previous government had signed with the PLO, while in fact desiring nothing more than to consign the agreement to the dustbin of history. This conflict put the Revisionist ideology and its continued viability to a real test. At first, all the MK heirs, led by Netanyahu, had opposed the accords. They attacked the agreement from every platform, portraying it as a catastrophe and an existential threat. Now, however, as Prime Minister, Netanyahu was forced to deal with the fact that any backtracking on a (previous) government agreement would lead to a schism within the nation and a crisis vis-à-vis the Clinton administration. In addition, cancellation of the agreement would lead to a huge wave of Palestinian terrorism, as well as harsh international criticism. The Israeli public was divided into two almost equal camps. The first was Netanyahu's own political base, which had opposed the agreement from the start and believed that implementation of its terms would represent a surrender – especially now that it was clear that Israel had been deceived and had paid with rivers of blood. The other was the "peace camp", which was enthusiastic in its support for the agreements and sought to keep the dream of peace alive. The veneration of Rabin was at its peak during this period, and the Israeli Left avoided blaming Arafat and the PLO for the blood spilled in terror attacks, preferring to point an accusing finger at Netanyahu for cutting short the peace that Rabin had sought to attain.

The controversy over the agreements had been apparent already in the months leading up to the elections, when Netanyahu declared publicly that he would honor the agreements if he was elected Prime Minister. This was an attempt to attract centrist voters: those who supported the agreements in principle, but wanted new, firmer security restrictions (like Netanyahu himself, who said that he would honor the agreements according to his interpretation of them). Already then, Netanyahu had been forced into a first ideological compromise – not happily and wholeheartedly, but as an electoral tactic. It ran contrary to his worldview, and it ran afoul of the prevailing stance among two generations of the Likud: the veterans and the second-generation, right-wing heirs.

The political patriarchs Shamir and Arens intervened and tried to set boundaries for Netanyahu. Professor Bentzion Netanyahu, too, was unhappy about his son's announcement regarding the contractual continuity of the agreements. It was precisely because of such compromises that Professor Netanyahu had avoided entering politics. The entire generation of underground veterans was opposed to Netanyahu's declaration but refrained from open revolt in order not to harm the electoral chances of their prized heir, who was in any case under such intensive attack after Rabin's murder. Attempts were made from every side to convince

Netanyahu that he was making a big mistake that opened the door to territorial withdrawal, but in the end everyone "agreed to disagree" quietly, hoping that after the elections Netanyahu would not be forced to put his words to action and actually talk to Arafat.

The younger heirs who were loyal to Netanyahu also had no wish to rock the boat on the eve of the elections. For Begin, Landau, Rivlin, and Ahimeir, Netanyahu's declaration was a hard pill to swallow, but as Rivlin explained to me, many years later: "We didn't want to harm the chances for his electoral run, which seemed hopeless."

The only Likudniks who placed ideology above election tactics were Yitzhak Shamir (who denounced Netanyahu in public) and Benny Begin (who, following Netanyahu's announcement, distanced himself from his election campaign). Meridor and Milo, whom Netanyahu had marked as rivals, favored continuation of the agreements, which sat well with their own growing tendency towards political appeasement.

Hebron Agreement – accelerating the ideological rupture

After Netanyahu's government was sworn in, in June 1996, the tension between Israel and the Palestinians reached new heights. The reason for this was the government's de facto non-continuation of the Oslo agreements. Firstly, Netanyahu refrained from speaking to Arafat. (It must be remembered that Netanyahu had won the election following a negative campaign that showed Peres walking arm in arm with this mortal enemy of Israel.) Secondly, he established the principle of reciprocity as a key element of his policy (the simple formulation has become everyday idiom in Israel: "If they give, they'll get; if they don't give, they won't get.") All his colleagues supported this policy, certain that it would take forever until the Palestinians would be ready to "give", and thus the issue of what they would need to "get" would never arise. But the day arrived sooner than expected, just a few months after the establishment of the new government.

One of Netanyahu's first decisions (at the initiative of Olmert, mayor of Jerusalem) was to open the Western Wall Tunnels to the public, following a lengthy period of archaeological excavation. Today, this network of tunnels, extending beneath the Temple Mount and the Muslim Quarter in the Old City of Jerusalem, is full of visitors all day, every day; the tunnels are regarded as fully part of the Western Wall complex. At the time, however, the decision led to three days of bloody rioting, with the Palestinians claiming that this was an attempt to "Judaize Jerusalem" and that the excavation and the opening of the tunnels were intended to cause the collapse of the Temple Mount. This utterly false claim, with a call for violent action to "defend the Holy Shrine", reinforced with quotes from the Quran, was propagated by Nobel Peace Prize laureate Arafat.

The violent confrontation that erupted threatened to sink the Oslo agreements. Within a short time President Clinton, who was committed to the collapsing agreement, intervened and forced the two sides back to the negotiating table. Netanyahu was under attack both in Israel and abroad. Everyone blamed him for stalling the peace process and kindling the fire that had taken the lives of seventeen Israelis as well as a number of Palestinians. Under Clinton's watchful eye the negotiations resumed, and there was even an encounter between Netanyahu and Arafat (a photograph of the two of them together haunted Netanyahu ever after; Sharon reminded him over and over of their "warm" handshake). By the end of the negotiations Netanyahu was forced to implement the next stage of the accords, in the form of the Hebron Agreement, which included a "redeployment" of the IDF in Hebron – meaning, a withdrawal of IDF troops from the only Palestinian city in which they still maintained a presence. The most that Netanyahu was able to obtain was the retention of IDF troops in the Hebron Jewish Quarter, to protect the inhabitants.

The agreement to withdraw from Hebron, the City of the Patriarchs, was hard for the right-wing public to accept, and certainly for both generations of the Likud. The decision was approved by the government only by virtue of the unbearable pressure that was being exerted by the American administration. The unrest within the Likud was nothing compared with the pressure of President Clinton, who watched as the ongoing bloodshed undermined the peace agreement for which he had received the Nobel Peace Prize. The first cracks heralding the ideological split among the heirs became manifest. Minister of Finance Meridor supported the agreement. Like Netanyahu, his arguments were pragmatic in nature, but he was far less averse to the agreement. Milo, who had already crossed the Rubicon, also expressed his open support. Other heirs who turned out unexpectedly in favor were Hanegbi and the new MK Boim, both of whom insisted that reality demanded pressing on. Thus, Netanyahu, Meridor, Boim, and Hanegbi, all loyal members of the Tagar Circle, adopted a pragmatic approach from the very outset. Until this point, the Likud veterans had witnessed such "pragmatism" only in the conduct of the Left.

A vast right-wing camp opposed the Hebron agreement, including all the veterans as well as MKs Begin, Rivlin, Landau, Livnat and, from outside the Knesset, Jabotinsky Jr. (grandson of the movement's founder). They all insisted that the agreement represented a surrender to terror and that there was no room for compromise with Arafat. It was the familiar Revisionist refrain: no compromise on the Land of Israel, ever. For Rivlin, the scion of a family that had fled its home in Hebron after the 1929 riots, the agreement represented an affront to the sacred family legacy.

However, there were only two senior Likud figures who took real action expressing their opposition. The first was the former party leader, Shamir. He was so incensed over the agreement that he publicly distanced himself from Netanyahu, accusing him of deviating from the Likud path, and cutting off contact with him. What hurt Shamir most was that Netanyahu simply ignored him. Shamir did not cut himself off from Milo or Olmert even when these heirs, who had been part of his close circle, moved much further to the Left. But the young Prime Minister did not show respect towards his predecessor, nor did he consult with him. For this Shamir could not forgive him. The Hebron Agreement marked the final split between them. The other Likud figure who reacted with actions and not just words was Benny Begin, who resigned from the government. After just a few months in office, this most royal of heirs found himself in an untenable situation. He decided to follow his truth, rather than remaining part of a government that was implementing leftist agreements. His resignation rocked the Likud and led to the formation of an ideological opposition bridgehead outside of the government. The great storm was about to break.

The Bar-On–Hebron affair

On January 10, 1997, the Netanyahu government approved the appointment of a new Attorney General: Roni Bar-On. The appointment astounded the political and legal establishment: legal experts and public figures alike expressed their opposition to the inexplicable promotion of a lawyer of no special stature, who happened to be a political activist in the Likud, to such a sensitive and senior position. In fact, it was Bar-On's friends from the Likud branch in Jerusalem – Meridor (who abstained) and Begin (who voted against) – who were among the most vociferous opponents. For Meridor, who had sat next to Bar-On many years previously watching endless Beitar Jerusalem soccer games, nominating Bar-On as Attorney General was tantamount to promoting a goal-keeper (and friend) who played in the junior league to star in the national team.

The media showed great interest in this controversial appointment. Netanyahu suspected once again that the withering criticism had emerged from the direction of Minister of Finance Meridor, who was close with legal circles. Matters reached a head when Irit Linor, a writer and publicist who was interviewed on a radio program hosted by Shelly Yechimovich (later to become a Labor MK and leader of the Labor Party), accused Bar-On of improper personal conduct (an allegation that was never proven). Bar-On succumbed to the devastating public criticism and resigned within less than forty-eight hours.

But all of this was just the prelude to a far more ominous story: the Bar-On–Hebron affair. On January 22, during the Channel 1 Television news broadcast, political correspondent Ayala Hasson dropped a bombshell that shook the country to its foundations. Hasson claimed that the surprising appointment of Bar-On had been part of a shady deal between Shas leader Aryeh Deri and Benjamin Netanyahu, in anticipation of the government's vote on the Hebron Agreement. According to the report, in exchange for Shas support, Netanyahu had agreed to appoint Bar-On as Attorney General, with the understanding that he would ensure good terms for a plea bargain in the corruption case against Deri at the time. The parties allegedly involved in this scheme were Prime Minister Netanyahu; Minister of Justice Tzahi Hanegbi; director general of the PMO, Avigdor Lieberman; MK Aryeh Deri; and businessman David Appel, whom we recall from Levy's camp in the Likud, and by this time a supporter of Shas. Each of these men denied the story at the time and ever since.

The Bar-On–Hebron story occupied the press and the public for many months. Israelis were shocked by what appeared to be a scheme to subvert justice, in return for a vote on the fate of the country. An investigation was launched, headed by police commissioner Sando Mazor, and for the first time in Israel's history a sitting Prime Minister was questioned under caution, along with other government ministers. At the conclusion of the investigation the police published its recommendation: indictments for the Prime Minister, MK Aryeh Deri, Minister Tzahi Hanegbi, and director-general Avigdor Lieberman. Netanyahu was now in real danger of facing trial on a count of criminal conduct and ending his career in the most humiliating fashion, behind bars. He was criticized and denounced day and night in the press by a chorus that included the majority of journalists, commentators, legal experts, and politicians – in other words, all those who had sat tight, since the elections, waiting for the moment when they could boot out Netanyahu and put right the historical wrong of his having inherited the premiership from Rabin.

Netanyahu knew the truth. He was innocent, and he had witnesses, too. Years later he told me in one of our conversations that he knew that if and when the case came to court, and State Attorney Edna Arbel was questioned, she would have to testify that Netanyahu had already announced to her his prior intention of appointing Dan Avi-Yitzhak to the position of Attorney General. It was only at the last minute, when he was prevented from appointing his preferred candidate and he had no ready substitute, that he had decided on Bar-On.

Since he knew that there was no truth to the accusations, Netanyahu viewed the entire episode as an attempt to target a democratically elected Prime Minister, and he blamed his enemies in the press, who had colluded with his enemies among the early heirs. He felt that they had crossed all boundaries by leading a legitimate political difference of opinion into the realm of criminal charges.

The right-wing camp felt that the days of persecution and public excoriation were back. This time, it was generated by a putsch aimed at "correcting" the election results which dictated that "Rabin's murderers" would inherit the rule of the country.

In the wake of the onslaught Netanyahu and Lieberman called an extraordinary meeting of the Central Committee, and they emerged with the body's firm backing. The gathering was attended by Meridor and Begin, too. They both sat silently in the tenth row of the hall, directly in front of the speakers, making no attempt to even present their position, given the general atmosphere, which recalled a noisy and impassioned soccer stadium. They were surrounded by hundreds of furious Central Committee members, who viewed Meridor as the main culprit behind this debacle, an enemy from within. Begin sat beside him and also absorbed a slew of accusations, but retained his regal dignity. The Likud Central Committee was no longer the warm home in which these two heirs had grown up. Their parents' movement was issuing them a final warning.

As described earlier on, Meridor had grown up in a home that sanctified both underground activism and democratic grandeur. With the eruption of the Bar-On–Hebron affair, he sided with his new reference group: the judges and the senior staff of the Attorney General's office, who had been shocked to the core by Netanyahu's election. Meridor was no longer attentive to his earlier reference group – the members of the fighting family, who viewed Netanyahu as the victim of political persecution. Meridor was already deeply immersed in the legal world and was convinced that Netanyahu's circle was leading him to wage war against the "old elites" including, especially, the legal system. Meridor feared that the threesome that seemed to be controlling Netanyahu – Lieberman, Appel, and Deri – was trying to seize control of the country. As he saw it, this was a nightmare that demanded immediate and clear-cut action.

The Bar-On–Hebron affair opened a Pandora's Box and ignited a world war between the early heirs and their camp, on one hand, and Netanyahu, on the other. All the jealousy, suspicion, and frustration that had accumulated now came to the surface and undermined the stability of the government. Different conflicts – political, ideological, moral, and personal – all converged in this drama. From this point onwards, personal and ideological issues became inextricably entangled and ultimately shattered the Netanyahu government from within.

The episode was a sobering lesson for the younger heirs, including Limor Livnat. Livnat belonged to the more right-leaning faction in the Likud and had worked closely with Netanyahu for four years since joining his campaign in 1993. She was well rewarded for her loyalty, and the first portfolio that she held was the Ministry of Communications (although she, too, had been enraged by the experience of the allocation of ministries: she had been forced to wait, tense and anxious, for hours until her turn had come to enter Netanyahu's office). She was popular as a minister and was held in esteem even by some who had opposed her in the past.

The Bar-On–Hebron affair caught Livnat in between Netanyahu and the early heirs, who were her friends from their days in the Likud Youth and the opposition: Milo, Meridor, and Begin. She chose to stay close to Meridor, who also received tremendous media support, and threatened to leave the government if the investigation of the affair pointed to corrupt behavior.

The closer Livnat drew to Netanyahu's adversaries, the further she distanced herself from her core of supporters in the Likud. The more positive attention was lavished on her by the media, the more of the veterans' anger was directed towards her. One morning, signs painted on sheets of fabric appeared on the bridges crossing the Jerusalem–Tel Aviv highway, with the inscription "*Livnat habala*" (literally, "demolition block", also a play on words involving her family name). The media chose to interpret this as a threat to Livnat's life, which obviously was not the intention. Those responsible for the signs had indeed threatened – but only her political career. They were youngsters dispatched from Likud headquarters, bearing a message that Livnat was "demolishing" the Likud.

The tension among the public ran high in anticipation of the decision of the (new) Attorney General Elyakim Rubinstein and State Attorney Edna Arbel. At the end of a tumultuous investigation lasting three months, the Attorney General published an unusual announcement in which he criticized Netanyahu's conduct but did not recommend indicting him.

Netanyahu seemed to have been saved by the skin of his teeth. He tried to bring the episode to a close and quickly moved to appease Meridor, both in private and in public, promising an overhaul of the way in which government business was managed. Meridor was mollified and continued to function as Minister of

Finance. Seemingly, tempers had calmed. But at this point it was already too late to stop the snowball that had begun rolling. On one hand, Netanyahu could not forgive what he perceived as an altogether fictitious libel. On the other hand, the fact that Meridor remained in the government turned him overnight into an object of scorn on the part of the Left. His decision not to abandon Netanyahu aroused great disappointment in the media, and for the first time Meridor was subject to vicious attacks. He was portrayed week after week on a popular satirical program on television as a weak and helpless kitten named "Mitzi". The satirical clips became a cultural cult favorite, casting Meridor forever more as a spineless object of derision.

A few months later, the inevitable blowup between Meridor and Netanyahu finally happened. It grew out of a difference of opinion on a side issue that simply became the last straw: an argument between economists relating to the linkage between the Israeli and American currencies. Netanyahu sided with the Governor of the Bank of Israel against his Minister of Finance, Meridor. The Prime Minister forced the hand of the minister whom he suspected as having initiated the plot against him. This time, Meridor decided against another display of weakness and submission. He resigned and became an opposition within the Likud. Both he and his good friend Begin Jr. found themselves out of the Likud government within its first year, owing to personal and principled opposition to Netanyahu – Meridor, citing the sanctity of the law, and Begin, citing the sanctity of the land.

The first opposition of heirs against Netanyahu

Of the four rebellious heirs – Begin, Meridor, Milo, and Livnat – it was Milo who was the most outspoken. For him, this was easy and also beneficial. As mayor of Tel Aviv, he was the only one who earned real points from his aggressive stance, since every word of criticism against Netanyahu increased his popularity in this secular-leftist city. In contrast, the ministers who formed the opposition to Netanyahu paid a political price within the party; two paid with their seats.

Milo's attacks were harsh and received wide exposure. He was a political commentator on Channel 1 Television, and week after week he denigrated Netanyahu from every possible angle, over every issue. Milo was also the first Likud member who declared that he would run for Prime Minister against Netanyahu. In May 1998, he reserved a party name, "Atid" (Future), hinting at his intention to establish a centrist party. In the background, rumors swirled concerning secret meetings that he held at the Tel Aviv municipality with the other heirs.

The last to join the heirs' opposition to Netanyahu was the mayor of Jerusalem, Olmert. Before he entered the Jerusalem municipality the press had called him a "dove in hawks' clothing", but as mayor he came across as decidedly hawkish. Throughout his years in the municipality he maintained a distinctly and even extreme right-wing stance; he struck an alliance with the right-wing/religious/ultra-Orthodox activist camp in Jerusalem, and it was he who urged Netanyahu to open the Western Wall Tunnels. The cooperation between him and the Prime

Minister seemed close and harmonious. They enjoyed excellent relations, since there was no personal or ideological conflict between them.

However, from the moment Netanyahu took office, Olmert worked to position himself as a more right-wing, nationalist alternative. He was constantly showing himself to be to the right of Netanyahu, pressing him to build in neighborhoods whose political status was a matter of controversy and thereby exposing the Prime Minister to diplomatic threats on the part of the American administration and the Palestinians. Olmert positioned himself as a loyal right-wing hardliner, while Netanyahu, by virtue of his title, was obligated to proceed cautiously. The riots over the Western Wall Tunnels, whose opening Olmert had pushed for, taught Netanyahu a lesson. And the results of the riots – a conciliatory agreement that included relinquishing Hebron, which in turn entailed a break with Shamir and Begin Jr. – left Netanyahu with a bitter wariness with regard to Olmert's displays of nationalistic fervor.

Olmert worked hard to fortify his position on the Right. He tightened his alliance with his Religious Zionist and ultra-Orthodox partners in the municipality, ever alert and looking to the future; he was the strongman behind the Beitar Jerusalem soccer team, with its important status in Jerusalem and in the Likud; he consolidated his hold on Likud branches; controlled the National Labor Federation (which his father had helped to establish); nurtured his connection with the veterans, by commemorating the leaders and casualties of the underground movements at sites throughout Jerusalem; and continuously worked at eroding Netanyahu's political base. To his great frustration, however, the Likudniks – veterans and heirs alike – remained loyal to their leader.

In September 1997, about two months before the Likud convention, Olmert changed his overt strategy, which had consisted of public support for Netanyahu while showing himself to be more inclined to the Right – a sort of bear hug that lasted until the right time came to compete for the leadership. That day arrived after Olmert was acquitted in court in a case concerning financial irregularities in the previous municipal elections (1988). Now, with the cloud of legal proceedings no longer hanging over his head, and in view of Netanyahu's weakened position, Olmert believed that the time had come to move to center stage. He therefore intensified the political and media pressure on the Prime Minister regarding the delay in construction in Jerusalem (which was due to American pressure), while at the same time cozying up to his friends who formed the internal opposition. Still, it was only after the Likud convention towards the end of 1997 that he spoke out openly against Netanyahu: only then, when it was clear to him that the break between the heirs and Netanyahu was irreparable, did Olmert feel confident enough to act openly to bring about Netanyahu's downfall.

Change of election system in the Likud – a Pyrrhic victory for Netanyahu

In the weeks leading up to the Likud convention of November 1997 (the "Convention at Stand 28", see later) there were frequent reports of meetings between

Olmert and Milo, Meridor, and Livnat. Everyone was talking about the axis that appeared to be forming, including also Begin. Three of the heirs – Meridor, Olmert, and Milo – considered themselves worthy of inheriting Netanyahu's seat.

At the same time, there were also rumors of a secret plan on Lieberman's part to change the election system in the Likud: instead of holding primaries in which tens of thousands of Likud members vote for MKs (the system introduced by Netanyahu four years previously), he proposed reverting to the "old" system, whereby the decision lay with the Central Committee of activists and power-brokers. The prevailing view was that this was how Netanyahu and Lieberman intended to solve the problems arising from lack of party discipline, including the defamation of Netanyahu by the early heirs and their attempts at a putsch. The change of electoral system was meant to ensure that the ministers would be subservient to the Prime Minister and that rival heirs would think twice before acting against him. There would be a clear message that if their subversion did not end, they would not be elected to the Knesset by the Central Committee which was loyal to Netanyahu and Lieberman.

The Lieberman initiative to change the electoral system was greeted with great satisfaction by the Central Committee members, who of course were glad at the prospect of having the choice of MKs returned to their hands. Meantime, Netanyahu refrained from declaring his position on the matter in public.

At the same time, the idea of abolishing the primaries antagonized the heirs who now formed an internal opposition. They argued that it was undemocratic, and enlisted the media in support of their position. For the first time, they realized that even their status as regular MKs was now at risk, and they would soon have to beg and plead with Lieberman and Netanyahu just to remain in the Knesset. At the same time, the only one who dared to stand up to the members of the Central Committee was Livnat, who spoke out against the phenomenon of political appointments and decried the erosion of character and integrity in Israeli politics in general, and in the Likud in particular. When she asked a rhetorical question, directed towards the Central Committee members – "Did we come to power so we could give out jobs?!" – and the answer was a resounding and decisive "Yes!", the Central Committee's image took a mortal blow. But her words earned a place among the immortal Likud speeches, and Livnat was treated to an even warmer embrace by the media.

Ultimately, Netanyahu and Lieberman succeeded in their endeavor. The primaries were abolished, and the choice of the Likud list for Knesset reverted to the Central Committee. The four rebels had aroused great anger among the veterans and the activists. The Likud public's loyalty to Netanyahu was almost blind; there was tremendous support for this Prime Minister who was so hated by the Left and the elites. The early heirs, who had once been such beloved figures among the Central Committee, were suddenly regarded as "subversive elements" at best, if not actual collaborators with the Left. The nationalist public, the veterans, and the religious sector forgave Netanyahu for his concessions in Hebron (especially after he later put a halt to the Oslo process), and the public in the periphery identified strongly with his abhorrence of the elites. All of these groups stood firmly behind him at the 1997 convention. They encouraged Netanyahu, turned their backs on his adversaries, and rejected the "rebels".

The absolute loyalty to the leader was typical of the Likud; it had characterized the movement since the days of Jabotinsky and Begin. From 1997 until the end of Netanyahu's first government, the Central Committee was dominated by Lieberman on behalf of Netanyahu.

The "Stand 28" episode had an epilogue that explains its name. The scandal broke when journalist Dov Gilhar revealed that during the course of the convention, a private video photographer had documented secret discussions among Central Committee members who opposed Lieberman's initiative. In the article that he published, Gilhar claimed that the photographer had been employed by a group associated with Lieberman, located at Stand 28 near the convention hall and working to change the election system. What this meant was that the official party apparatus (under the direction of the director-general of the PMO) had seemingly employed unlawful means in order to monitor Central Committee members. The exposé shocked the country. Netanyahu distanced himself from the incident and established a commission of inquiry to investigate the conduct of the convention, but once again his public image took a beating. Shortly afterwards, Lieberman resigned from his position as director-general of the PMO.

Later it turned out that the convention where Netanyahu had seemingly come out on top had actually harmed him. Following the change in the system of election, the heirs felt that they had no chance or future in the Likud. This led to the establishment of three new parties in the two years that followed. Lieberman, who had been "dismissed", now felt free to emerge from under Netanyahu's wing, and he proceeded to found a party of Russian immigrants. Meridor and Milo set out to conquer the center of the political map with their Hamerkaz (The Center) party. Begin Jr. attached himself to the Right and was one of the founders of the National Union party. The "Stand 28" convention of 1997 thus marks the turning point where the early heirs began to entertain serious thoughts of leaving the Likud – a prospect which they would previously have viewed as a nightmare. They were caught in a corner, a political dead end. They understood that they had lost their hold on their parents' movement and that they stood no chance of even serving as MKs so long as the Central Committee was with Netanyahu. Their options were either to topple Netanyahu or to establish a new political home.

Notes

1 The biblical expression of outrage directed by the prophet Elijah at King Ahab (1 Kings 21:19).
2 Yediot Aharonot, March 29, 2006.
3 Yisrael Hayom, June 13, 2014
4 Interview with the author, April 10, 2002.
5 Interview with the author, October 2, 2008.
6 Yediot Aharonot, December 4, 2011.
7 Interview with the author, April 21, 2002.

20 The fall of the first heirs' government

On October 23, 1998, following ten days of seclusion and intensive negotiations under heavy American pressure, the Wye River Memorandum was signed, in the presence of President Clinton, King Hussein of Jordan, Netanyahu, and Arafat. The aggressive goading of the American President forced Netanyahu into an agreement that in his eyes led to a flood of terror. The Wye Memorandum was the moment when the Likud was finally forced to implement the detested Oslo agreement against which the entire Right in Israel had protested and demonstrated. In its wake the Likud was torn to shreds, and elements from within went on to bring down the heirs' government.

The Wye Memorandum was intended to salvage, update, and implement the Oslo Accords and included an Israeli commitment to a three-phase redeployment, entailing withdrawal from about a tenth of the territory of Judea and Samaria (the "West Bank"). Netanyahu's political achievement in the new agreement was the principle of reciprocity, which demanded a commitment from the Palestinians to fight terror and prevent incitement, in return for the withdrawals (or "redeployments", to use the laundered language of diplomacy) set forth in the Oslo Accords. Netanyahu had to battle Clinton and his advisors on the issue of reciprocity. He argued that following the withdrawals from Jericho, Hebron, and other areas, the Palestinians had not fulfilled their obligations to collect illegal weapons, nor had they halted terror attacks, while he – Netanyahu – had been forced to negotiate with the head of a terror organization and to carry out territorial withdrawals (albeit initially on a minor scale). One can only imagine how difficult this must have been for the leader whose policy, as set out in his book, ruled out negotiations with terror organizations. As Prime Minister, Netanyahu had dreamed of implementing the worldview of his esteemed father, but instead he was forced to honor agreements that he opposed and to shake the hand of Arafat, the very symbol of bloodthirsty terror against Israel.

Two decades earlier, the peace agreement signed with Egypt at Camp David had led to right-wing MKs resigning from Begin's government, and the establishment of a new party under the leadership of MK Geula Cohen. Now it was Shamir who parted ways with the Prime Minister. Arens, the Likud veteran who had cultivated Netanyahu, was likewise adamantly opposed to the withdrawal. Now already seventy-three, Arens expressed his disappointment later on by submitting his (symbolic) candidacy against Netanyahu for chairman of the Likud.

Netanyahu made supreme efforts to explain his signing of the Wye Memorandum and to emphasize his achievements, including a reduction and postponement of the withdrawals and the stubborn insistence on reciprocity. Ultimately, he succeeded in doing what Begin Sr. had done after signing the peace treaty with Egypt: he persuaded most of the veterans against a radical break, such that they expressed only passive opposition to the agreement, within the party. Indeed, although former party leaders Shamir and Arens had declared an open war against Netanyahu, most of the veterans chose to remain part of the movement. They were disappointed, they were pained, but they did not leave – because the party was their family, and it was headed by an heir. The veterans, who had finally witnessed the realization of their long-held dreams, did not wish now to lose the government and their future.

Wye Memorandum – the heirs split into three ideological streams

For the heirs, the Wye Memorandum was a formative experience. For the first time, they were alone in power, completely independent, and trying to deal with a reality that had been forced upon them and now demanded that decisions be taken. Following previous challenges from which they had emerged (more or less) intact, they were now faced with the biggest test of all. It pitted the integrity of the Land of Israel against the Oslo Accords that handcuffed them.

In the absence of their biological and political parents and mentors, the heirs were free of the yoke of their Revisionist legacy and could respond individually, rather than having to conform to a unified stance. And thus, after two and a half years in power, and after fifty years of a shared heritage and shared values throughout their childhood, youth, and early political path, the heirs broke up into three groups.

The biggest news was the reaction of Dan Meridor. The man who up until now had spoken behind closed doors with friendly media personalities about the need for territorial compromise now stated openly and clearly the view that had always been categorically rejected by the fighting family: the Land of Israel had to accommodate two peoples. The vision of the Greater Land of Israel that had been nurtured by the parents must now be put to rest.

The first signs of Meridor's softening stance were manifest in his lukewarm and half-hearted opposition to the Oslo Accords. Meridor had criticized specific sections of the agreement but (in contrast to his colleagues) did not reject the essence of the agreements, which included repealing the blacklisting of Arafat. Now his position was given public expression in the form of unwavering support for the Wye Memorandum. Together with Roni Milo, mayor of Tel Aviv, who was already associated in the public mind with Oslo, Meridor presented Netanyahu with a moderate front. These two figures spearheaded the breach of the fighting family's ideological walls.

This time, the Tagar heirs were pragmatic and chose to support Netanyahu. Both they and Netanyahu continued to express their opposition in principle to the Oslo Accords but displayed a willingness to make tactical concessions that would allow the government to continue, based on the assumption that the agreements with the Palestinians would ultimately lead nowhere. They negotiated in the same way that Arafat did: they spoke, believing nothing of what the other side said; they signed, having no intention of putting the commitments into practice; they smiled for the cameras, believing that the true face of their enemy was about to be revealed, at which point the agreements could be discarded as the worthless pieces of paper that they had always known them to be.

Netanyahu and his supporters did not believe that the Palestinians, led by Arafat, were ready for compromise and real peace. They believed that Arafat followed a "salami strategy", working for incremental achievements that would cause Israel to shrink and become weakened, at which point it could be annihilated. Netanyahu found a loyal follower in Hanegbi, who had always been perceived as the most extreme right-wing element in the party. This was the same Hanegbi who, two decades earlier, following the peace agreement with Egypt, had left the Likud, together with his mother. Now, as Minister of Justice, Hanegbi understood and accepted the exigencies facing the Prime Minister.

The security situation and international pressure therefore led five heirs to support the new agreement, which included withdrawals from parts of the homeland. The two groups that were in favor – the moderate, conciliatory group and the activist-pragmatic group – comprised about half of the heirs serving in the Knesset. The Wye Memorandum showed that once the heirs were in the driving seat, they were far more pragmatic than they had been while sitting in the opposition.

The third group that arose as a result of the Wye Memorandum consisted of those who sought to continue the Revisionist legacy (and who, in their political maturity, became replicas of the parents' generation). First and foremost among these was Benny Begin, and he was joined by MKs Uzi Landau (chairman of the Knesset Committee on Security and Foreign Affairs) and Reuven Rivlin (chairman of the Likud faction); and, outside of the Knesset, Yossi Ahimeir and Ze'ev Jabotinsky Jr. Despite serving as Minister of Communications, Limor Livnat joined them, too. These "Land of Israel heirs" opposed outright the agreements with the Palestinians. The Wye Memorandum confronted them with an intractable dilemma. However, with the exception of one of them, these heirs chose not to break with their political home and destroy it. They allowed Netanyahu to pursue his path, despite their reservations. "I opposed Wye unequivocally," Rivlin told me in a conversation we had many years later.[1]

I told Bibi that it's bad enough that the Left gives away territory. [. . .] Will we do the same?! That's making things even worse. [. . .] I know that Bibi comes from a good home, but with the Wye Memorandum something happened between us.

When asked why he and the other Land of Israel heirs chose not to leave the government, he answered with characteristic frankness:

> We knew that our stance was worth between eight and fourteen mandates in an election, just as it was in the past, and so we had to maintain a large Likud as a way of preserving the most that we could of the Land of Israel.

The only one of the Land of Israel heirs who took action (for the second time in this term of office) was Benny Begin, who adhered to his consistent approach: no to a tactical willingness, prior to elections, to recognize the Oslo Accords; no to negotiations with the terrorist Arafat; no to the Hebron Agreement (at which point Begin resigned from the government); and no to the Wye Memorandum (which he referred to as an "unacceptable outrage").

In an interview with *Globes* financial newspaper, Begin said:

> Capitulation has become a value in its own right, even when everyone knows that the concessions don't achieve anything. If a right-wing government provides living space for terror, is it really a right-wing government? [. . .] More than anything else what we see here is the docility and weariness of the leadership in Israel, and the dissolution of the nationalist camp. [. . .] The readiness to concede land is turning the Likud into a party centered around real-estate.[2]

Despite the objections, the government approved the Wye Memorandum. Netanyahu was aided in this regard by none other than Sharon, who, within a few weeks, shifted from vehement opposition to the agreement, to wholehearted support. As in the implementation of the peace agreement with Egypt in 1981, Sharon, as a senior minister, switched sides the moment he became party to what was happening. In the earlier instance, Begin had needed a Minister of Defense who would evacuate the Jewish settlements in the Sinai, and Sharon carried out the task after receiving the appointment. Now the same scenario repeated itself: Netanyahu appointed Sharon as Foreign Minister and took him along to Wye River Plantation. There he sat with Arafat while the negotiations were conducted, although he refrained from shaking hands with him. Sharon helped to formulate the agreement and to obtain the approval of the government. In return for his support, he demanded (and received) an official promise of a senior portfolio in Netanyahu's next government. The assumption was that Netanyahu would be re-elected.

Division and downfall in the 1999 elections

The ideological and personal crises that buffeted the heirs did not break the government apart right away. The Wye Memorandum was supposed to bring back the more moderate heirs, Meridor and Milo, but it did not lead to reconcilement. Each for his own reasons had already made a final break with Netanyahu. At the other end, the Land of Israel heirs, who held senior ministerial positions, were not in a hurry to let the government fall.

Up until the Wye Memorandum, Begin Jr. had been an internal ideological opposition, but he took no part in the secret meetings of rebels against Netanyahu. Now, the signing of the agreement led him to lead the revolt and the most bitter confrontation between two heirs. After just two months, Begin broke the rules of the game and shocked the Likud veterans. He resigned from his father's movement and, from the opposition, joined with MKs representing the far-right, with the purpose of bringing down the government at the end of 1998. In the end it was the son of Menachem Begin, of all people, who caused the collapse of the most right-wing government that the country had known.

Begin's departure divided and weakened the group of Land of Israel heirs. They were left orphaned in the Likud, with no leader charismatic or powerful enough to lead the movement. Begin founded a movement that he named Herut, thereby signaling its direction: a return to the original ideal, to the historical Herut which would never relinquish an inch of the Land of Israel. The new-old name set Begin apart from the party he had left, which he felt had become submissive, unprincipled, and undemocratic. At the beginning of 1999, when his new party showed no ascent in the polls, Begin united with the extreme right-wing factions. Together they formed a new party: the National Union. Begin wanted to present his candidacy for direct election as Prime Minister, against Netanyahu, but withdrew following pressure from his partners, who were severely criticized by their voters for their part in bringing down a right-wing government. At this point they were not prepared for Begin to also split the right-wing vote for Prime Minister. They preferred that the contest be between Netanyahu and the Labor candidate, Ehud Barak. Their own battle with the Likud would concern the size of the Knesset lists.

Many of the heirs who were united in their hatred of Netanyahu parted ways the moment they needed to choose a leader from among themselves.

Meridor and Milo left the Likud and formed the Hamerkaz party. For a short time they allowed themselves to waft in the results of polls that predicted some twenty mandates for their new party, but their alliance was marred by frequent bickering over the leadership. Eventually, the number one slot was given to the popular Minister of Defense, Itzik Mordechai, who demanded this as his condition for leaving the Likud and joining them.

To the outside observer, the new party looked like a dream team. It included an esteemed and popular Chief-of-Staff (Amnon Lipkin-Shahak), who at different times had headed the country's Northern, Central, and Southern Commands and who had also served as Minister of Defense; mayor of Tel Aviv Roni Milo; and three heirs representing both sides of the political divide – Meridor and Milo from the Likud, and Rabin's daughter, Dalia Rabin-Pelossof, from Labor. Milo and Meridor thus found themselves sharing a political home with prominent leftist figures including not only Lipkin-Shahak and Rabin-Pelossof, but also Shimon Sheves, who had been director general of the PMO under Rabin; Labor MK Nissim Zvilli; and Peres's advisor for Oslo, Uri Savir. The idea that this diverse group could form a party together was, at the time, a revolutionary, new, and exhilarating prospect, especially as Netanyahu's government came across as an arena of endless strife and controversy. Indeed, the new party received much positive press coverage.

It soon became apparent that the team was less of a "dream" than it appeared. Each of the four heads of the new party viewed him/herself as a leader and not a follower. Each of them had left his/her previous political home and had joined the party not to serve as an MK but in order to be Prime Minister. There were leaks from each of the party heads concerning each of the others; the glue – hatred of Netanyahu – that held them together was no match for their personal ambitions, and the centrist party dream team ended up crashing. The party received six mandates, and each of the MKs drifted off in a different direction.

The only one who benefitted from this debacle was Labor candidate Ehud Barak. The dissolution of the Hamerkaz party ended with Itzik Mordechai retracting his candidacy for Prime Minister just prior to the elections, and Barak gained his voters, along with all those who had abandoned Netanyahu. Without having intended it, the heirs Meridor and Milo found themselves supporting the Labor candidate against the party in which they had grown up and served, against an heir who shared their same roots.

Everyone in the Likud was pained by Begin's departure. But even those who had agreed with his position disagreed with his decision. The fighting family opposed any form of internal revolt or splitting, even – perhaps especially – if it concerned the son of the party's founder.

Most of the heirs therefore remained in the Likud. However, they were not all of the same mind. Some were Netanyahu loyalists (Hanegbi, Boim, and the new candidate Tzipi Livni), while two heirs who opposed him and deliberated the options (Livnat and Olmert) decided eventually, only at the very last moment, to remain part of the Likud.

Whereas Livnat did not consider for a moment the possibility of leaving the party together with Begin, whose views were closely aligned with her own, she thought long and hard about leaving together with her good friends and fellow heirs: the moderates Milo and Meridor. She weighed up the party established by her friends against the party of her youth, whose chairman was on bad terms with her; the moderates' stance against that of the Land of Israel camp; a new and untested party against the well-established Likud. In a meeting of reconciliation held in January 1999, a few days before the internal Likud elections, Netanyahu persuaded her to remain, promising that he would work to improve the relations and interaction between them. Both must have known deep down that nothing could erase the scars of the past, but Netanyahu did not want another highly publicized desertion of another popular minister, and Livnat, for her part, was hesitant to join a centrist party – a move that would be interpreted as a betrayal of the party of her father, who was still alive and influential.

Olmert, too, remained in the Likud, aspiring to leadership but seeing the path blocked to him. He saw the admiration for Netanyahu that persisted despite everything and offered not the slightest chance of Olmert defeating him. On the other hand, no-one was inviting him to lead the new Hamerkaz party. Not only did his friends not want him as their leader; they were fighting between themselves over the leadership. Under these circumstances, he preferred to remain safely in his office as mayor of Jerusalem, waiting for the next round of internal elections in the Likud. Olmert saw that the Likud was being emptied of candidates for future leadership after Netanyahu and wagered that the Likud's defeat in the upcoming elections would lead to Netanyahu's downfall, offering Olmert the opportunity to succeed him.

In the elections for Likud chairman, held in 1999, none of those who had once been considered potential leadership successors was left in the party. The once-impressive cadre of candidates had managed to implode during what should have been a golden term of office. Begin, Milo, and Meridor had left. So had David Levy, who had now teamed up with Barak. Ariel Sharon was left weakened, the target of much acrimony over a decade of battles that had ended with the party's loss of power.

As though the desertion of the moderates was not enough, during the election campaign the Land of Israel camp made another symbolic gesture of ideological independence. At the start of the campaign, Uzi Landau announced that he would contend against Netanyahu for the party leadership. It was clear that he stood no chance, but in view of the concessions entailed in the Hebron and Wye agreements, he wanted the party to have an ideological alternative to Netanyahu. Then came an even bigger surprise: after seven years away from the political sphere, Arens reappeared and presented his candidacy against Netanyahu. Although he, too, was clearly not headed for victory, it was important to him to express his displeasure with the conduct and policy adopted by his protégé. In light of this development Landau retracted his candidacy and devoted himself to supporting Arens. Olmert, too, expressed support for Arens, in an attempt to weaken Netanyahu and build an opposition that would serve his own candidacy after Netanyahu's anticipated defeat in the elections.

Netanyahu responded by going out of his way to appease Arens. He appointed him Minister of Defense (replacing Mordechai, who had resigned), thereby offering the veterans a double bargain: by voting for Netanyahu, they would see an heir at the party's helm, along with a well-respected veteran as Minister of Defense.

Netanyahu, as expected, won the internal election with a very wide margin: seventy percent to him, twenty percent to Arens. Nevertheless, Arens's challenge was perceived as an expression of no confidence on the part of this veteran Revisionist towards the youngster he had nurtured, and it harmed Netanyahu in the general elections. The rest of the veterans continued to show unwavering support for Netanyahu. He was, in effect, the consolation for the terrible blow they had suffered with the desertion of the early heirs.

Elections of 1999 – the heirs lose power

For the second time, a right-wing government was brought down by the Right. Two Likud governments fell before completing their terms (1992, 1999), at the hands of internal elements, after their leaders (Yitzhak Shamir, Benjamin Netanyahu) were accused of spineless over-accommodation. Both leaders were replaced by heads of the Labor party (Yitzhak Rabin, Ehud Barak), who, upon taking office, each set about advancing negotiations towards unprecedented and far-reaching concessions.

Netanyahu's defeat to Barak in the general elections of 1999 was like a final chord in a symphony. Surrounded by enemies and burdened with accusations and libels, Netanyahu tried desperately to save his seat. But he was now up against hostile character witnesses who had been part of his own government. The support that Likud heirs displayed for Barak was impossible to counter.

It must be remembered that at the beginning of the campaign, even after all the events described earlier, Netanyahu was still the leading candidate, with widespread support among the public. Barak was unable to gain traction even among his own party. He was close to being replaced, with another candidate – the eternal Peres, ever-popular in the polls – breathing down his neck.

But in the months leading up to the election Barak surged in the polls, mainly owing to the warring among the heirs, which weakened Netanyahu. The Prime Minister endured a battering from within and without, absorbing all the acrimony that still remained from Rabin's assassination. Voters watched as Arens and Landau – figures close to Netanyahu and at the very heart of the Likud – were now turning their backs on him and running against him. Figures who had long been associated with the Likud – such as Begin, Meridor, Milo, and Levy, and even the newcomer, Mordechai – were not only deserting the party but warning against Netanyahu as Prime Minister, out of personal familiarity with him. Two heirs and two other senior Likud figures (Meridor, Milo, Mordechai, and Levy) expressed openly their support for the Labor candidate. The outcome was not hard to predict. Netanyahu was defeated in the direct elections by Barak, who won fifty-six percent of the vote to Netanyahu's forty-four. The Likud shrank to a mere nineteen mandates.

The veterans could only comfort themselves with the knowledge that ten heirs were now MKs. Seven represented Likud (Netanyahu, Livnat, Landau, Rivlin, Hanegbi, Boim, and – for the first time – Tzipi Livni); two represented the Center party (Milo and Meridor); and one represented the National Union (Begin). While the heirs were divided, they remained in the top tier of Israeli politics.

*

On election night, May 17, 1999, as the results emerged, Netanyahu announced his resignation from all offices he held in the party and in the Knesset. This was a show of personal accountability unprecedented in Israeli politics.

At three in the morning, as we stood with our wives, Sara and Tali, on the balcony of the Hilton Hotel in Tel Aviv, Netanyahu did not wallow in self-pity but instead launched into a review of his mistakes. Even his harshest critics in the press would not have subjected him to such cold, hard, searching analysis. Those who knew him well could see that on that very night he embarked on the long road of learning lessons that would restore the nation's faith in him.

What Netanyahu never imagined that night was that the road would be much longer than he imagined, and unbearably hard. He did not know that the next step would not be his own but rather the initiative of his adversaries who wanted revenge as well as a knockout blow. Immediately upon his departure from office, there was intensified persecution of Netanyahu along with his wife, and they were forced to defend themselves in two legal cases that were portrayed in the media as involving "corruption" (keeping official gifts and accepting favors from a mover). There were humiliating, public investigations which were concluded (once again) without any indictment, but which stained the reputations of Netanyahu and his wife.

The 1999 elections changed the fundamental axioms of Israeli politics. Up until 1996 the political map was divided into a distinct Right and Left. The Labor (Left) initiated and supported concessions in return for peace, while the Likud (Right) believed that security was bound up with the territories earned in 1967. In the 1999 elections, this clear division became blurred. The new centrist Hamerkaz party brought together MKs from both sides. This attempt at a political "restart" ultimately failed, but it left a lasting impression. For the first time, heirs of both political homes – children of Begin and children of Ben-Gurion – came together in opposition to the Likud.

The moment that MKs of the stature of Benny Begin, Meridor, and Rabin-Pelossof abandoned their parents' parties, the age of party loyalty came to an end. It was an historical moment that ushered in a new age of greater flexibility and movement among the different camps and parties. David Levy, who had been a Likud icon, was living proof of the new reality. In the 1999 elections he moved to the rival camp, joining Barak as number two on the party list which, for the benefit of Levy and other disillusioned Likudniks, was called One Israel, but was in fact the Labor list with some additions.

The first heirs' government marked the beginning of the recognition among the Likud that the dream of the Greater Land of Israel – the dream that had accompanied the heirs all their lives – was coming to an end. While the family rhetoric might still sound the same, it was clear that the Likud heirs had become more moderate in their political view and accepted a reality that ran counter to the old worldview.

Preface to the war of the elites

What Netanyahu faced after his defeat was described as follows by Amnon Lord, writing eighteen years later:[3] "In order to understand the basis for the claim that a regime of investigations can become a way of carrying out regime change, one has to go back to 1999." He quotes journalist Ari Shavit of *Haaretz*, who wrote (on June 18, 1999):

> Faced with what was regarded as a regime that was elected but dangerous, elected but not legitimate, it was only natural that the counter-action of the President, aimed at halting the regime, was perceived as protecting

democracy, rather than threatening it. And when over the course of the past year something substantial changed, and the Israeli elites decided that they had to eliminate this elected regime almost at any price, and that to this end they were ready to steamroll almost all professional and ethical norms, it was almost a foregone conclusion that the non-normative behavior of the President, and the flagrant intervention in the political process, would be viewed as a blessing. [. . .] However, now that this "enlightened putsch" or "democratic putsch" (as some people referred to it) has succeeded, now that the former regime has been banished in disgrace, the test facing all those who were part of this multi-pronged operation is whether they will be able to go back to regular civic life. Will the generals be able to go back to their fortresses; will the journalists be able to go back to their work? Will the government clerks and Shin Bet personnel and police officers all understand that now, with the task accomplished, the great mobilization is over? That now that enlightenment has once again taken the reins, the role of the enlightened ones is for each to go back to his place, to the clear boundaries of the role entrusted to him within the framework of the democratic division of authority?

Lord then commented:

Please note: "the generals"; "the Shin Bet personnel and police officers"; "inter-departmental operation". The unrelenting pressure of empty investigations and needless enquiries over the years since Benjamin Netanyahu's victory in 1996, and even since his defeat in the 1999 elections, has had its effect. And over the last year the dam has burst and once again it's the same loathsome, anti-democratic scenario all over again.

Just to elaborate a little on that "enlightened putsch" of 1999: here is an example of the advertisements published in the press the day before the elections, calling to "topple Bibi tomorrow or place Israel's future at risk". It's signed by former Mossad heads Zvi Zamir and Meir Amit; former Shin Bet head, Avraham Ahituv; by former senior Mossad personnel Avner Azoulai, Shmuel Toledano, Nahik Navot, and David Kimhi.

This was the sort of daunting pressure that that former security establishment personnel were constantly exerting on the public during the period leading up to the elections. Ari Shavit wasn't exaggerating. In the days following the election, Yoel Marcus, writing in *Haaretz*, called Netanyahu a "public criminal". Marcus asserted that his defeat in the elections was "the only thing that Bibi earned honestly."

Notes

1 Interview with the author, June 11, 2002.
2 Globes, December 29, 1998.
3 Yisrael Hayom, September 14, 2017.

Part IV

Likud breakaway becomes the party of Sharon, Olmert, and Livni

Netanyahu resigned his position after he lost in the 1999 elections but helped his old rival, the glorified General Ariel Sharon, against his fellow "Princes" led by Olmert, whom he feared would remain in power for many years. In the general election, Sharon surprisingly overcame another glorified general, the Labor party leader Ehud Barak, in the 2001 elections and was appointed Prime Minister. Netanyahu returned to politics and began five years of bitter rivalry with Sharon. Netanyahu stood at the head of the right-wing in the Likud, with most of the "Princes" on his side. Sharon, on the other hand, adopted left-wing views as Prime Minister and subsequently introduced a historical opponent, the Labor party, into becoming an integral part of the government. Sharon then initiated and carried out a one-sided retreat from the Gaza Strip. Consequently, another inner battle erupted in the Likud, this time triggering Ariel Sharon's resignation from the Likud. Sharon formed a new party (Kadima) and managed to take with him some of the "Princes" like the rising political star Tzipi Livni, Ehud Olmert, Roni Milo, and Dan Meridor, who left their parents' party. Netanyahu stayed and was chosen to lead the Likud in 2005, and he would do so for the next thirteen years.

When Sharon went into a coma after having suffered a stroke, his replacement was Ehud Olmert, and in the election of 2006 for the first time, two Princes fought for the leadership from two different parties. This would occur once again in 2008 when Netanyahu beat Tzipi Livni, Ehud Olmert's successor.

21 The Sharon-Netanyahu war

On the night of the dramatic defeat in 1999, Netanyahu announced his resignation as chairman of the Likud, astonishing everyone by unofficially handing the leadership of the party to Sharon, who was the only senior minister who had been smart enough to stand by Netanyahu at the critical moment. In the emotional speech that he delivered that night at the Hilton Hotel in Tel Aviv, Netanyahu thanked just two people: Sharon, for supporting him at this most difficult time, and his wife, Sara.

A great many Likud members tried to persuade Netanyahu to remain. Even after his defeat, Netanyahu – generally hated by the Left – still enjoyed an unparalleled level of support within the right-wing camp. Likud activists had trouble accepting the new political norm whereby a leader who loses an election assumes responsibility and resigns. Previous leaders who had found themselves in this situation – including Begin and Peres – had not taken this step.

It was not only Sharon's show of support for Netanyahu that caused the defeated leader to hand the reins over to him. Before the election Netanyahu had understood that he was going to lose, and had started preparing for the future, starting with his resignation, which would come as a surprise, and an astute transferral of power to his preferred replacement. In his estimation, the seventy-one-year-old Sharon was a better option than one of the younger stars who might make it more difficult for Netanyahu to make a quick political comeback. By the time the Likud recovered from the shock of Netanyahu's resignation, Sharon was already regarded as his natural successor.

Ten years earlier, the relations between Netanyahu and Sharon had started off well, despite the fact that Netanyahu belonged to the Shamir-Arens camp.

Unlike the early heirs, Netanyahu had not participated in the aggressive Likud battles of the 1980s, and the strong resentment that built up towards Sharon among the early heirs in the 1980s was foreign to him. During the First Lebanon War he had been stationed in the Israeli embassy in Washington. While Begin and Meridor worked behind the scenes against Sharon, the Minister of Defense who, to their view, had misled Menachem Begin, Netanyahu had been immersed in diplomacy and defending the Israeli position. Later on, when Olmert, Milo, and Meridor united against Sharon (and in support of Shamir), Netanyahu was serving as Israel's ambassador to the UN. Thus, he had not been involved in the bitter and acrimonious clashes that characterized the Likud conventions in 1986 and 1987. While remaining updated as to what was going on in Israel, he was not personally involved in the Likud's political battles. He held meetings with representatives of all the camps, thereby positioning himself as a consensual, non-aligned figure within the party.

When Netanyahu returned to Israel and re-integrated into the party in anticipation of the 1988 elections, he therefore held no resentment or ill-will towards Sharon. He had positive memories of Sharon as a courageous general during his military service in the Six Day War, the War of Attrition, and the Yom Kippur War. And so although he belonged to the Shamir-Arens camp, his relations with Sharon were good. In addition, it did not take long before they shared the same rivals: the early heirs. So it was that in his run for a Knesset seat, at the start of his political career, Netanyahu received support from Sharon's camp, even though Sharon gave no explicit directive in this regard. Sharon's followers viewed Netanyahu as a true leader who had entered politics after a sterling diplomatic career, and not as just another "heir" who had achieved his position simply by being a "son-of". (Netanyahu's Revisionist family lineage was not widely known.)

In the internal elections of 1992, Netanyahu was the initiator and the central axis of the temporary alliance between Shamir-Arens and Sharon, leading to the defeat of Levy's camp. He led the campaign on behalf of Arens, the intended successor, and managed to draw Sharon's sworn enemies (Begin, Meridor, and Milo) into a political alliance with him. Anyone watching the harmonious cooperation could see that Arens was ready to hand the leadership over to Netanyahu, bypassing the early heirs.

In the contest for the Likud chairmanship in 1993, Sharon was weak and his following had declined, and so he chose not to submit his candidacy. While not supporting Netanyahu openly, he allowed his people to vote as they wished, knowing that they would support Netanyahu rather than Shamir and Benny Begin. No doubt Sharon was not happy about being overtaken by an heir, but Netanyahu was the least objectionable option, considering that he had also sidelined Sharon's bitterest enemies among the early heirs.

In the struggle over the Oslo Accords, Sharon and Netanyahu maintained full cooperation and were the most active MKs opposing Rabin's government. Together they spearheaded the right-wing demonstrations, including the infamous demonstration at Zion Square, and they absorbed the brunt of the criticism both from without (the media and the Left) and from within (the early heirs) for their participation at those events.

In the 1996 elections Sharon was obviously not happy that Netanyahu was the Likud candidate for Prime Minister. At the same time, the moment he understood that the only options were Netanyahu and Meridor, he quickly blocked the efforts to replace Netanyahu. During the election campaign Sharon worked in favor of the Likud candidate, mobilizing the ultra-Orthodox to support Netanyahu and thus playing a central role in bringing him to power.

In Netanyahu's first government the relations between the two men were outwardly warm and grew closer in the wake of the efforts to subvert Netanyahu's position. The harder the early heirs worked against Netanyahu, the closer Sharon drew to him. As the internal and external opposition to Netanyahu grew more intense, Sharon's position within the party leadership grew stronger. In order to earn the support of the hawkish Sharon for the Wye Memorandum, Netanyahu appointed him Foreign Minister. Thus, following fifteen years of internal battles, Netanyahu became the first Likud leader to restore Sharon – by then widely regarded as a political "has-been" – to the senior leadership of the party and the country.

Netanyahu and the veterans take revenge on Olmert

Olmert had competed against Sharon in the primaries held in September 1999. He was the only heir who had submitted his candidacy to lead the party, since the four strongest contenders at the time (Netanyahu, Meridor, Begin, and Milo) were either outside of the party or outside of politics altogether. The only candidate among the younger MKs was Meir Sheetrit, who, while popular as one of the leaders of the Mizrahi revolution in the development towns, and as an articulate and unconventional MK, nevertheless stood no chance, in view of his conspicuously left-wing views.

The middle-generation leaders who had been expected to replace Shamir were likewise seemingly out of the way: David Levy had left the party and was now a member of Barak's government. Shamir's natural successor, the seventy-four-year-old Moshe Arens, had resigned seven years previously (although he did later make a brief comeback). The seventy-one-year-old Ariel Sharon, the sole candidate representing the middle generation, was perceived as an aging, tired leader. Olmert believed that the path to the top of the Likud was paved and ready for him. With some thirty years of politics behind him and a solid record as a hawk, he was certain that he could rehabilitate the crumbling party. In his campaign he presented himself as a candidate capable of reunifying the Likud after Netanyahu's divisive term in office, and bringing back the early heirs who had left the party – Begin in one direction, and Milo and Meridor in the other.

In fact, Olmert did not even wait until Netanyahu was actually defeated. A few days before the 1999 elections, with the rivalry between Netanyahu and Barak at boiling point, Olmert took a step that astounded the Likud: he allowed Barak's campaign managers to use the video of an interview that he had given as mayor of Jerusalem, in which he had declared that Barak had no intention of dividing Jerusalem (in direct contradiction of the thesis that formed the basis of Netanyahu's campaign). This was a stunning and humiliating blow to Netanyahu and his camp: Olmert was manifestly aiding the rival party's candidate. Olmert was so keen to replace Netanyahu and to clear the way for his own ascent to the top of the party ranks that he was willing to cooperate with the Labor party and to help bring victory to Barak.

But Olmert made three mistakes. Firstly, he failed to foresee that the strongest opposition to his candidacy would come from within the party, from the veterans and the fighting family. Secondly, he underestimated Netanyahu's power within the Likud. He thought that Netanyahu's future in the party was over, failing to grasp that the Likud would automatically rally around and embrace its leader who was being slandered in the media. (Olmert, of all people, should have remembered how the much-maligned and vilified Begin had survived three decades of electoral defeat and scorn in the Knesset.) Thirdly, Olmert miscalculated the potency of Netanyahu's response to his betrayal. Netanyahu was burning with revenge towards him for his subversive interference and for helping to bring Barak to power. In addition, he was eager to block a young candidate who could potentially obstruct the comeback he was already planning (at this stage, without anyone's knowledge).

Interesting evidence of Netanyahu's aid to Sharon in the primaries against Olmert is to be found in an interview that MK Eli Aflalo granted to Boaz Gaon of *Maariv*. Aflalo, who was one of the main activists in support of Netanyahu, was also responsible for setting up Sharon's election campaign for the primaries. "The person who requested of Aflalo to help Arik was Bibi, in his 1999 incarnation," Gaon wrote. "Netanyahu told Aflalo that Sharon was already old, such that his appointment as chairman [of the Likud] would not endanger [Netanyahu's] own status."[1] Netanyahu's camp, which comprised the majority of the Likud, did not vote for Sharon for the most part but were active on his behalf.

Olmert's loss to Sharon in the Likud primaries was another important milestone in the history of inter-generational relations in the Likud. It was yet another stage in the splitting of the fighting family. Olmert had not gauged the depth of the schism between himself and the veterans. He found it difficult to believe that they would prefer to stand on the sidelines and refrain from participating in the election – for the first time in their lives – rather than helping an heir who had fought at their side in the past to block Sharon, the "invader". After all, Olmert was the son of an Irgun fighter and MK, a born-and-raised Revisionist, and the only one among the candidates who knew the words to the Beitar anthem. He had proven his commitment to the legacy of the underground more thoroughly than any other heir had done by naming streets after the heroes and building monuments in their honor.

To his astonishment, however, the veterans turned their backs on him, acceding to Netanyahu's call to help elect Sharon (temporarily) instead. By abstaining from voting for Olmert, they allowed their bitter adversary to become the party's new leader. The rejection of Olmert by the veterans went beyond the punishments they meted out to other heirs. His betrayal of Netanyahu revived the hostile distrust that the veterans had harbored towards him since the days of Shmuel Tamir's revolt against Begin some thirty-three years previously. Although Shamir had forgiven Olmert and had repaired the relationship between them, the veterans seemed not to have forgotten or forgiven the "insolent upstart" for the speech he had given at the age of twenty-one. They had supported him when he defended Shamir, but their support had always been provisional and guarded. Even when he had made hardline right-wing decisions as mayor (such as opening the Western Wall Tunnels and building the Har Homa neighborhood) they suspected that his motivation was more electoral than ideological. They also read the articles that appeared in the media exposing his covert leftist views. They concluded that he was in fact a dove in hawk's clothing.

Olmert failed to attract the support of most of even his own generation. Rivlin, Landau, Hanegbi, and Livnat all supported Sharon, while Meridor, Milo, and Begin were by now all outside of the movement. Olmert was supported by just two new heirs: his childhood friend Zeev Boim and the young Tzipi Livni.

The previous leaders, Shamir and Arens, supported Olmert. They could not contemplate seeing their rival, Sharon, taking control of their old political home. In addition, they viewed Olmert as having been their full partner in the battles of succession in the 1980s. From their point of view, he was a born-and-bred member of the fighting family; he had built in Jerusalem and commemorated the Revolt. But this time, the veterans refused to toe the line. They already had a different leader, even though he was in the process of stepping down.

The beneficiary of the split among the fighting family was Sharon. On September 9, 1999, he received fifty-three percent of the vote (Olmert received twenty-four percent; Sheetrit twenty-two) and became the new Likud chairman. The Netanyahu camp, which had supported Sharon and led to this victory, viewed the new chairman as a mere substitute for the "real" chairman, Netanyahu. None of them dreamed that this "old" and "temporary" chairman would revive himself and become someone new.

Sharon assumes leadership of the Likud in the shadow of Netanyahu's return

Sharon himself could hardly believe that he had realized his dream and was finally installed on the twelfth floor of the Likud headquarters, in Begin's mythological office, from which he had been distanced for so long by Likud leaders.

Sharon, now aged seventy-two, achieved what he had aspired to for many years only after it already appeared (even to himself) that he no longer stood any chance with the public, owing to events of the past and battles of succession. He became chairman of the Likud after watching more and more heirs overtaking him, defeating him in internal elections, disparaging him in the media, and receiving senior appointments. He became the Likud chairman after watching Netanyahu, a full twenty-one years younger than himself, leaving him way behind. In the first heirs' government he had been relegated to a low-profile ministry, and it was only through supreme efforts, and by virtue of his experience and survival skills, that he had managed to remain on the Likud map. After thirty years of aggressive, combative, bellicose, intensive, and frustrating efforts, he had finally made it.

Sharon reaped the benefits of a rather rare situation: the heirs had in fact destroyed one another, leaving the road clear for Sharon. The competition among the heirs had eroded the unifying force that had blocked him for two decades. Following the generational revolution that brought the heirs to power, pushing the middle generation aside, leadership of the party suddenly fell into the hands of Sharon, the first "outsider" in the party's history who managed to penetrate the Likud headquarters.

But even as chairman of the Likud, Sharon was regarded as no more than a temporary fixture. The political discourse referred to him openly as "over the hill". People who held meetings with him during this period felt he was no longer the same Sharon: MKs reported that he would nod off during work meetings, and in encounters with young activists he would veer off the subject of the discussion and start recounting stories from his military past. When I was summoned, as chairman of the Public Broadcasting Authority, for a meeting with him at Likud headquarters, I was shocked to find an old man who kept returning to stories about the conquest of Beer Sheba. When I left his office, I called my father, who was Sharon's contemporary and had also participated in the battle for Beer Sheba. We both thought that it would have been more appropriate for my father to have had the talk with Sharon. They had much more in common. Sharon seemed exhausted after fifty years of bloody battles in the army and in politics. No-one believed there was any chance that he could win a general election. Anyone who met him felt that Sharon himself had trouble believing that Israelis would support him. *Maariv* described Sharon and Peres as standing together on the threshold, on their way out of political life. Sharon was described as "a temporary, abandoned, iso- lated head of the opposition."[2]

Like the political commentators, Sharon knew that the heart of the Likud belonged to Netanyahu. Netanyahu remained the uncontested leader, even after his defeat and his resignation, leaving behind a demoralized party with just a handful of MKs. It was after Netanyahu's departure that it became clear how powerfully he had conquered the movement's heart. Likud activists admired him and awaited his return. Once again, the pattern repeated itself: the more savagely the Likud leader was attacked from the outside, the more love he was shown within the movement. As in the days of Jabotinsky and Begin, anyone who spoke out against the leader was punished, suffering the revenge of the generation of the Revolt. Indeed, whoever harmed Netanyahu was simply rejected, to the point of banishment from the movement.

Netanyahu estimated that it would take a few years until he could return. He left the Knesset and turned to his own independent interests, but he maintained con- tact with the activists. He made no attempt to fend off the waves of support, which caught even him by surprise, and half a year after his resignation he already knew that he could soon be back. He set up an office with professional staff, referred to in the media as the "submarine" – an apt name for a body that was mostly out of sight, only occasionally surfacing. Netanyahu himself made appearances only at carefully chosen times and places.

The staff of the "submarine" included volunteer consultants specializing in media communications, politics, diplomacy, policy-setting, and law, who met with him on a weekly basis. His senior advisors included Ron Dermer (later to become Netanyahu's cabinet secretary and later ambassador in Washington), Gideon Saar (the outgoing cabinet secretary, later to serve as a minister), Dr. Dore Gold (the outgoing ambassador to the UN, and political advisor to Prime Minister Netanyahu), and Aviv Bushinsky (a well-respected journalist who accompanied Prime Minister Netanyahu as his media advisor). His lawyers, David Shimron and David Molcho, were also in constant contact, as was Amos Regev (later to become editor-in-chief of *Yisrael Hayom*). I accompanied Netanyahu during the 1993 primaries and joined the team prior to the 1996 elections.

The veterans waited for Netanyahu. He was their last hope. They had been disappointed by the betrayal, twice in a row, by the early heirs. For the first time in their lives, they had nothing to do but to wait it out while the foreign invader settled into headquarters. The veterans had to start cultivating a new cadre of heirs, to bolster the few loyalists who remained in the Knesset. The direction in which Netanyahu invested his greatest efforts was his connection with the veterans. Even now, he never refused an invitation to any of their events: he attended those events, delivered speeches, shared embraces. Of course, he was the regular guest of honor at the Rosh Hashana (New Year) event organized by the Tagar Circle, headed by Eli Sheetrit, which was attended by about fifteen hundred former Irgun fighters. The oldest members of the movement were still the most loyal to Netanyahu. It was clear that they were pressing him to return.

When Prime Minister Barak came crashing down in 2000, just over half a year after entering office, it was clear to all that Netanyahu would be back. Netanyahu had already branded himself in his "concerned citizen" speech, which portrayed him not as a politician seeking power, but rather as an involved citizen who was troubled about what was happening to the country under Prime Minister Barak. He made dignified, statesmanlike appearances that showed him off as a model of confident, articulate leadership.

Indeed, every time Netanyahu made an appearance against the backdrop of Barak's flailing collapse, the public felt greater longing for this concerned leader who displayed no desire to be Prime Minister. But the subtext, indicating that Netanyahu would return, came through loud and clear.

The Likud prepared to welcome him back. Polls showed that he would retake the Likud effortlessly. They also predicted that he would defeat the unpopular Barak in general elections. In retrospect, Netanyahu's term of office, plagued with invective and mistakes, already looked different. Right-wing voters felt that he had suffered an injustice. As after Rabin's assassination, they wanted to repair the injustice that his rivals in the Knesset and among the elite had perpetrated. The Knesset (which was contentious towards Barak and wanted Netanyahu back) even amended the law preventing anyone who was not an MK from running for Prime Minister.

However, just when Barak announced his resignation in December 2000 and announced new elections for Prime Minister, Netanyahu surprised everyone by making his return conditional on having not only the personal elections for Prime Minister moved forward but also the general elections for the Knesset. (We recall that at this stage there were still two separate ballots for the Knesset elections and for Prime Minister). He argued that he would not be able to function as Prime Minister if the Likud held only nineteen mandates. He expected his partner in the future coalition, the Shas party, to cooperate in this regard. But Shas refused. It was not willing to risk the record seventeen mandates that it had achieved in the 1999 elections; some of the party's new voters would likely go back to voting for Likud.

The entire political establishment was in shock. Israel had not previously encountered a leader who was willing to forego his certain election as Prime Minister. The veterans were profoundly disappointed but once again reconciled themselves to Netanyahu's decision. They even tried to explain his logic, but they were heartbroken. They were forced to live with the bitter reality of Sharon as chairman of the Likud and its candidate for Prime Minister. There was simply no-one else.

The Likud heirs who had already lined up at Netanyahu's side – including Livni, Hanegbi, Boim, and Landau – were caught unprepared. For them, this was one let-down too many. Now they would have to go back to the incumbent chairman, Sharon, and support him, in the hope that he would win the election and appoint them as ministers, despite their "defection".

And so Sharon won the premiership a second time and received the chairmanship of the Likud on a silver platter. There was no other candidate on the horizon: Silvan Shalom, the only strong contender who could have presented serious competition, had withdrawn his candidacy when it had seemed that Netanyahu would be returning, and had joined up with Sharon in return for a promise that he would be number two and would receive a senior ministry. The political situation also played into Sharon's hands, with the inexperienced Barak making every possible mistake and thereby losing most of his supporters and partners. Barak engaged in an unsuccessful round of negotiations with the Palestinians in July 2000, at Camp David. He aroused a thunderous public outcry when he offered Arafat the most far-reaching concessions ever (Israel would relinquish ninety percent of the territory of Judea, Samaria, and Gaza, and would grant the Palestinians sovereignty over the Arab neighborhoods in East Jerusalem and religious sovereignty over the Temple Mount). In his usual fashion, Arafat rewarded this generous offer by launching a second murderous Intifada, in September 2000, leading to Barak's downfall.

Barak had now lost his chance to make peace, and he stood for election in the midst of the bloody Intifada. Suddenly, everything lined up in Sharon's favor. He was portrayed as an alternative leader who was older and more experienced than the reckless Barak. Sharon awoke from his hibernation, filled with new and unexpected energy, and ready to make the most of the historical opportunity that had come his way.

2001 – Ariel Sharon is Prime Minister

On Tuesday, February 6, 2001, Ariel Sharon performed another political feat and defeated the incumbent Ehud Barak in the direct elections for Prime Minister. The old Likud moshavnik won a resounding victory (62.5 percent) against the young Labor kibbutznik (37.5 percent).

Even after taking office, Sharon was constantly watching for Netanyahu's shadow. He was fully conscious of Netanyahu's popularity and knew what a danger he would present in general elections, which were scheduled for another two years' time. "Sharon needs a wall against Bibi," was how *Haaretz* described the situation following his election.[3]

With this danger ever-present, Sharon changed his attitude towards his colleagues. Whereas in the past he had distanced anyone who was not completely loyal to him, he now opened his door to all and forgave anyone who had been close to Netanyahu in the past or in the present. He even reconciled with the heirs and appointed seven of them to his government, hoping that this would cement their commitment towards him and weaken Netanyahu.

The right-leaning heirs received sought-after portfolios: Livnat was Minister of Education; Landau became Minister of Internal Security; Hanegbi was awarded the Environment portfolio; and Livni, the new MK, was brought directly into the government as a minister without portfolio. Rivlin, who had been Sharon's main supporter and manager of his campaign, was appointed Minister of Communications. The two heirs who had split off and formed the Hamerkaz party, which was now a coalition partner, received less glamorous appointments: Meridor was a minister without portfolio, responsible for intelligence services, while Milo was made Minister for Regional Cooperation. These seven heirs received a warm embrace from Sharon, while the MKs who had been his main supporters were shocked to find themselves outside the government.

The Likud was back in power, but power had not returned to the veterans. They were still waiting for Netanyahu. Nevertheless, the "genetic replication machine" continued its work even at this difficult time. The heirs were in government, their prized protégé was waiting in the wings, and this gave them hope.

Netanyahu overtakes Sharon on the right

At the start of Sharon's first term, the Likud was an ideologically stable and well-consolidated party. All its factions were represented in the government, and although Sharon had softened his image and had defeated Barak with the help of the rhyming slogan, "*rak Sharon yavi shalom*" (Only Sharon can bring peace), the Likud members knew him as a hardliner who implemented large-scale construction plans in Judea and Samaria.

I remember well a condolence visit that I paid to Sharon at his ranch in March, 2000, following the passing of his wife, Lily. Sharon received his visitors in a mourners' tent and spoke about the dangers that the Arab enemies posed to the country. Oblivious to his audience's surprise at the timing of his speech, he declared that Israel's Arab neighbors could not be trusted, that there was no hope of making peace with them, and that it was important to settle Jews in the Negev, which was being taken over by Bedouins.

Now, during the election campaign, Sharon was presented as an affable grandfather, but the Likud heirs knew better than to fall for this image. They believed that Sharon was the most solidly reliable hawk. One might be wary of his manipulations, but his views were squarely on the right. Their reliance was based, in part, on the settlement enterprise to which Sharon had devoted his energies over the course of fifteen years. It was easy for the heirs to connect with his right-wing views – further to the right, it seemed, than Netanyahu. Sharon had always positioned himself to the right of Prime Ministers; he had always attacked from the right; he had refused to shake hands with Arafat; he had been the friend of the settlers and was viewed as the source of the slogan, "What goes for Tel Aviv goes for Netzarim" (a reference to an isolated Jewish settlement in the middle of the Gaza Strip).

As Prime Minister with elections looming, Sharon assumed a different image, seeking to project a more centrist posture in order to gain the support and the votes of many Israelis who still viewed him as an aggressive, war-mongering general.

From the moment Sharon started conveying a more centrist, moderate position, Netanyahu applied himself with full force to criticizing his policy of restraint. Israel was now in the midst of a new wave of suicide terror attacks. In March 2002, after 130 citizens had been murdered, and after the Passover festival attack in which dozens of innocent participants in the traditional Seder night were butchered at a hotel in central Israel, Netanyahu (ever the "concerned citizen") demanded that Sharon take action, re-enter the Palestinian cities that had been handed over to Arafat within the framework of the Oslo agreements, and move to isolate the PLO.

Netanyahu's initiative prompted Sharon to embark on Operation Defensive Shield, which entailed the IDF re-entering the Palestinian cities, confiscating the Palestinian Authority's weapons, eliminating hundreds of Palestinian terrorists, destroying the main PLO headquarters, and placing Arafat under siege. The military operation halted the wave of terror attacks – and at the same time halted Netanyahu's ascent. Operation Defensive Shield extricated Sharon from the paralysis that gripped him for fear of a repetition of the failure and subsequent excoriation he had experienced following the Lebanon War. It also fortified his status in the Likud as an active, powerful, and combative leader.

Despite the effective military initiative, Netanyahu continued to haunt Sharon. In anticipation of the 2003 elections, Netanyahu was well organized. Although the Likud was unified under the firm and vigorous Sharon, this time Netanyahu was determined to make his return.

His tactic was a sophisticated one: instead of attacking Sharon or organizing an active political opposition, he spoke at a number of conferences where he criticized the government's policy by proposing more resolute action. Unlike Sharon, who spent his time in his office and did not enjoy being interviewed, Netanyahu appeared frequently on television. Sharon was aware of his ubiquitous media presence. He sensed Netanyahu's shadow every day.

Netanyahu and Sharon engaged in a strange sort of dance: Netanyahu would demand action and set forth an activist policy towards the Palestinians, and Sharon reacted by toughening his policy. Netanyahu pushed for more, and Sharon became even more militant. Both adopted a firm position in view of the Palestinians' escalating violence. A few months before the general elections, the country was on fire. For the first time since Oslo, there was a complete disconnect between Israel and the Palestinian leadership. Yasser Arafat was effectively imprisoned and isolated in his headquarters in Ramallah.

The Likud was in power but was extremely uneasy. Everyone knew that the battle of the titans was approaching. For the third time in three and a half years,

Israel was headed to elections. The date was set for January 2003. The political calendar therefore anticipated primaries for the Likud leadership towards the end of 2002.

As Prime Minister, Sharon was no longer the weak and tired leader who had replaced Netanyahu. He took control of the Likud headquarters, aided by a professional and aggressive staff that responded promptly to every word that Netanyahu uttered. Sharon also wielded an army of powerful and experienced power-brokers who made hundreds of appointments in the public service, thereby shoring up Sharon's weak standing in the Likud.

The new Sharon was managed by his son, Omri, who had come to be with his lonely father after Sharon's wife, Lily, passed away. Unlike the rest of Sharon's staff, Omri was not obliged to appease the Prime Minister. He set about establishing a new policy of openness towards politicians with whom Sharon had waged fierce battles for years, and opened the doors to reconcilement with many journalists towards whom Sharon harbored great bitterness. He managed to overcome the historical hostility that many figures in the press– enemies who had slandered him for over three decades – felt towards Sharon.

Omri's formula for dealing with the elites and the media was simple: first he would meet, talk, soothe, and propose making a new start. Then he would convey the message that his father had become a new and different leader who was moderate and conciliatory. At the same time, he managed (where all others had failed) to persuade his father to orient himself towards new audiences who had been ill-disposed towards him for twenty years. These seeds started to germinate in the mind of his father, who at this time was still delivering tough speeches about Arafat and the murderous nature of the Palestinian enemy.

The media was still prejudiced against both Sharon and Netanyahu. Both were regarded as the most right-wing figures on the political map. The Israeli elites were still waiting for a promising leader to emerge from the Labor party. However, the Labor had been embroiled for some time in internal battles over the leadership. Ehud Barak had resigned in February 2001, and Labor entered the unity government under Sharon, with Peres serving as Foreign Minister and Benjamin Ben-Eliezer as Minister of Defense. The chairmanship was passed backwards and forwards, with legal proceedings along the way, and new primaries were called. In anticipation of the primaries, at the end of October, Labor pulled out of the government, ostensibly owing to its opposition to the budget. After all this turbulence, in November 2002, Amram Mitzna became the fourth chairman of the Labor party in less than two years.

Thus, Sharon was up against a rival party which systematically crushed its leaders, and a rival candidate who was open and candid in his left-wing views. Unlike other candidates of both the Right and the Left, Mitzna's integrity did not allow him to portray himself as a centrist for election purposes. Moreover, he chose to focus his campaign on a call for unilateral withdrawal from the Gaza Strip and Hebron, evacuation of isolated settlements, and a separation fence. Sharon and the Likud were delighted that the competition was a candidate who could easily be labelled as a yielding, spineless leftist in the midst of the murderous Intifada. The center of the political map was left with no representation. With Mitzna on the Left, and Sharon and Netanyahu on the Right, Israelis contemplated the ongoing Palestinian violence and sought a leader representing a responsible Right. Sharon wasn't there yet.

Sharon is investigated and moderates his stance

Ariel Sharon, the seasoned warrior, still faced two major hurdles on the way to serving a second term. One was the internal threat presented by Netanyahu, who had challenged him ever since handing over the chairmanship of the Likud. The other was the general elections. While Mitzna's openly declared policy seemed to increase Sharon's chances, he knew that the road to victory was still long and strewn with all sorts of difficulties.

Sharon had good reason to be concerned. Since September 2001, he and his two sons had been the subjects of various police investigations, which were given broad media coverage and troubled the Sharon family over the next three years. Starting at the same time, there was a dramatic change in Sharon's policy. As the investigations progressed, so his position moved further to the left. Suddenly this ultra-hawk of the IDF and of the political system began expressing positions that tended increasingly towards far-reaching concessions. The most militant general in Israel's history, the politician who had positioned himself as more right-wing than the former heads of the Irgun and Lehi, Begin and Shamir, the great builder of settlements, began voicing the sort of accommodating and openhanded state- ments that only leaders representing the Left dared to utter, and took action that no left-wing leader had ever attempted.

Much has been written on the question of whether there was a connection between the drama of the police investigations, on one hand, and the drama that was played out in cabinet meetings, on the other. Top-rate commentators expressed their opinions, especially after the Disengagement from Gaza. What- ever the case may be, it must be remembered that the media supported Sharon's concessions, and the further he went in accommodating the Palestinians, the warmer the embrace he received. The media coddled him and "cocooned" him, as Channel 2 commentator Amnon Abramowitz put it. What had started out as "spin" to placate the Israeli press brought such positive feedback, from Sharon's perspective, that he himself may have been swept up in this new and successful approach. He watched as his veering to the left lowered the intensity of the crimi- nal investigations, brought him positive media coverage for the first time in thirty years, and turned him into the darling of the nation. The harder Netanyahu and the Likud Central Committee fought against his betrayal of the principles that he and they had held dear, the greater the vigor with which he was defended, cleansed, and commended, and the more popular he became.

The investigations against the Sharon family had been launched in the wake of a report by State Comptroller and former Supreme Court Judge Eliezer Goldberg, asserting unlawful conduct in Sharon's fundraising for the Likud primaries in 1999. In the wake of the report Sharon repaid a million and a half shekels, while his son Gilad obtained a loan for the remainder of the sum that he owed. Part of this loan came from British textile magnate Cyril Kern, in apparent violation of the law against foreign contributions to election campaigns. For the next few years the ensuing large-scale inquiry dogged Sharon and his sons.

The biography *Ariel Sharon: A Life* documents some twelve different lawsuits and investigations against Sharon, starting from the issue of the ownership of his ranch, in the early 1970s, up to his terms as Prime Minister, in the new millennium.[4] Notably, none of these legal episodes ever led to criminal charges. However, the stain on the family name certainly grew increasingly problematic, and the pressure on Sharon and his sons was immense.

A watershed moment: the Likud Central Committee and the question of a Palestinian state

Three major developments took place over the course of 2002: the first was the Al-Aqsa Intifada (the "Second Intifada") and the Israeli response – Operation Defensive Shield; the second was Netanyahu's undeclared but undeniable return; and the third was the police investigations against Sharon and his two sons.

After an eternity spent on the fringes of the extreme and militant Right, Sharon now began making declarations that ran contrary to everything he had preached in the past. Leading up to the elections in 2001, his campaign ran the surprising slogan, "Only Sharon can bring peace", which was perceived as a tactic to placate voters who were concerned about Sharon's belligerence. The trend continued with a promise that he was ready for "painful concessions" – a message interpreted as targeting voters who were still deliberating. At a teachers' conference held in Latrun in September, 2001, Sharon said:

> The State of Israel wants to give the Palestinians that which no-one has ever given them [. . .] the possibility of establishing a state. Neither the Turks, nor the British, nor the Egyptians, nor the Jordanians afforded them this possibility.

This statement set the Right on edge.

The Left had not yet internalized the message or did not yet believe it. The left-wing camp continued quoting Sharon's erstwhile declaration, "What goes for Tel Aviv goes for Netzarim", and emphasized that while the statements now emerging from Sharon were more moderate, he was still implementing an aggressive military approach. The media was unconvinced by – even disdainful of – his new rhetoric. The prevailing view was that Sharon had not changed; he was merely paying lip service to the international community in general, and US President Bush, in particular.

On the Right, in contrast, Sharon's statements sparked outrage. Although Sharon was the "father of the settlements", a partner in the leadership of the Right over thirty years, and in the midst of a war against Arafat, the historical wariness towards him resurfaced.

Sharon's statements led to a seemingly minor initiative which ultimately brought about an historical split that changed the face of Israeli politics. A right-wing group within the Likud demanded that the party's Central Committee convene and vote on the proposition that no Palestinian state would arise. Although this was already enshrined as part of the Likud platform, for four months Sharon and his supporters tried in every way they could to avoid convening the Central Committee and the confirmation of the initiative. Eventually, the party's internal court forced them to allow the vote.

Sharon tried to put off the decision, fearing three outcomes: firstly, embarrassment before the international community; secondly, being forced to negotiate while his hands were tied; and thirdly, coming across as having surrendered to his opponents, first and foremost among them Netanyahu. He regarded Netanyahu as the party responsible for the initiative. Sharon believed (as did his son, Omri) that Netanyahu wanted to portray him as having lost touch with his own movement and party, in order to pave his own way back into power.

This is simply untrue. The fact is that Sharon was offered a series of compromises, but he rejected them – both out of concern that he would come off looking weak and out of reliance on his son's (erroneous) estimation that he could win over the ideological camp through deployment of his supporter-underlings throughout the party and the government apparatus.

Sharon approached the vote in the Central Committee laboring under two mistaken assumptions. The first was that he was going to win. In reality, he lacked the power to stand up to the Likud Central Committee on a question of such fundamental ideological importance. Had he come to the convention with a peace agreement that offered hope (as Begin had done), perhaps he would have stood a chance. Asking for the party's support to establish a Palestinian state in response to murderous terror attacks was a mistake. The second assumption that turned out to be incorrect was that Netanyahu was behind the initiative. It was true that Netanyahu had met with the group that proposed convening the Central Committee and he had told them that he would declare his support openly, but he was not eager to engage in battle. He was content to observe Sharon's predicament, but when Livnat and Hanegbi engaged in conciliatory discussions with Sharon, Netanyahu expressed his willingness to compromise.

The Central Committee meeting descended into the chaos that everyone had feared. As in all such clashes, the reason for the confrontation paled into insignificance the moment that the leaders walked onstage. It turned into a great open war – a war between two leaders who had not wanted to fight.

This great war erupted after two years of Netanyahu needling Sharon while maintaining a respectable, statesmanlike posture. On Sunday, May 12, 2002, the Charles Bronfman Auditorium in Tel Aviv was filled with hundreds of Likud Central Committee members. The strict security checks at the entrance were an attempt on the part of Sharon's camp to prevent the participation of opponents from the settlements who were not authorized to vote. (A number of other unauthorized parties were allowed in; apparently their support for the party chairman facilitated this deviation from the rules.)

The event was moderated by Omri Sharon. Despite his familiarity with the numbers, the camps, and the interests, he believed that Sharon would win. Omri took up a strategic but discreet position at the back of the first floor of the auditorium, looking down on the entire area. The members of the press, seated in the gallery, were able to discern his outline. His messengers came and went, updating him constantly. He was managing the show.

I saw right away that the crowd comprised four distinct groups. The first consisted of a few dozen noisy youngsters who had been bussed in by Sharon's party apparatus. Holding posters expressing support for Sharon, they took up their positions in the front of the auditorium, near the stage, very close to the television cameras and close enough to be seen and heard by both Sharon and Netanyahu. On television they were presented as Sharon's supporters in the Central Committee. The second group consisted of Central Committee members who supported Sharon. They sat behind the group holding the posters, quiet, almost embarrassed. The issue at stake was taboo in the Likud, and even Sharon's supporters were not ready to shout openly and enthusiastically that they were in favor of a Palestinian state.

Prior to the debate, while Sharon's youthful coterie was carrying on in the hall, the members of the third group – the veterans – were gathered in the lobby. They numbered in the hundreds, all in their seventies and eighties, faithfully showing up for the fight and, as always, making the most of an opportunity to meet with old friends. One of them mentioned that he had come by taxi, straight from some medical tests at Ichilov hospital; another responded that he had come especially by train, from the north of the country, since he could no longer drive. I stood next to another two veterans: one, a former Lehi fighter who was now a farmer in Zikhron Yaakov (my father), the other a former Irgun fighter who had become a successful Tel Aviv–based businessman (Chaim Eitani). They were updating each other about their children and grandchildren. Unlike past events, the veterans were now on their own, without their children, who had long since moved on from politics. Their support and companions were the heirs, the MKs, who were no longer so young themselves. As the session began, the veterans sat in the upper portion of the hall. Also at the back, but on the other side of the hall, were the Religious Zionists, with their knitted skullcaps, most of them bearded, in their thirties and forties. Unlike most of the Central Committee members, this group had not stopped to chat in the lobby. They did not mingle among the crowd but remained in their places from the beginning of the session to the end. Angry, impassioned, focused on the struggle, they stood throughout most of the debate, holding posters denouncing Sharon and rejecting a Palestinian state.

The Likud Central Committee had always included Religious Zionists. They had been integrally part of the underground movements and remained integral to the party. Throughout the years, they had been well-assimilated in the Likud, with members of all ages belonging to all the various factions. Now, for the first time in Likud history, observers from the gallery could discern a homogeneous group of about two hundred Central Committee members with knitted skullcaps who did not look familiar. These were the "Feiglin group": settlers who did not vote for

Likud. For the first time, the Likud was dealing with a camp that was different, more right-wing, severed from the history and day-to-day life of the party, and attempting a takeover from within. At this convention they joined forces with the Likud veterans and the many Central Committee members who were appalled by Sharon's new political path.

When Netanyahu entered the hall, the war erupted. He was greeted with applause from the back of the hall, while those in the front whistled and shouted abuse, as though they were in a soccer stadium. Netanyahu, in typical style, refrained from attacking Sharon personally, focusing on political and ideological criticism of and opposition to the Prime Minister's policy. He expressed his opposition to the idea of an international conference, which Sharon had started formulating; his opposition to the termination of Operation Defensive Shield; his opposition to the end of the siege on Arafat in his headquarters; and his opposition to the establishment of a Palestinian state. "Throughout the years under Begin's government, Shamir's government, and my own government, the Likud was vehemently opposed to the establishment of a Palestinian state in the heart of our homeland," Netanyahu declared.

> This opposition was part of the Likud platform for every election campaign, including in the last elections. It was on this basis that we appealed to voters, and it was on this basis that we received a mandate from the public. All leaders of the Likud are committed to that mandate.

Netanyahu went on to lambaste Sharon for adopting a policy that had not been approved by the party's democratic institutions:

> And now, without any democratic process – neither within the movement, nor within the government, nor within the Knesset [. . .] one of the foundation stones of our platform, and of our national security, has been uprooted. And thus the position of the Left, in support of the establishment of a Palestinian state – the position of Yossi Sarid and Peres – has become the supposedly official policy of the government of Israel.

The ugly scenes that had played themselves out in the 1980s were back. As Netanyahu spoke, dozens of youngsters stood just a few meters from him, waving their fists and chanting loudly in an attempt to disrupt his speech. Netanyahu fumed: "It's enough with these antics. It's enough with these pathetic stunts. Learn to listen." And then, glaring at the "mercenaries" who had been brought to the event, he added cynically that since he himself had been Likud chairman, "it's remarkable how the age of Central Committee members has gone down."

Sharon's speech likewise received a hostile reception, but this time the shouting came from the back rows. On one side stood the Religious Zionists with their posters; on the other side the veterans shouted in protest. Unlike Netanyahu, Sharon chose to attack his rival personally and directly. He cynically reminded the Likud that "the Oslo Accords were accepted on our part by one person," hinting to Prime Minister Netanyahu. He recalled the days of Shamir and pointed out that Netanyahu had participated as Deputy Foreign Minister in the Madrid Conference, while he was now opposing the international conference that Sharon was trying to put together. He took care to note that there had already been Prime Ministers who "warmly, perhaps innocently, shook hands with Arafat. One of them was ours. I did not shake Arafat's hand." Afterwards, Sharon surprised the participants by reading out a proposal not to hold a vote on the resolution that had been set forth in the invitation. This aroused much anger. Most of the Central Committee members demanded an immediate and explicit vote against a Palestinian state. The whistling and shouting showed that most of the Likud was not on Sharon's side in this matter.

Sharon's people drew out the meeting as long as they could in an attempt to tire the veterans and cause them to leave en masse. But although the event went on and on, every last one of the veterans remained. The voting was tense; everyone was sure that the result would be a razor-thin majority one way or the other. In the end, it was clear and unequivocal: fifty-nine percent against Sharon, only forty-one percent in favor. It was a major blow for a sitting Prime Minister, and a huge victory for the opposition – as well as for Netanyahu, who had not sought a conflict to decide that which was already known. The feeling was that Sharon had not just been defeated in the vote but had lost the movement.

Sharon had in fact left the auditorium prior to the vote, in a display of contempt for the members of the Central Committee. This, perhaps more than anything else, exposed the extent to which his status in the Likud had fallen. After the results were announced, Sharon said that he accepted the decision but added that he would continue "leading the State of Israel in accordance with the same considerations that have always guided me." Netanyahu ascended the stage as a magnanimous victor, announcing, "We shall continue to support the government in its struggle against terror." The remaining audience applauded.

I was sitting among the political correspondents in the press gallery. The talk around me reflected a sense that Sharon had been defeated within his own party, that he was politically finished, a lame duck, that it was only a matter of time until he disappeared. But within just a few minutes, before my very eyes, a new spin was created in the media gallery. I watched as, during a live broadcast, some of the correspondents offered advice as to how the defeat could be transformed into success. The message (in the guise of news) was already a headline: the defeat in the Likud Central Committee was in fact a victory among the public. The new analysis held that Sharon had displayed courage in the face of an extremist Central Committee. His failed wager had in fact been a calculated attempt on the part of the Prime Minister to connect with the centrist, moderate majority in Israel, and it had led to a break with the right-wing extremist settler camp. That night, and the next morning, the media was already portraying Sharon's colossal loss as a huge victory. The images of the Prime Minister subject to the derision of his own party were reframed to show his brave stand against the aggressive and corrupt Likud Central Committee.

A poll conducted by *Yediot Aharonot*, published after the coverage of the convention, concluded that "a decisive majority of Likud supporters prefer Sharon as Prime Minister."[5] According to the poll, two-thirds of Likud members had supported Sharon's proposal, while only one-third had supported Netanyahu's. Among the public, support for a Palestinian state stood at sixty-eight percent in favor versus twenty-eight percent against.

For the first time in many years, the press was on Sharon's side. Netanyahu, the big winner of the evening, was transformed into the biggest loser. In a single night, everything had been turned upside down: Sharon had moved to the center of the political map, while Netanyahu had been pushed into the extreme right – the spot vacated by Sharon. The Israeli public began to get used to the idea of Sharon as the candidate of the political center. This was the same leader whose army was dealing harshly with the Palestinians on a daily basis. When Sharon announced that he was going to ignore the vote of the Central Committee, the media praised him as a national leader who transcended the extremist and corrupt Central Committee.

Netanyahu, who had won the vote, found himself portrayed as having suffered a devastating loss that brought his popularity down below that of Sharon. Overnight, Sharon had turned into a popular Prime Minister who enjoyed the support of the Left, the media, and the centrist voters, along with half of the Likud. Perhaps it was at this moment that Sharon and his advisors fell in love with the formula that went on to lay a great many golden political eggs: an appeal to the Left, entailing a confrontation with the "self-satisfied" Likud Central Committee (which Sharon had helped to build) as a lever to increase his popularity among the broader population.

The split among the heirs deepens – Olmert veers to the left

Although the leaders had not meant for the question of the Palestinian state to arise as a subject for discussion, it led to an ideological split within the Likud, between the Netanyahu-Landau-veterans-settlers camp and the camp of Sharon and the party apparatus. At this stage the possibility of a contest between Netanyahu and Sharon was still just starting to be discussed, and the ideological dilemmas concerning a Palestinian state were conceived only in embryonic form. However, even at this early stage, three different trends could be observed among the heirs.

The first was identification with the hawkish position led by Uzi Landau and Netanyahu, who was now returning to his ideological roots after a term as a pragmatic and calculating Prime Minister. They were joined by Ze'ev Jabotinsky Jr., who now appeared on the Likud stage for the first time as one of the Land of Israel heirs.

The second trend was the moderate stream that had begun to consolidate itself at the meeting of the Central Committee. The new heirs Tzipi Livni and Zeev Boim had taken their first steps in Sharon's direction (albeit keeping a low profile) and expressed quiet support for the Prime Minister with regard to a Palestinian state, presenting tactical rather than strategic considerations (not support for establishment of a Palestinian state, but rather opposition to stating an unequivocal position early on, in what was really a subject for discussion much later). Unsurprisingly, they were joined already at this stage by the early heirs Roni Milo and Dan Meridor, who were on their way back into the Likud following the disintegration of the Hamerkaz party and had already long supported the idea of a Palestinian state. But the only one of the heirs within the Likud who was openly supportive of Sharon was Olmert. He took a political and ideological step that went against everything he had said in the past, and now expressed open support for a Palestinian state.

The third trend was more complex. The minister-heirs Rivlin, Livnat, and Hanegbi were caught between the ideological rock and a political hard place. The three of them wanted to break away with Sharon but were altogether opposed to a Palestinian state. In an attempt to resolve their predicament, they struggled against engaging in the debate at all and tried with all their might to prevent or postpone the vote at the Likud Central Committee. They tried to mediate, to persuade, to arbitrate – but to no avail. From that fateful evening the minister-heirs were caught between politics and their worldview, between prestigious membership in the government and their own ideological opposition, between Sharon and their parents and Netanyahu. Hanegbi and Livnat voted against Sharon but did not speak out against him. Rivlin was torn between his loyalty to Sharon and his loyalty to the ideology of his parents' home. On one hand, he was the minister closest to Sharon, the head of his election campaign, his confidant and right-hand man. On the other hand, he was loyal to the Land of Israel. Any compromise, any concession – even only symbolic – was traumatic for him. Rivlin begged Sharon to come to a compromise with Netanyahu and not to confront him over the issue of giving a state to the enemy that had launched a terror campaign against Israel. He pleaded with the Prime Minister not to force him and the Likud apart. He understood, from long experience, that Sharon would lose at the Central Committee, and that the Likud would be split. He also understood, with his sharp intuition, that Sharon could end up in places where Rivlin would not be able to continue with him.

The question of the Palestinian state produced a new Olmert, entirely different from the old and familiar one.

The old Olmert had stood with his fellow heirs against Sharon in the battles of the 1980s. Hefez and Bloom argue in their book *Ariel Sharon: A Life* that Olmert even exacerbated the struggle against Levy and Sharon, out of an aspiration to skip over their middle generation and become leader of the movement.[6] The relations between Olmert and Sharon became even more strained in 1988, when Prime Minister Shamir promoted the heirs – including Olmert – to the government in which Sharon retained his former position but received no promotion.

The "old" Olmert was the mayor who initiated construction of the controversial Har Homa neighborhood in Jerusalem and pushed for opening the Western Wall Tunnels. It was he who overtook Netanyahu from the right, joining up with the Religious-Nationalist camp in the capital that wanted construction over the Green Line, to the displeasure of the Americans. He was the heir who led the virulent campaign against Sharon leading up to the primaries for the Likud chairman-ship in 1999 – a campaign which Uri Dan, Sharon's confidant, described as the most aggressive in the history of Israeli politics. In a newspaper interview Olmert declared:

> If there's anyone who, over the course of his entire career, symbolizes fickle-ness, it's Sharon. [. . .] From the days when he worked directly and indirectly against Begin, via his imposition of constrictions on Shamir, and up to his words against Netanyahu.[7]

Olmert was not afraid to make criminal accusations, either: he accused Sharon of having employed private investigators to invent evidence against Olmert's team and to engage in character assassination. He lapsed into personal vendettas, too, as Hefez and Bloom record:

> [Olmert's] staff began spreading word about Sharon's advanced age and the improbability of a seventy-five-year-old man contending against Barak in the next elections. [. . .] Suddenly everyone talked about his age. Some reports had it that Sharon could hardly function in his day-to-day chores.[8]

After Sharon was elected chairman of the Likud and expressed a willingness to join a unity government with Barak, Olmert accused him of docility and a willing-ness to give up Likud principles in order to earn a seat in the government.

Perhaps the most significant turning point began with the 1999 contest, when Olmert understood that he stood no chance in the Likud and that if he was defeated by the weak and weary Sharon, it meant that the Likud had rejected him.

In 2001, when Sharon was Prime Minister, Olmert was nearing the end of his second term as mayor of Jerusalem and was looking for a way back into national politics. While Sharon started making his speedy and surprising turnaround at this time as a cynical political tactic, it may be assumed that Olmert had planned his own turnaround over the course of years. It seems that throughout that time he had not been willing to pay the price of his views and feared that his voters would turn their backs on him. Hence it was only when Sharon embarked on his political transformation that the new Olmert made his debut.

At the Central Committee convention to vote on the proposition against a Pal-estinian state, Olmert veered dramatically to the Left. He stood by Sharon in the same way that he had once stood by Tamir (in the late 1960s) and by Shamir (in the 1980s). He argued with the other side, challenged, and baited as though seek-ing a confrontation – as though his level of aggression against the other side, and defense of the leader whose side he had chosen, would enhance Sharon's commit-ment towards him.

Olmert fought with the Land of Israel camp over the issue of a Palestinian state as though he had never been a right-wing mayor of Jerusalem. He delivered a speech in the auditorium, and I heard the journalists around me asking, "What's happened to him? Why is he riling them up? Why is he stoking the flames, when most of the Central Committee wants to remain united?" It was only with hind-sight, some years later, that the answers made themselves apparent. In his speech Olmert was divorcing himself from the right-wing camp and from the ideology he had grown up with. From that evening onwards, he knew that he had little chance of ever being elected in the Likud, and consequently he distanced himself further and further from the movement and from his earlier views. Perhaps he was also seeking his way back to the moderate stance that he had cultivated during the 1980s and which he had suppressed during his campaign and his term of office in Jerusalem. Journalists Amnon Dankner and Tommy Lapid intimated that this had been their impression.

On the evening of the convention concerning the Palestinian state, Olmert joined Sharon's camp, embracing the leader in what some described as a bear hug. He defended him in the media and appointed himself as Sharon's right-hand man, in the hope of receiving some reward for his loyalty in the next government. He started pushing Sharon to spearhead some sort of compromise with the Palestin-ians, in a manner that annoyed most of the movement. From that evening it was no longer Rivlin who represented Sharon, but rather Olmert – Rivlin's bitter enemy. During the passionate debate it was clear that Olmert was not seeking to mediate and bridge the gap for the sake of maintaining peace within the Likud, but rather sought the opposite: conflict, confrontation, schism, and division, from which he could build himself up.

Primaries 2002: Sharon beats Netanyahu

It is surprising to note that the Likud primaries held in November 2002 repre-sented the first time that Netanyahu competed directly with Sharon. This was the moment when these two leaders, who had followed a convoluted dance inter-weaving personal cooperation and the struggles between the camps they repre-sented, finally confronted one another face to face.

In anticipation of the previous contest (which never happened, owing to Netan-yahu's decision to withdraw) it had been clear that Netanyahu would win. Now, on the eve of the new contest, Sharon was in a far better position than before. As Prime Minister and chairman of the party, he was also aided by the character of this movement which was generally protective of its leaders, as well as the backing of the party, municipal, and government apparatus. In addition, Opera-tion Defensive Shield had extricated him from the old, passive, powerless image which had attached itself to him.

Netanyahu, as noted, had kept up a constant pressure on the Prime Minister since his first day in office, but the two men were careful not to cross any red lines. For fear of losing the voters who admired both of them and wanted both of them, they avoided personal attacks and took care to run indirect, cautious, clever, seemingly focused campaigns.

Against the backdrop of the bloody Intifada, Netanyahu presented himself as a more determined and activist alternative. Sharon had the support of the elite and the media from the moment he had run afoul of his party. Just a few words from him alluding to territorial concessions were enough to evoke an abundance of op-eds in support of Sharon from those who had been his long-time enemies in the media. Everyone was on his side, while Netanyahu became the negative right-wing icon that Sharon had been. At the same time, however, as usual on the Right, the tighter the media embrace for Sharon, the more the Right opposed him and gave their support to Netanyahu.

The short campaign (as dictated by Sharon) did not allow Netanyahu the time he needed to break down the protective wall that the media had built around Sharon. Sharon was being treated to positive and cosseting press the likes of which he had never known, while Netanyahu, who already had experience of both positive press (when he first entered politics) and hostile, negative press (since Rabin's assassination) was up against a campaign whose essence was that Netanyahu stood no chance. Netanyahu's team was unable to place his agenda at the forefront; it was unable to introduce real discussion of the two failures for which it blamed the Sharon government: the economic decline, leading to acute recession, and a lack of proper response to the Intifada, which had led to an unprecedented number of terror attacks.

The entire election campaign centered solely around biased polls in favor of Sharon, which appeared daily on television and in the newspapers, creating the impression that Netanyahu stood no chance against the Prime Minister. Even my own attempts, as campaign manager, to communicate and publicize genuine polls showing Sharon's lead to be no more than a few points were met with a deluge of supposed results pointing to a gap of ten to twenty points in Sharon's favor. The frustration among Netanyahu's team grew; field activists were abandoning the campaign in favor of the rival camp. The major power-brokers sensed which way the wind was blowing and followed the age-old rule: if you can't beat them, join them.

The struggle between Sharon and Netanyahu had another unusual aspect to it: while the Left was having trouble producing popular candidates, the Likud fielded two leaders of real stature with a solid public image. Unlike previous contests, in which candidates were supported by well-defined camps, in the 2002 primaries many Likud members liked both candidates, were torn between them, and hoped that they would find some way to cooperate.

Sharon and Netanyahu were careful not to anger the voters and took care that their campaigns remained focused with no mud-slinging. This was the first time that an internal Likud election was conducted with such restraint.

When Sharon delivered his speech at the Central Committee, listing (as always in such addresses) the names of the ministers and other senior party members in the hall, but omitting Netanyahu, he was met with a deafening chant: "Bibi! Bibi! Bibi!" Caught unprepared, Sharon responded with a call that made a place for itself in the Israeli political pantheon: "Bibi too; Bibi too". He was well aware that while he himself enjoyed a newly found popularity among the general public, the Likud belonged to Netanyahu. And this overwhelming support for Netanyahu sparked a brilliant maneuver on his part.

A few weeks before the primaries, he approached Netanyahu and offered him the position of Foreign Minister, which had just been vacated following the Labor's departure from the unity government. Netanyahu was trapped: if he refused the offer, he would be perceived as having placed his personal ambitions above the national interest and as a leader who failed to show responsibility at such a difficult time, risking the Likud's hold on power. He would then be likely to lose in the primaries. If he accepted the offer, he would lose the primaries anyway, since the Likud voters would have their wish of "two for the price of one": by voting for Sharon, they would have Netanyahu as Foreign Minister, too, whereas if they voted for Netanyahu, Sharon would resign.

I was with Netanyahu when it became clear that the battle for the party chairmanship and the premiership was lost. Identifying the failure in advance, he was able to prepare himself accordingly. After a few hours spent deliberating Sharon's offer, he chose the lesser of two evils and entered the government as Foreign Minister. Thus he could be certain that even if he lost the primaries, at least he would be "on the inside". He also knew that joining Sharon would earn him renewed legitimacy and that following Sharon's departure he would go back to being the natural successor.

On November 1, 2002, Netanyahu was sworn in as Foreign Minister, returning to the government after three and a half years spent outside of it. Despite the imminent primaries, he entered the Foreign Ministry building looking pleased to be back in the government and in a role that was so natural to him.

Netanyahu sides with the veterans; Sharon has the support of the heirs

When Netanyahu competed with Sharon, the sitting Prime Minister, for the Likud leadership, he was also up against the power-brokers. Omri Sharon was on the scene with a long list of government jobs. As the polls tilted further in support of Sharon, the number of branch activists who remained with Netanyahu fell.

Those who remained his faithful supporters through the 2002 primaries were the veterans: the former underground fighters now in their seventies and eighties, who had come to know this heir as part of the Tagar Circle. Once again, they mobilized on his behalf – most likely being the oldest activists ever to run an election campaign. They were no longer as strong and healthy as they had been in their underground days and no longer stood as upright as they had during their years in the opposition, but they were still filled with the same determination and commitment to the cause. From morning to night, dozens of veterans manned Netanyahu's election headquarters, along with young volunteers with knitted skullcaps who looked like their grandchildren.

Even Professor Moshe Arens, now seventy-seven years old, made a comeback in support of his one-time protégé, from whom he had distanced himself some years earlier. Arens and Netanyahu (whose connection went back to before Netanyahu was born, to the home of Tzila and Bentzion Netanyahu) sat with me in my office in Tel Aviv – one the mentor, who had recruited his friend's son twenty years earlier to serve in the Israeli embassy in Washington, and the other the novice, who had since served as Prime Minister. Two generations with the same vision, speaking the same language. Two generations that had always suspected that Sharon's actions on the fringes of the Right and on the hills of Samaria were motivated by a belief that Sharon was good for the country and therefore what was good for Sharon was also good for the country. Two generations that had always suspected that Sharon would do anything to be in power and that he was devoid of any ideology and any moral constraints.

Sharon went on to beat Netanyahu in the 2002 primaries with a convincing fifty-five percent of the vote against Netanyahu's forty. The next step was the Knesset elections, and in February 2003, he led the Likud to an impressive victory over Labor and its leader, Mitzna. After twenty-five years of trying, with five consecutive defeats, this was Sharon's fourth victory in a row. He was also buoyed by the Likud's tremendous achievement: no less than 38 mandates for the party, out of 120 Members of Knesset.

After being disappointed twice by Netanyahu (his departure from politics and his withdrawal from the 2001 race), the heirs – with the exception of Landau – no longer supported him. With most of them now either neutral or in Sharon's camp, it was Jabotinsky Jr. who came to his aid. This Land of Israel heir took up a central role in mobilizing the core of long-time Likudniks. He appeared in election broadcasts that sought to distinguish the authentic Likud camp from the camp that was in power and that had drifted far from Jabotinsky's teachings. But this was not enough to help Netanyahu back into the party chairmanship.

The efforts of Jabotinsky Jr. aroused internal media interest but could not conceal the full picture. The veterans' generation was, as usual, consistent and united in its support of Netanyahu, but the younger generation was divided. Two heirs remained with Netanyahu: Landau and Jabotinsky. Two remained neutral: Hanegbi and Livnat. The others supported Sharon. Rivlin and Olmert were openly and actively behind him, and they were joined by Livni, Boim, and the returnees Milo and Meridor.

The struggle between Sharon and Netanyahu over the leadership was another important milestone in the inter-generational relations within the Likud. It marked the break between the veterans and the heirs, and the liberation of the younger generation from obligation towards the parents' generation. The heirs' independence led to different ideological, political, and personal choices, as demonstrated over the decade that followed.

Notes

1 Maariv, January 22, 2004.
2 Maariv, October 3, 2005.
3 Haaretz, March 7, 2001.
4 Gadi Bloom and Nir Hefetz, *Ariel Sharon: A Life* (Tel Aviv: Yediot Ahronot Publishing, 2005), 400–412.
5 Yediot Aharonot, May 14, 2002.
6 Bloom and Hefetz, *Ariel Sharon: A Life*, 6–265.
7 Yediot Aharonot, August 20, 1999.
8 Bloom and Hefetz, *Ariel Sharon: A Life*, 331.

22 Sharon

King of Israel

Sharon emerged from the elections in 2003 stronger and more popular than ever. At the age of seventy-three, he had reached his peak. No previous Prime Minister in Israel had managed to transform his image so dramatically, positioning himself at the center of the political map while maintaining a solid hold on the Right and mobilizing new support from the Center.

The early heirs, who now supported Sharon after years spent alongside the veterans fighting him, faced a barrage of criticism from their parents' camp. Olmert, Rivlin, Meridor, and Milo had infuriated the veterans, who had already given vent to their feelings in the Central Committee vote for the Knesset list.

Meridor was conscious of his position in the Likud. He knew that from the point of view of the "aunts and uncles" who had brought him into the Knesset, he was a write-off, and so he chose not to submit his candidacy at all. Milo returned to the Likud with the hope of receiving the support of all those who had been in the Shamir-Arens camp and had fought alongside him throughout so many battles. But the veterans were not forgiving of his defiant ideological digression. He was placed forty-fifth on the list and found himself outside of the Knesset. This was the first loss for an heir who had won every contest he had entered at university, in five Knesset elections, and in the race for Tel Aviv mayor. Olmert, who was close to Sharon and his large camp and had fancied himself as his successor, was surprised to be placed so low on the list – number thirty-two – that he was sure that he, too, was out of the Knesset. The shock and humiliation almost broke him, and he was on the verge of turning his back on political life. In the end he remained an MK, thanks to the astonishing Likud showing in the elections, which ushered a full thirty-eight Likud representatives into the Knesset.

Rivlin, too, was deprived of the veterans' votes and ended up in the thirty-sixth slot, which seemed to indicate clearly that he would be out of the Knesset. Rivlin, too, was crushed by this rejection on the part of the camp that he loved so deeply. Rivlin was incredulous that the veterans had supported heirs who had a role in the concessions made by Netanyahu's government, but had punished him, the most loyal of the heirs, who had never deviated from Revisionist ideology. His only crime had been his open and active support for Sharon. The veterans were willing to forgive those who wandered off the ideological path from time to time, but they would not forgive support for the adversary, Sharon, who had competed against their star.

With the results of the primaries it seemed that the era of the early heirs – who had now led the country for twenty years – was over. The veterans' generation had forcibly removed the same heirs it had previously loved, encouraged, and advanced. As if this rejection was not enough, Sharon, too, had a bone to pick with the early heirs. Milo was disappointed not only in his political forebears but in Sharon, too, who should have rewarded him for his support and his joining the coalition. But Sharon had no intention of helping the man who had overseen his public excoriation during the 1980s. Meridor, too, suffered humiliation at Sharon's hands. He received no backing from him, even though he had acquiesced to a request by Sharon's people, who needed his support in the primaries. (Sharon had needed Meridor to help shore up his moral and public image, in view of the police and media investigations against him and some of his staff.)

Hefez and Bloom suggest that "[as] a former opponent and staunch humanist, Meridor's backing put Sharon in the mainstream for the first time in his career."[1] Nevertheless, Sharon chose not to bring Meridor back into his second government. This represented a violation of the explicit promise he had given before his election. Sharon generally forgave most of his opponents, but it seems he could not or would not put behind him the antipathy shown to him by Meridor and Milo during the First Lebanon War and throughout the 1980s, in the struggles against Shamir and Arens.

Sharon's surprising embrace of the heirs

After the 2003 elections it looked as though many of the heirs would not be part of Sharon's government: two belonged to Netanyahu's camp; others were neutral; a few had fallen to slots on the Likud list that made them ineligible. But Sharon surprised everyone and brought most of them in (with the exception of Milo and Meridor), tightening his connection with them in the hope of reducing the animosity of the veterans' opposition. Eight heirs joined the government, four of them in high-profile positions. Out of twelve Likud ministers, six were heirs (Plus one deputy minister). The new chairman of the Jewish Agency, appointed with Sharon's support, was Dan Meridor's brother, Sallai.

Sharon offered Netanyahu the Finance portfolio and surprised his stubborn opponent Landau with an offer to serve as a minister without portfolio. The two neutral heirs, Livnat and Hanegbi, were appointed Minister of Education and Minister of Internal Security, respectively. The four heirs who had supported Sharon were rather disappointed with their rewards: Livni was Minister of Absorption, Rivlin became chairman of the Knesset, Olmert was Minister of Commerce and Industry, and Boim was Deputy Minister of Defense. Olmert, who had received Sharon's promise of the Finance Ministry, was deeply disappointed and announced that he would not serve in the government. At the last minute he was also given the ministries of Communications and Employment, as well as the symbolic (at least at that stage) title of Acting Prime Minister. Olmert was mollified.

While Sharon filled his government with heirs and others who had opposed him, another loyal ally was pushed aside: Minister of Finance Silvan Shalom, who was dismayed at being replaced. After a campaign waged by his many supporters, Sharon made a last-minute decision to appoint him as Foreign Minister.

The surprising appointment of Netanyahu as Minister of Finance

Despite his firm standing after being elected Prime Minister, Sharon was still looking over his shoulder – at Netanyahu. Sharon knew very well that being elected chairman of the Likud and Prime Minister was no guarantee of stability, or of peace and quiet. The electoral system in Israel allows a political rival to attack the head of the movement and undermine his position – as Sharon himself had proven over the course of many years.

Sharon knew that the Likud still loved Netanyahu. It was entirely possible that Netanyahu would try to seize the movement by "overtaking from the right" – a tactic favored by Sharon in the past. The admiration for Netanyahu at Likud head-quarters was as enthusiastic as ever. For the veterans and heirs alike, he seemed to embody the essence of Revisionism, the heart of the Likud. The polls showed Sharon to be a popular Prime Minister, but the Likud tradition was to love whom-ever the elites hated. With Netanyahu's support comprising a core group of about forty percent of Likud members, he was certainly a force to be reckoned with.

Sharon knew that Netanyahu had one single aim: the premiership. In media interviews he often expressed scorn for the "handsome" Netanyahu (this would amuse Netanyahu; upon hearing the "compliment" he would gesture towards his middle, indicating that he was well aware of his age) and his specialization in rhetoric. Nevertheless, he held him in high esteem. He knew that this graduate of the General Reconnaissance Unit was a stubborn and determined rival. Sharon had watched as Netanyahu, a political rookie, had quickly overtaken him as well as all the heirs. He had also watched Netanyahu achieve his incredible victory over the Labor candidate, Peres, after Rabin's murder. Sharon knew that Netan-yahu held a firm and consistent worldview that resounded with the nationalist camp in Israel. He was painfully aware that Netanyahu had grown up as part of the Revisionist movement – an environment in which Sharon was, and would always remain, an outsider.

It was out of consideration for all of the above that Sharon decided to offer Net-anyahu the most important ministry in his government and the task of addressing the country's acute economic recession. By doing so he disappointed and pro-voked his loyal allies Silvan Shalom and Ehud Olmert, each of whom had hoped for this appointment. Both had watched as, prior to the elections, the outgoing Chief-of-Staff, Shaul Mofaz, was promoted over their heads to become Minister of Defense, with a view to blocking Netanyahu. Now, they watched as Sharon invited Netanyahu into the government rather than leaving him outside.

It turned out that Sharon believed that Netanyahu was in fact the only one of the ministers who was capable of dealing with the economic crisis. Sharon was a skilled strategist, and this was a smart move: if Netanyahu refused, he would be regarded as a divisive figure while Sharon was trying to unify the party. If he accepted the position, Sharon would benefit, no matter whether Netanyahu succeeded or failed. It was clear to Sharon that even if Netanyahu succeeded, the road to saving the economy would entail fierce conflicts, bitter arguments, and painful cutbacks among sectors and population groups that would not forgive the tyrant who had decreed them.

Netanyahu understood all this and deliberated long and hard before responding to Sharon's offer. On February 26, 2003, he convened the "submarine" team for a consultation that ended up stretching on for days. Owing to an unusually heavy snowstorm, there was no way of entering or leaving Jerusalem. MK Yuval Steinitz made heroic attempts to join the meeting, but to no avail. We tried not to think about what might be happening to our cars, which were stuck in the snow. We sat in the new Foreign Ministry building, facing huge windows that looked out over the snow-covered city. It was a surrealistic experience: the children outside frolicked and played, the view was magical, and we sat there, not knowing if and when we would get home.

Netanyahu was well aware of the severity of the economic crisis, and how difficult it would be to extricate the country from it. He held a series of discussions with experts in the areas of commerce and industry as well as with economists in Israel and abroad. They all agreed that it would be an exceptionally difficult task. Most of the experts maintained that taking on the Finance portfolio would be a strategic risk to his career, almost an act of political suicide, in view of the anticipated clashes with many sectors of the public. His advisors and his wife, Sara, deliberated along with him, divided in their opinions, but mostly tending towards the view that this was a trick aimed at destroying Netanyahu. Despite all of this, and with all due respect to the consultants with their views and the warnings he heard over the telephone in Hebrew and in English, Netanyahu believed that he would be able to bring the country out of its recession and seemed excited at the possibility of instituting far-reaching economic reforms. On the other hand, he knew that without the backing of the Prime Minister, his efforts as Minister of Finance would be doomed. He feared that Sharon would not be able to transcend his own rivalry and would turn him into a lame duck.

Sharon's confidants were enlisted to convey to Netanyahu that the offer arose out of genuine concern that economic collapse was imminent. They emphasized that Sharon was committed to supporting the Minister of Finance and that Netanyahu would be regarded as the "financial Prime Minister". This message was confirmed in contacts between Netanyahu's advisors (David Shimron and Gabi Picker) and Sharon's representatives (Dov Weisglass and Asi Shariv). As the snow piled up on the hill around the Foreign Ministry, Netanyahu sat talking on the phone with experts in Israel and abroad and with the staff that was effectively imprisoned in his office. He wrote a list of all the (many) areas over which he would want authority, and it was this list, with its far-reaching demands, that Netanyahu's emissaries presented to Sharon's team. The estimation was that Sharon would agree to less than half. It was a litmus test of Sharon's intentions. But Sharon immediately agreed to every last item, promising him all the authority that he wanted. He even acquiesced to a last-minute addition: a second minister in the Finance Ministry as Netanyahu's assistant. The man Netanyahu wanted was MK Meir Sheetrit, who had supported him in the primaries. He was stunned at Sharon's immediate acceptance of even this most unusual request.

After Sheetrit's appointment had already been approved, another audacious request arose in the middle of the night: Netanyahu wanted to be appointed Acting Prime Minister. The "submarine" team knew that the chances of Sharon appointing a substitute for himself were next to nothing: what sort of leader appoints a successor while he is still in office? And all the more so when the candidate in question is his greatest rival! Nevertheless, the idea was raised.

At this Sharon baulked. He knew that Netanyahu had already agreed to join the government. Paradoxically, however (as it sometimes happens in politics) the idea of the title "Acting Prime Minister" sounded like a way of appeasing Olmert. And so the title was offered to Olmert, who had already notified Sharon that he was leaving political life. Olmert liked the idea of holding the position that Netanyahu had requested but had not received. Soon the news was announced: Olmert had decided to join the government, after receiving an offer to be Acting Prime Minister. At the time, it was a symbolic title, devoid of any practical importance. Only two years later would its significance become dramatically apparent.

Netanyahu went back to deliberating, up until the very last minute. Even after all his substantive requests had been agreed to, he was still concerned that as Minister of Finance he would be isolated in the government and a target for Sharon's barbs. The hands of the clock moved inexorably towards the hour when the government would be sworn in. At a critical moment, the front page of *Yediot Aharonot* newspaper was spread over the small hospitality table in the Foreign Minister's office. At its center were photographs of the various ministers. The question was, which of these ministers would quarrel with Netanyahu? Tzahi Hanegbi, the most committed of his supporters in the previous decade? Uzi Landau, his friend from university? Limor Livnat, who knew very well who was expected to succeed Sharon? It was a rhetorical question. Clearly, all the ministers would support and give their backing to Netanyahu.

Netanyahu looked at his list, thought for a moment, and then turned to his aide, Shimron, who was standing at the ready, uncharacteristically tense, glancing every few moments at his watch. The entire Knesset, the entire nation, was waiting. He said, "David, tell them I'm coming." A few moments later, Netanyahu was on his way to the Knesset, to be sworn in as Israel's twentieth Minster of Finance.

On February 28, 2003, Netanyahu entered the Ministry of Finance and started implementing a large-scale economic revolution aimed at lifting Israel out of its recession. He waged a fierce war with powerful workers' committees, with representatives of the Histadrut, and with various factions in the Knesset. Anyone who encountered him during this period sensed that Netanyahu was realizing his life's dream; that he was even more enthusiastic in this position than he had been as

Prime Minister; that he had stepped into the shoes of the great reformers whom he so admired – Margaret Thatcher and Ronald Reagan – who had saved the economies of Britain and the US, respectively, during the 1980s.

Netanyahu threw his whole being into the reforms. The Israeli public was constantly hearing of some new measure: a revolutionary budget to streamline the public sector, salvaging the pension funds, reform of the ports, and so on. Finance Ministry clerks were happy to discover that the new minister was interested in and familiar with every aspect of their work. They excitedly told anyone who would listen that all the plans that had been drawn up over the years, only to be consigned to filing cabinets, were finally being implemented. The ideological confrontation that developed between Netanyahu and the socialist faction in the Histadrut aroused Netanyahu's fighting spirit. He was resolute about shifting the national mindset away from handouts and towards reliance on work, from over-dependence on bureaucracy to favoring the business sector.

Netanyahu's efforts over the course of 2003 bore fruit. After years of criticism and slander from within and without, he finally won full and sweeping support for his decisions and could rely on an automatic majority for any reform he chose to institute. For the first time since his term as ambassador to the UN, he was also held in high esteem by the Israeli elite. Praise and appreciation were voiced by top journalists, by Finance Ministry personnel, and by economic experts. The new spirit that he brought to the Israeli marketplace succeeded in engendering change and began to have an impact on the recession.

Throughout this time, the relations between Netanyahu and Sharon remained strained. They still disliked each other and harbored mutual suspicions. In private conversations they put each other down, although in truth they also both appreciated each other's strengths (as they always had). However, the tension remained concealed beneath the surface. Netanyahu, the "Prime Minister of the economy", was immersed in the affairs of his ministry, while Sharon gave him backing that few Israeli Ministers of Finance ever experienced. In return, Netanyahu respected Sharon's authority as "political and security Prime Minister"; he did not interfere in these realms and did not act as an overt internal opposition.

It was clear to all that the political rivalry had not disappeared, but it seemed that Sharon and Netanyahu understood that a single spark would be enough to ignite a huge fire that would bring down the government. Hence, any tension that arose between them (and there were real issues, along with pseudo-issues created by interested parties) was swiftly handled by the trusted confidants of both sides. These loyal aides believed that discord could shatter both the government and the Likud and would harm their respective leaders. Hence, cooperation was essential for both sides.

The government ministers, including the heirs, likewise tiptoed around the volatile territory that lay between the Prime Minister's Office and the Ministry of Finance, proceeding with no overt bias towards either side. Their loyalties were divided: on one hand, they needed Netanyahu as a strong Minister of Finance and continued to view him as Sharon's successor – especially in view of the constant rumors emanating from the legal cloud that surrounded the Prime Minister. On the other hand, the now-popular Sharon had a magic touch that drew them towards him. Hanegbi and Livnat found themselves in the middle, trying to uphold both loyalties and, most importantly, avoid burning their bridges in either camp; Landau was on Netanyahu's side, while Livni and Olmert had committed themselves to Sharon.

But Netanyahu was still a politician. He followed Sharon's political moves with concern and at the same time was aware of the rumors surrounding the police investigations into the Sharon family's activities. He maintained contact with the MKs who were close to him and with the settler leaders, and remained a guest of honor within the Tagar Circle.

In his second and third year as Finance Minister, the cooperation between the two camps was undermined. Two factors led to the dissolution of the bond that had been forged out of necessity. The first was the recovering economy, in view of which Sharon was less fearful of imminent economic collapse. The second was Sharon's political path, which began to wander far from that of the Likud and forced Netanyahu back into the political realm. And the more Netanyahu challenged the Prime Minister on his political path, the more Sharon disputed Netanyahu's economic policy and placed obstacles in his path.

Sharon's leftward turn leads to confrontation with the veterans and the heirs

Sharon was determined to convert the Likud: to change the historical worldview of this right-wing movement that was committed to the integrity of the Land of Israel. He believed that as Prime Minister he had the power and authority to ignore the party's roots, its essence, and its historical platform. The response was sweeping opposition and the most devastating split in the party since its founding.

With the public declaration of his intention to carry out a unilateral withdrawal from the Gaza Strip, Sharon drew the Likud into a two-year period of acute instability, virtually a slow-moving earthquake. At first there was shock at his statements. Later, he took action that led to active opposition and acute crisis. Ultimately, when Sharon's unilateral Disengagement from Gaza brought the expulsion of thousands of Jewish families from their homes in the settlements at the heart of the Gaza Strip, the cataclysmic upheaval tore the Likud apart.

As Prime Minister, Sharon navigated between the two poles of the political map: he became tougher in his military operations while at the same time speaking of the need for "painful concessions" that would lead to the establishment of a Palestinian state.

Hefez and Bloom mark November 20, 2003 as an important milestone. It was on this day that

> the Bush administration announced it would cut back on loans to Israel in the face of "on-going building in the settlements". Sharon felt a political noose tightening around his neck. He was under pressure across the board – Peres, Bush, Arafat, police investigations, the economy, the political quagmire, the

persistent terror attacks, and, of course, the sudden vigor in the camp of his in-house rival, Netanyahu. It was his worst predicament since taking office in 2001.[2]

As regards the Disengagement, it all started with an opaque statement that surfaced on November 20, 2003, during an economic speech at a minor event. Sharon devoted some attention to the importance of the American "roadmap" and followed up with a sentence that almost no-one noticed: "In addition, I do not rule out unilateral steps." It was a statement devoid of any context, and it received no coverage in view of the more compelling terror attack that took place on the same day.

What no-one knew at the time was that this sentence reflected a well-planned strategy. Sharon's advisors had been thinking about how to disentangle the Prime Minister. They felt that the Israeli public was waiting for a genuine peace initiative. Sharon's long-standing confidant, Dov Weissglass, and his son, Omri, pressed him in the direction of a unilateral withdrawal from Gaza. The big surprise came two weeks later, when Olmert made a more concrete and far-reaching statement concerning the need to leave Gaza as part of the relinquishing of the dream of the Land of Israel. This was on December 5, during the annual memorial ceremony for Ben-Gurion. Olmert had been dispatched to represent the Prime Minister at the event.

A short while later it became clear that both declarations had been trial balloons. After both floated by in relative quiet, it was time for the bombshell. On December 18, during his speech at the Herzliya Conference (a prestigious annual event where national policy is set forth by the country's most prominent leadership) Sharon announced his support for a unilateral withdrawal from Gaza. He elaborated at length, telling the Palestinians:

> We have no interest in ruling over you. We want you to run your lives on your own. In your own state. [. . .] But if the Palestinians continue in the coming months not to fulfill their part of the roadmap, then Israel will initiate a unilateral security measure of disengagement. [. . .] The Disengagement Plan will include a redeployment of IDF forces, new security borders, and a change in the positioning of settlements [. . .] The relocation of settlements will be undertaken first and foremost with a view to drawing as effective a security border as possible, creating a disengagement between Israel and the Palestinians.[3]

Behind all the wrapping and all the commentary the fact remains that Prime Minister Sharon was the first to deliver a speech that mentioned the Disengagement as a possibility. It was a speech that could have emanated from the most left-leaning faction of the Labor party, or a party even further to the Left. When Mitzna, the Labor leader, had mentioned similar ideas, Sharon had raised a hue and cry.

The political establishment listened in disbelief. There was widespread skepticism as to the seriousness of Sharon's intentions. The Left viewed his statement as an attempt to evade a real peace settlement: a sort of smoke-screen intended to ward off left-wing peace initiatives or to pacify the American administration. Others viewed the announcement as "spin" aimed at halting the police investigations. Journalists Raviv Drucker and Ofer Shelah assert that the evacuation plan was born out of Sharon's conviction that the State Attorney was going to indict him.[4] There was widespread agreement between the Left and the Right that Sharon's motives were not pure. Yossi Sarid, a prominent left-wing leader, coined an expression that was quickly adopted by opponents of the Disengagement: "The uprooting [of the settlements in Gaza] will go as deep as the investigation." Moshe ("Bogey") Yaalon, who was replaced as Chief-of-Staff owing to his opposition to the move, argues in his book *The Short Long Road*[5] that the Disengagement was prompted by extraneous considerations and that it originated with the group of image consultants that came to be known as Sharon's "ranch forum". Yaalon claims that Sharon embarked on the Disengagement, with all its strategic damage to Israel, not because he believed in it but because he was trying to save his own skin, in view of the criminal investigations against him.

During the weeks and months following Sharon's speech, the Likud waited for some clarification or qualification of his declaration. No-one wanted to bring down a broad and stable government. Even the veterans were trying their best to tolerate Sharon, out of a desire to keep the heirs in the government. However, the Prime Minister's statements caused a dramatic rise in the level of tension and disquiet. Many MKs and activists were unable to accept the idea of a voluntary unilateral withdrawal, and they expressed their dissatisfaction in internal discussions.

For Netanyahu, the Disengagement was an aberration that stood in direct opposition to his worldview. In the past, he had fought together with Sharon and together with the heirs against Barak's initiative of a unilateral withdrawal from the security zone in Lebanon. But now they had no wish to rock the boat. They hoped, and tried to explain, that Sharon's statements were mere talk and nothing would come of them. They gritted their teeth at every new pronouncement, hoping that Sharon would come to his senses and return to his familiar positions. For Ministers Netanyahu, Livnat, and Hanegbi, the conflict of interest involved not only their beliefs but their parents: each had been inculcated with and deeply influenced by the Revisionist beliefs and views that their parents had imbibed directly from Jabotinsky, seven decades previously. The parents had always remained on the ideological Right, never deviating even in view of the peace agreements signed by Begin and Rabin. It was difficult for Tzahi Hanegbi to talk with his mother, Geula Cohen, with whom he had established the Tehiya party as a response to the imminent evacuation of Jewish settlements in the Sinai, so close to Gaza. Netanyahu opposed the Disengagement from the outset but was convinced that reality would bring its own awakening. He continually told us, his consultants, that he would not serve in a government that implemented the Disengagement. Limor Livnat, too, had kept her father in mind throughout the various milestones of the peace process, from the Rogers Plan, via Camp David and the Wye Agreement, leading up to the Disengagement.

To understand the depth to which the Likud was dumbfounded by Sharon's initiative, I quote the following story, which was recounted to me by Rivlin, one of the Land of Israel heirs.[6] After Sharon's victory in the 2003 elections, there was growing concern that the extremist image that clung to him from the past would lead to intensified international pressure on the government. Rivlin proposed a plan to Sharon, although he made it clear at the time that he himself would oppose it in public. The idea was for Sharon to bring Labor on board to form a unity government, the bait being the relocation of the isolated Netzarim settlement in the Gaza Strip so it would form part of the Jewish settlement bloc. This would ensure the stability of the government. Rivlin recounted that Sharon's response was his by now well-known slogan: "What goes for Tel Aviv goes for Netzarim." He then added, with a scornful smile, "I see that you Revisionists have started losing your resolve." It was less than a year later that Sharon changed his skin.

Likud referendum: veterans once again on active duty

The fundamental uneasiness that the heirs and veterans alike felt towards Sharon had never been related to ideology; Sharon had consistently expressed distinctly right-wing views. Rather, it arose from the fact that he was an "outsider" who had threatened the fighting family over the course of three decades. "We always knew that he was a disciple of Ben-Gurion, while we were disciples of Jabotinsky," Rivlin told me.[7] Despite the firm friendship between himself and Sharon, Rivlin stated that he had harbored doubts about him throughout their joint activity. In 2003, when Sharon invited Rivlin to join his government with a view to "doing great things", Rivlin responded, "That's exactly what scares me – that you're going to do great things." It was for this reason that Rivlin preferred to take up the position of Chairman of the Knesset, foregoing the offer to serve as a minister. He quickly decorated the walls of his new office with pictures of his mentors and guides: Menachem Begin and Ze'ev Jabotinsky.

It did not take long before the smoldering wariness of Sharon burst into flame. In February 2004, Sharon spoke again about the Disengagement initiative.[8] This time he made no effort to obscure his intentions but stated openly and explicitly the cost: seventeen settlements in the Gaza Strip and in northern Samaria would be dismantled.

The surveys that were published in the weeks that followed showed that Sharon's brilliant scheme – the Disengagement Plan – had been very well received. The plan had the support of around two-thirds of the public. The Gaza Strip was viewed as a distant and hated territory, and the settlements located in its midst were perceived as small, isolated, and of no security value. Just as the public had supported the departure from Lebanon under Barak's leadership, it was now glad of the opportunity to exit the Gaza miasma.

When the Likud began to internalize the fact that Sharon meant to carry out his declarations, two camps collaborated in a campaign which, over the course of about a year, colored the country orange. The veterans ventured beyond the confines of their usual circles and joined forces with the settler camp, including the Jewish inhabitants of Gaza. For the veterans, the Disengagement Plan marked their final disengagement with Sharon.

They had been willing to accept the withdrawal from the Sinai as part of Begin's peace initiative, and they had allowed Netanyahu's partial implementation of the Oslo Accords. They had been forgiving towards Prime Ministers belonging to the fighting family who had signed agreements entailing concessions and withdrawals. But they were not willing to forgive Sharon. They had had enough of his schemes. In their eyes, he was and had always been a Laborite disguised as a Likudnik, a treacherous politician who was now leading their movement to ruin. After more than thirty years of hopping from side to side, consistent only in his lack of loyalty, his true beliefs and political affiliation were now laid bare. For them, Sharon had "seized" the Likud headquarters and was spearheading a most significant withdrawal without the backing of a democratic decision via the appropriate government and party mechanisms. This they could not accept. They called for a revolt against Sharon and were quickly joined by a chorus of furious settlers as well as religious students and settler youth who aided the elderly veterans. This time, they did not wait for the heirs sitting in government. They understood the constraints facing the ministers. But for themselves, this was another link in the never-ending struggle of Jewish history.

Of course, the veterans were well aware of Sharon's popularity among the broader, secular, non-settler public, which was eager to be rid of the security burden of Gaza. The tactic they chose was therefore a demand that the Disengagement Plan be approved by a Likud referendum. This demand received broad public support. Most Israelis (including Likud Central Committee members) wanted a say in this fateful decision. In an attempt to force Sharon to accept democratic rules, the veterans and settlers convened a meeting of the Central Committee. Sharon resisted but eventually acceded to their will. This was the first victory of what was referred to as the "orange" camp, in view of the color that they chose for their campaign. The Central Committee resolved to hold a referendum among the entire Likud membership. Here, too, Sharon was certain that he would win, in view of polls that indicated sixty percent support for the unilateral Disengagement among Likud members.

The war that raged between the veterans and Sharon produced scenes that brought tears to the eyes of those of us who grew up as part of the fighting family. Throughout the country, a veritable army of underground veterans descended on major traffic junctions and distributed stickers to passers-by. Some, well into their eighties, manned telephones, explaining with great passion how dangerous the Disengagement would be for Israel. Thousands of grandmothers and grandfathers took part in the struggle. Their determination was powered not by ideology alone; they had an objective that until now had been concealed and suppressed: to get rid of Sharon. Regardless of who would replace him, they wanted this invader out. The spirit of the Revolt that once again animated the veterans soon spread, sweeping up many others along the way – among them, some of the heirs.

The Land of Israel heirs at the forefront – Benny Begin is brought back

It was the veterans who mobilized the heirs to help lead the struggle. It was they who pressed Landau to lead the right-wing faction of the Likud. The quiet, modest Landau had always preferred to leave center stage to his more extroverted companions (first Milo, Meridor, and Olmert; later on Livni, Begin, and Netanyahu). Now he stood at the forefront, in his serious, to-the-point style, reminding the veterans of his father, Chaim.

Landau, the man who now represented the internal opposition to Sharon, had for many years been the only heir who was close to him. He had fought under Sharon in two wars and had watched the general at close hand at the height of his intrepid military activity. After the Yom Kippur War he had hoped that Sharon would make a political debut, and from the moment Sharon joined the Likud the two maintained a close bond. Landau viewed Sharon as the father of the settlements. In the First Lebanon War he had remained loyal to him, and he had even tried to convince Shamir to reappoint Sharon as Minister of Defense. In the internal party elections Landau had received support from some of Sharon's camp.

However, to Sharon's disappointment, Landau had never extended their ideological and personal connection into the political realm; he had always remained loyal to his roots: the veterans' camp. After Shamir resigned as chairman of the party in 1993, Landau had supported Netanyahu as his successor, and after Netanyahu's defeat he had preferred to remain neutral, supporting neither Sharon nor Olmert. In the 2002 primaries he backed Netanyahu, the contender, rather than Sharon, the incumbent Prime Minister, even though Sharon had appointed him Minister of Internal Security in an effort to woo him over.

But Landau had grown distant from Sharon as Sharon had gradually distanced himself from his previous positions. With each step to the Left on Sharon's part, Landau turned up his oppositional tone another notch in his media interviews and in the Central Committee. When Sharon chose to disengage from the vision of the Land of Israel, he caused a break with Landau, who viewed Sharon's move as treason. Landau was more hurt by Sharon's "deviation" than were the other heirs, for he had genuinely believed that Sharon was a true Land of Israel loyalist.

Landau and the veterans managed to bring eleven MKs who opposed the Disengagement into the new opposition against Sharon. In contrast to the government ministers, who opposed the plan but whose hands were tied owing to their ministerial positions, the MKs felt free of any obligation to the Prime Minister. The MKs, who were immediately labelled by Sharon's people as "the rebels", had the support of many veterans and activists, and they were motivated in their opposition inter alia by the belief that in the next internal elections, they would enjoy the support of a large camp.

But the orange camp was still in desperate need of a charismatic leader who could tilt the scales. Everyone knew Landau as an heir who was upright, loyal, and conscientious, but to win this war a personality of Netanyahu's proportions was called for. Netanyahu, however, was tied up in government. He refused to accede to the daily supplications of the veterans, for three reasons. Firstly, he believed that he would be able to change the situation from within the government. Secondly, he maintained that the Disengagement was a gimmick to evade the legal entanglements in which Sharon found himself (and as such it was better that Netanyahu remain as a "spare wheel" in the government, rather than leaving). Thirdly, Netanyahu was enamored and committed with every fiber of his being to the economic revolution that he was implementing. Since serving as Israel's ambassador to the UN he had not held a position that allowed him to set politics aside and simply get work done, in a sphere that he enjoyed. He felt that there was a pact between him and the public, requiring him to rehabilitate the economy and to carry through the revolution that was only just beginning. Leaving now would have been a violation of that pact. For all these reasons Netanyahu hoped that Sharon would put a halt to his dangerous adventure, so that work in the Ministry of Finance could continue.

The leader whom the veterans approached was Benny Begin. At this time, Begin was out of the Knesset. He had returned to his work at the Geological Institute, seemingly disillusioned with the results of all his political activity. For five years he had had no contact with the Knesset or politics. He seemed to despair of his ability to convince the public of his worldview that was opposed to territorial concessions, and had given up on Israeli society, which preferred short-term solutions to security for the future. It therefore came as a great surprise that Begin acceded to the veterans' request – just as he had returned to the political arena in 1986, at the request of the fighting family, when he had arrived at the Central Committee convention to halt the takeover by the very same Sharon. Begin took the helm and broke his long silence, declaring:

> Whoever supports the Disengagement should prepare to see Hamas flags flying over the abandoned territory, while their leaders rejoice over the victory of the 'Shahids' (Muslim martyrs) and incite the masses, calling for continuation of the violent struggle against Israel.[9]

The two heirs, Begin and Landau, the sons of Irgun commanders during the Revolt, were at the forefront. Around them were other heirs such as Ze'ev Jabotinsky and Yossi Ahimeir. Jabotinsky described Sharon as an "extreme Leftist [. . .] to the left of Meretz [. . .] presiding over a democtatorship," while referring to the Disengagement as a plan for "Expulsion and Flight". Even Chairman of the Knesset Rivlin, who was constrained by his position, expressed his opinion. From the moment Sharon chose to deviate from the Likud path, Rivlin started to backtrack on his support for him. For a moment it seemed that the Land of Israel faction had come back to life.

The renewed pact between the veterans and the heirs astounded Sharon. On May 2, the results of the Likud referendum on the Disengagement were published: some sixty percent of Likud members were opposed; only forty percent were in favor. Once again, against all odds, the veterans had won yet another victory against Sharon.

In the wake of this victory the Likud veterans, the members of the Yesha Council (the Council of Communities in Judea, Samaria, and Gaza), and the "rebel" MKs approached Begin, asking him to lead the right-wing opposition to Sharon. He was manifestly the most natural choice. Polls found that he was the candidate with the broadest public support. It was also clear that his agreement would itself impact the political map: he would be the head of the opposition, and Netanyahu would have to choose between allying himself with Sharon or leaving the government to join the opposition, partnering with Begin and Landau. But Begin was not looking for glory, and he believed that the democratic victory would be enough to stop the Disengagement. He was wrong.

Notes

1　Bloom and Hefetz, *Ariel Sharon: A Life*, 354.
2　Ibid., 434.
3　Haaretz, December 17, 2003.
4　Raviv Drucker and Ofer Shelah, Boomerang (Hebrew) (Beit Shemesh: Keter, 2005).
5　Moshe Yaalon, Derekh Aruka Ktzara [A Short Long Road] (Tel Aviv: Yediot Aharonot, 2008).
6　Interview with the author, October 3, 2008.
7　Ibid.
8　Haaretz, February 2, 2004.
9　Yediot Aharonot, April 20, 2004.

23 From Disengagement from Gaza to disengagement from the Likud

Sharon's decision to ignore the results of the Likud referendum and to continue advancing the Disengagement opened the floodgates. The old animosity towards him rose up from the hidden recesses and washed over the veterans' camp. For the first time they expressed openly what they felt: Get out of here. Get out of this movement that belongs to us and our children.

The Tagar Circle leaders sent the Prime Minister a letter, calling upon him to resign. The letter was an open declaration of war on his leadership. It was written with great anger and without an ounce of diplomacy:

> You no longer have any part in the Likud. The Likud is our home, even if you grasp and hang on to it with all your strength. There is nothing for you to do but to go back to where you came from – the Left. [. . .] You have destroyed the Likud; you are willing to trample every rule of human, public, and moral conduct in this country in order to carry out at any cost what you desire to do: to uproot and destroy the Katif region; to uproot pioneering Jews from their homes and their land. [. . .] Likud Chairman and Prime Minister Ariel Sharon: enough of this tyrannical and oppressive conduct. [. . .] You no longer have any place in the Likud. You have become a stranger in the nationalist camp. It's enough of you. Get up and resign. [. . . .] See what we have become. Who are your supporters today? The Labor, the Leftist elite, and the Arabs, who urge you on to implement the platform of Mitzna and the Left.[1]

The heirs become replicas of their parents

The collision between the Likud veterans and Sharon deepened the rift which, since the mid-1990s, had separated the heirs into three groups. On the right were the Land of Israel heirs, the standard-bearers of Jabotinsky's legacy, who maintained that there should be no territorial concession whatsoever (Begin, Landau, Rivlin, Jabotinsky, Ahimeir, and Aryeh Eldad, who was already to the right of Likud). On the left were the heirs who favored compromise for the sake of peace (Meridor, Milo, Olmert, Livni, and Boim). This group supported Sharon's initiative. In the middle were Netanyahu and the Tagar heirs (Livnat and Hanegbi).

The Land of Israel heirs were already in their sixties. Outwardly, many of them were almost exact copies of their fathers. It was widely noted that when Benny

Begin delivered an address, the audience had the sense that it was his father's voice that spoke through him. Towards the end of 2012, when Yair Shamir, the last of the heirs to enter politics, joined Lieberman's Yisrael Beitenu party, many observers caught their breath – it was as if his father, Yitzhak Shamir, had returned to public life.

The physical resemblance between the fathers and sons was a tangible representation of the almost miraculous replication of the founding generation in its younger offspring: the latter spoke with the same words and in the same serious and modest tone; there was the same ideological rigidity, the same dignity. The Land of Israel heirs held fast to the Beitar principles set down by Jabotinsky and took care to maintain the Revisionist legacy, adhering strictly to right-wing positions. They drew their inspiration from Begin Sr., adopting his approach wholly and comprehensively. When pressed for responses to challenges of the new millennium, they went back to Jabotinsky's teachings and Begin's speeches and found their answers.

Rivlin describes this well: "For me, and for Benny, Uzi, Zeev, and Yossi, Jabotinsky's teachings were holy."[2] Just as a religious Jew accepts the Torah unquestioningly, without trying to propose changes and corrections, so the Revisionists chanted excerpts of Jabotinsky's writings, seeing no need to invent a philosophy of their own. Rivlin avoids dealing with practical questions arising from Israel's control over Judea and Samaria (how to maintain a Jewish, democratic state in a reality that includes millions of Palestinians), preferring always to remain safely within the framework of the "Jabotinsky-Begin legacy". While he held a political office, he stated openly and honestly that he was in politics in order to uphold the liberal Jabotinsky ideal, along with protecting the integrity of the land. He told me that the generations to come would have to deal with the other questions – indicating, as it were, that perhaps there is room for some amending and updating of the ideology, but that this would be the task of the next generation.

In an interview he gave in 2003, Rivlin was asked about his decision to refrain from joining Sharon's government as a minister. He answered:

> As a disciple of Jabotinsky I believe that "Zion is all ours." Even if people tell me that it's impossible today, and for the next at least ten generations, I can't lift my hand against the principle that Zion is all ours. If I were one of the ministers in the government, I would find it very difficult to vote on such an issue against my conscience, and the moment I had to assume ministerial responsibility, I would have to get up and resign.[3]

In a different interview, just after the Disengagement, Rivlin described his feelings when he heard Sharon speaking against the settlers during the annual memorial for Ben-Gurion:

> When I heard what Arik said at Ben-Gurion's grave, I was heartbroken. His words tore a hole in my heart. From that moment I told myself that the rupture between us could not be repaired. I was deeply pained that I couldn't love him any more.[4]

Yossi Ahimeir, too, remained loyal to the worldview of his father and of Begin. In a piece that he published on his blog in October 2008, Ahimeir offered a cynical exposition of his worldview by contrasting it to that of a different heir:

> Just five years ago, in 2003, Olmert wrote the following, out of complete identification with Menachem Begin, o.b.m: "For years, when people wanted to attack Begin and tell him, 'You're no longer relevant; you're cut off from reality; you live in a different world,' they would say, 'You still believe in the Land of Israel [. . .]' and they attacked him over and over, just because he dared to dream, to educate, and to talk about our connection with the places that are the cradle of our nation's existence; the symbols that preserved our national bonds. And he went stubbornly on," Olmert writes about Begin, "in a manner that sometimes appeared strange to those close to him and to his supporters. He never gave up. Until it turned out that it was he who had been the realist; it was he who had been practical; it was he who had had vision; that it was he who had understood the more profound processes [. . .] rather than all the various pragmatic experts who advised him – for the sake of public relations, for the sake of gaining votes, for the sake of achievements, for the sake of elections – to forgo this inner truth, without which there would have been no purpose, nor any inner strength, nor any ability to fight for what this nation needed to fight for."[5]

While the heirs who favored compromise broke down the walls that isolated the fighting family, the Land of Israel heirs worked to reinforce the ideological scaffolding – even at the expense of positions of power, even where forced to resign. Those who were unwilling to "update" their beliefs generally remained in the opposition, or at home, such that the number of ministers who were part of this group was relatively small. While other heirs, younger than them, were already taking up ministerial offices and other senior positions in the movement and the public service, the Land of Israel heirs were forced to compromise (at best) and take more junior positions; in many cases they resigned over political moves by the leaders of the party. One example is Benny Begin, who resigned from the government in the wake of the Hebron Agreement and later left the movement in the wake of the Wye Memorandum. Uzi Landau likewise gave up his ministerial seat when he voted against the Disengagement. Rivlin, as mentioned, gave up the offer of a seat in Sharon's government, choosing to serve as Chairman of the Knesset instead.

The bitter struggle against Sharon took the Land of Israel heirs back to familiar, cold outbacks – this time, in the internal opposition. When the wheels of the Disengagement continued turning, despite the vote of the Likud Central Committee and even after the referendum, the heirs prepared for all-out war.

Sharon the "Bulldozer" paves the way for the Disengagement

The results of the Likud referendum in May 2004, caught Sharon completely by surprise. He was upset; he had not expected this loss. His newfound popularity, and the encouraging polls, had made him complacent. Now this referendum had upended everything. At first, Sharon sounded like he would accept the will of the voters and would make changes to the plan. In effect, he simply ignored the referendum and continued with his plan. Democracy was no obstacle for him.

From this moment, and for the next year and a half, Sharon and the orange camp engaged in a prolonged war of many battles, which also drew in the heirs of the opposition. Each of Sharon's moves provoked the orange camp anew, leading to an intensification of the conflict, until the final, predictable ending. Having suffered a stinging defeat in the party arena, Sharon submitted the Disengagement Plan for the government's approval on June 7, 2004. But by this stage the government presented a problem: Sharon no longer had a majority. And so it was that forty-eight hours before the vote was to take place, Sharon unceremoniously sacked two right-wing ministers – Avigdor Lieberman (Yisrael Beitenu) and Benny Elon (National Union) – who vigorously opposed the plan.

Even after these dismissals, there remained a core of opposition in the form of ten ministers, headed by Netanyahu. In many conversations between them, Netanyahu had expressed his clear and consistent opposition to the unilateral withdrawal, arguing that such a move would strengthen Hamas and lead to barrages of missiles on the south of the country. Sharon made special efforts to appease the Likud ministers, especially Netanyahu. He enlisted Livni as a mediator for contacts with Netanyahu, Shalom, and Livnat, and Livni indeed managed to consolidate a compromise agreement according to which the Disengagement would take place in three stages, each to receive separate government approval. In other words, the government would vote on each stage (a commitment which Sharon ultimately did not fulfill). Fourteen ministers supported this compromise (including Netanyahu and Livnat); seven were opposed (including Hanegbi and Landau). Although the ministers were still hesitant, and the agreement was tentative rather than final, Sharon issued an announcement that made huge headlines in the press ("The Disengagement Plan Gets Going!"), reinforcing his image as a courageous leader. The ministers who were opposed to the Disengagement – Netanyahu among them – were stunned by the headlines and the commentary that portrayed them as having compromised and effectively agreed to the Disengagement Plan. This public perception haunted them for years to come.

This was the first failure of the internal opposition. The pact broke up into two groups: the opponents, headed by Landau, and the so-called "compromisers", headed by Netanyahu. A third group consisted of Sharon supporters, with Livni now a prominent player thanks to the compromise that she had achieved. She was now perceived as having "unified" the Likud and brought Sharon an important victory.

About a month later, in June 2004, Sharon launched another initiative that stood in complete contradiction to all of his prior political activity: the man who had built the isolated settlements – sometimes using controversial means – now ordered that a report be prepared listing all the unauthorized outposts in Judea and Samaria. The task was entrusted to Talia Sasson, former head of the State Prosecution Criminal Department. Three elements of this absurd initiative aroused the ire of the orange camp: first was the decision to appoint an external legal expert who was openly identified with the Left; the second was that Sasson was known to have supported indicting Netanyahu in a legal suit that had later been closed by the Attorney General; the third was that Sharon instructed Sasson to investigate irregularities in the construction in Judea and Samaria, for which he himself had largely been responsible.

Another month or so went by, and in August 2004, Sharon made waves all over again. Although he had a broad and stable coalition, Sharon decided to invite Labor to join a unity government, so as to earn their backing for the Disengagement. This step was broadly opposed by the Likud, and especially by the ministers, who understood that they would become a minority in the diluted government (if not losing their positions altogether). The anger towards Sharon found expression at activists' meetings and in various petitions. This time it was not only silver-haired veterans and knitted skullcap-wearers who were against him, but even his own ministers.

Landau led the opposition against Sharon, with energetic help from Netanyahu's people. Netanyahu himself avoided direct confrontation with the Prime Minister, so as not to cause an explosion of the already fraught relations between them. He was on an overseas trip, and from afar he expressed his opposition, arguing that the Labor party would destroy the process of rehabilitating the economy. Landau also had the backing of the "rebel" MKs and ministers, including Foreign Minister Silvan Shalom, Sharon's erstwhile loyal ally, who understood that in a unity government, he would be replaced by Peres.

Sharon tried to avoid a Likud Central Committee convention, claiming that the decision as to the merger fell squarely under the authority of the Prime Minister. But with the Likud agitated and seething, Sharon was forced back into the now-uncomfortable party arena. He placed on the agenda a shrewd proposal that was intended to bypass his opponents: to allow him as Prime Minister to engage in coalition negotiations with all Zionist parties. His proposal would be brought to the vote along with the opposing proposal submitted by Landau.

Sharon's people worked non-stop to avoid losing the vote. Omri Sharon exerted strenuous efforts among the ministers and MKs. Claims were made about threats that the Prime Minister's people used against office-bearers, and about organized gangs that disrupted opponents' speeches. Sharon and his son believed that they would win, even though this time the opposition included Sharon's former ally who now found himself hanging by a thread: Silvan Shalom.

Sharon countered his opponents with Ministers Livnat and Livni. His new argument was that the Likud could not be seen to be blacklisting Labor – because in the past, Likud had been blacklisted by the Labor. Livnat sided against those who should have been her natural partners (the veterans suspected that she had received a promise that she would not lose her position as Minister of Education.)

Despite his calculating move, Sharon once again lost the vote. The Central Committee voted separately on the two proposals, and Sharon lost both. Landau's proposal, which opposed bringing Labor into the government, won, with 843 votes to the 612 of Sharon's camp. Without Silvan Shalom, Sharon was now clearly in the minority. Sharon's proposal received 760 votes, but 765 Central Committee members voted against it. Immediately after the voting, Omri Sharon maintained the same defiant stance: "From the Prime Minister's point of view, nothing happened here." And indeed, Sharon once again ignored the democratic decision of his party, and, in January 2005, brought Labor into a unity government. Shimon Peres agreed to join, in return for the symbolic position of Deputy Prime Minister.

Sharon emerged triumphant. The media was glad of the reinforcements to the compromise camp in the government, even if democracy had once again been trampled. In the public view, Netanyahu had lost again.

Disengagement Plan is approved by the Knesset – Sharon moves further to the left

On October 8, 2004, Sharon embarked on the next step of his venture, submitting the Disengagement Plan for the approval of the Knesset. In the Knesset he had the support of his faction in the Likud, along with the centrist and left-wing parties, and it was therefore clear that in this forum he was assured of a sound victory. Nevertheless, one big question remained: what would the Likud ministers, first and foremost among them Netanyahu, do when the time came to vote? (A minister's vote against the government is effectively a resignation.) The trap of the Disengagement vote increased the pressure on Netanyahu from his political base – the orange camp and the veterans.

The Knesset session that day was described as a "banana putsch" and is remembered as a farce. Netanyahu (along with Livnat, as well as Ministers Danny Naveh and Israel Katz, and the ministers of the National Religious party) announced moments before the vote that he would resign within two weeks unless the Knesset passed a bill setting a referendum to decide on the fate of the Disengagement. Now all eyes were on the two leaders: would Sharon bend, or not? If he accepted the demand of Netanyahu and his circle that the nation decide, rather than the Knesset, then he would have "surrendered" and would thereby have lost the leadership. Sharon did not accede. A few minutes before the voting, urgent consultations were still going on in the corridors between Netanyahu and his companions.

Netanyahu, Katz, Naveh, and Livnat retracted their demand. They voted in favor of the plan and watched as Minister Uzi Landau and Deputy Minister Michael Ratzon voted against and were dismissed by Sharon. Sharon won the Knesset vote, with sixty-seven votes against forty-five. The victory had been achieved with the votes of all the MKs of the Left, as well as some from the Likud.

In February 2005, the Evacuation-Compensation Bill passed. This was in fact the first real step in implementing the Disengagement, and it represented Sharon's sixth straight victory in the government and the Knesset.

Another step to the left came in the same month, in the form of the publication of the Sasson report on unauthorized outposts in Judea and Samaria. It looked like a document that had been prepared in the offices of the ultra-left Meretz party for a left-wing government. Its conclusions were blistering:

> Ongoing, blatant, institutionalized violation of the law by the institutions themselves, undermines the rule of law. Moreover, the acts of violation of the law become ingrained and turn into accepted behavioral norms. [. . .] These acts must no longer be accepted. There must be reform, and I believe that you are capable of undertaking it.[6]

Among the Likud and the Right, the report gave rise to indignation and a sense of betrayal. The Left rejoiced.

Netanyahu resigns from Sharon's government

This was a trying period, especially for Netanyahu. Sharon was riding a wave of tremendous public support, while Netanyahu was the target of media criticism. Other Likud ministers, who were deliberating between remaining in the government and openly opposing the Disengagement Plan, were given a free pass: the media allowed them to hide behind Netanyahu's back; all fire was aimed at him. He was portrayed as indecisive and irresolute, even though he had opposed the Disengagement from day one.

Now he also found himself in a hostile government, as Minister of Finance without the Prime Minister's backing. Sharon had started involving himself in the economic sphere; the Likud veterans were calling upon him to resign immediately; the orange camp raged over his serving in the Disengagement government – but he insisted on remaining in the Finance Ministry, determined to complete his important economic reforms. Netanyahu knew that the public still viewed him as a successful Minister of Finance who had saved the economy. He had tremendous support from economic experts, commentators, and senior figures in the world of commerce. Some of them were less than enthusiastic about Netanyahu the politician, but they showered him with praise as an economic leader.

On the Saturday night preceding the Disengagement, Netanyahu reached a decision: he would not sit in the Disengagement government. He would not be part of a government that carried out an operation to which he was fundamentally opposed. In his eyes, this was a bargain-basement sellout of state assets in return for legal peace and quiet for Sharon. When he resigned the next day, he was already determined to bring down Sharon and to replace him. The "imprisoned" heir was freed from his golden cage on the very threshold of the Disengagement. Now he turned into an overt and sharp-tongued opposition. He attacked relentlessly, warning that Gaza would become "a base for terror that will endanger Israel's security"[7] and that the Disengagement would bring disaster. What appeared then to be politically inspired doomsday prophecies turned out, just a few years later, to have been entirely accurate.

It was a last-minute resignation, a moment before losing his political basis, and a little too late for his image not to suffer some damage. During the

Disengagement Netanyahu was given a lukewarm reception in the Likud. There was bitterness over his having refrained from fighting the Disengagement Plan for a year and a half, and his not having been part of the orange camp. The MKs who had opposed the plan were resentful towards him. Their candidate for leadership against Sharon was Landau, who had paid for his principles with his ministerial seat. The media, which had praised Netanyahu for the economic turnaround but opposed his political views, now discarded all restraint and attacked him savagely. A moment before his resignation he had been the Minister of Finance who had saved Israel; a minute later, as he attacked the Disengagement over which they were so giddily excited, he became a target to be roasted, an enemy of the people. Even in the economic columns where he had so recently been feted and praised, he was transformed in an instant into the man who had abandoned the economy for political gain.

Netanyahu convened a press conference in which he announced his intention to run for chairman of the Likud and called for early elections. The event was held at Sokolov House in Tel Aviv, home of the Israeli Journalists' Association, in a small hall intended for journalists alone. But dozens of Netanyahu's supporters arrived, turning the press conference into a rather embarrassing debacle. The journalists were treated to rude comments about their attitude towards Netanyahu; there was much noise and commotion, and on top of everything else, the air-conditioning failed in the middle of this searing hot summer day. Tempers flared accordingly.

The journalists left the press conference with a damning headline: "Netanyahu is sweating." Their anger towards the Likud activists who had gate-crashed the event was directed towards Netanyahu. He was portrayed as stressed, as panicking, and as acting out of personal motives, out of a desire for power. His statement that he could not be part of a government that led to the creation of a missile base in the south and the forsaking of Israel's security was completely ignored.

A second night of the microphones – Sharon's last victory in the Likud

In September 2005, about a month after the Disengagement and Netanyahu's resignation, another round of fighting took place in the Likud Central Committee. The camp opposed to Sharon tabled a resolution seeking to bring forward the party primaries by a few months, so they would precede the general elections for the seventeenth Knesset.

On the face of it, this was a procedural matter. In fact, however, it was a critical fight over the path of the Likud: a direct and all-encompassing battle over whether the Likud would bring forward Sharon's certain ousting, or whether it would yield and wait for the fixed time. After the three defeats that Sharon had suffered at the Central Committee, the meeting would show whether Sharon still had a movement behind him, or whether he was a satellite that had lost all contact with its mother-base. After a series of indirect and restrained altercations, Netanyahu now openly challenged Sharon: a former Prime Minister against a sitting Prime Minister; a successor against his own successor.

The meeting was also meant to decide whether two camps that were so different from one another in terms of ideology were capable of dwelling together in
the same party. The speeches that Sharon and Netanyahu delivered at the meeting
left no room for doubt: there was no chance for coexistence. The personal and
ideological rift was too deep and too wide.

Crowds of infuriated Likud veterans arrived at the Exhibition Grounds. Their
prized protégés, Netanyahu and Landau, were no longer serving in Sharon's government, and so the veterans felt free to express their loathing – not only towards
Sharon but also towards the heirs who had followed him: Olmert, Livni, and
Boim. The veterans felt like parents whose children had stolen the family heir-
looms and handed them to their enemies.

The outrage over the Disengagement was still running high. The veterans and
the settlers detested Sharon, whom they viewed as a dictator who had stolen the
movement, uprooted democracy, and thrown Jews out of their homes and off
their land – all for the sake of evading punishment for the corruption of which
he was suspected. Landau, in contrast, was viewed as a trustworthy leader, and
despite their reservations concerning Netanyahu, who had not joined them in
their fight, their faith in his ability to save the movement and take it forward was
still intact.

The Sharon camp was comprised mostly of power-brokers. Most of them had
not supported the Disengagement – very few of the Central Committee members
had been in favor – but what motivated them now was the imminent danger of
Sharon being thrown out of the Likud and the loss of the power that his position
afforded them.

Sharon arrived at the convention fully aware that he had lost the movement,
having made a complete break with its core and essence. He knew that his level of
acceptance in the media and among the elite was in inverse proportion to his level
of acceptance in the Likud. For this reason, just prior to the convention Sharon's
people started spreading the news that he was considering leaving the Likud and
setting up a new party. Polls predicted a landslide victory – between thirty and
forty mandates for the new party.

In this way Sharon tried to hold the Likud Central Committee hostage: if
it behaved properly, Sharon would remain in the Likud and the Likud would
remain in power. If the party opposed him, Sharon would leave, and the Likud
would crash. The Central Committee members saw, heard, and read what the
political pundits had to say. They understood the significance of the moment and
the risks. A vote against Sharon might be a vote in favor of and commitment to
Likud ideology, but it bore a heavy price. For the veterans and the orange camp,
the decision was simple. But for the power-brokers, it was a political life-or-
death question.

Netanyahu spoke first. At eight in the evening he took the stage, accompanied
by a cacophony of calls from supporters and opponents alike. He started off by
addressing Sharon's threats to leave and for the first time showed him the door,
firmly and fearlessly: "Someone is threatening us with leaving. First of all, we
don't take threats of leaving [. . .] but if someone wants to leave, let him do

so right now." He then went on to attack Sharon and the Disengagement with extraordinary ferocity:

> Are we the Likud, or are we to the left of Meretz? That's the question. We're the Likud, not Meretz! [. . .] In violation of an explicit promise to the voters, entire families have been uprooted from their homes. I want to know: What did we receive in return? What did we get for all this suffering? I'm sorry to say the answer is clear; it's just as the security people warned: Hamas has seized control of the Gaza Strip. [. . .] A terror highway is pouring weapons into the area.[8]

The next speaker was Uzi Landau, who expressed his disappointment and anger when he attacked Sharon personally:

> *We're* ousting *you*, Arik? You make me laugh. *You* ousted the Likud members who voted in a referendum. For two years you've ignored the Likud and its institutions. You've had nothing but scorn for all of us. Just this weekend we saw about forty Qassam missiles. Didn't you promise that if a missile fell, there would be a painful response, and Gaza would shake? That day has come; we see that they're firing and firing and firing on Sderot, and there's no serious response at all. Is this the Likud?[9]

Then came Sharon's turn. The version of the speech that had been distributed in advance to the press[10] included an unbridled attack on the opposition:

> This is a move that is meant to oust me, and an expression of no confidence in the way in which the Likud has led the country. It's all out of a desire for revenge, and uncontrolled personal ambition. This will be suicide; it will smash the Likud and lead only in one direction – to the opposition. [. . .] Tomorrow we shall decide whether this will be a Likud that is at the heart of the national consensus, or an extremist Likud that has been pushed to the fringes; a large and influential governing party, or a small party with no influence, in the opposition, like the party I received six years ago.

But as Sharon started speaking, with the entire country watching on their television screens, a hiccup in the amplification system cut off his words. The Prime Minister stood before the Central Committee of his party, voiceless. He waved, and walked offstage. On television it looked like a malicious act planned by Sharon's opponents. There was no other way of understanding it: who would sabotage the amplification system while the Prime Minister was giving his speech? Obviously, his violent gangster opponents. And so the opposition suffered a heavy blow to its image: the Likud Central Committee looked and sounded just as Sharon's people presented it in the media: violent, vociferous, lacking respect, and more divisive than ever. The Likud looked like a party making a mockery of an experienced and beloved Prime Minister. It was "a movement committing suicide", as Shamir had exclaimed in the 1980s.

Once Sharon's speech was interrupted, it was clear to Netanyahu that the battle had gone the other way. The prevailing view among Netanyahu's camp was that Sharon had planned the sabotage of the microphone himself, just as he had been behind the incident in the 1990s. After all, he was the only one who gained anything from the incident. Several hours were spent carefully reviewing the footage again and again, in an attempt to find proof, but with no success. Only the shame remained, and it was attributed to the opposition. Netanyahu was surprised by the sudden turn of events but understood immediately that the great majority of the Central Committee was now swayed against the early elections. They would not want to continue the humiliation of the Prime Minister with the vote that was scheduled for the next day.

The vote was held the next day – this time, with no ceremony and no speeches. As expected, Sharon won. There was still a surprise, though, and that was the very slim margin. He received only fifty-two percent of the vote. This reflected the fact that Sharon no longer had a majority in the Likud. Had it not been for the unfortunate incident the night before, he would have been defeated.

This was Sharon's first and last victory in the Likud Central Committee over the entire course of the battles he waged with the orange camp. In his last fight, he managed to portray the bringing forward of the primaries as a personal initiative on the part of Netanyahu, who was eager to bring down a sitting Prime Minister. He managed to put off the inevitable ending – the primaries – until December 2005.

Splitting of the Likud – Sharon leaves, taking Olmert and Livni with him

The Central Committee meeting conveyed a sense of impending divorce. Shortly afterwards, the final battle was waged: the battle for the Likud faction in the Knesset. It came in the wake of the resignations of Landau and Netanyahu from the government, and Sharon's demand that they be replaced with two of his supporters: Zeev Boim and Roni Bar-On.

The Likud rebels fumed, arguing that this was clearly a matter of "buying" MKs with a view to gaining control of the Likud faction. Sharon had already advanced his people at the expense of those who had opposed the Disengagement: Meir Sheetrit had been appointed Minister of Transport; Gideon Ezra had been promoted from the Ministry of Tourism to the Ministry of Internal Security; Avraham Hirschsohn was now Minister of Tourism; and Tzipi Livni had been promoted from the Ministry of Absorption to the Ministries of Housing and Justice. The rebels refused to approve the new appointments. Sharon was left with a hostile faction.

During this period (September-October 2005) there was an uptick in the rumors that Sharon was planning to leave the Likud and establish a new party. The polls predicted widespread public support. Nevertheless, Sharon deliberated. An experienced and wily politician, he knew what had happened before to popular leaders who had left their parties to form new ones, only to end up crashing and disappearing: Ben-Gurion, Dayan, Tamir, Weizmann, and so on. However, the positive polls and the growing hostility that he was encountering in the Likud boosted his motivation to leave. He felt trapped in a party whose political worldview was completely different from his own. He knew that there was such anger towards him in the Likud that he would never be re-elected as chairman. He and his advisors knew that his situation among the Likud membership was nothing like his situation among the general public, and that Netanyahu was sure to beat him in the approaching primaries.

His advisors urged him to make the most of the historical opportunity and to set up a new party that would shatter all the conventions of Israeli politics. Sharon already controlled a fair-sized army of followers, all just waiting for his orders. His advisors had come to agreements with several Likud MKs who were ready to leave together with Sharon, in return for reserved places in the next Knesset. The media for the most part mobilized to promote the establishment of a sort of "Likud B": a party whose platform would read, "Two states for two peoples"; a new Likud that would destroy the old one that was so hated among the elite and the media. The trend in the media at this time was to glorify Sharon and back his measures against this recalcitrant has-been party ruled by a corrupt Central Committee. Sharon received requests from all sides – pleas, almost – to break the Likud for once and for all.

During this turbulent period there were those who feared the dissolution of the movement; others tried to implement various measures, believing that Sharon was against division and preferred to find a solution within the Likud; that he did not wish to leave but rather just to maintain his status as both chairman of the Likud and the Prime Minister. The estimate of these supporters was that Sharon was truly deliberating, that he was not blinded by the advice of his consultants and survey results. He still felt the sting of his independent party that had run for the Knesset in 1977 with the polls predicting a great future: it had barely scraped two mandates. Such mistakes are not forgotten.

Tzipi Livni faced a thorny dilemma. She knew that if Sharon left the Likud and set up a new party, she would hold a senior position in the new party and in Sharon's new government. She also knew that if the Likud remained united, she would have a difficult time with the Central Committee – a right-wing body that included Religious Zionist opponents of the Disengagement, and the veterans. She could expect confrontations with most of the movement and most of all with the "aunts and uncles" who would not forgive her for having followed their enemy, Sharon.

Nevertheless, even if Sharon's departure would guarantee her ministerial status, while remaining in the Likud would risk even her Knesset seat, Livni was troubled by the sight of her parents' movement being torn apart. She therefore took action against her personal interests, out of concern for the fate of the Likud, seeking a formula that would keep the party united. Knowing how small the chances were, she discussed with Sharon the possibility of a compromise that would leave him as chairman of the Likud, while Netanyahu would be the Likud's most senior minister as well as chairman of the Likud secretariat, which manages the movement. The proposed compromise also stipulated that the choice of Likud candidates for the Knesset would be made via primaries and not by the super-right-wing Central Committee. All members would have a vote, such that Sharon's supporters would stand a better chance. (If the Central Committee were to choose, they would stand no chance at all.) Livni wanted to assure Sharon the chairmanship of the party and the premiership, to assure Netanyahu his status as successor, and to assure the MKs who had supported the Disengagement the preservation of the primaries system for internal elections, so as to increase their chances of remaining in the Knesset.

The answer that Livni received from Sharon the next day was surprising – and up until the publication of this book was never made known. The fact is that Sharon was willing to compromise. Just six days before announcing his resignation, he still preferred to stay within the Likud, on condition that his status as chairman and Prime Minister was assured, and on condition that Netanyahu would promise not to challenge him in the primaries.

However, the response that Livni received from the other side was an unequivocal "no". The Likud was already de facto split. The opponents of the Disengagement wanted to see Sharon out. The leaders of the opposition were not prepared to support Sharon as chairman of the party or as Prime Minister. The Likud believed that even after the split, it would still hold more than twenty mandates, while Sharon and his new party would crash, as many political stars and their new parties had crashed in the past. Not for a moment did it occur to Sharon's opponents that it might be the Likud that would crash, that Sharon was at a unique, one-time political peak where he could create a major party that would annihilate his previous political home. Such moments are rare for any leader. The Likud believed that the moment would pass and that the reality that Sharon had created in Gaza would blow up in his face.

On Saturday night, November 19, 2005, Sharon's close circle – his sons, his advisors, and Tzipi Livni – gathered at his Sycamore Ranch. From the information that emerged later on it seems that they were divided as to whether to break away. They looked at the up-to-date, optimistic polls. Sharon had huge support in the media for a centrist peace party that would effect a "big bang" in Israeli politics. Tzipi Livni was the only MK who participated in the meeting – the only one of all the ministers and MKs whom Sharon trusted.

It was at this meeting that Livni first announced her full and unqualified support for the creation of a new centrist party (which was to be called Kadima – "Forwards"). Later on, the other participants said that it was Livni's support that decided the matter. From Sharon's perspective, if an Irgun heiress, the daughter of Eitan Livni, had reached the conclusion that there was no hope in the Likud, then there was no choice but to leave.

Livni told me later on that the platform of the centrist Kadima party was born out of the document entitled "Principles for the Unity of the Likud": the document with which she had sought compromise and unity within the Likud. After the other side rejected it, the title was changed to "Principles for the Establishment of a New Party".

The next day Sharon announced his decision to leave the Likud. He met with President Moshe Katzav and asked him to disperse the Knesset. The same day, Sharon convened his new faction. The momentum was breathtaking.

The Israeli public was behind him. All hopes were pinned on the new party which still had no official name, no offices, no bank account. But fourteen MKs from the Likud (a third of the Likud Knesset faction, as required for a breakaway party) had already signed membership in the new party, thereby officially breaking up the Likud into two parties. The greatest split in Likud history had just occurred.

Figure 23.1 The general who joined the Likud, Ariel Sharon. He fought with the veteran generation, resigned from the Likud, and divided the Princes between two parties. Here with Tzipi Livni, who served as a minister in his government.

Figure 23.2 Ariel Sharon with Ehud Olmert. Olmert was elected to the Knesset more than
forty years ago, fought against Sharon on the leadership, lost, joined his government, resigned with him from the Likud, and succeeded him as PM.

Notes

1 Founders of the Likud party call Sharon to resign (2005). Retrieved from https://www.
   inn.co.il/News/News.aspx/113209
2 Interview with the author, April 18, 2002.
3 Yisrael Hayom, June 13, 2014.
4 Haaretz, May 10, 2005

5 Yossi Ahimeir. (October 4, 2008). Kadima Lanesiga (Hebrew) [Web log post]. Retrieved from https://www.news1.co.il/Archive/003-D-32317-00.html
6 Haaretz, March 9, 2005.
7 Yediot Aharonot, August 7, 2005.
8 Yediot Aharonot, September 25, 2005.
9 Ibid.
10 Maariv, September 26, 2005.

24 Most of the heirs break with their home

After thirty years of unsuccessful wooing, Sharon took his revenge on the Irgun veterans who had caused him such headaches. With his departure, the battles that the veterans had waged against the middle generation came to an end. Forty years previously, the veterans had blocked the first of the eligible successors of the middle generation: the moderate Shmuel Tamir. In 1972 they had blocked another eligible successor: the moderate Ezer Weizman. During the '80s and '90s they had exerted mighty efforts to block Levy, Sharon, and Modai. After Sharon seized control, they managed to expel him, too.

This was the end of the fight against all who had threatened the hegemony of the fighting family over the course of fifty-five years. It had started with the struggle against the older generation; it had continued with the struggle against competing groups of their contemporaries; and it had extended to the struggle with the younger middle-generation leaders. Now the veterans had succeeded in their mission of ridding the party of Sharon – albeit at the expense of losing the government. Finally, they had a Likud that was free of threats, and they could once again coronate their ideological heir: Benjamin Netanyahu.

The rejected middle generations had produced competing parties, which were active in the political Center and attracted Herut/Likud votes: Shmuel Tamir had set up his Free Center; Weizman had started the Yachad (Together) party, which joined up with Labor; Levy had established Gesher (Bridge); Sharon had once founded Shlomtzion (Peace of Zion). Nevertheless, there remained an important difference between these other parties and Kadima, the party that Sharon created now: Sharon was the only one among these leaders who left the Likud as Prime Minister, the only one who managed to take half of the Likud with him, including mayors, MKs, and most of the party's voters.

Sharon had taken Israel back in time by building a huge ruling party. The Labor had once stretched from the moderate left, via the center, to the moderate right. Now Sharon's Kadima was a moderate ruling party supported by the main political Center. This was achieved thanks to Sharon immediately bringing on board prominent Labor figures, including Shimon Peres, who served as Sharon's stamp of approval for the centrist and left-wing public.

Like the historical Labor, Kadima now pushed the Likud into the opposition corner. For the veterans, the new millennium was a return to the 1950s. Once again, they belonged to a small, marginal, homogeneous, and impoverished party that was positioned at the extreme Right of the political map. They were not disheartened by this reality; they had lived to rid their political and ideological home of foreign invaders. The opposition was in their genes; it was not something to be feared. Moreover, they had as their leader a well-admired heir, a son of the fighting family, who gave them hope for rebuilding the ruins.

It was during November 2005, as Sharon was consolidating Kadima, that the diamond in the crown of the veterans – their younger generation – was shattered. The chain was broken. The children who in the past had fought side by side to restore their parents' honor now found themselves in rival parties. Sons and daughters of members of the Irgun high command were split and headed down diverging paths. For the first time, most of the broader circle of the Likud's younger generation – sons and daughters of veterans – left their political home and moved over to Kadima.

While Sharon's departure had been greeted by the fighting family with a sigh of relief, the defection of their sons and daughters to Kadima left them dumbstruck and crushed. The veterans had trouble dealing with the new reality in which the Likud now faced a rival party headed by their own sons and daughters. Each day more of them joined the rival camp; every week another of the faces that had been a party symbol was missing. The veterans were horrified that the finest of their offspring had joined their historical adversaries – Sharon and Peres. The feeling pervading the Likud headquarters was that the world was falling apart, that the foundations were crumbling. This was the hardest – and last – blow that Ariel Sharon dealt to the veteran camp: the younger generation's widespread abandonment of their cherished political home.

The first to leave, already some years back, had been the "compromise" heirs: Meridor, Olmert, and Milo. Since the 1999 elections there had been bad blood with them. Now, in the last two years, the veterans had been deeply disappointed in the heirs whom they had cultivated just a decade previously and who had grown closer to Sharon, both personally and ideologically. As they were promoted from one government to the next, the disappointment turned into anger and censure over their chasing the senior positions that Sharon offered them. The departure of Meridor, Olmert, Milo, and Livni along with Sharon caused great pain to the parents who felt themselves torn from the "children" they had nurtured, mentored, and advanced with their own hands. They had cultivated them believing that the heirs would remain loyal to them, to the movement, to the Herut worldview. The veterans had rebuffed and rejected many different groups and individuals simply because they did not trust them. They did not trust anyone from the "outside", because they knew that outsiders could surrender to the pressure of the elite and the media and hence could end up betraying the movement and the Land of Israel. It was for this reason that even an Irgun commander like Shmuel Tamir had been warded off; even a hawk like Weizman. In both these men, as in many others, the veterans had detected the early signs of media influence. The beginnings of a move to moderation.

They were even more thunderstruck by the second, unexpected wave of departures, when sons and daughters from the very heart of the camp – the heart of the Beitar worldview – shifted their allegiance to Kadima.

The walkout by Minister Tzahi Hanegbi, chairman of the Likud Central Committee, was a bitter and painful blow. This most right-wing of heirs, son of the renowned Lehi fighter, opponent of the Disengagement, left everyone flabbergasted when he announced that he was moving from Likud to Kadima. While Meridor and Livni had drifted slowly away, Hanegbi's departure was a blitz. There had been no warning.

A confidant of Hanegbi explained the move in terms of personality: Hanegbi felt he could rely on Sharon; he viewed him as a leader who could guide Israel to safe shores. But in retrospect one could see that Hanegbi had also undergone a change in his worldview while he served in the heirs' government under Netanyahu. There the principles that he had imbibed at home collided with the complicated reality of international agreements. Hanegbi had loyally followed Netanyahu, even where compromises had been involved: in the Hebron Agreement and in the Wye Memorandum. In Sharon's government, Hanegbi had been firmly opposed to the Disengagement but had not taken drastic steps. As chairman of the Likud Central Committee he did all he could to maintain unity. He tried to persuade Netanyahu to limit the struggle so that Sharon would not leave and break the Likud apart. At the same time, he tried to convince Sharon not to leave, leveraging his senior position to mediate between the two camps. Hanegbi was involved in most of the attempts at compromise. After his move to Kadima, Hanegbi said in an interview:

> I changed. It didn't happen all at once; it's a lengthy process. You weren't monitoring me, but it happened. Today, now that I'm involved, knowing what's going on, aware of the exigencies, I'm prepared to compromise on things I wasn't prepared to in the past. [. . .] My ideological maturity is the product of the last few years.[1]

Every day there were rumors of new desertions from the outer circle of the younger generation that had grown up in the movement. The names were not familiar to the general public, but they were well known among the movement: sons and daughters whose parents had fought in the underground; youngsters who had grown up on Jabotinsky's teachings, had fought against the Left, had been student leaders . . . until the Likud rose to power, and something in their political identity had come unstuck.

Note

1 Maariv, December 8, 2005.

25 The Likud

At the height of its decline

On January 4, 2006, just a few weeks after establishing Kadima, Ariel Sharon, aged seventy-eight, suffered a massive stroke and was left in a coma.

The tragedy shook the country and the new party, which had lost its founder. Knesset elections were approaching, and the unexpected loss of the highly popular Sharon threw the political system into turmoil. The country was rife with rumors and speculation: would Kadima survive the crisis? Would its leaders, who had all come from different parties, remain united? Acting Prime Minister Ehud Olmert took immediate action. The moment Sharon was declared incapable of carrying out his duties, Olmert took over all the Prime Minister's areas of authority. Although Peres and Livni, his colleagues in the new party, enjoyed a far greater level of public confidence, they did not challenge his candidacy for the premiership as the representative of Kadima.

A short while later, a new chapter began in the story of the heirs: for the first time, two Likud heirs were competing for the Prime Minister's seat. Netanyahu and Olmert had grown up on the same heritage, and their contest reflected the schism among the heirs.

Likud primaries 2005: Netanyahu vs. five other candidates

When Netanyahu left Sharon's government and split Likud loyalties, it was clear that he was king of the right-wing faction and that he would be the natural Likud candidate for Prime Minister. However, immediately upon his resignation, Netanyahu fell from his lofty status as Minister of Finance. He was once again a political target and was lambasted by journalists and politicians at every level. He was portrayed as a man whose lust for power had caused the Likud to split and who had lost his magical touch for attracting votes. The Likud power-brokers were resentful of him when they found themselves out of the centers of power. Many sought to stay close to the favors that accompany the regime, and chose to follow Sharon. Others remained, frustrated and angry, joining the broad and simmering internal opposition.

Netanyahu found himself in a bloody political struggle for survival against no less than five other candidates, three of them powerful ministers with organized political camps behind them.

The first was outgoing Minister Uzi Landau, who was now occupying Netanyahu's designated spot: an heir who was prized by the veterans, held in esteem for his absolute loyalty to the Likud ideology and his readiness to give up his seat in the government. Landau was already the leader of the orange camp that had opposed the Disengagement: the Land of Israel loyalists and veterans along with Religious Zionists inside and outside of the Likud. Although serious and somewhat lacking in verve, Landau was viewed as consistent and determined, and the hundreds of orange activists were now his faithful followers. Landau set himself apart as the most authentic and faithful representative of the Likud, having fought Sharon with the greatest determination and having paid the full price – as opposed to Netanyahu who, from this perspective, had squirmed and deliberated leading up to the Disengagement and had left the government only at a very late stage.

To the right there was Moshe Feiglin, who, during the Oslo Accords period, had been the leader of the radical right-wing Zu Artzenu (This is Our Land) movement. Later on he had joined the Likud and established the Jewish Leadership Division within the party. He had the support of extremist settlers who conducted themselves as an insular faction aiming to taking over the Likud.

Minister Israel Katz surprised everyone when he announced his candidacy, challenging his patron, Netanyahu. Up until now he had been the head of Netanyahu's political office; at this point he simply uprooted his camp of supporters and drew in all the headquarters leaders and branch heads, leaving Netanyahu dumbfounded, devoid of activists, and devoid of staff – as though he had just landed on Planet Politics, alone and empty-handed.

Minister of Defense Shaul Mofaz was another surprising candidate in these elections. While everyone had expected that he would move over with Sharon to Kadima, after having supported the Disengagement, Mofaz created a stir by remaining in the Likud. He knew very well that almost half the Likud members supported Sharon. He knew that they were angry at Netanyahu and would try to hurt him and the Likud in any way they could. Hence, he expected to attract the support of a great many supporters of Sharon and thereby take control of the Likud from within, following which he would then unite the Likud with Kadima, either before or after the elections. Mofaz was a popular and powerful Minister of Defense, as well as a Mizrahi candidate – an immigrant from Persia who had climbed all the way to the top of the IDF and Israeli politics. In addition, since he enjoyed the support of many of Sharon's people, the general feeling was that Mofaz was a candidate with good chances.

But all of a sudden, in the midst of the internal elections, Mofaz announced that he was moving over to Kadima. Two factors prompted this decision: firstly, the polls predicted results less rosy than he had expected (the Sharon camp was divided between him and Silvan Shalom), and secondly, Prime Minister Sharon promised that if he moved, he could continue as Minister of Defense. Mofaz's clumsy turnaround is remembered as one of the most awkward moments in the history of Israeli politics.

The fifth candidate, Silvan Shalom, benefitted from Mofaz's departure, since he could now attract more votes from among Sharon's wheeler-dealers in the Likud who were looking for a leader who could defeat Netanyahu, their nemesis. Over the course of the five years of Sharon's premiership, Shalom has been a close ally, and with skill and hard work he had built up a following. He was now the candidate who presented the greatest threat to Netanyahu. Shalom had in his favor his loyalty to the Likud and his Beitar roots, as well as his long climb as a Mizrahi youngster from Beer Sheba to Minister of Finance and Foreign Minister. But his closeness to Sharon proved to be his Achilles' heel.

The veterans are called to Netanyahu's aid

Netanyahu, who had embarked on his political career seventeen years previously, was back to square one. In fact, he was way behind his original starting point: whereas from the outset he had been considered a most promising star and was widely popular in Israel, he had since been battered and bruised, and pundits now held that his political career was over. Sharon's hacks were more than willing to keep punishing him. He made supreme efforts to regain his regional coordinators but discovered to his disappointment that they were already committed – either to Sharon (in both the Likud and Kadima) or to Katz. At the same time, he faced the orange camp with its two candidates who were both well-organized after an epic battle over the Disengagement.

Netanyahu had to reinvent himself and rebuild his camp from scratch, one activist at a time. Once again, alone and isolated in his office, he demonstrated full confidence in his ability to rehabilitate his status and to win. Even his closest circle was amazed at his willpower, willingness, and determination.

Netanyahu convened his team and got to work. I was there and was part of the search to find activists who would help to re-establish Netanyahu's camp. The branch heads and major power-brokers were already committed to his opponents to the right and to the left: they were now either with Sharon, whose power brought obvious benefits, or with Landau or Feiglin, the orange leaders who had offered non-stop action over two years of ideological struggle. The few who had remained with Netanyahu had now been whisked away by Katz.

The first to come on board was Tzahi Braverman, one of the leaders of the Nes Tziona branch (a decade later he became Netanyahu's cabinet secretary). Within a few days, Braverman had set up a command center that was in dire need of manpower. Next was Yoav Horowitz, who was clearly capable, in view of his highly successful management of the orange leadership against the Disengagement and his familiarity with the orange activists (a decade later he would be head of the PMO). A new activist who was discovered and recruited was one of the more prominent and ideological leaders of the Likud Youth: Yariv Levin. (As mentioned previously, he was of Irgun stock, and his mother's uncle, Lenkin, had been commander of the *Altalena*. He became an MK four years later.) Another notable figure was Yossi Sheli from Beer Sheba who, after an hour's conversation with Netanyahu, had a command center at the ready. It takes no effort at all to recall the names of the activists. They were few in number, lone figures in a vast and desolate wasteland.

As if all this was not enough, Netanyahu also had to deal with the savage assault on his image among the public. From the moment he set himself against Sharon, against a Palestinian state, and against the Disengagement, the Likud Central Committee had been branded as a corrupt, aggressive body with extreme right-wing views. It remained a Likud Central Committee in which Sharon had many supporters, thanks to the methods of operation he had relied upon (including the large-scale recruitment of questionable – not to say criminal – groups).

Within a few weeks, a malicious and effective campaign implemented by Sharon's consultants and the press succeeded in turning Netanyahu into a persona non grata, an extremist politician affiliated with the detestable Central Committee. The venerated Minister of Finance was transformed into a dangerous, volatile, and irresponsible figure. Even his term at the helm of the Finance Ministry was now portrayed as a series of blows to the weaker sectors, including – and especially – Likud voters. This brutal campaign saturated the media, to the point where no-one was willing to listen to Netanyahu. He and his party were abhorrent – just like Ahimeir's Strongmen's Alliance; just like Jabotinsky's party following the murder of Arlozorov in 1933, or the Irgun and Lehi during the Revolt and surrounding the *Altalena*; just like Begin's Herut concerning the German reparation payments.

Given these circumstances Netanyahu had to encourage and reinforce even his hard-core support. Even the veterans were no longer firmly behind him. Many of them had been drawn into Landau's orange camp. At best, the veterans were straddling the fence. Netanyahu, in his typical style, did not give up on them, but rather wooed them back. Oren Hellman, Netanyahu's advisor at the time, recounted to me with amazement his impressions of the unforgettable evening when Netanyahu visited the home of his long-standing champion, Eli Sheetrit. Five of the Tagar Circle leaders were there, including Eli's brother, Yossi Sheetrit, and Sami Samuel. These abiding supporters of Netanyahu spent several hours questioning him about his political path, his signing of the Wye Memorandum during his first term, and his lingering in a government that was headed towards the Disengagement. Netanyahu sat and patiently responded to this loving but concerned ideological commission of inquiry. He spoke at length about his parents' home, his father, the legacy of the generations, the tradition that he carried with him. Hellman told me:

> It was clear that this was all out of love. He treated the veterans with the sort of respect that he had never shown to anyone else. I never saw him so respectful, so loving, so strenuous in his efforts.[1]

The veterans' value was more moral than electoral. Netanyahu wanted them with him just as they had been with him over two decades. They asked searching, penetrating questions but desperately wanted to be persuaded. They wanted Netanyahu to convince them that Wye, Hebron, and the Disengagement would not be repeated. He spoke like a son explaining matters to his beloved parents. It was clear that, as in any family, the temporary disagreement would be erased for the sake of family unity. Netanyahu also visited his mentor Avraham Appel. Appel, in poor health, welcomed Netanyahu while leaning on a cane. They sat together for hours in family-like intimacy. Netanyahu explained that he had remained in the government in order to save the economy, although he had opposed the Disengagement from the moment it was first mentioned. Appel wanted to be convinced. There was never a moment's doubt what would emerge from these encounters.

And indeed, as in the past, it was the veterans – now in their eighties and nineties – who mobilized in support of Netanyahu. They were not prepared to lose the movement all over again. They viewed his competitors (with the exception of Landau) as Sharon's agents and believed that if any of them was elected, Likud would end up being swallowed by Kadima. It was this prospect that prompted many of them to head out to battle with a single, clear purpose: to ensure that now that Sharon had been dispensed with, a Likud heir would replace him.

Netanyahu's rare ability to adapt to changing situations manifested itself once again. As had happened when he "stood no chance" after Rabin's assassination, and when he was "finished" following the defeat in 1999, he looked only forwards. He believed in his path, he believed that the public would listen to his truth, and he believed that despite everything, he would win. His enthusiasm spilled over onto the lone initial activists, and they brought in others. The command center was overflowing with veterans, headed by Eli Sheetrit and his elderly companions. Unbelievable as this may seem, these old-timers fought like lions. These veterans of the Revolt were in the office morning, noon, and night, telephoning, writing letters, persuading – and all in their humble and quiet manner, as though this were the most important task in the world for these fighters who had driven out the British and had brought independence for Israel. I knew that this was their last political battle, and I watched them with a mixture of admiration and sadness.

As always, the veterans turned inwards, among the fighting family, to the candidate who was the closest and most loyal representative of their worldview. They applied tremendous pressure on Landau to convince him to leave the race. Their argument was simple: a splitting of the vote among the Land of Israel camp could lead to a second round, in which Sharon could defeat the Likud from the outside. As they saw it, there was no doubt that if it came to a second round, Mofaz, Shalom, and Katz would join forces and defeat Netanyahu.

Persuading Landau was not easy. Twice before, he had foregone submitting his candidacy. Now he was a strong and well-organized contender. The polls showed he had a significant following, and his real strength was far greater, in view of the legions of orange and veteran activists at his disposal.

Surprisingly, Landau agreed. He decided to support Netanyahu in order not to split the right-wing camp. He knew that his supporters wanted a merger with Netanyahu, seeking to form a large camp and thereby save the Likud as a national movement. He also knew that Netanyahu was the only charismatic national leader who could win the great battle against Sharon. He withdrew his candidacy and immediately set to work in support of Netanyahu. Not many candidates would be able to pull out of a race and then devote themselves in such a forthright, wholehearted manner in favor of the former competition. Within a few days he had connected Netanyahu with the orange camp, uniting its troops around the chosen heir. On the day that Landau's orange activists arrived at the united headquarters, a volcano of activity erupted. The same energetic camp that had fought tooth and nail against the Disengagement was now committed to the Netanyahu-Landau cause, undisturbed by power-brokers and vote contractors, and unaided by the other heirs, who were now either in Kadima or watching from the sidelines.

Netanyahu won the primaries outright, thanks to an extraordinary voting turn-out (ninety-one percent) which hit hard at the power-brokers and expressed the will of the rank-and-file Likud membership. Netanyahu was now Likud chairman for the second time, after six years under Sharon. Just when it seemed that the fighting family dynasty had come to its end, it was back at the helm of the party.

A first duel between heirs in the general elections: Olmert vs. Netanyahu

The 2006 elections witnessed the first duel for the premiership held between two heirs of the same generation. For the first time, two groups of heirs, representing both sides of the ideological rift, confronted one another. They shared the same roots but diverged into two worldviews, each side convinced that it was the guardian of Jabotinsky's legacy.

A total of eight heirs appeared on the Kadima and Likud lists, four for each party. The Likud list featured Netanyahu, Rivlin, Livnat, and Landau. (Landau ultimately refused to enter the Knesset, offended at his low placement on the list, although he knew that it was the remaining Sharon loyalists in the Likud who had exacted their revenge.) The Kadima list boasted Olmert, Livni, Hanegbi, and Boim, with the external support of Meridor and Milo. Another heir, Dr. Aryeh Eldad, appeared on the National Union–Mafdal (Religious Zionist) list. Nine heirs on the Knesset lists, out of 120 MKs – for the sixth time.

Kadima, under Olmert's leadership, ran for election from a position at the heart of the Israeli consensus: an internally united ruling party with one leg on the Right and the other in the Center. Although Sharon was out of the race, his aura still clung to Kadima. In contrast, Likud, under Netanyahu, was perceived as an opposition party in decline, torn, destitute, on the fringes of the Right, and far removed from the national consensus.

Notwithstanding the antagonism that had built up between them over the years, Olmert and Netanyahu were surprisingly similar: both belonged to the generation of Israel's independence; both had grown up in strongly Revisionist homes; the fathers of both had held key positions in the movement. Their fathers had belonged to the first "middle generation", whose leader had been Jabotinsky. And although both fathers had aided the Irgun during the Revolt, neither belonged to the closed group of Irgun commanders.

Bentzion Netanyahu had been a statesman. He had contributed to the Revolt as the "ambassador" of Jabotinsky's movement to the US, but had not been among those who fought for the land, through fire and water, with Begin. After the establishment of the state he had focused on the academic research that he so loved. He never sought a political career in the Knesset, nor was a Knesset seat ever offered to him by Begin despite (or perhaps because of) his status and closeness to Jabotinsky.

Mordechai Olmert had likewise not been part of Begin's coterie and the Irgun military arm. He had supported the Irgun, like everyone in his moshav, in the other Beitar moshavim and in the National Labor Federation. These were the spheres in which he was active throughout his life.

The fathers of these two men had been divided in their view of Begin. Olmert Sr. had upheld the banner of Jewish settlement alongside the banner of the Greater Land of Israel. He had criticized the party's almost exclusive focus on the political vision, to the exclusion of other values – such as the Beitar focus on education, and settlement. Professor Netanyahu had likewise disliked the single-dimensional orientation of the party that focused exclusively on parliamentary activity. He believed in Jabotinsky's model of a decentralized movement that possessed depth and breadth, including a political arm.

Ehud Olmert and Benjamin Netanyahu, their sons, had followed their fathers' footsteps. Each felt that his father deserved a greater status than that which he held, on both the party and national levels.

Both fathers had also experienced first-hand the clash with the oppressive Labor establishment, which persecuted them and placed obstacles in their paths. Olmert Sr. had represented a minority in Israel's settlement movement, the great majority of which was socialist in orientation. Netanyahu Sr. had represented an oppressed minority in the leftist academic sphere. This might explain why both sons exhibited an unusual measure of political motivation.

The contest between Olmert, leader of Kadima, and Netanyahu, leader of Likud, was therefore a battle between two "brothers" who had emerged from Jabotinsky's "family". Both were men of the wide world, fluent in English, smart, well educated, energetic, experienced, media animals (and media victims), ambitious, and controversial.

Both were also strongly family-oriented. Olmert, who was torn between his political and biological family and the family he built, made a final choice at the age of sixty-one and threw his lot in with the Left. Netanyahu, in contrast, lived in ideological harmony both with his biological family and within his own home. His father Bentzion, his mother Tzila, and his brothers Yoni and Ido, while not involved in party politics, were strongly and profoundly committed to the Zionist nationalist ideal in the Jabotinsky mold. His wife, Sara, came from a family with strong nationalist roots: her father, Shmuel Ben-Artzi, was buried in the Irgun fighters' section of the Mount Herzl military cemetery. Sara and Benjamin Netanyahu shared the same worldview, and their sons, Yair and Avner, continued their nationalist-activist path. The families established by Olmert and Netanyahu were ideological standard-bearers on both sides of the political divide.

Up until the departure of Shamir and Arens, Netanyahu and Olmert had fought on the same side, along with the veterans. They were second-generation fighting family heirs who halted the Sharon-Levy offensives, worked in cooperation against the Oslo Accords, and presented a single, united, activist front against the governments of Peres and Rabin. But from the moment that the political patriarchs, Shamir (for Olmert) and Arens (for Netanyahu) stepped aside, the countdown began to a confrontation over the party leadership. From that time, the relationship between the two had its ups and downs. Along with tactical coopera- tive initiatives against Oslo, against Peres, and in favor of a unified Jerusalem, there had also been strategic rivalry over the Likud chairmanship.

Olmert had suffered two decades of frustration on account of Netanyahu. He could not forget how Netanyahu had arrived from the US and bypassed him – the most senior of the heirs in Knesset. He could not forgive Netanyahu for skipping over twenty years of Sisyphean political work, managing to make his way to the highest levels of the Likud list on his first try, while Olmert had fought every step of the way and had earned his seat in the Knesset through struggles, deals, and reserved places. Olmert could only observe with envy the tremendous popular- ity enjoyed by this new heir. He found no consolation in the fact that he was appointed a minister in Shamir's government in 1988, while Netanyahu was not. He knew that in a future confrontation, Netanyahu would stand far better chances, owing to his greater popularity among the movement and the public at large.

In 1993, when the battle over succession took place, earlier than expected, Olmert was not ready for the fight and chose not to engage. The more popular heirs, Benny Begin and Netanyahu, were before him in line, and Sharon, Levy, Sheetrit, and Katzav were also waiting in the wings. Netanyahu's election forced Olmert into the Jerusalem municipality for a frustrating period of waiting, during which he made sure to attack Netanyahu from the right whenever he could.

On the surface, the two men had been partners since Netanyahu's election as Likud chairman. However, as we have seen, Olmert had a dual relationship with Prime Minister Netanyahu. From his office in Jerusalem he maintained a complex dialogue with the Likud chairman, dragging him into clashes over political and security issues with the opposition and with the US. When Netanyahu, as Prime Minister, was forced to compromise, Olmert was ready with an uncompromising, nationalist response.

From the outside, the two men seemed to be in harmony. But when Netanyahu found himself in trouble, in his first term, vis-à-vis the other heirs and in relation to the media and the elite, the entanglements bore the fingerprints of the mayor of Jerusalem. And as the revolt of the Likud heirs against Netanyahu grew in its intensity, so the rumors multiplied that the mayors of Jerusalem and Tel Aviv – Olmert and Milo – were organizing a putsch against him. Ultimately, Olmert left it to his fellow heirs to confront Netanyahu in the open. Thereafter he waited for Netanyahu to depart from political life, and for Meridor, Milo, and Begin Jr. to head for more centrist and right-wing parties, after it had seemed, for a while, that he would be leaving with them. The outcome of all these moves against Net- anyahu was that of all the heirs, only he remained to challenge Netanyahu over leadership of the Likud.

There is no question that Netanyahu's departure after the 1999 defeat was a relief for Olmert. But Olmert's indirect support for Barak, which brought a counter-maneuver on Netanyahu's part, distanced him from his dream of leading the Likud at the moment when this great opportunity presented itself. And when

Sharon was elected in his stead, with Netanyahu's support, the antagonism that Olmert felt towards Netanyahu reached irreversible proportions. By the beginning of the new millennium each felt that the other had betrayed him.

When Netanyahu reappeared on the scene, after two years away, Olmert did his best to obstruct his progress. He spoke out against him at every opportunity and made him a central target for his sharp attacks. Netanyahu, for his part, ignored Olmert, not viewing him as a serious contender. Sharon was the only adversary that concerned him. After the declarations about a Palestinian state in 2002, the personal clashes overlapped with the political turnaround that Sharon and Olmert had undergone. The attacks on Netanyahu were now both personal and ideological.

And then, when it was clear that Sharon would run against Netanyahu while Olmert patiently awaited his turn, Sharon was unexpectedly eliminated from the scene and Olmert was catapulted into the league that he had thought he would never reach. He was now Acting Prime Minister and head of the largest party, running for Prime Minister. Just a short while previously it would have sounded altogether unreal.

Elections of 2006: the greatest defeat in Likud history

The events of 2005 and early 2006 should have led to a decline for Kadima and a mass return of Likud voters to their former party: the leader of Kadima, Sharon, had left the stage; his replacement, Olmert, did not enjoy the same level of public confidence; and in Gaza, Hamas seized power and all the bleakest prophecies of Netanyahu and the opponents of the Disengagement were coming true.

Inexplicably, these dramatic events did not help Netanyahu in any way. He kept talking, and no-one was willing to listen. Even committed Likud supporters would not listen to him in the months leading up to the 2006 elections. When he warned that the Disengagement would strengthen Hamas (which is what in fact happened), everyone was focused solely on his mistakes. When he predicted that Gaza would turn into a huge weapons depot (which indeed it did), no-one listened. When he declared that Gaza would turn into a terror state and a base for shooting missiles into Israel's south (which is exactly what it became), Israel closed its ears to the truth. When his election broadcasts illustrated his forecast with red balls of fire headed from Gaza towards Tel Aviv, even those closest to him told him that the public had had enough of hearing prophecies of doom. Kadima was viewed as a successful, responsible, centrist, optimistic option, while Netanyahu and his companions in the Likud were regarded as extremist, old-fashioned, wretched politicians.

The preliminary election results publicized on television on March 28, 2006, took the Likud and the country by surprise. Up until the elections, the prevailing view in the Likud was that the party would receive around twenty mandates, perhaps slightly less. The first preliminary result to appear on the screen therefore came as a crushing shock to the Likud and especially the veterans: just eleven mandates, placing Likud as the fifth-largest party in the Knesset. As the counting progressed, they prayed that the Likud would receive another one or two mandates, inching up to third place, so that at least Netanyahu would head the opposition (the assumption being that Labor and Shas would be part of the coalition). The final results were not much of an improvement: twelve mandates, just one more than Lieberman's party, by a margin of just 116 votes. Netanyahu was head of the opposition, but this consolation prize did little to assuage the shock of this colossal upset.

The changeover of leadership and the failure of the Disengagement certainly had an impact on Kadima, too. The polls had predicted forty-four mandates, but following the Hamas takeover in Gaza, support for Kadima plunged and the party received only twenty-nine mandates. Still, Kadima emerged as the big winner, while Likud was at its lowest point in fifty years. Netanyahu had led the party back to the days of political isolation, almost losing even the leadership of the opposition. The experts pronounced him finished and declared that the Likud era in Israeli politics was over.

Olmert became Prime Minister and had little trouble forming a coalition without the party of his youth, which was not even invited to negotiations. Kadima seemed to be consolidating its legacy as the first party in Israel to succeed in breaking the historical Left-Right model, uniting former leaders and members of Labor and Likud in a single major party, and breathing new life into the political Center. Previous centrist parties had all been warmly received by the public but had collapsed in the elections.

In retrospect one might say that a rare combination of circumstances saved Likud from an even greater walloping. The sudden disappearance of Sharon prevented the Likud from sinking below ten mandates, while also preventing Kadima from growing to forty. Olmert's self-confidence tripped him up: he could have split and destroyed the Likud by drawing another three or four Likud MKs in the direction of Kadima, but apparently he saw no point in investing further efforts in dismantling a party that seemed irreparably broken. At that point, in early 2006, he was self-assured and complacent.

The veterans return to the days of the small and isolated Herut

The Likud faction in Knesset was despondent and divided. Almost all of the "rebels" against Sharon now found themselves outside the Knesset, thanks to Sharon's power-brokers and voters who had remained members of Likud long enough to vote them out and only then officially moved to Kadima. Landau, disappointed that the movement had not rewarded him for his political courage over the course of the Disengagement and his agreement not to run against Netanyahu, refused to serve as an MK. Like Benny Begin before him, he too turned his back on politics, greatly disillusioned and concluding that there was no place for upright, principled idealists in an age of wheeler-dealers and self-interest.

The shrunken Likud faction now included a disgruntled core of former ministers (Silvan Shalom, Limor Livnat, and Israel Katz) who had lost their government seats and were back to being regular MKs.

The veterans looked as though they had lost their entire world. They had lost the battle against the Disengagement, and now they had lost the leadership of the country, too. They were back in the opposition, having lost half of their heirs along the way. The dream that had come true with the consolidation of a dream team of heirs was now just a memory, and all because of their confrontation with Sharon. They had now lost not only the heirs that Sharon had taken with him but also the two stalwart Land of Israel heirs: Benny Begin, who had declined to run for office, and Uzi Landau, who had walked out. Overnight, the elderly veterans found themselves transported back to the 1950s, when the Likud had been a small and embattled party. They found themselves back in the period of pure ideology, on the benches of the virtuous opposition. Perhaps that was some comfort.

Netanyahu is saved from a putsch by the skin of his teeth

On the night of the elections in 2006 there were only about fifty Likud activists in the auditorium at the Tel Aviv Exhibition Grounds, which had been reserved for use by the Likud party overnight as the results were publicized. Half of those present were veterans, the others were parliamentary aides. As the preliminary results began emerging, there was talk that originated with the party's voters, blaming Netanyahu for the defeat. Incoming telephone calls from activists spoke of a major wave of protest against the party chairman, who was held solely responsible for the debacle. There were rumors (which were never officially confirmed) of a putsch that was being organized by the ministers whom Netanyahu had forced to resign prior to the elections.

The former ministers in question – Katz, Shalom, Livnat, and Naveh, along with MK Eitan – stayed away from the hall, thereby adding fuel to the rumors. However, the MKs who were present – Rivlin, Gideon Saar, Gilad Erdan, Moshe Kahlon, and Yuval Steinitz – spoke among themselves (and with Sharansky, by phone) and decided to give Netanyahu their backing and save his chairmanship. All in all there were six MKs in the hall (one connected by phone) against five MKs who were absent. These critical moments decided Netanyahu's fate and the path of the Likud moving forward.

The six MKs in favor preferred Netanyahu's political vision to that of Silvan Shalom, whom they regarded as having supported the Disengagement and as close to Sharon. They wanted a Likud that was clearly distinguished from Kadima, not a Likud that resembled Kadima. Later on, observers claimed that the MKs – especially the younger ones – preferred Netanyahu over a new chairman such as Silvan Shalom, fearing that a new chairman would occupy the leadership for many years ahead.

While all this was going on, no-one in the hall knew what Netanyahu was thinking. No-one knew whether he was even willing to deal with the wave of revenge that was going to wash over the media. No-one knew if he had the strength to withstand the anticipated putsch. No-one knew how he would react to the greatest defeat in the history of the Likud. And, of course, no-one knew if he stood a chance of emerging from what looked like the end of his career.

Within a few minutes, Netanyahu, who had been watching the results from his headquarters, in central Tel Aviv, made a dramatic leadership decision. He decided to stay, to fight. He knew that, within minutes, activists would be arriving at the hall carrying signs reading "Resign! Resign!", and that this would be the image that the public would see on its television screens. He knew that twenty or thirty raucous troublemakers could spark a revolt in the devastated party. All it would take was thirty activists and thirty critical minutes. Netanyahu got into his car and headed for the Exhibition Grounds. During the fifteen minute journey he wrote his speech, using his trademark thick blue felt-tip. He even managed to rehearse the speech with his consultants over the phone before striding into the small hall.

His close circle had managed to convey a quiet message to the small circle of loyalists: "Netanyahu is on the way." The thirty-odd veterans and twenty parliamentary aides applauded warmly as he ascended the stage and stood alongside the senior heir, Rivlin, and the younger MKs, Erdan, Saar, Steinitz, and Kahlon. He began to speak, but, to the great surprise of the hundreds of thousands of spectators watching the event live on television, he did not resign.

Instead, he delivered a short ideological address in defense of the cause. It was a Beginist speech that called on the activists not to give up. It was an emotional, patriotic speech by the leader of a small, beleaguered, and slandered faction on the brink of collapse – just like the speeches that Begin had given in the 1950s. "I received the party in its darkest days," he said.

> We shall rebuild the movement; we shall continue on our path and adhere to it. We have seen better times, and we shall see better times. [. . .] We have taken a major blow – but our path is the right one, the only one, leading to security for our country.

Following his address, in which he announced his intention to remain in his position and to continue the struggle, Netanyahu left the hall. The event as it appeared on television was quite different from what it was in reality. It had been a forlorn, gloomy, depressing spectacle, no more than fifty shell-shocked activists watching aghast as the results appeared. Most of those present were journalists. But what the television footage showed was Netanyahu arriving to warm applause, surrounded by a loving and supportive faction. On the screen, it looked like a show of support.

In the months following the elections the veterans formed a veritable protective shield around Netanyahu at all the party conventions and Central Committee gatherings. They arrived early at every event and occupied the front rows, so as to push back the Kadima activists who were still interfering in the Likud. Most of the Likud MKs also showed their support and helped to turn the mood in his favor. Ideological Likud activists liked the right-wing, nationalist ideology that he represented, and remained loyal to him. The MKs who had saved Netanyahu now served as a critical political safety net. They constituted a majority of one vote, which served to block any move towards a split or any vote of no confidence during the bleak months of Olmert's government.

Netanyahu, recovering from the third major defeat in his political career, displayed confidence that strategic adherence to the Jabotinsky worldview would overcome any tactical crisis.

Note

1 Interview with the author, August 12, 2014.

26 The rise and fall of the Olmert government

Olmert got off to a magical start: he presided over a large and disciplined faction, the media showed him favor, the opposition was shrunken and divided, while the coalition numbered seventy-eight MKs.

The constitution of Kadima was formulated in such a way as to prevent any undermining of the status of the founding leader. This protection, originally meant for Sharon, now stood Olmert in good stead. In addition to his stable and secured position at the helm, he also fielded an attractive and diverse team. The senior Kadima leadership included new political stars such as former director of the Shin Bet, Avi Dichter, and Professor Uriel Reichman, as well as well-respected public figures including Shimon Peres, Tzipi Livni, and Chief-of-Staff Shaul Mofaz. There was no visible threat on the horizon.

For the second time in Israel's history, an heir of the fighting family was Prime Minister of Israel. At his side was another heiress, Tzipi Livni, who was appointed Acting Prime Minister. In addition, Zeev Boim was Minister of Immigrant Absorption, and Tzahi Hanegbi was chairman of the Committee for Foreign Affairs and Security.

Olmert: peace talks and two wars

The restlessness that had characterized Olmert up to this point – tending alternatively towards conciliation and militarism – continued into his term as Prime Minister.

On one hand, he surprised the country even before the elections by evacuating the Amona outpost. The manner and the suddenness of the move gave the impression that he was trying to create an intentional confrontation with the settler public. While the bitter results of the Disengagement were playing themselves out in Gaza, Olmert ran an election campaign that was spearheaded by the evacuation of nine houses in a place that Israel's citizens had never heard of. The evacuation reopened raw wounds among the settlers, who this time put up physical resistance to the police batons. Two right-wing MKs and dozens of settlers were injured. Olmert also continued to engage in negotiations, adopting the most submissive posture ever displayed by an Israeli Prime Minister. He declared his readiness for an almost-complete withdrawal from Judea, Samaria, and the Golan Heights.

At the same time, Olmert approved three offensive military operations within three years, two of which developed into full-blown wars. He started his term with the Second Lebanon War (summer of 2006) and concluded it, after already resigning, with Operation Cast Lead against Hamas in Gaza (winter of 2008–2009). In between, according to foreign reports, on September 6, 2007, Israel launched a courageous attack that destroyed a nuclear reactor in Syria. Syria's lack of response prevented a third war.

In the south, Olmert failed to halt the Gaza takeover by Hamas, following which the inhabitants of Israel's south became hostages of the terror organization, exposed to its missiles and rockets. The tension in the south intensified after the kidnapping of a soldier, Gilad Shalit, in June 2006. The kidnapping became a central topic of public discourse in Israel, with mounting frustration over the failure to free the soldier by means of either a military operation or negotiations.

Two weeks after Shalit was kidnapped, two soldiers on reserve duty on the northern border were kidnapped by Hezbollah. In response, Israel launched the Second Lebanon War. Leaked reports described heated arguments between the military brass and the government, and military experts were unsparing in their criticism of Olmert's handling of the war. The Lebanese paid dearly, and Israel counted 160 casualties, along with thousands of missiles raining down on an unprepared home front.

After the war Olmert was roundly criticized from all directions. There were demonstrations against him throughout the country. On the streets and in the media there was growing pressure to set up a state commission of inquiry. Eventually Olmert established a government investigation committee, headed by former Justice Eliyahu Winograd, but declined to set up a commission with the authority to reach binding recommendations concerning dismissals. Still, the preliminary report of the Winograd Committee, published on April 30, 2007, caused a major stir with its harsh condemnation of Olmert's handling of the war. The Prime Minister refused to resign, and the demonstrations grew larger and louder. Surprisingly, those calling for his resignation now included Tzipi Livni, his own Foreign Minister.

A war of heirs at the center: Olmert vs. Livni

From the high point of forming his government, Olmert had slipped downwards in the polls. Following the Second Lebanon War his popularity dropped even lower, and he was unable to regain the trust of the public. At the same time, the popularity of two other heirs, whom the polls showed to be regarded as more worthy of the premiership, was on the rise. One was the leader of the opposition, Netanyahu, who, it now appeared, had been right in his warnings; the other was Acting Prime Minister Livni, who had climbed to the number one favorite for chairmanship of Kadima. Yossi Verter wrote in *Haaretz*: "In contrast to Olmert, Acting Prime Minister and Foreign Minister Tzipi Livni – perhaps one of the most popular politicians of all time – enjoys an abundant measure of public support.[1] In May 2007, Livni was featured in *Time* magazine as one of the world's one hundred most influential people.

Olmert heard the voices in the press and in Kadima anticipating the day when Livni would replace him, and concluded that Livni was undermining him. Livni, for her part, thought that she deserved gratitude, not suspicion. She expected Olmert to express thanks for having supported him after Sharon suffered his stroke (after all, she could have questioned his leadership and dragged Kadima into a primaries race, in which she would have stood a good chance at being elected) and for having served as his "stamp of approval" in the elections. But after coming to power, Olmert no longer regarded Livni in terms of her contribution; all he could see was her rising popularity in the polls. Like other Prime Ministers before him, he was not happy to see another politician behind his back whom the public wanted as his successor. And thus, after the Second Lebanon War and the publication of the Winograd Report, the low-key rivalry that had simmered between them since the beginning of Olmert's term now became overt. Livni was no longer willing to offer Olmert her blind support through wars and investigations.

During the war, Livni had disagreed with the Prime Minister, who had been inclined in the direction of continued hostilities. In closed discussions between them she demanded a speedy political settlement and voted against an intensification of the attacks. After the Winograd Committee published its interim report, Livni let it be known that in a meeting with the Prime Minister she argued that in view of the report, "resigning would be the right thing to do on his part."[2] The country was in uproar; the conflict was in full view, and everyone started discussing the mutual loathing and lack of trust between the two.

Livni found herself in a political pickle, because Olmert did not resign, and she was still serving in his government. Olmert's loyalists in the PMO and in the media were pushing Livni to resign, but she was well aware of the fragility of Olmert's position and decided not to give up her title of Acting Prime Minister, which ensured that she would be his certain successor if he quit (as anticipated) after the final Winograd Report came out.

Livni herself was now the target of fierce criticism, for the first time since her election to the Knesset. This squeaky-clean heiress who had known only victories and praises was now condemned by many who had formerly been enthusiastic fans. The media was suddenly full of discourse about her "lack of experience", her "weakness", her "hesitation" and "inability to make decisions". Ben Caspit, writing in *Maariv*, opined that she was "fit to serve as Secretary General of Naamat (the Movement for the Advancement of the Status of Women in Israel) or, at most, the WIZO (Women's International Zionist Organization) presidency."[3] Livni's popularity plummeted, but for the first time she demonstrated her grit as a politician: she took in the criticism, kept her silence, and continued serving under the Prime Minister in whom she had lost confidence.

Prime Minister Olmert – between investigations and court cases

Starting in mid-2006, Olmert became entangled in a series of police investigations and legal troubles, which concluded eight years later with a conviction on charges of bribery. Olmert underwent more investigations and was involved in more legal suits than any other politician in Israel, and he ended up in jail.

Some among his close circle maintained that Olmert suffered all this as a result of the reforms that he tried to introduce into the justice system via his Minister of Justice, Professor Daniel Friedman – suggesting that a special effort was made to indict Olmert and to oust him from the PMO.

The first case broke in August 2006: the State Comptroller issued a critical report focusing on suspected political appointments to the Center for Small Businesses while Olmert had served as Minister of Commerce and Industry. In October 2006, the State Comptroller announced that he had gathered enough evidence to justify a criminal investigation into the "Tender for the sale of Bank Leumi" affair. In September 2007, another investigation was launched by the State Comptroller, this time surrounding possible bribery involved in the sale of Olmert's house (the "house on Cremieux Street"). October 2007 witnessed yet another criminal investigation concerning the "Investment Center" (a body which puts millions into private-sector projects that meet specific criteria), where Olmert was suspected of having shown preferential treatment to clients of a close confidant and partner. In April 2008, the Attorney General recommended opening an investigation into the "money envelopes" affair involving Jewish-American businessman Morris Talansky. Olmert announced that if criminal charges were pressed, he would resign as Prime Minister.

In June 2008, yet another investigation was launched, this time surrounding suspicions that Olmert had financed private flights for himself and his family with funds he had received through deceptive charging of public bodies (the "Rishontours" affair). In September of that year the police recommended that Olmert be prosecuted, and in November, Attorney General Meni Mazouz decided to put him on trial on three separate counts (Rishontours, the money envelopes, and the Investment Center), and to close two other cases (Bank Leumi and the house on Cremieux Street). In September, 2008, Olmert announced that he had decided to resign so he could direct his energies to addressing the criminal charges. He continued to insist that he was innocent.

In April 2010, a new investigation was launched – the Holyland apartment complex affair – and in January 2012 criminal charges were laid. The Holyland trial received widespread media attention, especially in view of such dramatic developments as betrayals and the death of a key witness. In July 2012, Olmert was acquitted in the Rishontours affair, the evidence deemed insufficient to prove his guilt beyond reasonable doubt. He was also acquitted in the "money envelopes" affair. For his role in the Investment Center irregularities he was charged with breach of confidence and was given a suspended one-year sentence, along with a fine. The State Attorney appealed both acquittals, as well as the sentencing in the case for which he was found guilty.

Olmert remained mired in his legal battles for another five years, as we shall see. However, he remained involved in political life, even while under heavy police and legal fire.

Olmert: the most acceding Prime Minister in history

As Prime Minister, Olmert left his mark on two diplomatic fronts: he stepped up the pace of negotiations with Abbas and engaged in secret negotiations with Syria. During his election campaign he had caused a storm by declaring his plan for a unilateral withdrawal from Judea and Samaria. His Convergence Plan was meant to lead to the concentration of Jewish settlement in settlement blocs, while outlying communities would be evacuated and the land handed over to the Palestinian Authority. As the former militant mayor of Jerusalem became the Prime Minister of Israel, he even questioned (in October 2007) the need for Israel to maintain sovereignty over all parts of the capital.

Seven years after the outbreak of the Second Intifada, Olmert decided to reboot Israel's relations with the Palestinian Authority. In November 2007, the Annapolis Conference was convened to reignite the peace process. The conference, initiated by Livni and others, took place in the US, with the participation of forty countries, including Arab states and the Palestinian Authority. It concluded with a declaration of the renewal of negotiations on the basis of the American "Road Map".

MK Haim Oron, head of the Meretz party, to the left of Labor, greeted Olmert's new position with great enthusiasm: "These are very important, courageous statements. Especially in view of the positions that Olmert held in the past."[4] Journalist Ben Caspit offered a mordant interpretation of Olmert's idea of separating Israel from the Palestinians: "It now turns out that Olmert has turned into Beilin (a symbol of the Israeli Left). Unlike Beilin, Olmert saw the light at the end of his career."[5]

In the end, it was the police investigations that put an end to Olmert's initiatives. His senior coalition partner, Labor chairman Ehud Barak, announced in mid-2008, after the eruption of the "money envelopes" affair, that he could not remain in the coalition in view of the investigation. He broke up the coalition, forcing Olmert to announce, at the end of July, that he would vacate his post immediately after the election of a new Kadima chairman.

Olmert devoted his final cabinet meeting mostly to a farewell to the vision of his forebears from Nahalat Jabotinsky: "The Greater Land of Israel is finished. There is no longer such a thing, and anyone who talks this way is deluding himself."[6] In an interview he granted to *Yediot Aharonot* shortly afterwards, he stated candidly:

> I used to think that from the Jordan to the (Mediterranean) Sea was all ours, because wherever one digs, one finds Jewish history. But ultimately, after doubts and deliberation, I reached the conclusion that we have to divide it with those who dwell here with us, if we don't want a bi-national state.[7]

Olmert's parting interview also marked this heir's final separation with his ideological home. Here he prided himself on being the leader who had made the greatest concessions to the Palestinians, taking pains to portray himself as outdoing the Labor in this regard:

> What I'm telling you now is something no Israel leader before me ever said: there has to be a withdrawal from almost all of the territories. From East Jerusalem, too. And from the Golan Heights.[8]

He went on to say that in order to arrive at a peace agreement,

> There has to be a withdrawal from most of the territory of Judea, Samaria, and the Golan, as well as East Jerusalem. [...] We have to give up parts of Jerusalem. [...] I want to see a single serious person in Israel who believes that we can make peace with the Syrians without ultimately relinquishing the Golan Heights.

In his final days in the PMO, Olmert undertook painful introspection concerning his father's legacy. "I want to say something personal," he said at the Herzliya Conference in 2008.

> I myself was often engaged in formulating reasons why we could not concede. [...] Now we have to understand that there's no more time. We've been fighting courageously for sixty years [...] in order not to end up in a bi-national reality.[9]

The sixty-three-year-old Olmert went so far as to declare that he had embraced Ben-Gurion as his new ideological guide:

> I grew up and was educated in Nahalat Jabotinsky, in a Beitar family. [...] My father Mordechai, of blessed memory [...] was vehemently opposed to the Partition Plan, out of loyalty to and genuine love for the entire Land of Israel. I bow my head in humility and admiration of him and his memory, as I say something that would perhaps cause him to sigh, but I say it anyway: Ben-Gurion was right.

From heir to heir – Kadima is passed to Livni

The Kadima primaries were held on September 17, 2008, with the general assumption being that the new chairman would be Prime Minister. Tzipi Livni held a solid lead in all the polls, rating better than any of her former Likudnik rivals Shaul Mofaz, Meir Sheetrit, and Avi Dichter. The preliminary results of the election showed the same trend, but the final results showed that Livni had defeated Mofaz by a very slim margin: forty-three percent to Livni, forty-two percent to Mofaz – a difference of only about four hundred votes. It was a bitter victory that left Livni with a powerful internal opposition whose leader, Mofaz, was committed to ousting and replacing her.

As chairman of Kadima, Livni approached the task of putting together a government coalition. On the face of it, she had at her disposal a bloc of sixty MKs (representing Labor, Meretz, and the Pensioners' Party) out of the total of 120, along with the left-wing fringe, including ten MKs representing the Arab parties. The opposition consisted of only fifty MKs, divided among warring factions, which would seemingly be easy to tempt and bring into the coalition: there were eighteen ultra-Orthodox MKs, Lieberman's party with another eleven, and the Likud and the right-wing with a total of twenty-one. Livni could have based her coalition on sixty MKs representing the Center and the Left but declined to do so, fearing both the fragility and the left-wing inclination of such an alliance. Instead, she wanted to include an ultra-Orthodox party (Shas) so as not to be dependent on the Left and on lone MKs. However, the difficult and drawn-out negotiations with Shas ended in failure. Some claimed that Livni had not been sufficiently flexible; Livni herself claimed that she had already come to an agreement with Netanyahu that they would jointly seek general elections.

In any event, Livni's failure to build a coalition created a second wave of negative sentiment against her – especially among her own party, which had become addicted to power. Livni's failure was presented as evidence of her lack of experience and lack of skill as a politician, while Livni herself was proud of her refusal to bow to ultra-Orthodox demands. She returned her mandate to the President on October 25, 2008, paving the way for general elections for the eighteenth Knesset in February 2009.

Livni champions just one cause: peace

Sara Livni passed away in 2007. At the start of the funeral, her daughter, Tzipi, sang the Beitar anthem, together with the other mourners gathered in the courtyard of the Likud headquarters. Seemingly, it was more of a song of memorial for her parents and their legacy, and less of a declaration that those gathered felt a sacred commitment to the Land of Israel, as had the Beitarists.

Already in April 2002, shortly after her first appointment as a government minister, Livni declared that in order to fulfill the dream of a Jewish homeland, "We are obliged to relinquish parts of the dream of the Greater Land of Israel." Five years later, she said:

> I am doing this [. . .] not as a responsibility towards my parents, but rather as a responsibility towards my children. I think that I am actualizing an ideology that is more complex than simply "the Greater Land of Israel". I am not giving up the ideology I was educated with, but rather implementing it.[10]

During the decade following the Oslo Accords, as the political system and the Israel public came to despair of the possibility of making peace with the Palestinians, Livni underwent a transformation in the other direction. This Irgun heiress, who had entered politics precisely because of her misgivings concerning the Oslo agreements, emerged as a leader who upheld mainly – almost exclusively – one banner: peace.

While the left-wing parties had already downgraded the peace process to a low-profile issue, emphasizing security and social issues instead, Livni became an enthusiastic proponent of negotiations with the Palestinians. In every interview and in every speech she expressed herself in favor of renewing negotiations, emphasizing their necessity and urgency: "This is the Livni paradox," declared Yossi Beilin in an interview. "She arrived seeking to halt the Oslo process, but became a central part of the process and of the negotiations with the PLO leadership for an agreement to establish a Palestinian state."[11]

With reference to Livni's focus on the overall aim of peace, in an age when most of the parties had already given up on it, Aluf Ben wrote:

> Tzipi Livni is a stubborn woman. Journalists who met with her in recent years, while she was still a low-level minister, followed her on her climb to the top, listening to her speeches and declarations, and hearing the same message ad nauseum: I'm here because of an over-arching aim, which is a Jewish and democratic state. Therefore I support the establishment of a Palestinian state, on condition that it is the national solution for all the Palestinians, just as Israel is the national solution for all the Jews.[12]

As the Kadima primaries approached, an editorial was published in *Haaretz* that was supportive of Livni.[13] The newspaper, which Livni's parents and their generation had regarded during the Revolt as the mouthpiece of the British Mandate, was now touting the daughter of the Irgun Operations Officer. The editorial stated that

> Foreign Minister Livni is unique insofar as from day one she took the political platform of Kadima seriously, and has been trying ever since to advance it. As someone whose biography is an embodiment of the awakening from the dream of the Greater Land of Israel, she manages to create the impression that a political solution is a matter of profound importance to her, and that she understands how urgent it is that an agreement between Israel and the Palestinians is reached, while each of the two nations has a leadership that is ready for it. [. . .] Livni is the most profound and clearest spokesperson in favor of a Jewish and democratic state.

When I interviewed her,[14] Livni recounted with emotion a symbolic encounter that had taken place in February 2007. Prime Minister Olmert and Foreign Minister Livni met with the head of the Palestinian Authority, Abbas, and with the American Secretary of State, Condoleezza Rice. Also present was Rafiq al-Husseini, scion of the famous al-Husseini family of Jerusalem, which was well represented in the Palestinian leadership. During this "meeting of heirs", Livni asked al-Husseini whether he, too, had undergone a moderation of his views, as she had, and whether he, too, had traded the militant worldview of his father and grandfather for a recognition of the necessity of peace. This was her way of explaining her change of position.

Despite her newfound insights, though, Livni took care to set firm boundaries for a peace agreement. While Olmert had grown increasingly yielding and magnanimous towards the Palestinians as the challenges and complications of his term as Prime Minister had grown and multiplied, to the point where he offered concessions that no Israeli Prime Minister had ever imagined, Livni had much clearer red lines, recalling her Revisionist roots. For instance, she would not agree to discuss the issue of the refugees. As she saw it, allowing a return of the refugees would shatter her view of two nation-states, one of which was to be Jewish. She also maintained firm boundaries as to Israeli concessions, thereby distinguishing herself from both Olmert and Barak.

During the election campaign in 2009, in an interview with Ari Shavit published in *Haaretz*, Livni offered the following explanation of the difference between herself and Netanyahu:

> Bibi thinks that we have to choose between security and peace. I think that's a terrible mistake, which will lead to us not having security, either. There will be neither hope nor security. I believe in a very clear stance, based on both of these pillars. Both security and peace. Both Jewish and democratic. Therefore, only a government over which I preside can really create unity.[15]

Notes

1 Haaretz, June 8, 2006.
2 Yediot Aharonot, May 5, 2007.
3 Maariv, May 3, 2007.
4 Yediot Aharonot, October 2, 2007.
5 Maariv, October 6, 2007.
6 Yediot Aharonot, September 14, 2007.
7 Yediot Aharonot, September 15, 2008.
8 Yediot Aharonot, September 21, 2008.
9 The Prime Minister's speech at the Hertzelia conference (2008). Retrieved from https://mfa.gov.il/MFAHEB/PressRoom/Pages/Address%20by%20Prime%20Minister%20Ehud%20Olmert%20to%20the%208th%20Herzliya%20Conference%20230108.aspx
10 Haaretz, October 2008.
11 Maariv, October 19, 2007.
12 Haaretz, September 18, 2008.
13 Haaretz, October 23, 2007.
14 Interview with the author, February 22, 2007.
15 Haaretz, January 30, 2009.

Part V

The father, the son, and the Iranian nuclear threat

From 2009, Netanyahu has been the Prime Minister. In 2018 he would count ten years as the Prime Minister of Israel; this is the second longest "reign" of any Prime Minister in the history of Israel. During his last two terms as Prime-Minister, he waged a tireless battle fighting against the Iranian nuclear program. He was inspired by the views of both his father Bentzion Netanyahu and his spiritual father Ze'ev Jabotinsky. Netanyahu learned and understood intuitively from the example of the Nazi perpetrators that when a nation openly declares that the Jews will be annihilated, while the rest of the world chooses to ignore it and remain silent, you had better take them seriously. He quoted his mentor Churchill when he went on a worldwide campaign to forever halt the Iranian nuclear program, while directly confronting the US President Barack Obama.

In Israel today, Netanyahu is struggling against the political, military, and judicial elite. Although Netanyahu is under investigation in a number of legal cases, he enjoys an unprecedented support from the right-wing public. They feel that he is being hunted down just as the "Prince's" parents were presented as fascists who were violent and dangerous, while they fought the British Mandate as they won and established Israel's independence.

Today Israel is being led by two "Princes", Netanyahu as Prime Minister, and Reuven Rivlin as President (Rivlin was elected against Netanyahu's will). The Israel of 2018 had seen besides them other "Princes" in key positions, such as a former Prime Minister (Ehud Olmert), a former Foreign Minister (Tzipi Livni), a senior minister (Tzahi Hanegbi), a new minister (Yariv Levin, Minister of Tourism), MKs, and mayors.

The father, the son, and the Iranian nuclear threat

27 Netanyahu's second government

Leading up to the contest against Livni in 2009, Netanyahu worked feverishly to recruit new stars who would restore some of the Likud's former attraction. First he brought on board "non-political" (formerly Labor) security figures: former Chief-of-Staff "Bogie" Yaalon, Major-General (res.) Uzi Dayan (nephew of Moshe Dayan), former Police Commissioner Assaf Hefetz, and Major-General Yossi Peled, who had previously been a Likud member. He also added new stars from other spheres, including former IDF spokeswoman Brigadier-General (res.) Miri Regev; a young and promising journalist, Tzipi Hotovely; and the legendary basketball player, Tal Brodie. And indeed, these new additions, especially the security heavyweights, did bring Netanyahu the impetus that he sought.

It came as a surprise when Netanyahu decided to transcend past rivalries and to also bring back two heirs who symbolized upright integrity: the "heir of heirs", Benny Begin, and the champion of the rule of law, Dan Meridor. Netanyahu knew that their return would enhance his candidacy and restore his status as the legitimate leader of the heirs' generation. Since Livni was being portrayed as a symbol of clean politics, he sought out individuals who shared similar prestige. There was also additional benefit to bringing these two heirs back into the Likud: the gap between their respective political worldviews (from Meridor's Left-Center to Begin's Right) was wide enough to attract a broad segment of voters. Furthermore, Netanyahu believed that having Meridor on his team would weaken the extreme-right image that adhered to the Likud in the media in the wake of Feiglin's drive to enlist extremist Religious Zionists into the Likud en masse.

The reappearance of the two heirs did have significant impact. The Likud list now included top-class names, veterans and younger stars alike. The Likud had returned to itself and to its roots, with five heirs in the senior leadership (Netanyahu, Begin, Meridor, Rivlin, and Livnat), along with four esteemed Major-Generals, and additional young and promising names: Gideon Saar, Gilad Erdan, Moshe Kahlon, Silvan Shalom, and Yuval Steinitz. The Kadima list, following Olmert's resignation, would feature only three heirs: Livni, Hanegbi, and Boim.

Primaries 2009: the return of the early heirs

In November 2008, after a lengthy political exile, Benny Begin announced his return to politics and his candidacy for the Likud Knesset list. This came as a

surprise. Some ten years had passed since he had left the party. In a press conference held at the Likud headquarters, Begin explained: "Bibi has matured by ten
years, and I've grown ten years older." This was his way of expressing a matura-
tion of the relationship between the two heirs, and their ability to overcome the
scars of the past.

Netanyahu opened the Likud doors wide to welcome Begin back. He did not
merely view him as a moral and electoral reinforcement; he was genuinely happy.
Their reunion showed no signs of mutual suspicion or resentment; rather, it was
the reconcilement of two heirs who were already mature, experienced leaders.

Netanyahu had always admired Benny Begin above any other political contemporary. Even when he was the target of Begin's harsh criticism, he had appreciated
his integrity and his values. He did not view Begin Jr. as a potential party leader
but did value his contribution as a moral and ideological compass who was good
to have on hand in leading the party and the country.

Begin had been approached by his friend, Reuven Rivlin. Rivlin, in the midst
of his own campaign for the primaries, had set aside his personal interest and set
about bringing Begin back to the Likud. The possibility of having him rejoin the
party filled Rivlin with great hope: he viewed it as a rare opportunity to repair
an historical injustice. He regarded Begin and Meridor as "brothers" who had
brought the Likud not only electoral strength but also ideological steadfastness
and fortitude.

The return of Benny Begin to political life energized the Likud. He led in all
the polls preceding the primaries. He enjoyed the support of all sectors of the
party, especially the veterans, and was a sought-after guest at conferences and
panels of candidates that sought to attract voters. A visit that I paid to his headquarters, located on the second floor of a neglected building in the Bnei Brak
industrial area, was like a journey back in time, an encounter with the Likud
of three or four decades earlier. What I found there was the small, warm movement that the Likud had once been, with the best and most loyal of the younger
generation along with the veterans, in their nineties, who had long since given
up political activity but were excited to see Benny Begin back, excited to see the
reunion of the heirs.

While Begin's return was quick, Netanyahu wooed Meridor for months, in
secret, before the primaries. During their meetings they discussed a broad range
of economic and, especially, diplomatic topics. The talks produced a renewed intimacy between them, the old wariness replaced by general agreement concerning
Israel's situation and its needs. Despite the gap in their political views, the common interest prevailed: Meridor had dedicated himself to public service for four
decades; Netanyahu was looking to reinforce his list and to win the elections. The
two men rediscovered all they shared in common as the sons of parents who had
been inspired by Jabotinsky, living just a few hundred meters apart in Jerusalem
of the 1950s.

Meridor had suffered great disappointment from Sharon and Olmert, whom he
had supported over three general elections. He felt that they had both used him
as a "stain-remover" at election time, promising him a government portfolio and

then reneging on the commitment. Unlike Begin, who deliberately distanced himself from politics, Meridor had politics literally flowing through his veins. He had an eager appetite for public service; anything else bored him, including the big money of the business world.

While Sharon's violation of his promise to Meridor might be explained in terms of old misgivings going back to the First Lebanon War, the similar treatment at the hands of Olmert and later, Livni was deeply frustrating and disheartening. These were fellow heirs and shared similar views to his own. Olmert had been a personal friend for forty years. Livni shared the same squeaky-clean image that Meridor enjoyed. But each of them in turn gave in to Sharon's close circle who vetoed their appointment (according to some, it was his son, Omri). After all, each of them wanted the support of Sharon's people. In his autobiography, Olmert, who offers few confessions or regrets, offers an apology to "my good friend Dan Meridor", claiming that he was forced "to disappoint Dan and myself, too."[1] He lays the blame on Sharon's circle.

Paradoxically, Begin's unexpected return to the Likud made Netanyahu's offer less attractive to Meridor. The party now already boasted an esteemed, upright heir who refreshed the leadership. In addition, Meridor had never enjoyed participating in the party's internal elections. He disliked the sweating, the shouting, and the obsequiousness that characterized the Central Committee experience. This explained the difficulties he had encountered in getting himself elected by the power-brokers of the new Likud ever since his stint as the liberal Minister of Justice, since the internal elections of 1992 when he had been elected only by virtue of the Sharon-Arens deal. Meridor also refused to bend his worldview and adopt a right-wing guise that would help him in the primaries. His positions were fundamentally opposed to those of many in the Likud.

During the primaries, Begin's sole concern was the situation of his friend Meridor. He knew that Meridor's views would work against him, and he begged his activists to "take care of Meridor", insisting that this was important for the Likud. Anyone who met Begin during this period, expecting a solicitation for his vote, was surprised to hear the same message that Begin had maintained seventeen years previously, in the second round of the internal elections of 1992: "Dan must be elected. A vote for him is more important than a vote for me."

Netanyahu came to Meridor's aid when he saw the polls. He was afraid of a scenario in which Meridor would run for the primaries but fail to be elected. This would paint the Likud as an extremist party, trapped in the clutches of extremist candidates. Netanyahu therefore extended the primaries for an extra day and transmitted a clear message in the media and in conversations with activists: the Likud needs a compromise-minded heir in order to exhibit openness and diversity. The veterans were the first to answer the call and vote for Meridor. This time, their considerations were tactical and political, rather than emotional and generational, as they had been in the past.

The result was gratifying: Meridor and Begin joined Netanyahu, who took care to let the public know that the heirs were designated as ministers in his government.

Elections of 2009: once again, two heirs competing to be Prime Minister

Leading up to the 2009 elections, one Jerusalemite heir was campaigning to bring the Likud back to power. He was accompanied by an impressive Knesset list including youngsters, generals, and five additional heirs. Together they embarked on an efficient campaign to regain the leadership.

Competing against this Tagar Likud heir was the heiress championing Kadima and diplomatic compromise. This was the third time that heirs were in line to assume leadership of the country. First there had been Netanyahu, in the 1996 elections; then Olmert versus Netanyahu, in 2006. Now in 2009, once again, two heirs headed the two major parties and one of them would be taking office.

The polls indicated clearly that the Likud was doing better than Kadima. During October-November 2008, the Likud had jumped from twenty-six mandates to a projected thirty-three, a gap of six over Kadima. The return of Begin and Meridor had ignited the Likud camp, and Netanyahu was enjoying the highest level of support he had seen in a decade.

Netanyahu's campaign focused on the heirs and new stars who now surrounded him. In comparison, the Kadima list featured Haim Ramon and Tzahi Hanegbi, both of whom were embroiled in legal issues; Shaul Mofaz, regarded as an opposition figure; and some drab MKs who brought Livni no particular prestige. The shadow cast by Olmert's forced resignation further hindered her chances. Netanyahu's campaign of stars was particularly effective because it eroded Livni's main advantage in the public mind: the fact that she was untainted by scandal and corruption.

From the moment he took the lead in the polls, Netanyahu shifted gears into a "safe" campaign that would not put his advantage at risk. Livni did not give up; even when the gap between them widened, she aired her views unapologetically and launched an underdog campaign that damaged Netanyahu's position. She waved the peace flag, branding herself as the candidate who offered the public hope. Netanyahu, in his typical style, promised voters his truth: the hard Middle Eastern reality of blood, sweat, and security as the only path to survival.

Livni's slogan towards the end of the election campaign – "Tzipi or Bibi" – was aggressive and populist, but it drew voters only from the Left, not from the Center-Right. The more Livni attacked Netanyahu, reminding the "white tribe" of her long struggle with him, the more warmly he was embraced by the Center.

Although Netanyahu saw that the right-wing parties were attracting Likud voters, he preferred not to react to their campaigns against him, in order not to sabotage his future coalition. He was willing to forego Likud MKs at the bottom of the party list if that would ensure his attainment of the important goal: the premiership. While everyone was talking about the drop in the number of projected mandates for the Likud, Netanyahu kept his silence. It was only after the elections that everyone understood why he had not fought harder against the right-wing parties, the religious parties, and the ultra-Orthodox parties.

In the Knesset elections held on February 19, 2009, Kadima received twenty-eight mandates, making it the largest party in the Knesset. Netanyahu, who had held a projected advantage of six mandates, lost a great number of votes to satellite parties, ending up with twenty-seven mandates.

As the preliminary results started to emerge, Kadima seemed to be nearing thirty, two more than Likud. The celebrations commenced. In her victory speech, Livni called upon Netanyahu to acknowledge his defeat and to join a unity government:

> What remains is to respect the voters' decision, to do what is right at this time and to join a unity government under our leadership, based on Israel's major parties, both to the left of Kadima and to its right.[2]

The same night, Netanyahu sat with his advisors, watching all three television stations awarding the victory to Livni and "burying" him for the umpteenth time. He was perhaps the only one who knew how right the television presenters Amit

Figure 27.1 PM Benjamin Netanyahu with his father and spiritual role model, Bentzion Netanyahu. A rare relationship of love and admiration.

Segal, Ilana Dayan, and Yaron Dekel were when they countered the preliminary results with confident, unambiguous analysis ("Netanyahu has a decisive bloc"). Now the country observed another absurd spectacle, the likes of which had played out in the past, starring Peres and Rabin (1981) and Shamir and Peres (1984), with each of the contestants claiming victory. Both heirs, both winners, both delivering victory speeches. Netanyahu hurried to the Exhibition Grounds and declared victory in order to prevent Livni from consolidating her status as victor and dragging in one of the less-reliable parties he was counting on for his coalition of sixty-five mandates. The activists at the Exhibition Grounds were surprised, having just watched preliminary results that declared Livni the winner.

It took weeks until everyone understood that Netanyahu's election strategy had been focused on a bloc, rather than on his party (in contrast to Livni, who had worked to maximize the number of Kadima mandates, hoping that the Kadima victory would bring other parties to support her bid to be Prime Minister). The disappointed Livni was unable to mobilize even her own bloc to support her candidacy, and the President entrusted Netanyahu with the business of forming a government.

Figure 27.2 Young Benjamin Netanyahu rose to the head of the Likud in the 1993 primaries, only five years after arriving from the UN, where he served as an ambassador. Here with his enthusiastic supporters.

Figure 27.3 Benjamin Netanyahu with the head of the Tagar Circle of the Etzel Veterans, Eli Sheetrit (on the right). Sheetrit and his friends sponsored Netanyahu, crowned him, fought for him, and defended him for twenty-five years after 1988.

Netanyahu forms a government with Labor rival Barak, rather than with Livni

Netanyahu already had a small but solid and harmonious right-wing–ultra-Orthodox coalition wrapped up and ready to proceed. However, he had learned his lesson from past experience and knew that the Right could bring down a right-wing government. He wanted a broader coalition. He therefore made supreme efforts to bring in Livni, but she was too caught up in her disappointment and frustration over having the election victory snatched from her. Her close circle, including Sharon's "Sycamore Ranch team" and Netanyahu's detractors, assured her that Netanyahu and his government would fall within a year.

Livni continued to champion the cause of peace. By this time the idea was no longer a central issue in Israeli public discourse: Oslo was generally regarded as a failure, and the generous concessions offered by Barak and Olmert in negotiations had been answered with terror. In her negotiations with Netanyahu she demanded (and received) the political negotiations portfolio and then made her entry into the government conditional on Netanyahu's agreement to the principle of "two states for two peoples". The daughter of the Irgun's "Minister of Defense" was now demanding of the son of the Revisionists' "Foreign Minister" that he agree to the establishment of a Palestinian state. Netanyahu refused. This diplomatic difference of opinion was the (overt) reason for the breakdown of negotiations.

Nevertheless, Netanyahu was so eager to have Livni in the government that he continued secret talks with her. Although he already had a coalition, he went so far as to agree to a rotation of the premiership after three years. In order to lead the country with a government that would represent the majority of the public, Netanyahu was ready to give Livni a share of the Prime Minister's role, along with an equal number of Kadima ministers as Likud ministers in the government and the cabinet. But Livni refused. She demanded that Netanyahu relinquish one of his other coalition partners, so that he would be dependent on her and would not "snatch" her faction in mid-term. Livni had good reason to be wary of such a scenario. She knew her faction colleagues and their appetite for power.

The result of the failed negotiations was the formation of the "no option" right-wing and ultra-Orthodox coalition. Once again, two heirs confronted each other as Prime Minister and head of the opposition. But now Livni had a problem: domestic politics no longer interested her. Over the course of a decade in the Knesset, she had spent eight years as a minister, and what she enjoyed was dip-lomatic activity. She grew increasingly frustrated in the opposition, as did her faction colleagues: they had joined a party that had promised an eternal reign; they had already held high-ranking positions and were accustomed to power, and they held Livni responsible for the fact that they were now in the opposition. Mofaz, her main rival, rushed to fill the vacuum that she had left. He returned to the Sisyphean work at which he excelled, devoting attention to the party's power-brokers, who received him with open arms.

The surviving underground veterans watched their children's generation, headed by Netanyahu, inching closer to power again, exactly a decade since Net-anyahu's ouster. There were now eleven heirs installed in the Knesset, but they were spread over three right-wing parties and one centrist party. Six represented the Likud: Netanyahu, Rivlin, Begin, Meridor, Livnat, and Yariv Levin, a new MK. Two represented right-wing parties: Uzi Landau and Aryeh Eldad (son of Yisrael Eldad). Three more represented Kadima: Livni, Hanegbi, and Boim. Alto-gether, eight children of the Irgun and three of Lehi. Five of these were children of the Irgun high command during the Revolt: Begin, Meridor, Livni, Lenkin and Landau. Sixty-five years earlier, their parents had been united in the leadership of the Revolt.

The Irgun veterans were proud to see eight of their heirs among the country's leadership: a Prime Minister, five ministers, a former Prime Minister (Olmert) who was still exerting influence from outside the government, the head of the opposition (Livni), and Chairman of the Knesset (Rivlin).

During his second term as Prime Minister, Netanyahu took to heart the les-sons of his first term and tried to unify the country and the party around him. He went to astonishing lengths to create a broad coalition that would include at least one party representing the Center-Left. He tried hard to bring in Livni (and later her successor, Mofaz), and also managed (surprisingly enough) to bring in Labor, now under the leadership of his old rival Ehud Barak. Netanyahu now had a hawkish Foreign Minister (Lieberman) and a dovish Minister of Defense (Barak). The latter appointment was a conciliatory message directed towards the international community, ensuring that Netanyahu would be able to get on with the job. Netanyahu and Barak, his former commander from the General Reconnaissance Unit, maintained a firm alliance that survived even the Labor's decision, later on, to leave the government: Barak split the party and formed a new faction, which remained part of Netanyahu's coalition, maintaining that the war against a nuclear Iran took precedence over any other interest. This son of Kibbutz Mishmar Hasharon became Netanyahu's closest partner in his second term, while the Prime Minister's harshest critics were the Irgun heirs Livni and Olmert.

During this term, relations between Netanyahu and Livni became so fraught that they were unable even to schedule meetings for coordination and updating, as required by law between the Prime Minister and the leader of the opposition. A third heir had to intervene and mediate between them: Chairman of the Knesset Rivlin.

Netanyahu's second government proceeded to work in harmony and with mutual confidence. Meridor, Begin, and Rivlin moderated the more radical right-wing tendencies in the Likud and the government, maintaining the rule of law and democracy. The policy of judicial activism of former President of the Supreme Court, Aharon Barak (whom the prominent legal scholar Richard Posner referred to as a "legal buccaneer") had led to a popular backlash, and the Knesset debated legislation aimed at limiting the power of the Supreme Court. The three heirs were central players in the war on what they viewed as the tyranny of the majority and anti-democratic legislation.

Netanyahu and the heirs showed themselves to be more mature, more attentive, and more cooperative than they had been in the past. Now in their sixties and seventies, they maintained a narrow security cabinet numbering between six and nine ministers, which operated with a rare level of confidentiality, discussing the most critical issues (Egypt, Syria, and Iran) and remaining unified in pursuit of their well-considered policy. With the help of the heirs, Netanyahu was a responsible, cautious, and restrained Prime Minister. As a statesman who believed strongly in the power of deterrence, he ended up, over the seven years of his two terms, relying less on military force than had any of his predecessors, including those who had declared peace as a priority.

Notes

1 Yediot Aharonot, January 27, 2011.
2 Yediot Aharonot, February 11, 2009.

28 The Netanyahu dynasty

From the Nazi threat to the Iranian threat

Netanyahu carried the legacy of two generations. Both Jabotinsky (his spiritual or ideological grandfather) and Natan Milikowsky (his biological grandfather) were a presence in his life. Their guidance merged with the profound and decisive influence of his father, Professor Bentzion Netanyahu.

Unlike other Jewish leaders of their time, Bentzion Netanyahu and Jabotinsky had warned of the approach of the Holocaust and had emphasized the urgent need to declare the establishment of a Jewish state as a concrete objective. The most important insight that Netanyahu received as a real living legacy from his forebears was the memory of the failure of Jewish leadership in the wake of the rise of Nazism. Jabotinsky's warnings had been met with apathy and indifference on the part of Jewish leaders in Europe and in the Land of Israel, who denounced him for sowing hysteria, terror, and despair. Netanyahu Jr. could not forgive or forget this repression in response to danger. Speaking out was his motto and his mission.

The same frustration that Netanyahu's forebears had felt with the approach of the Holocaust, as they tried to deal with the hopelessly optimistic and impossibly submissive leaders of the western powers (Chamberlain first and foremost among them), rose up in Netanyahu Jr. as he dealt with successive presidents of the US. As his forefathers had opposed the policy of peace, restraint, and compromise adopted by the leaders of the Yishuv (Weizmann, Ben-Gurion, and others), so he opposed the policies of previous leaders of Israel (Rabin, Peres, Barak, Sharon, and Olmert). During his second term, Netanyahu regarded the developments in the Middle East with concern, while his political rivals viewed them as positive opportunities. While they regarded Arafat as a partner for peace, he viewed him as an unreformed and irredeemable terrorist. What they regarded as the "Arab Spring" Netanyahu perceived as the spread of extremist Islam over Egypt and its neighbors. Where Obama and Kerry saw a rosy future, he saw darkness.

Above all, Netanyahu was troubled by the threat of a nuclear Iran. For the sake of addressing this threat he was willing to show flexibility on what he considered to be tactical issues, such as a temporary freeze on construction in Judea and Samaria, and even agreement to a demilitarized Palestinian state. (Political commentator Amit Segal heard from Netanyahu Sr. in 2009 that his son had promised him that the possibility would never come to fruition, since the terms he set down for the Arabs would never be met.)

All the while, Netanyahu had to deal with an American administration that cherished a vision of world peace. This administration pressured him to make concessions to the Palestinians both in his first term (President Clinton) and in his second and third terms (President Obama). He, of all Israeli Prime Ministers, had to contend with American leaders whose worldview was the opposite of his own. They believed that the way forward was to appease and persuade the Muslim world to make peace with the West, while Netanyahu had predicted and warned thirty years earlier of the rise of extremist and violent Islam under the patronage of terror states.

Netanyahu's whole life and worldview were shaped by the memory of the historical lapse of Jewish leadership in the face of the approaching Holocaust. The motif that was passed from generation to generation in his family was a constant vigilance against the blindness of Jews who, laboring under the sickness of exile, repressed and ignored the bitter truth: they were not wanted in Europe. What Herzl, Jabotinsky, Milikowsky, and his son Bentzion Netanyahu had seen, most of the Jewish leadership was not willing or able to see. Jabotinsky and Milikowsky decided to act. They abandoned their comfortable, everyday lives and devoted themselves to saving the Jews of Europe. They were the first to declare openly, as early as the mid-1930s, with Hitler's rise to power, their sacred (and controversial, at the time) aim: the establishment of a Jewish state.

Netanyahu also carried with him his father's charge: to overcome the Jewish instinct to look away from danger, and not to fear the loneliness and isolation that are the lot of prophets of doom. In a column entitled "The Loneliness of Netanyahu III", political commentator Ari Shavit described eloquently Netanyahu's feelings in the Iran age:

> The Prime Minister of Israel was and remains an outsider who feels that outside of his home there is no-one whom he can really trust, nor is there any Israeli who understands the challenges that he is forced to address. From the point of view of this Jerusalemite historian's son, a severe lapse on the part of the elites, acute media distortion, and dangerous national blindness have resulted in his standing altogether alone on the navigation bridge of the Jewish state.[1]

After the death of Netanyahu Sr. on April 30, 2012, Shavit wrote that he had been

> the most influential figure in the Prime Minister's life. The son's life is an ongoing tension between his father's hawkishness and the exigencies of reality. [. . .] Bentzion Netanyahu loved the Jewish People, but did not believe in the Jews. He thought his fellow Jews were children who did not understand history and had no idea how to act within history. Bentzion Netanyahu was committed to the State of Israel, but he did not appreciate Israelis. He thought we lacked the sense of sovereignty of clear-headed nations, and the warning mechanism that alerts every living thing to great danger. [. . .] Benjamin is not

Bentzion. He is far more moderate than his father, far more open to compromise, and slightly less pessimistic. Nevertheless, the son's life is an ongoing discourse between his father's moral core, and a changing reality.[2]

In his eulogy, the love and great and rare admiration that Netanyahu felt for his father were manifest. While he spoke of his father and of the past, he was also speaking, to a considerable degree, about himself and the present:

> You did not hesitate to set out to confront the storms that would befall the Jewish People. [. . .] In 1937, at the age of just twenty-seven, you wrote: "Herzl saw that the smoldering coals of the fire of primal antisemitism were destined to be rekindled. He saw in his mind's eye a vision of catastrophe. It was clear to him that the nation was headed for annihilation." You wrote this a few years before the Second World War; before the Holocaust that befell our people. Not only did you agree with Herzl about the danger; you acted to the best of your ability to ward it off. You acted to precipitate the establishment of the Jewish state, by enlisting the US. [. . .] You went, alone, to dozens of senators and members of Congress [. . .] and told them that the Jewish state, when it arose, would not be defeated by the Arabs, and that it would be the pillar of Western culture in the Middle East.[3]

In 1996, at the beginning of his first term as Prime Minister, Netanyahu was the first to warn, openly and publicly, of the danger posed by a nuclear Iran, during a visit to the Bergen-Belsen Nazi extermination camp.

Netanyahu was castigated by pundits and publicists for invoking the memory of the Holocaust and using it in this way. He had already heard criticism from his opponents – experts, generals, politicians – who warned against independent Israeli thinking and planning. The American administration, too, expressed misgivings when Netanyahu began planning a military option against a nuclear Iran.

But as Netanyahu saw it, this criticism was just like the criticism that had been aimed at Jabotinsky when he warned of impending annihilation, and like the threats of the American administration, the high-ranking Israeli security personnel, and the opposition when Begin had attacked and destroyed the nuclear reactor in Iraq. The flood of negative feedback in the media and academia actually reinforced his resolve. No-one was proposing any practical solution to the nuclear threat other than further reliance on the international community, which had been of little help throughout history, from the Expulsion from Spain, via pogroms in Russia, all the way to the Holocaust.

In the previously mentioned article,[4] Shavit analyzed Netanyahu in the Iranian context:

> From Netanyahu's perspective, the hostile world has not changed: Iran was the existential threat up until 2013, and it remains the existential threat from 2013 onwards. To his estimation, it was specifically the tough policy adopted by his previous government, and the "red line" speech that he delivered at the

UN, that deterred the Iranians last year, and bought the little time that remains in which to act. [. . .] The challenge is not to dwell on the previous Holocaust, but to prevent the next one. It is difficult to do this while the security establishment believes wholeheartedly in the American messiah, and while the political and media discourse is not serious. [. . .] But Netanyahu III does not mean to give up. As he sees it, Iran is not behind us, but rather before us.

The source of the misunderstanding is Netanyahu's agenda – an agenda that does not sit well with the social agenda which the media, and much of the public, often places at the center. The agenda of the Israeli Prime Minister is not the agenda of the Israeli public. What he thinks about is not Rikki Cohen's overdraft, but rather Iran, the Arab chaos, the Palestinian question, and the need to maintain the economic miracle of the last decade. [. . .] The new, unsettled, Islamist Middle East is the real problem which the lonely man Netanyahu intends to address in the coming years.

Netanyahu threatens to bomb Iran – in front of his generals and the Obama administration

Netanyahu's campaign to halt the Iranian nuclear program was conducted in three dimensions: international diplomacy, focusing especially on the US; extensive preparations for an Israeli military attack; and a channel that was and remains secret, although the explosions, sudden deaths, and computer viruses affecting the nuclear industry in Iran have been noted and discussed the world over.

During his second term, Netanyahu became a leader who had a greater influence than most on the world agenda. He caused the world – almost forcibly – to face up to the Iranian threat, his words demanding attention and consideration. The Prime Minister of the tiny country became a regular fixture on television screens throughout the world, as he threatened and planned, together with his Minister of Defense, Ehud Barak, a military option. This served to accelerate the imposition of increasingly restrictive sanctions by the US and other world powers during 2011-2012. Netanyahu and Barak, the former soldier and commander from the IDF General Reconnaissance Unit, the ousted and the ouster in the 1999 elections, had met up again, in the same government, as Prime Minister and Minister of Defense. They were alone in Israel and in the world in their determination to deal with the Iranian threat which they regarded as a supreme and tangible danger. The general opposition they faced only intensified their efforts.

Much has been written about the huge confrontation over the question of an Israeli attack on Iran. The American and Israeli media focused extensively on this issue which troubled the world leaders. Netanyahu and Barak guided the security establishment and provided billions in budgets in anticipation of an unprecedented strike on a distant country, such as Iran. This sparked an ongoing conflict with the American administration, which was fed by the American and Israeli media. A second source of opposition was the top-ranking officials of the Israeli security establishment. From material that has been made public it appears that in 2011–2012 Israel came very close to launching an attack.

Twice the Netanyahu-Barak duo was challenged by a Chief-of-Staff/head of Mossad duo who adopted every possible measure, including collaboration with the Americans, the media, and the opposition, to sabotage an operation which, to their view, was likely either to fail, or to accelerate the Iranian nuclear program, or to postpone it for only a limited time. Chiefs-of-Staff Ashkenazi and later Gantz, and Mossad heads Meir Dagan and later Tamir Pardo, along with Shin Bet director Yuval Diskin, and later Prime Minister Olmert, were all opposed to a military strike. The Chiefs-of-Staff expressed their views and discussed them in security forums, but the Mossad and Shin Bet heads admitted to having acted to sabotage orders in real time. After their terms of office were over they joined with Olmert in a public campaign against what they viewed as a dangerous initiative.

It was a well-coordinated collaborative effort, with a media assault advanced by political commentators who were fed information by former members of the security establishment, in cooperation with the American administration and the American media, led by Thomas Friedman of the *New York Times*. He criticized and warned Netanyahu on a regular basis, with messages that appeared to originate with the American President himself. At the end of 2011 the details of the secret operation were spread all over the press, the Internet, and television in Israel and the US.

At the start of the Knesset's 2011 winter session on October 31, Netanyahu declared that "a nuclear Iran would be a serious threat to the Middle East and to the entire world. Of course, it would also be a direct and grave threat to us." The head of the Labor party and of the opposition, Shelly Yachimovich, called upon Netanyahu "to listen to the heads of the security establishment", declaring that his statement "sounded like preparing the ground for a wild and megalomanic adventure. [. . .] We warn you in advance, Mr. Prime Minister, and you too, Defense Minister Ehud Barak – beware."[5]

There are two ways of understanding the battle to prevent Israel's attack on Iran. One is that the Prime Minister and Defense Minister ordered preparations for an immediate bombing of the Iranian nukes, but the IDF and Mossad brass twice scuttled the attack, through various means, some of which might be described as a putsch against an elected government. Israeli history offers only one previous recorded case of generals rebelling against the government. It was during the period prior to the Six Day War (May-June 1967), when the Chief-of-Staff ostensibly forced the Prime Minister into a pre-emptive strike against the Egyptian and Syrian armies, which were threatening the country's south and north. Official documents that have been published expose the heavy pressure exerted on the government and Prime Minister Levi Eshkol, who was accused of hesitancy and indecisiveness, by a series of generals: Chief-of-Staff Rabin, Deputy Chief-of-Staff Weizman, Major-General Sharon, and others. When it came to Iran, the scenario was reversed: it was the government that sought to initiate action, while the heads of the security bodies opposed it, refused to cooperate, and obstructed the military initiative.

The other interpretation holds that Netanyahu and Barak did indeed plan for a strike but never ordered its execution. Their aim was to convey a message to the American administration and to the world that if the Iranian nuclear project was not halted, Israel was ready to bomb the sites, with or without American approval or backing. According to this interpretation, Netanyahu knew that operative preparations would be leaked by opponents of the plan to the press and to the Americans, who would have no choice but to take decisive action – which is what happened in any case.

Ben-Dror Yemini, writing in *Yediot Aharonot* on June 3, 2018, sums up the following conclusion:

> The problem is the suspicion that certain high-ranking individuals in the defense establishment planned a putsch. They sabotaged an order by the political echelon, because they held a different opinion. It is not clear that their opinion was more correct.[6]

Surprisingly and extraordinarily enough, three top-ranking security personnel acknowledged – not to say boasted of – having obstructed two explicit orders to embark on preparations for an attack on Iran. The testimonies of former Mossad heads Dagan and Pardo, and former Shin Bet director Diskin, indicate that twice Israel readied itself and was close to attack. The former top security men were met with a forgiving attitude on the part of the media, which portrayed them as having saved Israel from an unnecessary war. Nevertheless, if their testimony is correct and reliable, they actually refused an order by a Prime Minister elected by the people of Israel.

The first refusal was exposed on the television program "Uvda" (Fact), presented by investigative reporter Ilana Dayan, on November 5, 2012. According to Dayan, the head of the Mossad at the time, Meir Dagan and Chief-of-Staff at the time, Gabi Ashkenazi, came to Jerusalem sometime during 2010, and according to their "close circles" the Prime Minister gave an order: to place the security establishment on "P+ alert" – a code signifying preparedness for a possible strike. They protested. Ashkenazi is quoted as saying, "It's not something that you do if you're not certain that in the end you'll want to go through with it." Ashkenazi's people claimed that he was concerned that the very act of moving to "P+", even without embarking immediately on the operation, could create facts on the ground that could lead to war. The report claimed that Mossad director Dagan did something that no-one had ever done to a Prime Minister and Minister of Defense: "You are about to make an unlawful decision to go to war," he rebuked them. "Only the cabinet is authorized to make that decision." Later, Dagan leveled an accusation that has probably never been made by someone at the executive level, in Israel or anywhere in the world, against an elected leader: "The Prime Minister and Minister of Defense just tried to slip a war in." Ilana Dayan quotes Barak's claim that Ashkenazi told Netanyahu and Barak that the "P+" order could not be carried out since the army lacked operational ability. Now, it is not clear whether the military did or did not actually possess the operational ability to carry out the strike at that time, but from Barak's perspective Ashkenazi failed in not preparing the option, such that it was not possible to carry out the "P+" order. Dayan quotes a contradictory response by Ashkenazi: "Barak isn't telling the truth. I prepared the option, the army was ready for an attack, but I also said that an attack at this time would be a strategic mistake." Barak responded, maintaining his version of events:

> The decisions you are talking about are the government's responsibility. The assumption that if the Chief-of-Staff doesn't recommend something for which the operational ability exists, then there can be no decision to carry it out – that has no basis. The Chief-of-Staff has to build the operational ability; he has to tell us, from a professional point of view, whether it is possible or impossible to execute, and he can – and must – add his recommendation. But it can be carried out against his recommendation.[7]

This, then, was the second instance of military and intelligence brass forcing their will on an elected Prime Minister. The third instance in Israel's history was exposed on the same television program, "Uvda", on May 31, 2018, seven years after it took place. This time, former Mossad head Tamir Pardo admitted that he had tried to block an order by Prime Minister Netanyahu. During 2011, he claimed, the Prime Minister had instructed him and Chief-of-Staff Benny Gantz to activate "P+15" – in other words, to have the defense establishment at the ready for an attack on Iran within fifteen days of the order. In an interview with Ilana Dayan, he was asked whether he believed that the attack would indeed take place. He replied:

> If someone does this, it can be for two purposes. One possibility is that he really means it; the other possibility is that he's sending a message. Someone out there will know about it. Perhaps someone in the US will get to know about it one way or another, and it will cause him to do something.[8]

Pardo testified that he had decided to take the most unusual step of checking whether the Prime Minister of Israel was in fact authorized to give an order which might, to Pardo's mind, lead the country to war. (This effectively opened every bombing in Gaza or Syria, and every Mossad operation in enemy territory, to the same question.) He acknowledged sharing this confidential information with others:

> I checked with previous Mossad directors; I checked – starting with Yitzhak Hofi, all the way to Meir Dagan. I checked with legal advisors. I consulted with everyone I could speak to in order to understand who is authorized to issue instructions in all matters pertaining to starting a war. As part of this unprecedented series of consultations, I also approached the Attorney General.[9]

The Chief-of-Staff at the time, Benny Gantz, had spoken to a group of new army recruits in 2012, denying his involvement:

> Not one of the statements that was published was made by me, nor was any one of them issued in my name. [. . .] Iran continues to exert efforts to attain

military nuclear ability. This is something that should not be ignored. Iran is the only country in the world that calls for the annihilation of another country – Israel. The IDF is prepared and ready to act, and as far as we are concerned, "all options are on the table" is not a slogan, but rather a work program.[10]

Statements by Prime Minister Netanyahu concerning military plans in general, and concerning Iran in particular, are almost non-existent. In a televised interview in July 2012, he made rare reference to the opposition to the strike that the media attributed to the Chief-of-Staff, the Shin Bet director, and the director of the Mossad:

I hear their opinions behind closed doors. The media discourse that pretends to reflect their views is irresponsible, and it harms state security. The proper discussion of such a sensitive subject takes place behind closed doors. There are many aspects that are not given expression [in the media]; the external discourse is most inappropriate, and very superficial. [. . .] In the Israeli democracy, as in any democracy, it's the political echelon that decides, and the professional echelon executes the decision. I have not yet made a decision.[11]

In interviews Netanyahu cited the example of Prime Minister Begin's decision to destroy the Osirak nuclear reactor in 1981:

Others in the security establishment at the time, including the head of the Mossad and the head of Military Intelligence, were adamantly opposed, but the political leadership made the decision, because it had the overall perspective, and it bore the supreme responsibility. The same applies today. The decision that is made, when and if it is made, will be the decision of the political echelon. Iran's nuclear armament is something that I will not allow to happen. The Ayatollah regime is working on nuclear bombs to destroy us! So far as it is up to me, I will not allow it to happen.[12]

Netanyahu made this commitment openly and publicly. For the benefit of his audience in Washington, he added, "I'd be very glad if the international community would do the work in Iran."

There is no question that Israel's threats of a strike, whether uttered by the Prime Minister, the Minister of Defense, or the Chief-of-Staff, were picked up loud and clear in Washington. Proof of this is the fact that the American Secretary of Defense at the time, Leon Panetta, landed in Israel within twenty-four hours of Netanyahu's interview. The same month, Secretary of State Hillary Clinton and National Security Advisor Tom Donilon also visited. Also within twenty-four hours of the interview, President Obama signed in new sanctions which gradually intensified the restrictions on Iran over 2011-2012.

President Obama and Prime Minister Netanyahu moved on two separate but related axes. Netanyahu threatened, while Obama applied sanctions and engaged in negotiations. Netanyahu pursued his campaign, focused on New York and

Washington, in Congress and at his dramatic annual appearances in the UN, which carried his warnings about Iran to the entire world. Obama responded by tightening sanctions, leading to economic crisis in Iran, along with negotiations in which the Western powers (P5 + 1) demanded an Iranian commitment to halt the nuclear project in return for sanctions relief.

The final stage of negotiations between the world powers and Iran, in late 2014–early 2015, brought on the most potent confrontation ever between Netanyahu and Obama. In the past the disagreements between the two countries had been one-directional, with the US expressing disapproval of Israeli policy or action, occasionally threatening or applying sanctions, initiating plans for Israel concessions, or interfering in Israeli elections. This time, the disagreement was initiated and driven by Israel.

For five years, Netanyahu had tried to sway the world and the US President, in meetings, via the press, and through the agency of opinion leaders and US Congressmen. This effort went against the position of the US President and other world leaders, and against the economic interests of huge corporations that were pressuring the European states to open up commercial ties with Teheran. Thus, it became an open war between the Prime Minister of a tiny country and the President of the mightiest world power, with the former fighting against the latter's intention to remove sanctions.

The drama developed once the US administration had already come to an agreement with Iran, and needed only to neutralize congressional opposition. At this point, Netanyahu announced his intention to address a joint session of the US Congress. He had accepted an invitation by the Republican Speaker of the House of Representatives at the time, John Boehner, via Israeli ambassador, Ron Dermer, in January 2015. Boehner invited Netanyahu despite the unequivocal opposition of the US President, who announced that, in a departure from protocol, he would not meet the head of state visiting Washington. Netanyahu endured weeks of withering criticism for antagonizing the President and for the potential disastrous impact on Israel-US relations. The entire opposition, along with almost all political commentators and experts, flooded the country with doomsday predictions about the historical Israeli-US rift that Netanyahu was causing. They all pressed him to make do with the smaller victory – the imminent agreement to halt Iranian nuclear development – and to stop trying to win the war (which was lost in any case) over the cancellation of sanctions.

The US media that was loyal to President Obama, led by Thomas Friedman of the *New York Times*, had spearheaded a campaign against Netanyahu since 2011. Friedman was interviewed on Israel's army radio station in February 2015, prior to Netanyahu's visit to Washington. He warned the Prime Minister and tried to apply pressure via Israeli public opinion:

> I would suggest that Netanyahu stay home. It's a very bad idea, from start to finish, with very negative repercussions for Israel-US relations. [. . .] There are many Democrats and Republicans alike who don't like it that a [foreign] leader is coming to the US at the invitation of just one party. [. . .] This

represents further erosion of our relations; another crack in the wall. [. . .]
It's not a good precedent, and it's likely to harm the relations between our
countries in the coming decade.[13]

Responding to a question about the relations between Obama and Netanyahu,
Friedman answered crisply, "They apparently can't stand each other; it certainly
looks that way. Bibi thinks Obama is naïve and incompetent, and Obama thinks
that Bibi is going about things in the wrong way."

Washington wanted Netanyahu to suffice with the achievement of halting a
nuclear Iran and warned him against measures that would look like a provocation.
Pressure was applied on him personally, as well as on Democratic Congressmen,
who were urged not to attend Netanyahu's address. Such a situation had never
arisen between the two countries: the Prime Minister was going to appear before
Congress, a few hundred meters away from a fuming US President in the White
House.

Only a Prime Minister with a sense of fateful, historical mission, and armed
with confidence in the unparalleled status that he had built for himself among the
public and in the Congress over decades, could proceed with such a visit. Israeli
ambassador to the US, Ron Dermer, who had coordinated the anti-Iranian campaign in Washington, did not hesitate to declare openly (at a Bonds convention in
Florida):

> It is a supreme moral obligation to speak before the Congress concerning the
> existential threat that Iran presents to Israel. [. . .] The Prime Minister has one
> single objective in the US: to speak out so long as it is still possible to speak
> out. To speak out so long as it is still possible to change the reality.[14]

After Netanyahu's visit, too, in March 2018, when Dermer was asked by interviewer Thane Rosenbaum what he thought of Netanyahu's speech in Congress,
he replied that it was "the moment that I was proudest of, during my entire term."
When asked whether it was right for the Prime Minister to have appeared before
Congress, Dermer answered that this was the Prime Minister's supreme duty:

> I know that it was controversial for a lot of people. I never thought that it was
> controversial, because Israel's Prime Minister has a duty to speak up clearly
> about a subject that involves the nation's security and Israel's survival.[15]

He summed up Israel's position concerning the negotiations for an agreement
with Iran using the well-known aphorism, "If you're not at the table [and indeed,
Israel had not been party to the negotiations], you're on the menu." He added:

> The reason why it was a disaster is that it paves the path to Iran having a
> nuclear arsenal in fifteen years. It places temporary restrictions on ura-
> nium enrichment today in exchange for unlimited enrichment tomorrow –
> essentially sacrificing the future for the present. This is why the PM said in

Congress that a decade may seem like a long time in the life of politics, but it is a blink of an eye in the life of a nation. The issue of Iran conquering the Middle East – enabled by sanctions relief – is also terrible. But had Iran's nuclear program been fully dismantled, we would have accepted the deal, knowing that at least it resolved the existential threat to us. But it did not resolve that threat. It did the opposite. It gave a regime that threatens us with annihilation a clear path to the bomb – only a delayed path.

Netanyahu himself responded to critics at the Presidents' Conference in Jerusalem on February 16, 2015:

The Congress fulfills a critical function in applying pressure to the Iranian regime, and is able to influence a final deal with Iran. [. . .] The answer to all three questions is actually the same. Why Washington? Why the Congress? Why now? Because of the grave dangers posed by the deal that is currently on the table.[16]

On March 3, 2015, Israelis and Americans were glued to their screens, waiting to see whether the Congress would empty out before Netanyahu's speech. To everyone's surprise, 477 Congressmen were present; only fifty-eight absented themselves in a gesture to Obama. Despite the mood emanating from the White House, Congress greeted the Prime Minister who had come to warn against an historical mistake on the part of the US administration with an enthusiastic four-and-a-half-minute standing ovation. In his speech, Netanyahu said: "For over a year, we've been told that no deal is better than a bad deal. Well, this is a bad deal. It's a very bad deal. We're better off without it."[17] Turning to Elie Wiesel, the Holocaust survivor and international icon who was present in the Congress to show his support for Netanyahu, he said:

Your inspiring life and work give meaning to the words, "Never Again." And I wish I could promise you, Elie, that the lessons of history have been learned. I can only urge the leaders of the world not to repeat the mistakes of the past. Not to sacrifice the future for the present; not to ignore aggression in the hopes of gaining an illusory peace. But I can guarantee you this, the days when the Jewish people remained passive in the face of genocidal enemies – those days are over.

House Speaker Boehner presented Netanyahu with a bust of Winston Churchill, a symbolic gesture alluding to the fact that Churchill was the only other foreign leader who had addressed Congress on three occasions.

However, even Netanyahu's dramatic appearance in Congress could not stop the US President from obtaining the thirty-four signatures he needed to push through the JCPOA (Joint Comprehensive Plan of Action) agreement. Despite the Republican majority in both Houses of Congress and the fact that the Congress had displayed its support for Netanyahu's position, the Iranian agreement train had already left the station. Four months after Netanyahu's speech, in July 2015, the agreement was signed, lifting the sanctions on Iran in return for a halt on Iranian nuclear development. It was a heavy blow for Netanyahu, who had fought and warned against an agreement that would liberate Iran from sanctions and simultaneously free up vast sums that could now be directed to the spread of the Khomeini Revolution in all directions. Indeed, the results were not long in coming – in Yemen, Iraq, and Syria. Iran wasted no time building territorial continuity via Iraq to Syria and Lebanon, right up to Israel's northern border. Netanyahu had to content himself with the knowledge that at least he had succeeded in introducing into the American public discourse the idea that Iran was a danger to the world. He hoped to reap the fruits of this labor when the next administration was installed – as indeed he did.

The struggle over Iran was Netanyahu's supreme struggle, and he threw his all into it. At the same time, however, he had to deal with internal squabbles at home, and the election campaigns of 2013 and 2015.

Notes

1   Haaretz, April 11, 2013.
2   Haaretz, May 1, 2012.
3   Yediot Aharonot, April 30, 2012.
4   Haaretz, June 13, 2014.
5   Pinchas Wolf. (2011, October 31). MK Yachimovich: We won't back Netanyahu and Barak for an adventure in Iran. Walla news. Retrieved from https://news.walla.co.il/item/1873160
6   Yediot Aharonot, June 3, 2018.
7   Ruthy Shteinberg (Producer) (2012, November 5). *Uvda* [Television broadcast]. Tel Aviv, Israel: Keshet Broadcasting Service.
8   Ruthy Shteinberg (Producer) (2018, May 31). *Uvda* [Television broadcast]. Tel Aviv, Israel: Keshet Broadcasting Service.
9   Ibid.
10 Yediot Aharonot, July 31, 2012.
11 Yisrael Hayom, August 1, 2012
12 Ibid.
13 Globes, February 19, 2015.
14 Gil Tamary. (2015, January 26). Israel's ambassador to the US: It is a supreme moral obligation to speak before the Congress. Channel 13 news. Retrieved from https://13news.co.il/item/news/domestic/ntr-1106063/
15 Ron Dermer (2018, March 8). Defending the Jewish State (Thane Rosenbaum, Interviewer). Retrieved from https://www.92y.org/archives/israeli-ambassador-ron-dermer-thane-rosenbaum-defending-jewish-state
16 Yisrael Hayom, February 16, 2015.
17 Maariv, March 3, 2015.

29 The heirs fulfill their parents' dream

President and Prime Minister

Netanyahu's easy 2013 elections

By the time the 2013 elections came around, the heirs were already mature, well-established leaders. Four decades had passed since they had entered politics. The young heirs who had made their way into the government a quarter of a century earlier were no longer young. Most were now in their sixties and seventies. Their children were now the same age that they themselves had been when they were first elected to the Knesset, the same age that their grandparents had been when they directed operations in the underground. Only when one calculates the total years of public service accumulated by the heirs together with their parents does one appreciate the degree to which both generations took this on as a lifetime commitment.

Netanyahu persisted, despite the opposition, the attacks, the persecution, and the bumps in the road, and in 2013 was elected Prime Minister for the third time. He was sixty-three and ready to start a new term twenty years after becoming chairman of the Likud.

The party that should have put up the most significant competition to the Likud was Kadima, which had received more mandates than the Likud just four years previously. But Kadima was no longer the same party.

Former Prime Minister Olmert had tried, against all odds, to make a comeback as the leader of the centrist bloc. Olmert viewed himself as the most senior, most experienced, and most worthy candidate to take on Netanyahu. He regarded the other center-left candidates as youngsters who would do well to take shelter under the broad wings of a leader with forty years of experience in the Knesset, including twenty years as a minister and Prime Minister. Even as he remained immersed in legal troubles and recovering from illness, at the age of sixty-eight, Olmert remained a vociferous opponent to Netanyahu, carrying out popularity surveys, reading supportive op-eds in most of the press, and preparing to run for Prime Minister in the 2013 elections. He discussed, instructed, checked, and deliberated, but in the end his legal troubles put a halt to his ambitions. He left the political stage some fifty years after making his appearance with the speech attacking Begin in 1966.

Olmert's legal drama reached its peak on March 31, 2014, when Justice David Rozen convicted him of receiving a bribe in the Holyland affair. The conviction described the entire group that had been involved in the affair as "the country's elite" and as acting out of "avarice, not to say greed." Olmert's prison term commenced in February 2016, but he maintained the same determination that had accompanied him over forty years of activity and walked free in July 2017, having published a book in which he reviewed his political life and settled scores with each of his rivals. The book received huge coverage in the mainstream media, as though the author were not a former Prime Minister who had just been released from prison. Olmert went back to appearing at cultural events, sporting events, and other venues, where he received an enthusiastic welcome from those who still remembered in his favor (as detailed in the book) his struggle against the enemy and target of the Israeli elite and media: Netanyahu. There was even discussion of the possibility of Olmert's return, but he declined the suggestion, knowing that this would be going one step too far in the eyes of the public. He preferred to keep away from the political swamp where he would have to deal with unforgiving factions and a police and legal system that would place obstacles in his path.

Kadima had by now ousted Olmert's successor, Livni, who proved unable to deliver on her promises, having failed to leverage the 2009 victory to ensure the party at least a share in the government. The hungry power-brokers replaced her with her rival, former Chief-of-Staff Mofaz, who had listened to and empathized with them for four years.

Mofaz, the new chairman of Kadima (the fourth in five years) performed an about-face that destroyed the party that had intended to rule the country for many years. He broke with Livni and moved directly from being a venomous opposition to Netanyahu into the arms of the government, resigning from Kadima with no explanation. Left without Sharon, Olmert, or Livni at the helm, the party that had started out with such a seemingly bright future quickly disintegrated.

After eighteen years of activity in the Knesset and the government, the Livni of 2013 was no longer the same snow-white heiress that she had been in 2009. After losing the chairmanship of Kadima, she resigned. However, shortly afterwards, she returned to politics at the head of a new party, Hatnuah (The Movement), which was the final nail in the Kadima coffin. Livni enlisted two former Labor chairmen who had also since been replaced (Amram Mitzna and Amir Peretz). Theirs was a single-issue (peace) party which looked and sounded the most oppositional to the party of Livni's youth. While all the other major parties were cautious and guarded towards Netanyahu, who was now the leading and fairly certain candidate for Prime Minister, Livni was fearless in her criticism.

Although Hatnuah was led by three former party leaders who should have been able to attract the Kadima electorate as well as a good share of the Labor votes, the party failed to gain traction and ended up receiving only six mandates. Both Livni and Peretz had made too many transitions. This was the third party for each of them, and this fact dented their credibility.

Netanyahu was challenged by three parties that all filled the same niche: simply being anti-Netanyahu. In contrast to previous election campaigns, in which two major parties had competed against each other, there were now three party leaders who insisted on leading the challenge to Netanyahu: Shelly Yachimovich of

Labor, Yair Lapid of Yesh Atid, and Tzipi Livni of Hatnuah, which had replaced Kadima.

For Netanyahu, who had come through four general elections with two victories and two defeats, this was the easiest campaign to navigate. He sailed through the primaries, after having gone through hell in the past to arrive at chairmanship of the Likud. He had endured six rounds of internal elections, three of them particularly difficult primaries, and had emerged victorious from five of them, with one nearing defeat to Sharon.

Up to now, Likud candidates (Begin, Shamir, Sharon, and Netanyahu) had won seven general elections to become Prime Minister. Each time, the battles had been close, hard, and uncertain, ending in a narrow victory for the party or even for the bloc. The elections had always featured a candidate of the Right against a candidate of the Left. In 2013, Netanyahu competed against a divided camp that fielded three candidates. Throughout the campaign he worked to maintain a dramatic gap that demoralized the opposition.

Netanyahu, ever wary of threats, and fearing a unification of the Center and Left against him, went to great lengths to have Lieberman's party, Yisrael Beitenu, join the Likud. When political reporter Amit Segal revealed the scoop that Netanyahu and Lieberman were merging their parties, it seemed to make no sense: why would Netanyahu be willing to pay Lieberman such a high price – a third of the combined Knesset list – in return for a union? It was perhaps double what Lieberman could achieve on his own. What the pundits failed to understand was that this move effectively decided the elections in advance. By showing off a party which polls predicted would receive forty mandates, Netanyahu sowed despair among his rivals of the Center-Left bloc. They had not managed to unite and were running as three separate parties which could collectively receive forty mandates, but taken separately they showed in the polls as two medium-sized parties and one smaller one.

Now that the Right was assured of victory, thanks to the Netanyahu-Lieberman union, religious right-wing voters permitted themselves to vote for the religious parties – Bayit Yehudi and Shas – which together received twenty-three mandates, at the expense of Likud–Yisrael Beitenu, which dropped to thirty-one mandates, eleven of them to Lieberman's party. Lieberman profited from the agreement with Netanyahu which (as in 1996) prioritized victory (even with a lower number of mandates) over a race for every seat, which might end in defeat. Experience had also shown that MKs who were placed low on the list were not necessarily worth fighting for; they sometimes caused embarrassment to the party or rebelled against its leader.

The coalition negotiations, following the elections, should have been smooth sailing, considering that almost all the parties were eager to be included in the government. However, Bayit Yehudi leaders Naftali Bennett and Ayelet Shaked (both former Netanyahu aides) had old accounts to settle, and adversaries from the past tried to ensure that they would not be part of the coalition. In order to bolster their position they joined forces with the centrist Yesh Atid party, despite the absence of any ideological connection. The Bennett-Lapid alliance proceeded to dictate the choice of coalition partners, the exclusion of ultra-Orthodox parties (which had been the focus of a negative campaign by Lapid), and the numerous major portfolios which they sought to hold.

The manner in which the government was formed was a recipe for disaster. Netanyahu could not manage a government in which he was Prime Minister, but the Minister of Finance (Lapid) and Minister of Economic Affairs (Bennett) were actually in charge. He found himself in control of only the twenty Likud mandates, while his partners – Bennett, Lapid, Lieberman, and the Shas party – each controlled factions of over ten MKs.

Netanyahu could already identify a phenomenon that became manifest later on: one axis of the coalition (Bennett-Lapid) was developing into an internal opposition to Netanyahu, with the active support of the media. This media trend was countered by *Yisrael Hayom*, a highly popular daily newspaper distributed for free, founded by Netanyahu supporter Sheldon Adelson. *Yisrael Hayom* was accused of siding with Netanyahu and against his rivals on the Left and the Right. Its widespread distribution, causing readers and advertising budgets to be diverted from other media, along with its pro-Netanyahu stance, created huge Knesset support for a law that would limit its influence. Such a move would serve the political interests of all the parties (except for Likud) as well as all of the other media, which enthusiastically promoted the law.

Netanyahu's third government, which should have been stable and harmonious, and under his absolute control, ended up lasting only two years. In the end it was the media that brought it down, leading Israel into an era characterized by the merging of politics and the media – or, to put it differently, an era of Netanyahu vs. the media (and most of the parties). The center-left ministers Livni and Lapid were dismissed in December 2014, and new elections were declared. Netanyahu was already eager to be free of this government in which he felt trapped.

During its shortened term in mid-2014, the government had to deal with a deteriorating security situation on the Gaza front. Despite being the most militarily cautious and restrained of Israel's Prime Ministers, Netanyahu was forced to respond to Hamas provocation, and he launched Operation Protective Edge, which lasted from July 8 until August 26.

With an eye on the northern front and the threat from Iran (and later Syria), Netanyahu sought to prevent an escalation that would lead to a full-blown war in Gaza, but stage by stage he was forced to intensify his military response. At first, Israel responded to the kidnapping and murder of three teenaged boys. Then Hamas and the Islamic Jihad intensified their aggression, shooting rockets not only into the southern Israeli kibbutzim and towns surrounding Gaza, but into Beer Sheba and the center of the country, and digging tunnels for the purposes of infiltrating Israel and carrying out terror attacks inside the southern towns. The Israeli response began with aerial bombings, but eventually there was no choice but to send in ground troops. The result was a fifty-day war that claimed seventy-three Israeli casualties, with somewhere between 1600 and 2800 casualties on the Palestinian side. Following efforts by Egypt, the US, and the UN, a ceasefire was obtained, bringing four years of relative quiet to the south. With Hamas now closed in from the north, east, and west by Israel and from the south by Egypt, refusing to disarm, and plagued with large-scale unemployment, it was clear to all that Gaza was a ticking time-bomb.

Netanyahu oversaw Operation Protective Edge along with Minister of Defense Yaalon and Chief-of-Staff Gantz. The three men displayed a united front which had the backing of the Israeli public, unlike the Second Lebanon War under Olmert, which had been characterized by a disagreement among the generals which eroded public confidence, and unlike the battle over the Iranian nuclear program, which had pitted the elected political echelon against the military leadership. Criticism of the government emanated this time from the two right-wing ministers Avigdor Lieberman and Naftali Bennett. Both focused their faultfinding on Minister of Defense Yaalon, whose position each of them sought to inherit. Despite their ongoing censure, the political establishment on the Left and Right, along with the media, was behind the government, the army, and the Prime Minister. He was regarded as acting responsibly and judiciously in not being drawn into a war that would lead to the reconquest of Gaza.

Netanyahu emerged from Operation Protective Edge with his "Mr. Security" image intact, despite the missiles that had been fired on Tel Aviv and Beer Sheba, despite the fact that the operation had lasted longer than expected, and despite the fact that the bodies of two soldiers, Oron Shaul and Hadar Goldin, remained in Hamas's hands. In the years that followed, their families ensured that Netanyahu would not forget them.

Heirs' government of 2013 – without the veterans

Four and a half decades after the heirs first appeared on the political map, their rise to power continued to display singular historical characteristics. Their rivals had originally regarded their advancement by their parents as nothing more than nepotism and assumed that the heirs would soon be out of the way. However, the heirs remained. Long after Sharon, Modai, and Levy had left the scene, they were still being elected to every Knesset.

Now, for the first time, they were on their own, without the veterans, most of whom were deceased; only a few of the younger fighters in the Revolt, now close to ninety, were able to get to the voting booths to show their support for their protégés. My father, who had been an Irgun commander at the age of seventeen, was already eighty-five. I watched as he arrived at the voting booth to fill in his slip with the names of all the heirs. Netanyahu was his choice for Prime Minister, to form what he hoped would be a fourth heirs' government, continuing the ninety-year Revisionist tradition of Jabotinsky-Begin-Shamir-Netanyahu and a twenty-eight year reign by just two generations since the 1977 Upheaval.

Thirty-six years after the first of the heirs became MKs, eight were in Knesset after the 2013 elections. And twenty-five years after Milo, Olmert, and Meridor had first joined the government, six heirs were now cabinet members: Prime Minister Netanyahu, Livni (who joined as minister for negotiations with the Palestinians), Livnat, Landau, Yair Shamir Jr., and Deputy Minister Tzahi Hanegbi – three from Likud, two from Yisrael Beitenu, and one from Hatnuah. In addition, in the Knesset, Yariv Levin served as chairman of the coalition.

The parents' generation had endured in the Knesset by means of "replacements" from among contemporaries, and the heirs' generation adopted the same strategy. This time it was the two most symbolic heirs who took their leave: Benny Begin and Dan Meridor. Begin, aged seventy, had maintained a love-hate relationship with politics and chose the age of seventy as the point where he would retire, like his father. But after a harmonious previous term, Netanyahu wanted him on the Likud list again. Meridor and Rivlin also begged him to submit his candidacy. Although Begin truly wished to retire, he acceded to the request but refused to campaign actively. He did not appear at the branches, refused media interviews, and disappeared from the public eye. Consequently, he lost his place on the Likud list. The voters understood that he had lost the will to fight. Had he actually competed, it would not have required much effort for him to obtain a place near the top of the list.

However, Begin surprised everyone two years later, returning to politics at the age of seventy-two and illustrating the extent to which the heirs were committed for life. Just a few hours before the Knesset list was confirmed, on January 29, 2015, Netanyahu announced that he had succeeded in persuading Begin to come back. The moment that Begin showed his willingness, he was included on the list and he went on to serve another term in which he demonstrated both his commitment to public activity and his adherence to the old grandeur of Jabotinsky and Begin. He was the only Likud MK who acted against the right-wing government's efforts to diminish intervention by the Supreme Court, to diversify the views dominating this body, and to advance initiatives such as the Nationality Law. Although he acted against the movement, he continued enjoying the universal adoration and deference that only an heir of Beginist lineage could receive.

Begin had served eighteen years in five Knessets. He and his father sat in a total of fifteen Knessets – fifty-three years of a Beginist presence and sixty-three years of political leadership from Beitar in Poland up until the new Likud; from the days of the Nazis and the Revolt against the British, until the period of Google and Facebook.

As we have seen, the heirs had started their activities at a very young age, and they remained active in the party and in politics over most of their lives. They devoted themselves to public service, even if they eventually diverged in their views. Perhaps one might say that they were addicted to their public activity, refusing to leave. The early heirs Milo and Olmert, who were forced to leave, would have preferred – even after forty years of continuous activity – to stay. Now it was the turn of the third of the early heirs. Dan Meridor had no wish to leave, even after forty-eight years of activity in the movement, thirty-two years since becoming Cabinet Secretary in Begin's government, and twenty-three years in the Knesset, of which fifteen were spent in the government. But this time, although Meridor was a candidate in the primaries, he did not become an MK. He was no longer the Likud, and the Likud was no longer Meridor. In fact, ever since his first term in the Ministry of Justice in 1988 he had been effectively disqualified. When he did receive a seat (in 1992 and in 2009) it was with the help of a major push by the leaders of the Likud. This time, he was not elected. Unlike the situation in 2009, when the Likud was lacking in confidence and seeking to return to power, this time the party was in power and fielded a great number of promising young candidates who had grown up in the movement and interacted with the party's branches. They included Gideon Saar, Gilad Erdan, Moshe Kahlon, Israel Katz, and Danny Danon. Meridor, in contrast, was occupied with security and diplomatic activity in the government, and did not appear at events where he could mingle with party members. In addition, he still maintained his stance favoring compromise in the Israeli-Arab conflict and was considered (justifiably) close to and protective of the Supreme Court, towards which the Right was apprehensive.

Meridor regretfully said goodbye to the Knesset, but he did not hide his urge for involvement in and influence on the public agenda. After the 2013 elections, journalist Nahum Barnea, who had followed Meridor over two decades, succinctly summed up a four-hour interview: "Politics is still in his blood."[1] Meridor might have recalled with some satisfaction that he and his father had served in a total of nine Knessets. The two Meridor generations, like the two generations of Begin, Olmert, and Landau, had been influential on the national level from the days of Hitler and Chamberlain in the 1940s all the way through to the second decade of the new millennium.

Even when the heirs were already grandparents, there were those who joined or returned, continuing the reign of the Revisionist second generation.

At the same time that the Irgun heirs left the Knesset, two new Lehi heirs joined the Likud: one was Yair Shamir; the other was Tzahi Hanegbi, who returned to the party of his youth. Netanyahu gave him a warm reception, forgiving him the desertion to Kadima eight years previously that had left the party broken-hearted. It helped that Netanyahu held him in high esteem and that Hanegbi had been Netanyahu's earliest supporter, visiting him at the UN in 1987 and serving as the head of his campaign headquarters in 1993. Hanegbi was also highly popular among the party's rank-and-file and was perceived as a symbol of tradition, continuing his mother's path, and as a symbol of the struggle for Yamit. Unlike Begin and Meridor, Hanegbi was also willing to invest in the requisite fieldwork. He visited every branch office in every corner of the country and disarmed his opposition. He adapted remarkably well to the demands of candidacy in the primaries, returning twenty-five years in time to the period when he had first run from branch to branch, from one potential party member to the next. Watching him one might have thought that he was the youngest candidate in the party. And indeed, contrary to expectations, Hanegbi earned a place on the Likud list and was later appointed Deputy Foreign Minister.

At the age of sixty-eight, Yair Shamir, son of the late Prime Minister Yitzhak Shamir, decided to take on the role bequeathed to him by his parents, who had been Lehi commanders. Shamir Jr., the new Land of Israel heir, replaced Begin in the Knesset – a son of a Lehi commander taking the place of a son of an Irgun commander. Shamir knew that if he did not take this opportunity, it would be too late. As Amira Lamm wrote in *Yediot Aharonot*, "From a certain perspective, this was also the fulfillment of a last will. [. . .] It was an open secret that his father had wanted to see him there."[2] Or, as Shamir Jr. himself stated, in the same interview: "My father's death was perhaps the push that brought this to fruition. I have no doubt that he would have welcomed it. He wanted very much for me to go into politics." In the Knesset he sounded just like his father, who had been born a century earlier, when Kaiser Franz Josef still reigned over Austro-Hungary. "The sea remains the same sea, and in my opinion the Arabs, as of now, remain the same Arabs. Unfortunately, the great and celebrated spring of the nations has only strengthened that."

Thanks to the combined Likud–Yisrael Beitenu List, Uzi Landau – son of Chaim Landau, a member of the Irgun General Command – also sat in the government.

With the end of this shortened term of office, and in anticipation of the elections in 2015, there was a wave of resignations by veteran heirs.

Following Milo (sixty-six), Meridor (sixty-eight), and Olmert (seventy), Limor Livnat (sixty-five) announced her resignation before the primaries. Livnat had clocked forty-five years of political activity, starting in her student days at the demonstration in 1970. After twenty-three years in the Knesset, most of them spent as a government minister, she had participated in nine election campaigns.

Another heir with a long political resume was Uzi Landau (seventy-two). After thirty-eight years of intensive activity since the Upheaval of 1977, and after twenty-nine years as an MK, he decided that it was time to step down. Uzi and his father, so similar in their worldview as well as in their outer appearance, had served a total of sixty years in the Knesset – almost the entire history of the country, from the establishment of the state until 2013.

Following one term in the Knesset, Minister Yair Shamir (seventy) felt that he had carried out his filial duty. Having spent most of his life in security- and economic-related activity, he had now also carried out the request of the only parent of the veterans' generation who had wanted his son to be active in politics.

Following all these retirements, after the 2015 elections there were still five heirs, including some younger representatives who had entered politics long after the early heirs. Tzahi Hanegbi (fifty-eight) had accumulated thirty-six years of activity with twenty-five years in the Knesset, of which fourteen were spent in the government. He and his mother, Geula Cohen, served an impressive total of forty-five years in the Knesset – some of them concurrently. Tzipi Livni (fifty-seven) had been active in politics for twenty years, fifteen of them spent in the Knesset. Yariv Levin (forty-six) was a third-generation heir who had earned a place among the Likud core despite having no genealogical connection. In addition, there were another two senior heirs, whom we shall discuss later.

Two long-time Jerusalemite heirs succeeded in achieving their very highest aspirations. Netanyahu had already become Prime Minister. Now, his neighbor, Reuven Rivlin, the oldest of all the heirs, sought to close a circle in the President's Residence, close to the home in the capital where he had grown up.

Reuven Rivlin, the first heir-President

Rivlin seemed well past his prime in 2013. The seventy-four-year-old heir had served seven most significant terms in the Knesset, with twenty-one years in government. Born in 1939, the year of Jabotinsky's death, his early years had been the period of the Second World War. He had a very full public record and was well liked in the Knesset and on the street. During the preceding two years he had been greatly disappointed at being replaced as Chairman of the Knesset, such that he was back to being a regular MK again, as he had been in the 1980s.

Rivlin was the heir with the longest history: sixty-nine years previously, at the age of five, he had already been smuggling Irgun weapons. From his earliest infancy he had imbibed belonging and commitment to the Irgun, Herut, and Begin. He had covered the longest, hardest, most Sisyphean road since his childhood in Beitar. For decades, the old Herut branch in central Jerusalem was his second home. He was an inseparable part of Herut, Likud, Beitar, and the Jerusalem municipality. The city knew him and loved him. Known by his nickname, "Ruby", he knew every Herut and Likud activist, whether he or she was born in 1920, 1940, or 1980. Not a single election campaign went by without his presence and involvement – as a child distributing Herut slips before the national elections, in the first elections in which Herut campaigned at the Hebrew University, in the town squares with Menachem Begin in the 1960s and '70s – until he watched his beloved movement win the elections and its leader, Begin, sworn in as Prime Minister.

Rivlin put his heart and soul into the Beitar Jerusalem soccer team. This had once been the team of the Irgun fighters. It was the team that was tightly bound up with the underground, with the Herut branch, with Likud of Jerusalem and of the country. In every game they played outside of the capital they encountered hundreds of fans who loved Beitar as Jabotinsky's team, Begin's team, the team that represented the opposition to the Labor establishment regime and its Hapoel team, which ruled over sports the same way that the Labor party ruled over the country.

Along with his brother Lazie, Rivlin managed to cultivate the neglected "opposition team" and led it to impressive achievements and a place in the mainstream consciousness. There are those who remember 1976 as the first time Beitar won the State Cup; many of them remember an image of the team's chairman, Rivlin, weeping with joy. I remember witnessing the mutual affection between him and the activists from all over the country when he first ran for the internal Likud elections in 1984. They viewed him as a Beitar symbol.

It was only at the age of forty-five that Rivlin moved into activity on a national scale. It happened when he was called upon to help save the Irgun veterans' camp in the seemingly hopeless battle of inheritance after Begin's resignation. While up until that point Rivlin had been Jerusalem and Jerusalem was "Ruby", he now became part of the war of the camps, fighting alongside Shamir and Arens in anticipation of the convention of 1986. Rivlin mobilized all his friends, many of them sons and daughters of Irgun and Lehi fighters, and together with the veterans he won over the Jerusalem branch, the largest in the country, thereby saving the veterans. This positioned him as a central player, and he became the leader of the most important and most influential branch in the country (which was, and remains, located in an old, neglected downtown building).

Rivlin himself, on the other hand, was destined to follow the hard road, along with Prime Minister Shamir. He was pushed aside by a different Jerusalemite heir who maintained a rivalry with him over decades. Olmert snatched Rivlin's dream by becoming Likud's candidate for Jerusalem mayor. The rivalry with Olmert drew Rivlin towards the camp of David Levy, who competed with the veterans' camp to which Rivlin was so firmly attached. This led him to hard years of contention with the veterans whom he loved, and they – despite their love for him – left their "ideological son" out of the Knesset in 1992.

In 1993, the great battle of inheritance erupted after Shamir's defeat and resignation. Once again Rivlin was committed to David Levy in the latter's struggle – this time against Rivlin's Jerusalemite neighbors, friends, and fellow heirs, Begin and Netanyahu. And then, outside the Knesset and aligned with Levy, Rivlin found himself abandoned when Levy left the Likud in 1996. Rivlin, ever loyal, took the difficult route and remained in "his" Likud, knowing that he would pay the price of his association with Levy, who was so despised by the veterans. Indeed, he paid a price and once again was not placed high enough on the party list to become an MK (he was number thirty-three, and the Likud received thirty-two mandates). Once again left out of the Knesset, and this time without a camp, it seemed that his political career had come to an end. But then there was a stroke of luck and a Likud seat in the Knesset was vacated. Rivlin was back, and he remained in the Knesset for the next two decades.

In the next battle of inheritance, in 1999, after Netanyahu's defeat and resignation, Rivlin was once again up against rival heir and fellow Jerusalemite Olmert, who sought election as Likud chairman. Rivlin led Sharon's camp to a decisive victory against him. Now he was a major player in the winning camp within the Likud, and when Sharon surprisingly also became Prime Minister, Rivlin became a minister for the first time, holding the Communications portfolio.

When Netanyahu made his return and competed against Sharon, Rivlin was on Sharon's side. For the third time he was pitted against a fellow Jerusalemite heir, in the service of a middle-generation "outsider" who was disliked by the veterans. In the 2003 primaries the veterans made him pay for this all over again, even though he had remained loyal to the Revisionist path and had not deviated from the Land of Israel ideal. The veterans liked him, but they would never forgive anyone for supporting opponents of their leaders (Begin, Shamir, and Netanyahu). Once again, he was back at the bottom of the list. And when it was clear that he again stood no chance of entering the Knesset, just as in 1992 and in 1996, another miracle happened: this time, Sharon succeeded in leading Likud to a stunning victory with thirty-eight mandates. So at the last minute, Rivlin was in.

The roller-coaster journey continued. From a hair's breadth away from losing his Knesset seat, Rivlin was catapulted from the bottom of the party list right into the role of his dreams: Speaker of the Knesset. He preferred this over-arching post, unaffiliated to any party, because of his love of the Knesset. In addition, as he told me at the time, he had begun to discern Sharon's deviation from Likud ideology. He did not want to sit in a government in which he would have to bear joint responsibility for "painful concessions" involving parts of the Land of Israel, which Sharon was already beginning to discuss.

Once again, the leader with whom Rivlin had been aligned decided to make a complete break with the Likud. When Sharon embarked on the Disengagement, Rivlin stood firmly with the veterans. And when Sharon walked out and formed Kadima in 2005, Rivlin once again displayed loyalty and stayed, although he would have been assured a good position with Sharon in his new party. Netanyahu was elected Prime Minister and finally Rivlin could stand together with an elected heir – two Jerusalemite heirs whose parents had been friends and neighbors. However, very soon afterwards, in 2006, Likud was defeated by Kadima, headed by Olmert, and Netanyahu came close to being ousted. His defense during the critical time following the defeat came from Rivlin, the oldest of the Likud MKs, who consolidated the group of younger MKs and saved the party chairman.

And so it was that when Netanyahu became Prime Minister again in 2009, it was only natural that Rivlin would be restored to the position he so loved: Chairman of the Knesset. Finally, at the age of seventy, it seemed that he had attained the pinnacle of his aspirations. Both men were happy to be back in their former positions – one in the more panoramic, symbolic role, at the helm of the Knesset, and the other in the executive role, at the helm of the state.

However, this term in office, with its demands for cooperation between government and Knesset, led to tension between the two men, as a result of which Netanyahu chose, in 2013, not to renew Rivlin's appointment, nor to appoint him as a minister. Rivlin's roller-coaster brought him back down to the level of a regular MK, while his friends served in the government. Netanyahu claimed that Rivlin had not cooperated with him, preferring to maintain good relations with the opposition, including the Arab parties, all with the intention of receiving their support in the future elections for President. As an example of his recalcitrance, Netanyahu's circle pointed to Rivlin's opposition to revoking the parliamentary immunity of MK Haneen Zoabi, of the extremist United Arab List, following her participation in the violent flotilla that attempted to break the naval blockade on Gaza. (Rivlin maintained in his defense that he had fulfilled his role as befitting Chairman of the Knesset.)

When President Shimon Peres decided against running for a second term, Rivlin announced his candidacy. He sought Netanyahu's support but received no response. All he heard were the leaked rumors in the press about a possible cancellation of the institution of the presidency – just so that Rivlin would not be appointed. In light of the tension between the two men, efforts were made to calm the situation, mediate, and restore relations between them, but to no avail. Netanyahu would not forgive Rivlin for what he viewed as a lack of loyalty. He was certain that if Rivlin was President, and it came time for him to assign the task of forming a government after the next elections, he would do everything in his power to choose anyone other than Netanyahu. At the same time, Netanyahu did not declare his support for any of the other candidates, either. Every day brought new rumors, but Netanyahu maintained a stony silence, and to Rivlin it seemed that there was no chance of receiving the appointment in view of the Prime Minister's opposition.

In the meantime, MKs were starting to sign up in support of the various candidates. First in line to support Rivlin was MK Gideon Saar – a move that later proved to be a significant factor in his own rupture with Netanyahu. It was a complex race, owing to the number of candidates and multiple rounds of voting. Tension reached a peak in the final round, held on June 10, 2014, in which Rivlin (with the official support of Netanyahu, despite his misgivings that were well known to all) vied with MK Meir Sheetrit, the candidate fielded by Livni's Hatnuah.

The forecast was that Sheetrit would win, and Rivlin was already preparing to congratulate his rival when the Knesset and the entire country discovered that he had received the votes of sixty-three MKs, while only fifty-three had cast their vote for Sheetrit. This was a personal victory, reflecting the longstanding friendship and esteem that MKs from the opposition felt for Rivlin, causing them to vote with some of his old friends from the coalition.

Reuven Rivlin, the heir who had spent a long and difficult half-century on Sisyphean work in the Jerusalem branch, the other Likud branches, and the Knesset, had now – against all odds – reached the office that he had dreamed of since his father had submitted his own candidacy for the presidency but had lost, owing to the "stain" of his affiliation with the Revisionists. He had triumphed in the race for the venerated office that his party had never yet managed to conquer. For Rivlin, his victory was a closing of three circles: for his party, for his parents, and for himself. After the results were announced, he went to visit his father's grave on the Mount of Olives, to tell him that a Rivlin would be occupying the President's Residence.

On one hand, Rivlin's road to the presidency symbolized the sense of duty that had been inculcated in the second generation of the fighting family. On the other hand, his candidacy illustrated the breach that had opened between the heirs when they reached the country's top leadership. On the way to victory he had had to overcome two senior fellow heirs: firstly, Netanyahu, the leader of his own party, with his unstated opposition, and secondly, Livni, the heiress who headed Hatnuah and fielded a different candidate. According to pundits, in the secret ballot only three heirs had cast their vote in favor of Rivlin: Uzi Landau, Yair Shamir, and Tzahi Hanegbi, who contravened the official instructions of the heads of their parties – Netanyahu and Lieberman.

The meeting of (temporary) reconciliation that was held after Rivlin's election was another indication of how close his roots were to those of Netanyahu, as well as how far they had grown from each other; how they had started out as neighbors, friends, "grandchildren" of Jabotinsky – and how political battles at the top had divided them, just as their fellow heirs had gone their separate ways in terms of their votes, parties, and worldviews.

Yossi Verter of *Haaretz* quoted Rivlin's portrayal of the situation: "It was a dispute between brothers [. . .] and the resolution of the anger was also [undertaken] between brothers." After a moment's reflection, he added, "Hatred between brothers is worst of all."[3] In a different interview, with Nehama Dweck of *Yediot Aharonot*, Rivlin again mentioned the common background:

> I have known some members of the [Likud] faction for a few years. Others I have known for ages, and there's one whom I've known longer than all the rest. His name is Bibi. I've known him for sixty-five years. I was at his circumcision. For fifty-five out of the sixty-five years we were almost like brothers. For the past ten years there have been ups and downs. When he started out, I helped him. I told Benny Begin, Dan Meridor, and Roni Milo that Bibi was coming from New York, and that he would be the party chairman. They were angry at me, but I insisted, and I was among those who supported him. [. . .] Bibi helped me to become Chairman of the Knesset.[4]

Netanyahu congratulated Rivlin in the Knesset in the same spirit:

> Ruby, I wish to congratulate you on your election. [. . .] You draw from the deep well of Jewish tradition and Zionist tradition. I am very familiar with these values. We recognize and appreciate the long journey that you have made; that your father, of blessed memory, made.

In their meeting, he added: "We have known each other for decades. [. . .] We are both Jerusalemites, sons of professors, educated on Jabotinsky's teachings, and we have much else in common – for instance, our soccer team."

The day after his election, Eitan Haber published an opinion piece entitled, "Ruby is still Ruby", in which he wagered:

> Last night he was probably already humming the Beitar anthem, whose words were penned by Jabotinsky: ". . . Though a slave or a tramp/You were created the son of a king/adorned with David's crown." Rivlin is one of the few individuals in the Likud faction [. . .] who does not need to learn by heart the words of the song which he regards as the ultimate anthem. He absorbed it with his mother's milk.[5]

Predictably, the first event that Rivlin attended after his election was the annual memorial for the casualties of the *Altalena*. In attendance at the Nahalat Yitzhak cemetery were the Prime Minster and the President, and both reiterated the same promise that had first been uttered by Begin sixty-six years previously: "Never a civil war." Veterans in their eighties and nineties wiped tears of pain and pride, deeply gratified that the speakers commemorating the fighters of the Irgun, the *Altalena*, the legacy of Begin and Jabotinsky, were the President and the Prime Minister of Israel. Both heirs.

The reconciliation did not last. Although Rivlin and Netanyahu shared the same legacy, the same veneration of the underground fighters who had been killed by the British, and seemingly similar political views, there had been too much antagonism between them.

Figure 29.1 Two "Jabotinsky Princes", neighbors, sons of distinguished Jerusalem professors, brothers, and opponents: President Ruby Rivlin and PM Benjamin
Netanyahu.

They were now two Revisionists who had become Prime Minister and President: a right-wing Prime Minister in an age of political, social, and national polar-
ity, and a President who chose inclusive and all-encompassing civic statesmanship
as the banner of his office. A Prime Minister who was constantly being attacked
by – and attacking in return – the elite and the media, and a President who was
embraced and courted by the elite and the media (even turning a blind eye to his
visits to settlements and his repeated oath of loyalty to the Land of Israel). Netanyahu and his government, as we shall see, would launch a struggle to balance and
limit the powers of the Supreme Court, while the President would consistently
take the side of the court and of the Arab minority.

Throughout their term they were at odds, as though Jabotinsky was not their
common teacher and guide; as though they had not grown up in the same ideological movement.

Elections of 2015 – the world vs. Netanyahu

Netanyahu ran for the 2015 elections with an astounding record of thirty-three
years of public service, starting in the Israeli embassy in Washington, followed by
twenty-four years in the Knesset, including sixteen in the government and seven

as head of the opposition. He had run seven times for Likud chairman (achieving success six times) and six times for Prime Minister (achieving success three times) and had served as Prime Minister for nine years.

However, it quickly became apparent that nine years was far too long in the eyes of those waiting to succeed him, all those waiting for his downfall, all his opponents in the Likud, on the Right, in the Knesset, and in the media. He ran for elections with almost the entire Knesset wanting him to leave, especially those who opposed him for economic, ideological, or political reasons.

There were so many who had accounts to settle with Netanyahu. First and foremost, there was the media, which had always opposed the leaders of the Right who questioned the existing order and disturbed the elite, which sought to maintain the status quo. This had been the case since the days of Jabotinsky, continuing through the terms of Begin and Shamir, in the days of the underground, the Herut, and the Likud, and up until Netanyahu. Netanyahu had initially received a warm reception from the media lasting for about a decade from the days of the embassy in the US and at the UN until his entry into Israeli politics. But everything changed when he opposed the Oslo Accords, and the hostility towards him reached a peak after Rabin's assassination. After that, as far as the Israeli media was concerned, it was he who had destroyed the dream of peace. Not Arafat, not the terrorists who brought rivers of blood to the streets of Israel, not even Rabin's assassin – Yigal Amir – but rather Netanyahu. His first term as Prime Minister (1996–1999) consisted of three years of venomous coverage that enlisted all who viewed themselves as having been mistreated by him or who coveted his seat. The campaign continued year after year and reached a climax in 2013 with efforts to pass a law that would place limitations on *Yisrael Hayom*, the newspaper that attempted to defend Netanyahu against all the negativity. The television channels, too, were unhappy, owing to the policy of competition that Netanyahu sought to implement with the aim of decentralizing the media.

Within the Likud, his successors were getting tired of waiting for his retirement. Likud ministers were grumbling. After six years in government, being in power was taken for granted, and every minister sought to upgrade his or her status. As an example, Moshe Kahlon, Minister of Communications, who introduced reform in the cellphone industry that brought Israelis considerable savings in their monthly payments, had left the Likud two years previously. In 2015 he headed a new Knesset list that he had formed – Kulanu (All of Us) – which now threatened to take a share of Netanyahu's votes. Another eligible heir, Gideon Saar, had left the Knesset and was waiting quietly in the wings. On the right there waited two successors who had started off with Netanyahu in the Likud. One was Avigdor Lieberman, who had been director-general of the PMO in 1996 but had been "dismissed of his own accord". Since then he had headed his own right-wing party, whose voters were mostly Russian immigrants, and had maintained a cycle of entering and leaving the governments of Sharon, Olmert, and Netanyahu. Another was Naftali Bennett, who had been Netanyahu's chief-of-staff when the Likud was in the opposition, and who, in 2013, had been elected chairman of the Religious Zionist Bayit Yehudi party. Both Lieberman and Bennett had accounts to settle with Netanyahu, both on the personal level, in the wake of their dismissals, and also in the wake of Operation Protective Edge in Gaza, in which they had formed a vociferous opposition from within the government. In addition, they were also unhappy about the clear bias of *Yisrael Hayom* in favor of Netanyahu, to the exclusion of anyone else.

The opposition, of course, fought Netanyahu and the Likud as expected in an election campaign. This time, however, in addition to the left-wing opposition and the new parties discussed earlier, Netanyahu was also faced with parties headed by former partners whom he had dismissed from the government and who now sought revenge. These included Lapid's Yesh Atid, Livni's Hatnuah, and Labor, which had been split apart five years earlier by Netanyahu and Barak when Barak entered the government.

Netanyahu thus stood almost alone against powerful forces in politics, the elite, and the media. This state of affairs seeped into the public sentiment, and the general ambiance of the 2015 elections was "Enough of Netanyahu". This time his wife, Sara, was targeted too, with endless negative publicity about her and her family.

Labor and Hatnuah were united behind a single candidate, under the collective name Zionist Union. Thanks to the reinforcement provided by the Revisionist heiress, daughter of Sara and Eitan Livni of the Irgun, the Zionist Union candidate – Labor chairman Yitzhak Herzog – led the polls, ahead of Likud and all the other parties. The other center-left party, led by Yair Lapid, who had just served a term as Minister of Finance (a sure recipe for losing popularity), now trailed behind.

Behind the scenes, a deal began to form among most of the parties, aimed at ousting Netanyahu at all costs. There were intensive discussions, and a quiet understanding was reached between parties of the opposition and the coalition that the day after the elections, they would join forces – even if this required a rotation between two or even three heads of parties, who collectively brought ten or more mandates to the table. The main objective was just to be rid of Netanyahu.

The Zionist Union – the new Labor – continued to lead in the polls up until four days before the elections. A week before the fateful date, Israel's best-known public surveys expert, Mina Tzemach, predicted twenty-six mandates for Labor and twenty-two for Likud. Even on the morning of election day, the prevailing view was that the Likud would receive twenty mandates or just slightly more, while the Zionist Union would receive between twenty-five and thirty. Given that Herzog was acceptable to most camps within the Knesset, including religious and right-wing parties, the result seemed certain – especially in light of the open secret that most of the parties had already agreed among themselves to form a coalition that would bring an end to Netanyahu's reign after nine years and three terms as Prime Minister.

A selection of quotes from the days prior to the elections testifies to the degree to which Netanyahu was detested by the media, and the general consensus that his seat was lost. Six days before the election (March 11, 2015), Ben Caspit, a senior political commentator for *Maariv*, wrote: "As things are looking right now,

Netanyahu is going to finish the elections with less than ten mandates." The next day, the political correspondent for *Globes* financial paper wrote:

> The man who hasn't had dealings with regular people for the past six years, was unaware of what was actually happening here. He continued talking about Iran, failing to note what was happening to the Likud and what was happening to his popularity. He was the last to realize what was going on. Six years spent in the ivory tower of Balfour Street [the Prime Minister's Residence in Jerusalem] with its torn carpets disconnected him from the Israeli reality. [. . .] If someone in Netanyahu's environment would have had the courage to tell him to his face how he was perceived outside of this aquarium, and to provide him a real picture of the situation, perhaps he would not have ended up shortening his term in office with his own hands.[6]

The following day, Sima Kadmon wrote in *Yediot Aharonot*:

> At the end of the last week of this election campaign, the party in power is in a negative slide, and one has the impression that Prime Minister Netanyahu is not managing to do anything in the meantime that could stop it.[7]

Her colleague Nahum Barnea wrote:

> Israelis have had enough of Netanyahu. They have had enough of him; he has had enough of them. After nine years at the head of the government – three plus four plus two, and after twenty-two years in the headlines, the magic has worn off.[8]

The same day, the longtime economic correspondent for *Haaretz*, Nehemia Strassler, wrote: "The people want a change. The collective mind understands that it can't be that one person is in power here for nine years – of them, six consecutive years – and then continues for another four."[9] Alon Idan, also writing in *Haaretz*, opined: "Netanyahu will not win this election."[10]

Three days to go (March 14) and Uri Misgav wrote in *Haaretz*, "Read my lips: Herzog will head the next government. My mandates forecast has changed: Zionist Union – 26; Likud – 19."[11] The next day, Ben Caspit summed it up in his column in *Maariv*:

> Right now, his situation looks bad. These elections are not about Iran or Hamas; they're not even about the housing crisis. It's a referendum on Benjamin Netanyahu. It seems to me that the public doesn't want him anymore. Right, Left – it doesn't matter. He has worn us down; we have worn him down.[12]

On election day (March 17), Barak Ravid Of *Haaretz* wrote, "Whether Netanyahu has internalized this or not, the election campaign showed how cut off he is from public opinion."[13]

Netanyahu could always smell danger. He knew when he was about to lose in 1996, and he won his victory after turning the world upside down to get two parties to join him, at tremendous cost. He knew that he was going to lose in 1999, when he was unable to get Minister of Defense Itzik Mordechai to remain, and his departure was the last straw that turned the voters against him. In 2015, too, Netanyahu saw what was going on. However, the pundits failed to realize two things. The first was that Netanyahu had already come to an agreement with the two ultra-Orthodox parties. The second was Netanyahu's ability to mobilize in the final week.

In the days leading up to the election, Netanyahu embarked on an "SOS" campaign, warning right-wing voters that he was going to lose. The jubilant media were only too happy to spread his message far and wide. Not only did it match their own forecast, it also reinforced their hope for his imminent downfall. And thus Netanyahu appeared day and night on every television program or radio interview that was willing to host him.

Netanyahu also made extensive, ground-breaking use of his Facebook and Twitter accounts, disseminating his call to mobilize. A year after the elections, Amit Segal revealed in an investigative report on News 2, "This is how Netanyahu won the 2015 elections", how Netanyahu built a war machine based on the assumption that the classic media would be biased against him and his party. The solution was, in the words of Tzuriel Sharon, manager of the mobile content for the Likud campaign, "to operate in relation to our audience through channels that bypassed filters."[14] Segal revealed a detail he learned from the election campaign manager, Momo Filber (later to become a state witness in the Bezeq-Walla-Elowitz affair): no less than a hundred thousand SMSs were sent out in the week before the elections with a message from Minister Miri Regev and MK Benny Begin.

On the morning of the elections, things looked bad for Netanyahu following Livni's announcement the previous evening that she was foregoing the rotation agreement and would agree for Herzog alone to serve as Prime Minister. Segal revealed that on election day, five million SMSs were sent, along with a million recorded telephone messages. (For the sake of comparison, in Britain this would equal seven million SMSs; in the USA – thirty-three million phone messages.)

On election day Netanyahu also exposed a campaign by his opponents that had American funding (the V15 movement), which was urging voters from sectors generally negative towards Netanyahu, including Arabs, to go out and vote. Netanyahu's message to his voters – "The Arabs are flocking to the voting booths" – will forever be remembered as the reason for his victory, although it was just one factor, and it was uttered at six in the evening, just before election day drew to a close.

In almost every election campaign in which the candidate of the Right emerged victorious, there was a left-wing artist or entertainer who spoke at a Labor election rally in a manner that was pejorative towards the Mizrahi population, which was generally supportive of Likud. Perhaps the example that comes most immediately to mind is the case of Dudu Topaz, discussed earlier in this book. In the 2015 elections it was the left-wing artist Yair Garboz who managed to offend anyone who was religious or Mizrahi, making disdainful reference to the "amulet-kissing, idol-worshipping" supporters of Netanyahu. Once again, the Mizrahi and religious sectors were being portrayed as primitive and ignorant, and once again they were incensed.

The imminent rise of the Left to power was feared most of all among the settlers of Judea and Samaria. For this reason, in the last days of the campaign the Religious Zionist sector mobilized in full force. Just days before the elections, the well-known settler leader Daniella Weiss organized an event at the same square in Tel Aviv where Garboz had spouted his hateful words. It seems to have been on that Saturday night that the election pendulum starting to swing in the other direction: a great wave of activists inspired the right-wing camp with the urge to vote. This was also the point where the Religious Zionist camp deviated from support for its natural party – Bayit Yehudi – and voted for Netanyahu instead. I remember that I spent the day after the rally in Jerusalem, as part of the sales campaign for my first book in Hebrew – *Hanesikhim* (The Princes) – and spoke with young religious saleswomen in several bookshops. The astounding statement that I heard from the first saleswoman was repeated by the second, the third, and the tenth: "I'm for Bennett, but I'm voting Netanyahu," or "I'm with Bayit Yehudi, but I'm voting Likud."

Once again, the voters of the Right, the periphery, and the religious sector were coming to the aid of the embattled Likud leader, just as they had in 1981 for Begin and in 1996 for Netanyahu. In all three instances, the polls pointed to a crushing defeat, and the general feeling among the public was that Begin and Netanyahu (twice) were "finished".

At the close of election day, as Israelis sat watching the preliminary results, they were once again presented with a draw, which gradually broke as the night went on, with the number of Labor mandates dropping and the Likud climbing until it reached thirty – somewhere between five and ten more mandates than had been predicted. It turned out that Netanyahu had drawn in voters from the satellite parties in the very last days of the campaign, with the Bayit Yehudi party suffering the greatest loss.

Now, with Likud holding thirty mandates, there was no party among the Right or the Religious Zionists that could go against the will of the voters and form an alternative government, in accordance with the original plan. Netanyahu was no longer anxious that President Rivlin would entrust the formation of the new government to a different candidate. And this time he did not repeat the mistake he had made two years previously: he invited the natural right-wing and religious coalition partners to join Likud. At first he arrived at a narrow majority of sixty-one MKs; later, Lieberman also joined after being promised the Defense portfolio, even though his faction had only five MKs.

Netanyahu's fourth government featured only three heirs: himself, Tzahi Hanegbi, and Yariv Levin. Begin was an MK who focused his efforts on the Foreign Affairs and Security Committee, and on the struggle for minority rights. President Reuven Rivlin was another center of power. The last of the surviving veterans saw their two heirs – two disciples of Jabotinsky – occupying the

President's Bureau and the Prime Minister's Office. They ignored the differences of opinion between the two men, preferring to focus on the achievement that they represented. Rivlin and Netanyahu continued to appear at the memorial for the casualties of the *Altalena* – the annual event that symbolizes perhaps more than any other the persecution of the Irgun. By their presence and their words, the two leaders showed recognition for the event that had been presented over many years as a putsch by Begin and the Irgun, while the blood of the fighters and Holocaust survivors, injured and killed by fire at Ben-Gurion's command, flowed into the sea. My father and the father of Ofer Eitani, fighters of Lehi and the Irgun, were proud.

Unstoppable in his fourth government – Netanyahu III

On May 14, 2015, Netanyahu presented his fourth government. This was a new, "third generation" Netanyahu. Netanyahu I had been a diplomat, a feted ambassador to the US and the UN in the 1980s. Netanyahu II had been chairman of the Likud and leader of the nation intermittently during the 1990s and at the beginning of the new millennium. Now, he was no longer held back; he was freed of any obligation to those who had stood in his way at home, all those inside and outside the party who had undermined him, all who had competed or incited against him in politics, or in the media, or among the elites. He no longer had any hopes or expectations of them.

As "Netanyahu the diplomat" he had enjoyed support, esteem, and even admiration in the media and among the elite. In his second phase, "Netanyahu the politician", he had been given the cold shoulder by the media, the elite, and the Left, which ever since his lead in the polls over Rabin, and certainly since Rabin's murder, had been bitterly hostile. Still, even during the twenty years of his three terms as Prime Minister, as head of the opposition, and as Minister of Finance and Foreign Minister, there was still some sort of relationship and interaction (albeit antagonistic) between the two sides. The elections of 2015 managed to cut off all connection. The blowup with the media over legislation relating to the media and its decentralization had destroyed the bridge between them. The conflict had climaxed with most of the parties aligning against Netanyahu and with the media, leading to the dissolution of the government and the difficult election campaign in which Netanyahu appeared to stand no chance. With constant attacks by the media, which viewed him as endangering their economic future and as blocking the peace process (the emphasis varying from one source to the next), painting a consistently abhorrent picture of the Prime Minister, his wife, and his family, Netanyahu reached the end of the election campaign with nothing left but anger.

The end of the 2015 elections witnessed the final dialogue between Netanyahu and the mainstream press. As mentioned, the latter had been eager to host the desperate Netanyahu on any program and any channel. It had been a sort of game, with every question posed to him meant as a blow, and every response he gave intended as a counter-blow. It was a fight between the side that was close to a win, finally, after twenty years, and the other side, who had fought all his life, knowing that he was lost from the outset and that only a transcendent effort or a miracle would change this reality.

In the end, it was this reality itself that turned out to be the miracle. It was this bare-fisted fight that led Israel's "underdog tribes" to unite around Netanyahu. The more the presenters and commentators bashed him, and the longer he stayed in the fight, answering them, the more votes he gathered among the right-wing bloc (which grew demographically from one election to the next). By the time he emerged from the 2015 elections, he was a changed man: his consultants and close circle were no longer significant influences. He stood alone now, crowned with his experience, his success, his wife at his side, suffering along with him, and also his elder son, Yair, who also pulled no punches during the campaign.

The new Netanyahu put together an unequivocally, unapologetically right-wing–religious coalition that was quite different from all its predecessors. It was the first Likud government that liberated itself from the right-wing "inferiority complex" that had developed over four lonely, demoralizing decades in the opposition, causing it – when it came to power – to fear ruling alone. Electoral victory had, until now, been followed by apologies, or compromise, or an invitation to moderate individuals or parties, which invariably led in the direction of a centrist, rather than right-wing, government.

Begin had built a coalition with a large centrist party of ex-Labor figures and brought in the Laborite Moshe Dayan as Minister of Defense. Shamir had twice chosen to form a unity government with Labor. Netanyahu had formed a right-wing government in 1996, but he had learned his lesson after the elite fought him from his first moment in office until he was ousted. Sharon had brought Labor on board and had eventually adopted the Labor ideology. Netanyahu had brought elements of the Labor party – Kadima, Hatnuah, and Yesh Atid – into both of his previous governments.

This time he had no choice but to establish a right-wing government with no "stamp of approval" from the other side. The opposition parties were already set against him. Even in mid-term, when he was ready to appease the Labor leader, Herzog, with the Foreign Ministry and the Ministry of Defense in order to introduce a moderating factor that would balance the pressure from the right, Herzog faced a storm of protest from his own party and the media. And so Netanyahu had to live with a right-wing–religious–ultra-Orthodox coalition, with no counterbalance, even though in principle he maintained that the Prime Minister should be situated in the center of his cabinet, with at least one party on both his right and his left.

From the moment he formed his government, Netanyahu was at war with the elite, just as the underground and Herut had been under constant attack eighty years previously, and just as Netanyahu himself had been a target after his victory in 1996. Once again he faced a media storm on an almost daily basis. As in 1996, the situation quickly escalated to the level of police investigations: case 1000, 2000, 3000, 4000. Every few weeks a new case broke, with a different figure in his close circle being questioned and another of his advisors being offered immunity if he agreed to be a state witness and help to incriminate his boss. Every evening the news broadcast on television opened with senior reporters sharing leaked allegations and quotes, filling the public sphere with ballooning condemnation of Netanyahu and his wife, and later on even allusions to allegations against his son.

Hot on the heels of the investigations and reports came the demonstrations in the streets and outside the home of the Attorney General, Major-General (res.) Avihai Mandelblit, who was urged to pursue the investigations and indict the Prime Minister. There was no restraint and no respect for the legal process; just heavy, ongoing pressure on the legal establishment and specifically on the Attorney General. Although Mandelblit approved and oversaw the extensive investigations and the unprecedented recruiting of state witnesses, he was himself "suspect", insofar as he had been Netanyahu's cabinet secretary and was the son of an Irgun veteran. As far as the media and the public were concerned, Netanyahu was guilty even before the investigations were concluded. Calls for his resignation accompanied his entire term in office, of which hardly a day went by without police questioning and news headlines.

When it started to appear that public pressure alone would force Netanyahu into resignation, what happened was, surprisingly, the opposite. Netanyahu liberated himself completely from any dependence on positive press, deciding that there was no longer any point in trying to explain himself to journalists or political experts. He stopped appearing on television, on the radio, and in the press, since cooperation only helped his attackers by lending credibility to the media.

From this point onwards Netanyahu was in open confrontation with the media. The masks that had been the outward representation of their relationship for two and a half decades were removed. The fiction of an objective press that criticized Netanyahu on substantive issues was laid to rest. The Prime Minister was simply no longer willing to cooperate. In the past, with each new scandal that made the news he would appear, meet, explain, and request fairer treatment. Now everything was in the open. Netanyahu told the country flatly that the media was trying to bring him down. He responded to reports by police and legal reporters with direct, written statements in which he accused the press of attempting to oust him, and the police of leaking material with the intention of harming him and his family. He had a following of millions on his Facebook, Instagram, and Twitter accounts, where he posted messages on a daily basis. He also used these platforms to showcase his activity, which was not reported anywhere in the press. The press was now forced to quote the Prime Minister's Facebook posts in its coverage of him.

Amnon Lord, writing in *Yisrael Hayom* on September 14, 2017, minced no words describing this situation:

> It is highly doubtful whether there is any moral validity at all to an investigation that is being undertaken against someone – the Prime Minister – who has had an unprecedented, intensive campaign of incitement, hatred, and character assassination maintained against him for more than twenty years. All the investigations are products of the "law of preservation of hatred". They would never have come into existence were it not for the impetus of

the character assassination. [. . .] One might have expected, after the Prime Minister stabilized the country in the wake of the defense catastrophes caused by politicians and defense personnel, and after launching Israel into an age of growth, success, and a solid international standing, that a bit of the credit would adhere to him personally. That he would finally be treated to legitimacy. It is a great wonder: After eight and a half years as Prime Minister, this past year has marked a dramatic change in discourse, and from complete de-legitimization of the State of Israel we find ourselves in a situation of complete de-legitimization of the Prime Minister.[15]

The all-encompassing alliance that formed against him in the 2015 elections was maintained, and this changed Netanyahu, freeing him from the rules of the game which he had adhered to for so many years. He felt no obligation towards his coalition partners (who had planned to topple him), nor to his ministers, most of whom contributed little in terms of either action or solidarity. He certainly owed nothing to the academic, business, and cultural elites, who constrained and harassed him from every direction and in every possible way.

While by all accounts it seemed that the public had been swept along in the hurricane of the media, police, and legal system and would reject its recently elected leader, what happened was the opposite. As during the election campaign, the massive, overt, nightly attacks on Netanyahu caused his popularity to rise. While before the election campaign the polls had predicted just over twenty mandates, the Likud climbed, under fire, as it were, to thirty. Suddenly it seemed that the Prime Minister had the trust of most of the nation, which did not believe in the investigations and the political commentary. Sometimes it seemed that the television pundits were Netanyahu's greatest asset: while Amnon Abromowitz boosted television ratings with his ferocious criticism of the Prime Minister, he brought Netanyahu an extra ten mandates. The more combative, venomous, and direct the attacks were, the more the Right united around him.

The Left and Center, too, underwent a shift – from opposition and criticism to full-blown hatred and war. However, the campaign against Netanyahu showed that this was not the same Israel. The country was now decidedly right-wing, having lost its illusions of peace after all the Israeli offers that had been answered with terror: Arab missiles launched from Iraq in 1990, ongoing attacks, two Intifadas, and a record number of horrific terror attacks specifically after the concessions signed in Oslo and after the Disengagement from Gaza. This was the Israel whose cities had now experienced missiles raining down on them for the first time since the country's establishment and that no longer followed blindly the slogans of the Left and the Center promising a political settlement. This Israel wanted a right-wing government whose policy would not be based on illusions. From a distance of just a two or three hours' drive, Israelis followed with horror the killing of hundreds of thousands in Syria and the beheadings by ISIS. They no longer had any patience for the rational, accommodating messages of the Left and the Center, and became increasingly supportive of Netanyahu. He was the only person who had warned decades previously of the danger of Iran; the only person who had insisted on focusing on Iran, even if this entailed conflict with world powers. He was the man who, together with his right-wing camp, had warned of the dangers of the Oslo Accords and of the Disengagement. This was the leader who had almost been flattened in the 2005 elections when he warned of fireballs being launched from Gaza towards Tel Aviv.

After losing seven aides who were subjected to questioning, three of whom had been persuaded by the police to become state witnesses against him, Netanyahu was left almost alone (except for Ron Dermer, ambassador to the US; Tzahi Braverman, cabinet secretary; Yoav Horowitz, head of his bureau; and some new, ideological young activists). He could have recruited new aides, consultants and experts, but by this stage he preferred to handle the battle himself. He trusted only himself and engaged in the fight of his life alone, with his wife Sara.

The first "Netanyahu effect" that developed out of the 2015 elections was that the media adopted a defensive pose, to counter its image as being affiliated with the left-wing, anti-Netanyahu camp. Right-wing (and generally religious) journalists and commentators were given room to express their views. Some spoke up openly in support of Netanyahu; others sufficed with criticism of their Left-affiliated colleagues who made his life a misery.

The second "Netanyahu effect" of 2015 was that his opponents now directed their energies mainly in the direction of police and legal channels in the hope of toppling him, since it seemed impossible to defeat him in elections. The road to removing Netanyahu from the national agenda seemingly no longer passed through the voting booth; now it was a matter of police investigations, state witnesses, arrests, and demonstrations against the Attorney General.

The third effect was felt especially after the ongoing barrage of reports about police investigations not only failed to weaken Netanyahu but strengthened him. The media, giving up on leaders of the Left and Center who had proved to be no match for Netanyahu in either the elections or the polls, began to cultivate anyone on the Right who was not Netanyahu and who might stand a chance of taking him on and inheriting his seat one day. Perhaps, if and when charges were pressed against him, other right-wing leaders – perhaps even in the Likud – would announce that they could not sit in a government whose leader faced such serious allegations. Thus, leaders of the Right and of Likud began to receive positive coverage and exposure of the sort that right-wing figures had enjoyed up until now only if they changed their views or made statements against their parties. Those on the Right who had been cultivated and embraced by the media up until now were the "moderates", or the opposition to Begin, Shamir, or Netanyahu, or those who had deserted the Likud for the Center or the Left.

Like Netanyahu personally, his right-wing–religious government also felt increasingly liberated vis-à-vis the legal system, which was perceived as biased in favor of the Left and as undermining the authority of the government and the elected Knesset. In his first two terms, Netanyahu had taken care to show the proper respect towards the Supreme Court. But after confrontation with the legal system and the media, in which he found himself mired in endless investigations, a close encounter with electoral defeat, and then the threat of being put on trial,

Netanyahu was now in his fourth term and both sides were engaged in open battle. On one hand, there were investigations and leaks throughout the Prime Minister's term; on the other hand, the Right accused the Supreme Court of functioning as an operations base for the left-wing parties and movements.

Minister of Justice Ayelet Shaked of the Religious Zionist Bayit Yehudi party set as an objective the appointment of conservative judges. They would serve as a counter-balance to the judges of the "judicial activism" stream, which arrogated to the courts areas of authority that belonged to the government. With the assistance of Likud minister (and fighting family heir) Yariv Levin, Shaked managed to bring about a revolution in the composition of the courts, including the Supreme Court. The committee for the appointment of judges, which she headed, instituted a revolution the likes of which had not been seen since the rise of the Right to power, forty years previously. In an interview published in *Yediot Aharonot*, Shaked summed up the revolution as follows:

> From a body responsible for interpreting the law, the court has transformed itself into the body responsible for policy. [. . .] In the past, there were sectors of the population that felt that the Supreme Court did not represent them. Today it represents everybody. It is more diverse, more conservative. [. . .] not a branch of Meretz.[16]

The reaction from the left-wing opposition and media was not long in coming. Former president of the Supreme Court Dorit Beinish declared, "There is a misunderstanding here as to what democracy is. These are demagogic statements that belong to a different system of government."[17]

The movement founded by the generation of veterans, which had rebelled against the Mapai socialist establishment and against the British occupiers, was once again back to rebelling against the establishment – this time, the legal establishment. A number of laws were legislated which aroused the ire of the opposition and the media. One was aimed at constraining bodies that received funding from foreign countries that were trying to interfere in Israeli politics. Another was the Nationality Law, a Basic Law establishing that Israel is a Jewish state, and defining its anthem and flag. With regard to the latter, Yariv Levin, addressing the Knesset in place of the Prime Minister, proposed the law as "expressing with great clarity Herzl's vision, according to which Israel is not a state like any other, but rather, first and foremost, the nation-state of the Jewish People."[18]

Most of the opposition parties and most of the media were opposed to the law. Former Labor Prime Minister Ehud Barak spoke of a war against it, "for which we should enlist with heads held high."[19]

The Nationality Law exposed once again the extent to which the heirs had gone their different ways, in both personal and ideological terms. When it came to the Arab-Israeli conflict, there were two camps: on one side were President Rivlin, the Prime Minister, Minister Yariv Levin, MK Begin, and the heirs who had left the party: Landau and Shamir; on the other side were the "moderates" – Livni – and those no longer in the Knesset: Meridor, Olmert, and Milo. On "internal" questions concerning democracy, minorities, and relations between government and the courts, the division was different, with Rivlin and Begin joining the "moderates". President Rivlin, leading the battle alongside the other long-time Jerusalem heirs Meridor and Begin, entered into direct personal and ideological conflict with the Prime Minister, declaring, "If I sign the Nationality Law, I will do so in Arabic."[20] He went on to explain his opposition:

> This atmosphere of de-legitimization, this atmosphere in which "everything is political", is filtering down to the public, which is getting the message that there's no longer any overall consideration of the good of the state; there's only governance. And democracy, in such an environment, means that the majority decides. Democracy means that the power of whoever happens to be the majority, has the final say. And having lived in the days of "no Herut and no Maki [the Communist Party]" – I know what that means.

In his speech at the opening of the twentieth Knesset's winter session, the President invoked his ideological forefathers Jabotinsky and Begin against his opponents:

> I see no reason to bring support for what I am saying, in the form of quotes from Jabotinsky or Begin, concerning the essence of democracy and the importance of its institutions. The reason for this is that the revolution that is taking place before our eyes is not a continuation of Revisionism, or of Beginism. On the contrary: this political revolution has scorned Jabotinsky-style grandeur. It views Begin as someone who only aspired to recognition on the part of the old elite; who wanted nothing more than a positive editorial in *Haaretz*; above all – someone who was not sufficiently courageous to come to terms with the Upheaval of 1977. Therefore, despite all these years in power, according to the architects of this political revolution, the upheaval is not yet complete. The bastions of power of institutionalized Israeli democracy – the defense bodies, the media, and the professional administration – headed by the legal system – have yet to be conquered.[21]

Finally – the American administration gives its backing

The next major liberating development was the election of the new US President. Netanyahu had struggled for ten years with Presidents Clinton and Obama, whose worldviews were profoundly opposed to his own. They had believed that the Israeli-Palestinian conflict was the crux of the problems of the Middle East and had followed a policy of pressuring Israel into withdrawals and concessions in order to achieve peace. Netanyahu, on the other hand, had always believed that the root of the problem of the Middle East was Islamist extremism and violence, which was cultivated in and exported from Iran. He believed that history proved that concessions – to the Nazis, to Arafat's PLO, to the Iranians – always brought additional demands, intensified violence, and more terror.

With the rise of President Donald Trump, who viewed Israel as the best friend and most reliable partner the US had in all the world, as an asset and not as a burden, Netanyahu was freed. Finally, there was a US President who came to Israel to offer encouragement, rather than to pressure for withdrawals. There was a Vice President, Mike Pence, whose ideological views, as evidenced throughout his years of service in the Congress and as Governor of Indiana, were extremely close to Netanyahu's own. The Vice President was regarded in Washington as a symbol of pure traditional conservatism. He had maintained his faith in the US-Israel alliance throughout his years in the public service, viewing Israel as a strategic asset and a partner in values. He had supported Israel's right to strike and destroy the Iranian nuclear program while the Obama administration had vehemently opposed this. As governor, he had signed a law prohibiting trade with companies that boycotted Israel. His perception of Israel was based on his evangelist Christian faith that Israel was "divinely promised".

Israel's standing in Washington changed dramatically. The Israeli ambassador in Washington, Ron Dermer, reaped the fruits of the intensive efforts he had invested in relations with the Republican Party even during the Democratic presidency. Despite his modesty and the fact that he had only rarely made appearances in the Israeli media, it was clear to anyone familiar with the situation in the US that he enjoyed a rare status in the Congress and, now, in the US administration. With a President like Trump, a Vice President like Pence, and a National Security Advisor like John Bolton, Dermer was set to become the most well connected and most influential of all ambassadors to Washington. He shared with the leaders of the world's great power a similar worldview which he had consolidated many years previously as a Jewish-American boy growing up in Florida.

President Trump surprised the world with unconventional decisions. He appointed David Friedman, an avowed and unapologetic supporter of Israel, as his ambassador to the country. Friedman responded to the appointment by declaring that he looked forward to fulfilling his role from the embassy "in Israel's eternal capital, Jerusalem."[22] It was no longer the "objective" State Department that was dictating the tone, but rather the ambassador, representing the administration. He landed in Israel, drove straight to the Western Wall in Jerusalem to pray, and immediately announced that he would be residing in Jerusalem. Following the murder of an American-Israeli by a terrorist with a knife, Friedman chose to visit the victim's home town of Efrat, in the Gush Etzion Bloc, where he delivered a eulogy that stirred the country: "America grieves as one of its citizens was brutally murdered by a Palestinian terrorist. Ari Fuld was a passionate defender of Israel and an American patriot."[23]

Trump placed his son-in-law, Jared Kushner, and Jason Greenblatt – two representatives of his innermost circle – in charge of Middle East negotiations, signaling the importance that he attached to reaching an agreement, but at the same time indicating that he did not subscribe, as his predecessors had, to the view that the responsibility for making peace lay mainly with Israel. Netanyahu welcomed the gesture, while the Palestinians responded with anger, as expressed in Abbas's ultimatum to the Americans that he would return to negotiations only if Greenblatt was replaced with an "objective" mediator.

On December 6, 2017, Trump delivered another surprise, in the form of his "Jerusalem speech", in which he announced that he would carry out forthwith the election campaign promise that no-one had believed he would honor:

> In 1995, Congress adopted the Jerusalem Embassy Act. [. . .] Yet, for over twenty years, every previous American president has exercised the law's waiver, refusing to move the US embassy to Jerusalem or to recognize Jerusalem as Israel's capital city. Presidents issued these waivers under the belief that delaying the recognition of Jerusalem would advance the cause of peace. [. . .] After more than two decades of waivers, we are no closer to a lasting peace agreement between Israel and the Palestinians. It would be folly to assume that repeating the exact same formula would now produce a different or better result. Therefore, I have determined that it is time to officially recognize Jerusalem as the capital of Israel. While previous presidents have made this a major campaign promise, they failed to deliver. Today, I am delivering. [. . .] This is a long-overdue step to advance the peace process and to work towards a lasting agreement. Israel is a sovereign nation with the right like every other sovereign nation to determine its own capital.[24]

Trump's announcement was denounced in the strongest terms by Abbas and by Turkish president Erdogan, and received a cool reception from the European Union, but Netanyahu was grateful: "This is an historic day. The announcement by US President Donald Trump is an important milestone in the history of Jerusalem."[25]

The ceremony marking the American embassy's move to Jerusalem was fixed for a date much sooner than had been expected, despite the emphatic opposition of many countries, especially in Europe. On the symbolic date of May 14 (the English date of Israel's declaration of independence), 2018, the President's daughter, Ivanka Trump, and her husband, Jared Kushner, arrived in Jerusalem for an occasion that aroused excitement throughout the country. This was a heartwarming moment for Netanyahu and for all of Israel, after long years of broken promises.

The next arena to be turned around was the UN. While the previous US administration had isolated Israel in this forum, signaling to the Europeans and others that pressure on Israel would help to advance negotiations, the appointment of Nikki Haley as the US ambassador to the UN brought dramatic change. Haley immediately befriended the Israeli ambassador to the UN, Danny Danon, who had expected a hostile environment and had planned to wage war on Israel's behalf, but now found that he had reliable support. Haley, armed with a clear ideology, did not allow the nations of the world to blur the distinctions between democratic, peace-seeking countries (such as Israel) and dictatorial, terror-producing countries (such as Iran). She pointed out the irony of the UN Human Rights Committee including countries that systematically abused human rights, while denouncing

Israel. The world realized that the courageous ambassador would not allow them to bash Israel with impunity. Danon was no longer constantly under attack by the Arab countries, backed by the Europeans, with a wink from the Americans. Haley became a most popular figure in Israel.

The American president surprised the world once again when he cancelled US aid to UNRWA. This agency, originally created to rehabilitate Palestinian refugees, had ended up perpetuating their dire situation for seventy years, despite a budget of tens of billions of dollars devoted over the decades to this specific cause. Trump's decision indicated that he would not agree for the refugees to be used any longer as pawns and as an excuse for the Israeli-Palestinian conflict. He would direct funds towards the refugees' rehabilitation, instead of intentionally prolonging their plight, as UNRWA had done. Haley expressed fierce criticism of UNRWA and stated that the agency would need to undertake far-reaching reform, including reassessing the number of Palestinians actually eligible to be called refugees, before the US would go back to cooperating with it.

Shortly thereafter, on September 19, 2018, the US administration announced additional startling measures, including closing the PLO mission in Washington, owing to the Palestinian refusal to engage in discussions about the peace plan that was being prepared. State Department spokesperson Heather Nauert said:

> The PLO has not taken steps to advance the start of direct and meaningful negotiations with Israel. To the contrary, PLO leadership has condemned a US peace plan they have not yet seen, and refused to engage with the US government with respect to peace efforts and otherwise.[26]

Netanyahu, who had endured ten years of American administrations that believed that advancing peace was up to Israel, the stronger party, announced immediately that "Israel supports the American actions aimed at making it clear to the Palestinians that refusing to negotiate, and efforts to attack Israel in international forums, will not advance peace."[27]

The Palestinians fumed all over again, denouncing American "bullying" and "spitefulness" (and ignoring the end of the State Department announcement: "We are not retreating from our efforts to achieve a lasting and comprehensive peace.") National Security Advisor John Bolton commented, "The United States will always stand with our friend and ally Israel."[28] Such unequivocal statements about Israel had not been heard in Washington for some years. Bolton informed the Palestinians in very clear terms that Washington would not leave the PLO mission open so long as the Palestinian Authority refused to return to negotiations with Israel. PLO Secretary General Saeb Erekat immediately announced in response that the Palestinians would not "submit to US threats and bullying" and repeated the calls to the International Criminal Court (ICC) in the Hague to open an investigation into Israeli war-crimes. The Palestinians closed their ears to the President's promises that his administration was working on the "deal of the century" for peace in the Middle East, which would require painful concessions on both sides. At an election rally in West Virginia, the President said, with reference to the US recognition of Jerusalem and the relocation of the US embassy to the capital:

> It was a good thing to have done, because we took it [the issue of Jerusalem as Israel's capital] off the table. [. . .] In the negotiation, Israel will have to pay a higher price, because they won a very big thing. [. . .] If there's ever going to be peace with the Palestinians, then this was a good thing to have done.[29]

At the same time, he promised that "the Palestinians will get something very good, 'cause it's their turn next."

There was no official Israeli response to this disturbing statement. The Palestinians, meanwhile, maintained their stony refusal of any contact with the administration, which continued to impose penalties on the stubborn Abbas.

The good relations between the two leaders also found expression in what was, for Netanyahu, the most important area of all: the Iranian nuclear program. In an unforgettable presentation that was broadcast live from the Ministry of Defense in Tel Aviv on April 30, the Prime Minister showed the world the documents and materials which had been delivered to him by the Mossad, comprising Iran's secret nuclear archive. At this climax of the anti-Iran campaign that he had waged since 1996, he displayed definitive proof of the Iranian nuclear weapons program that no-one had been willing to believe existed. It was clear that Netanyahu was one of the few leaders who could attract a world audience for such a speech. He had surpassed his father and his ideological teachers in applying Jabotinsky-style statesmanship, using the most up-to-date technology.

The European countries, which were desperate to maintain friendly ties with Iran, were horrified at the possibility that Netanyahu's exposé had been coordinated with President Trump, just a few days prior to the deadline for Trump's decision as to how to proceed concerning the 2015 JCPOA Iran deal. Angela Merkel, Emmanuel Macron, and Boris Johnson all visited Washington in the fortnight that followed. All three tried to convince the US President that there was no strategic alternative to the existing deal, and warned that its collapse would be a blow to diplomacy, strengthening the extremists in Teheran.

On May 8, 2018, President Trump astounded the world all over again, announcing that the US was pulling out of the Iran deal and would reapply all the sanctions that had been revoked. Israeli ambassador to the UN Ron Dermer listened as Trump realized Netanyahu's dreams. It was a moment of gratification and relief after years of uphill struggle and after watching President Obama and Secretary of State John Kerry take the opposite route and sign an agreement with Iran that would only temporarily slow down the Iranian nuclear program, while granting the Ayatollah regime the resources and freedom it sought to send money, missiles, and Iranian soldiers into every part of the Middle East.

The US President's announcement signaled a dramatic strategic change in American policy:

> The United States no longer makes empty threats. When I make promises, I keep them. [. . .] This was a horrible, one-sided deal that should have never, ever been made. It didn't bring calm, it didn't bring peace, and it never will.[30]

Trump referred to the "decaying and rotten structure" of the agreement, calling it "defective at its core". He said, "A constructive deal could easily have been struck at the time, but it wasn't." He asserted that

> at the heart of the Iran deal was a giant fiction that a murderous regime desired only a peaceful nuclear energy program. Today we have definitive proof that this Iranian promise was a lie. Last week, Israel published intelligence documents long concealed by Iran, conclusively showing the Iranian regime and its history of pursuing nuclear weapons. [. . .] If I allowed this deal to stand, there would soon be a nuclear arms race in the Middle East.

In the discussion at the UN, Ambassador Haley backed up the president:

> The list of [Iranian] violations is longer than I can enumerate. Resolution 2231 precludes the transfer of weapons from Iran, but we see Iranian weapons throughout the region, from Yemen to Syria and Lebanon. UN Resolutions 1701 and 1559 called upon Hizbollah to disarm, but it has built a military arsenal of weapons provided by Iran. [. . .] Hizbollah leaders speak openly about the support they receive from Teheran.[31]

The world understood very quickly that the US viewed Israel and its Prime Minister as important and close allies. The diplomatic effect followed: Netanyahu, continuing Jabotinsky's policy of reliance on a world power, strengthened ties with the American administration. He became the head of state closest to the American president, and the message to the world was clear. Netanyahu began to receive warm welcomes in many countries. In Europe, he was no longer on the defensive. He began to overtake larger and longer-established countries by means of mutual visits with south-eastern and north-western Europe. Within a year he had been to Hungary, Poland, Lithuania, Latvia, and Estonia, and the leaders of Hungary and Austria had visited Israel. Netanyahu also began to halt the flood of European anti-Israel initiatives.

Netanyahu, with his political orientation that he had learned from his father, who had been politically active in the US, became one of the best-known and most-esteemed leaders in the world, thanks to his rare capability and his experience. The leader of the world's second great power, Vladimir Putin, also made Netanyahu his partner for many talks and visits, during which they discussed Syria and Iran.

During the years 2016–2018 Netanyahu met with the leaders of the US and of Russia more often than any other head of state. In addition, he met with the leaders of China and India, powers that had never shown an interest in Israel. It was a dramatic change from the period when Obama's administration had provided unprecedented defense aid but had pressured Israel heavily, causing other countries to take the hint and keep their distance.

Netanyahu had been the Prime Minister who, more than any previous leader of Israel, had avoided resorting to the country's considerable military force, for examples the restraint he showed during Operation Protective Edge and also while facing the Hamas provocations in 2018, including violent demonstrations, knifing attacks, attempts to infiltrate the country, and incendiary balloons that burned vast areas of farmland.

But now, with Iran's military infiltration into Syria and its presence on Israel's northern border, Netanyahu felt freer to act, with US backing. (This was a necessary precondition, according to the teachings of both Jabotinsky and Bentzion Netanyahu, who had acted to enlist the support of the Great Power – Britain, and later the US – for the establishment of the Jewish state.) In view of the Iranian aggression, which was approaching to within an hour's drive from Tiberias and the Sea of Galilee, Israel began attacking Iranian bases and weapons on a regular basis. While there was no official Israeli acknowledgment of responsibility for these strikes, the residents of Damascus and Latakia were frequently woken by the sound of explosions, and there was no doubt in their minds as to where the planes flying overhead had originated.

Netanyahu maintained a cooperative relationship, for the first time in the country's history, with Russia. The courageous Israeli operations deep in Syrian territory met with no interference or disturbance by the Russian planes that were constantly circling over Syria. It was clear that this was the result of unprecedented coordination between the two militaries, as well as with the American administration. As Bolton expressed it: "Our aim is to get Iran out of Syria."[32] In an interview with ABC News, he declared that the aim of the US administration, Russia, and Israel was to push Iran out of the Middle Eastern countries:

> Certainly the objective of the United States, of Israel, President Putin said it was Russia's objective, to get Iran – Iranian forces, Iranian militias, Iranian surrogates – out of the offensive operations they're in in both Syria and Iraq, and frankly, to end Iran's support for Hezbollah.[33]

Bolton said, "I think the president's decision to withdraw from the Iran nuclear deal has put a real crimp into the Iranian economy. I think they're feeling it in their capability [. . .] to conduct offensive operations in the region here."

Netanyahu would have a hard time expressing "Jabotinsky-speak" better than President Trump, Vice President Pence, UN Ambassador Nikki Haley, and National Security Advisor John Bolton. After ten years of ideological struggle with two administrations (which also developed into personal tension) Netanyahu could now share a firm bond with the world's greatest power, as well as with the second world power. The dream of his father, Bentzion Netanyahu, and of his ideological "grandfather", Ze'ev Jabotinsky, had come true.

Notes

1 Yediot Aharonot, March 29, 2013.
2 Yediot Aharonot, June 13, 2014.
3 Haaretz, June 13, 2014.
4 Yediot Aharonot, June 13, 2014.
5 Yediot Aharonot, June 11, 2014.
6 Globes, March 12, 2015.
7 Yediot Aharonot, March 13, 2015.
8 Ibid.
9 Haaretz, March 13, 2015.
10 Ibid.
11 Haaretz, March 14, 2015.
12 Maariv, March 15, 2015.
13 Haaretz, March 17, 2015.
14 This is how Netanyahu won the elections [Video file]. (2016, January 25). Retrieved from https://www.mako.co.il/news-military/politics-q1_2016/Article-d22b77e844a72 51004.htm.
15 Yisrael Hayom, September 14, 2017.
16 Yediot Aharonot, September 6, 2018.
17 Haaretz, September 5, 2018.
18 Israeli Knesset (April 30, 2018). Minister for tourism Levin: the Nationality Law-Herzl's vision. Retrieved from https://m.knesset.gov.il/news/pressreleases/pages/press 30.04.18ll.aspx.
19 Maariv, August 6, 2018.
20 Maariv, July 30, 2018.
21 Yediot Aharonot, October 23, 2017.
22 Globes, December 16, 2016.
23 Yisrael Hayom, September 16, 2018.
24 Yediot Aharonot, December 6, 2017.
25 Ibid.
26 U.S. Department of State (September 10, 2018). Closure of the PLO office in Washington: press statement. Retrieved from https://www.state.gov/closure-of-the-plo-office-in-washington.
27 Haaretz, September 11, 2018.
28 *The Wall Street Journal*, September 10, 2018.
29 Haaretz, August 23, 2018.
30 *The New York Times*, May 8, 2018.
31 United States Mission to the United Nations (October 18, 2017). Ambassador Nikki Haley U.S. Permanent Representative to the United Nations U.S. Mission to the United Nations New York City. Retrieved from https://usun.usmission.gov/ambassador-nikki-haley-u-s-permanent-representative-to-the-united-nations-u-s-mission-to-the-united-nations-new-york-city-october-18-2017-for-immed/
32 Yisrael Hayom, August 19, 2018.
33 *The Times of Israel*, August 19, 2018.

Postscript

I write these words at the end of 2018. The underground commanders are no longer with us. Most of the parents' generation of the fighting family has passed on and lies buried alongside brothers-in-arms and comrades for life. Only the youngest of the Irgun and Lehi fighters are still alive, in their nineties. After playing a dominant role in Israeli history for seventy-five years, the remnant of the generation of the Revolt now sits back, watching the second generation lead the country. Finally, the veterans are at rest, after lives full of battles. It was only after coronating Netanyahu and bringing him and the heirs back to the helm of the country in 2009 that the veterans were able to enjoy their old age and celebrate with their children, grandchildren, and great-grandchildren. With heirs installed as Prime Minister and President, they were finally free to visit the Jabotinsky Institute, the Begin Heritage Center, and the Lehi Museum to meet with the last of their beloved brothers and esteemed fighters.

The veterans had been proud of the children of their fellow fighters already half a century previously when the children had waged their battle against their teachers. They felt that the children of the fighting family were truly their continuation. They believed that Rivlin, Milo, Olmert, Livni, and thousands more children of underground veterans were fighting their fight in the schools, against the "perfidious pens", against history books that distorted and violated the memory of the Revolt and its heroes. The generation that was raised on the story of Jabotinsky's war against Socialism watched with pride as boys and girls like Olmert and Livni fought against the same detested red flag. In the 1960s, when the movement's branches had been destitute and isolated, with Israelis fearing to enter them lest the slightest degree of association destroy their income and future, the veterans had happily embraced their "nieces and nephews" – Rivlin, Naor, Meridor, and others. They were proud of the thousands of children who accompanied their parents and their "aunts and uncles" in distributing voting slips showing Herut during the election campaigns in the 1960s. Thousands of parents and children, alone against all the world.

Later, the parents had proudly saluted the combat soldiers and outstanding officers who went to battle in the three wars of the late '60s and early '70s. Twenty years after the Revolt, they saw "Begins", "Shamirs", "Meridors", "Rivlins", and thousands of children of Irgun and Lehi fighters once again on the frontlines, in defense of the country. Menahem Begin and his generation wiped tears and saluted the Herut heroes who fell in battle, including the pilot Lieutenant-Colonel Avi Lanir (Lenkin), and commander of the Entebbe Operation, Lieutenant-Colonel Yoni Netanyahu.

Former Irgun and Lehi generals now saw before them IDF generals who were children of the fighting family, far removed from politics but devoting their lives to military public service. A very high percentage of the Irgun and Lehi second generation fought in combat roles and climbed their way up the ranks. Five of them became generals in the same army that had shot at the parents aboard the *Altalena*, the army that had turned away the underground fighters with the most extensive combat experience, who had so longed to devote their lives to it. Major-General Ido Nehushtan became Commander of the Israeli Air Force; Major-General Yohanan Locker, Deputy Air Force Commander and Military Secretary to Prime Minister Netanyahu; Major-General Yaakov Amidror, head of the Research Department of Israeli Military Intelligence and National Security Advisor to Netanyahu's government; Major-General Avihai Mandelblit, squarely in the public eye as Attorney General to the government whose head he was investigating; and Major-General Hertzi Halevy, head of the Southern Command responsible for dealing with Hamas in Gaza.

The veterans of the Revolt contemplated the leaders of the country and knew that they had succeeded in their task of replicating their generation. They had managed to continue their hegemony among the Revisionist movement and the Likud, setting a record for the democratic world: some eighty years of dominance of the movement, since the days of the Revolt, by two generations. They were proud of the thirty-eight years of government under the veterans and the heirs, of which twenty-five years featured three Prime Ministers from within their ranks (four, if Olmert is included). They also lived to see an "Irgun child" become President of Israel in 2014.

They were painfully aware of the fact that the heirs, nearing middle age, were split between right-wing and center-left parties, between the priorities of security and peace, between conservatism and liberalism. Above all they were aware of the personal rivalries over leadership of the movement and of the country. And they were crushed every time an heir looked to concessions for the sake of peace, while their own philosophy called for an "iron wall" as a precondition for peace. They wanted all the heirs to follow in their ideological footsteps. But they understood that the complex situation was the result of the encounter between their ninety-year-old ideology and the reality of the new millennium. They were therefore forgiving of "their" Prime Ministers, Begin and Netanyahu, who opted for concessions. It was hard for them to watch heirs compromising on the ideology of the parents' generation. It was hurtful for them to see heirs abandoning the camp of Begin and their own parents. Hardest of all was to observe an ideological shift accompanied by a departure from the sacred framework of the movement and party. Thus, the Center Party heirs of 1999, the Kadima heirs of 2005, and the Hatnuah heirs of 2015, who joined up with Labor, were viewed as having betrayed their heritage.

Nevertheless, every last one of the veterans was comforted at having lived to see an heirs' government for the second, third, and fourth time, in 2009, 2013, and 2015. They had lived to see ministers with the names of their beloved commanders, sitting in Israel's government: Begin and Shamir, Landau, Meridor, Livni. The aged veterans watched their television screens in wonder as Begin and Shamir, Landau and Rivlin were reborn before their eyes, speaking the same words, expressing the same faith, the same worldview, as seventy years previously.

Most of all, they were proud of Netanyahu, the heir who connected them back so powerfully with the movement's founder, Jabotinsky, and who faced a similar all-out onslaught by the country's elite. They were deeply proud of the heir who led their opposition party to four terms as the Prime Minister of their heirs' government. They even accepted his right to interpret and update the teachings of his father and his spiritual grandfather, adapting them to the exigencies of the changing geopolitical reality.

The veterans of the Revolt helped to save their chosen heir the first time from the abyss, in which he found himself following Rabin's assassination, and prior to the 1996 elections. They embraced him when he was pronounced politically dead after being unseated from the Prime Minister's Office in 1999; and they accompanied him through the years of exile and waiting under Sharon. When they were already well advanced in age they saved him (for the third time) in the cutthroat primaries of 2005, when he was at a low point and up against five other candidates. And then again, a few months later, when he was declared politically finished for the fourth time, after the massive defeat in 2006, with only twelve mandates and the general expectation that he would go home.

The veterans who were still around celebrated with Netanyahu when he won the election and returned to the PMO in 2009. And they watched him come back to life for the sixth time, when everyone had already launched into their political eulogies, in the 2015 elections. This time he succeeded without the help of the veterans. But after this heartening high point, the veterans watched him heading into police investigations, with the media already counting down the days to a plea bargain and the end of his career, or even time in prison. The veterans were transported back to the days of the incitement of the regime, the media, and the elite against their earlier leaders – Jabotinsky, Begin, and Shamir.

Few of them were left to see Netanyahu stand up to the hurricane of police questioning, leaks, and media investigations. Together with the rest of the country, they were surprised when this treatment earned him the backing and support of millions of Israelis who were outraged by what they viewed as an attempt at an anti-democratic ousting of a Prime Minister.

The veterans were reminded of Jabotinsky travelling between the world capitals, as they watched his "grandson", the Prime Minister, shuttle between Washington and New York, between speeches at the UN and speeches to Congress, between leaders of countries with which Israel had never shared diplomatic ties. They looked on approvingly as Netanyahu nurtured the closest relationship of all time with the US President and Vice President, while simultaneously maintaining

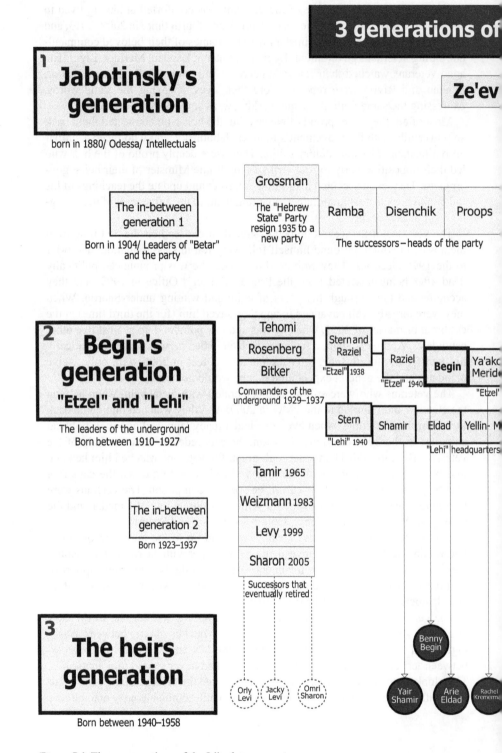

Figure P.1 Three generations of the Likud movement.

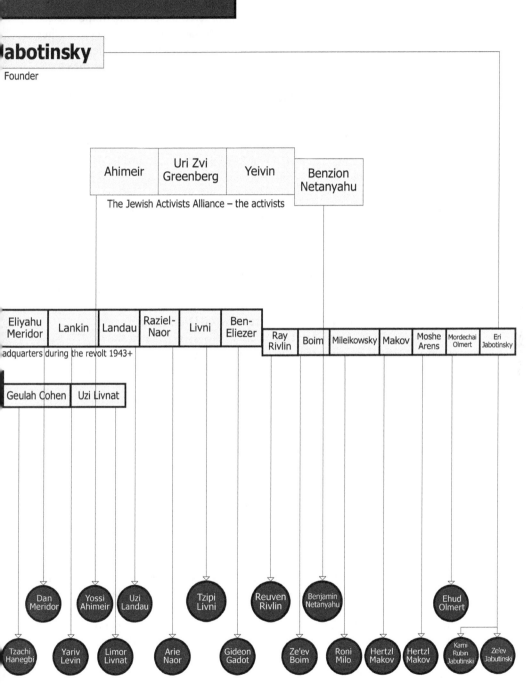

the Likud movement

Jabotinsky
Founder

Ahimeir	Uri Zvi Greenberg	Yeivin	Benzion Netanyahu

The Jewish Activists Alliance – the activists

Eliyahu Meridor	Lankin	Landau	Raziel-Naor	Livni	Ben-Eliezer	Ray Rivlin	Boim	Mileikowsky	Makov	Moshe Arens	Mordechai Olmert	Eri Jabutinsky

adquarters during the revolt 1943+

Geulah Cohen	Uzi Livnat

Dan Meridor   Yossi Ahimeir   Uzi Landau   Tzipi Livni   Reuven Rivlin   Benjamin Netanyahu   Ehud Olmert

Tzachi Hanegbi   Yariv Levin   Limor Livnat   Arie Naor   Gideon Gadot   Ze'ev Boim   Roni Milo   Hertzl Makov   Hertzl Makov   Kami Rubin Jabutinski   Ze'ev Jabutinski unprecedented relations with Putin, president of the power that had been hostile to Israel since the early days of the state.

Those who had heard Jabotinsky warn about Hitler before anyone else had, those who had been at Begin's side when he ordered the bombing of the nuclear reactor in Iraq, felt history reliving itself when Netanyahu spoke out before other world leaders about the dangers of a nuclear Iran and of the Iranian terror super-power, despite the insubordination of Israel's military elite and despite the efforts of the US administration to squash and suppress his message. They were proud of him when he spoke before the American Congress and received prolonged applause, despite the strong disapproval of the US President. They were proud of his spearheading Israel's numerous strikes on Iranian weapons in Syria.

The veterans wept tears of joy and pride when their heir Reuven Rivlin, son of Ray Rivlin of the Irgun, became the first Revisionist president of Israel. They still remembered the five-year-old child who had smuggled weapons for them. They had the longest acquaintance with this heir who had joined the cause some seventy-four years previously, who had endured the long years of loneliness together with them, and who had remained loyal to the teachings of Jabotinsky and Begin.

Indeed, Rivlin was true to Jabotinsky's values of grandeur and resolve. As president he was connected to the settlements of Gush Etzion and at the same time to Kibbutz Misgav Am in the north; he was popular in Jerusalem, the national, traditional, religious capital that was also his home, and also in secular Tel Aviv; he was the president of Right and Left, of immigrants from East and West, of the religious, the ultra-Orthodox, the secular, Jewish, Druze, Arabs.

When Eli Sheetrit and his Tagar Circle friends celebrated their 2012 Rosh Hashana party, they knew that they were marking the end of an era. Nevertheless, they were satisfied. Despite all the rivalries, their heirs had fulfilled the supreme task: in the Israeli national consciousness, the Irgun and Lehi were no longer regarded as terror organizations; Begin was no longer viewed as having been a dangerous fascist; and Stern was not a gang-leader. They observed how Israel now remembered Begin as a worthy and well-loved leader, alongside his adversary, Ben-Gurion. They observed how their great-grandchildren learned in their official school history books that the Irgun and Lehi had fought bravely for Israel's independence and that Begin had prevented a civil war over the *Altalena* affair. They observed how the mayor heirs, Olmert and Milo, commemorated the underground movements and their heroes, along with Begin and Jabotinsky. They saw the country full of monuments, museums, streets, neighborhoods, and towns preserving the memories of the Revisionist leaders and fighters who had once suffered ignominy and disrespect. They were appreciative of the heirs who dedicated themselves to commemorating the Revolt and the underground organizations: Yossi Ahimeir, Herzl Makov, and Professor Arye Naor. As of the last count, Israel boasts fifty-five roads named after Jabotinsky (the most commemorated figure in the country), forty-two named after Begin (despite the family's opposition), and many named after the underground prisoners executed by the British. Four towns are named after Jabotinsky and Stern.

A hundred years after Begin's birth (and 133 years after the birth of Jabotinsky), the last remaining representatives of the fighters of the Revolt beheld a Prime Minister and President who formed a replica of their own generation. They saw two leaders of Israel who had been born with the Beitar anthem on their lips and who spoke of Jabotinsky and Begin on television and on the radio, describing them as their guides and teachers.

The last of the underground fighters saw, in their last days, how the heirs who had come to the aid of their shunned and isolated parents in the Israeli opposition had ultimately inherited the kingdom, achieving the pinnacles of power and symbolic legitimacy: the premiership and the presidency.

Bibliography

Books

Begin, Avinadav. *Ketz Hasichsoch*. Tel Aviv: Ahuzat Bait, 2010.

Begin, Menachem. *The Revolt: Story of the Irgun*. Netanya: Achiasaf Publishing, 1977.

Bloom, Gadi and Hefetz, Nir. *Ariel Sharon: A Life*. Tel Aviv: Yediot Ahronot Publishing, 2005.

Dan, Uri. *Ariel Sharon: An Intimate Portrait*. Tel Aviv: Yediot Ahronot Publishing, 2007.

Drucker, Raviv and Shelah, Ofer. *Boomerang*. Beit Shemesh: Keter, 2005.

Hagar, Ester. Erev hatzdaha l'aisha Halocchemet. *Be'eretz Israel*, Tel Aviv: January–February, 1988, 18.

Jabotinsky, Ari. *My father, Zeev Jaboutinsky*. Petah tiqwa: Stimatski, 1980.

Lebel, Udi. *The Road to the Pantheon: Etzel, Lehi and the Borders of Israeli National Memory*. Jerusalem: Carmel Publishing, 2007.

Livni, Eitan. *Hamaamad*. Jerusalem: Idanim, 1987.

Mannheim, Karl, *The sociology of knowledge* (London: Routledge & Kegan Paul, 1952).

Niv, David. *Etzel Military Campaigns*, vol. 1, p. 300. Tel Aviv: Hadar Publishing, 1980.

Ya'alon Moshe. *Derech Aruka Ktzara*. Tel Aviv: Yediot Ahronot Publishing, 2008.

Interviews

Appel, Avrum. Interview by author. October 10, 1987.

Haber, Eitan. Interview by author. July 21, 2007.

Hanegbi, Tzachi. Interview by author. May 31, 2002.

Hellman, Oren. Interview by author. August 12, 2014.

Kadishai, Yehiel. Interview by author. March 5, 2007.

Kulits, Haim. Interview by author.

Landau, Uzi. Interview by author. May 23, 2002.

Livnat, Limor. Interview by author. July 5, 2002.

Livni, Tzipi. Interview by author. February 22, 2007.

Meridor, Dan. Interview by author. April 10, 2002.

Milo, Roni. Interview by author. April 21, 2002.

Naor, Arye. Interview by author. August 20, 2014.

Nathan, Avraham. Interview by author. April 2, 2014.

Netanyahu, Benjamin. Interview by author.

Rivlin, Reuven. Interview by author. April 18, 2002.

Shamir, Haya. Interview by author.

Israeli Newspapers

Davar
Globes
Haaretz
Hai'r
Israel Hayom
Maariv
Makor Rishon
The Times of Israel
Yediot Ahronot

World Newspapers

The New York Times
The Wall Street Journal

Israeli Websites

Channel 7 News

https://www.inn.co.il/News

Channel 13 News

https://13news.co.il/

Ministry of Foreign Affairs
https://www.gov.il/en/departments/ministry_of_foreign_affairs
Walla News
https://www.walla.co.il/

World Websites

U.S. Department of State
https://www.state.gov/
United States Mission to the United Nations
https://usun.usmission.gov/

Israeli TV programs

Channel 12 News
Uvda, with Ilana Dayan, Channel 12.

Index

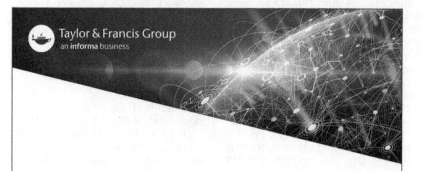